THE
WESTERN
READER

Henry Fonda as horizon-gazing Wyatt Earp in My Darling Clementine.

THE WESTERN READER

Edited by
Jim Kitses
&
Gregg Rickman

LIMELIGHT EDITIONS
New York

First Limelight Edition July 1998

Library of Congress Cataloging-in-Publication Data

The western reader/edited by Jim Kitses and Gregg Rickman. — 1st Limelight ed.
      p. cm.
    ISBN 0-87910-268-3
     1. Western films—History and criticism.
     I. Kitses, Jim   II. Rickman, Gregg.
PN 1995.9.W4W39   1998
791.43´6278—dc21   98-18452
                                                   CIP

The editors are grateful for permission to reprint copyrighted material as detailed in the Acknowledgments.

Printed in Canada

Text design by Jeff Fitschen

For my pioneers, who came West from Greece,
and
For Paula and Angela, Jesse and Anastasia,
I sure like those names . . .

Jim Kitses

For my father, who likes Westerns,
and
For my mother, who prefers a good musical

Gregg Rickman

CONTENTS

PART 3: REVISIONISM, RACE AND GENDER

ACKNOWLEDGMENTS

A part from our contributors, we'd like to thank many friends and colleagues for their support, interest, and assistance with text and visual illustrations: Ken Bowers, Claire Brandt of Eddie Brandt's Hollywood Matinee, Edward Buscombe, Steve Chack of San Francisco's The Naked Eye, David Chierichetti, John Fairchild, Tag Gallagher, Linda Gross, Margaret Henry, Tim Hunter, Margo Kasdan, Blake Lucas, Bob McLeod, David Meeker, Bill Nichols, Lowell Peterson, Janey Place, Lee Sanders, Scott Simmon, Bob Stephens, Jane Veeder, Christopher Williams, and Doug Williams. All photos of *The Ballad of Little Jo* are by Bill Foley. Alain Silver was always a generous source of information and wise advice. We are of course indebted to Mel Zerman for his enthusiastic support for the project.

With this book we would like to remember two distinguished film teachers who left us much too soon. The influence and contribution of Paddy Whannel are addressed in the Introduction. A colleague of the editors for many years at San Francisco State University, Christine Saxton's high regard for the Western is inscribed in her M.A. thesis on *Stagecoach*, as well as in the memories of her many students.

Essays are published as originally written, with the exception of a few silently corrected errors and also emendations by the authors on a few of the reprinted pieces. Edward Buscombe, Tania Modleski, Barrie Pattison, Christopher Wicking, and Robin Wood graciously allowed us to edit portions of their essays. For stylistic reasons we have brought the essays in line with the same forms of punctuation and referencing, although contributions that employ a "Works Cited" format have been allowed to stand. Captioning on the stills is ours.

Sherman Alexie, "My Heroes Have Never Been Cowboys" and "Reservation Drive-In" from *First Indian on the Moon*. Copyright © 1993 by Sherman Alexie. Reprinted by permission of Hanging Loose Press.

Peter Lehman, "Looking at Look's Missing Reverse Shot: Psychoanalysis and Style in John Ford's *The Searchers*," *Wide Angle* vol. 4, no. 4,1981. Copyright © 1981 by Peter Lehman. Reprinted by permission of the author.

Tag Gallagher, "Angels Gambol Where They Will: John Ford's Indians," *Film Comment* September-October 1993. Copyright © 1993 by Tag Gallagher. Reprinted by permission of the author.

Robert Baird, "Going Indian: From *Deerslayer* to *Dances With Wolves*," from *Dressing in Feathers: The Construction of the Indian in American Popular Culture*, edited by S. Elizabeth Bird. Copyright © 1996 by WestView Press. Reprinted by permission of WestView Press.

Pam Cook, "Women in the Western," from *The BFI Companion to the Western*, edited by Edward Buscombe. Copyright © 1988 by the British Film Institute. Reprinted by permission of the British Film Institute and the author.

Blake Lucas, "Saloon Girls and Ranchers' Daughters: The Woman in the Western." Copyright © 1998. Printed by permission of the author.

Janet Peterson, "The Competing Tunes of *Johnny Guitar*: Liberalism, Sexuality, Masquerade," *Cinema Journal* vol. 35, no. 3,1996. Copyright © 1996 by *Cinema Journal*. Reprinted by permission of the author and the University of Texas Press.

Janet Thumim, "'Maybe He's Tough But He Sure Ain't No Carpenter': Masculinity and In/Competence in *Unforgiven*," from *Me Jane*, edited by Pat Kirkham and Janet Thumim. Copyright © 1995 by Lawrence & Wishart. Reprinted by permission of St. Martin's Press and Lawrence & Wishart.

Tania Modleski, "Our Heroes Have Sometimes Been Cowgirls," *Film Quarterly* vol. 49, no. 2, Winter 1995-96. Copyright © 1996 by the Regents of the University of California. Reprinted by permission of University of California Press.

Jim Kitses, "An Exemplary Post-Modern Western: *The Ballad of Little Jo*." Copyright © 1998. Printed by permission of the author.

Gregg Rickman, "The Western Under Erasure: *Dead Man*." Copyright © 1998. Printed by permission of the author.

INTRODUCTION:
Post-modernism and The Western

Jim Kitses (1998)

"It Ain't Like It Used To Be, But . . . It'll Do!"

1

Someone is always trying to bury the Western. If a marker had been erected every time the genre's end had been proclaimed over its long history, the Western's gravestones would now overflow even Tombstone's cemetery, "the biggest graveyard West of the Rockies," as Doc Holliday (Victor Mature) informs Wyatt Earp (Henry Fonda) in John Ford's *My Darling Clementine*. Why all the wakes for the Western, the insistently gloomy taking of the genre's temperature? The Western has no peer for premature anticipations of its demise.

Paradoxically, this negativity may be seen to reflect the exuberant good *health* the genre has enjoyed over its history, both ancient and modern. Jaundiced dissenting opinions periodically generated by a lull or downswing in the business are understandable, but ultimately testify to the long and gloriously vital run of the genre, to just how central and dominant the Western has been from its silent days on. Film for film, pound for pound, the form has been the heavyweight champ of popular genres. Although comparisons may be invidious, it is difficult to entertain seriously the claims of other popular forms as having produced comparable creative traditions, frameworks as richly supportive of as many gifted film makers, and as uplifting of so many

15

modest talents. Of course, the dominating presence of John Ford, arguably America's greatest director, alone lifts the genre to a highwater mark of achievement.

Mention of Ford, fashioner of so many poetic images of America, points to a key source of the genre's power, longevity, and achievement. The Western is not just another movie type. As some of the earlist writings on the form (those of Warshow, Bazin, my own, all included here) stress, the Western's myth has provided a national myth and global icon, a cornerstone of American identity, its roots in history and the frontier providing a unique, rich body of signs and meanings. These meanings can be said to extend far beyond the boundaries of celluloid, no fences possible for the West as state of mind.

Still, you may say, things have changed—the genre is no longer what it was. We would of course agree—the Western no longer occupies a central place. Indeed, as post-modern theory insists, and our daily experience often reminds us, there no longer are centralities, privileged myths or canonical authorities. Jean-Francois Lyotard, in answer to the question famously put by Paolo Portoghesi—"What is Postmodernism?"—postulates the end of "master-narratives," legitimising overviews, "meta-narratives." Myth and art are clearly examples of Lyotard's *"epistemes,"* of Fredric Jameson's "cultural dominants," and the traditional Western—a totalizing system with its iconic representation of America in the cowboy, its nostalgic celebration of a heroic masculinist individualism and racist Manifest Destiny—appears to have been one such casualty.[1] Clearly, as well, an era of radical capitalism with its relentless global commodification, downsized status of the individual, and increasingly technological, mediated world of experience, has solidly positioned science fiction and neo-noir as the post-modern genres of choice, with their hybrid, the formidable "tech-noir" (*Blade Runner, The Terminator, Alien*), logically the post-modern genre *par excellence*.

Such developments can be seen to mesh with the end of the line of the genre's main standard bearers, a tradition of specialist Western directors and stars—both, in Clint Eastwood's case—now fading into history. But if the Western is now no longer privileged, it is still gloriously alive, as a distinguished run of remarkable films in the 90s—from *Dances With Wolves* and *Geronimo: An American Legend* to *Unforgiven* and *The Ballad of Little Jo*, from *Wyatt Earp, Tombstone, The Last of the Mohicans,* and *The Quick and The Dead*, to *Wild Bill, Posse* and *Dead Man*—vividly demonstrate. Blending mythology and demythology, revisionism and nostalgia, many of these films rework ancient conventions with panache and imagination, to incarnate the post-modern Western. An increasingly code-savvy image-culture persistently fine-tunes the Western now to define its frontier in racial and gender terms.

Two patterns predominate. Whatever the limitations of its white narrative voice, it was undoubtedly the inspiring *Dances With Wolves* that, against all odds ("Costner's folly," "Kevin's Gate") provided the decisive breakthrough, blazing the trail that other enterprising minority appropriations of the myth were quick to take. Much more modest in scale, although not in achievement, was Maggie Greenwald's vastly underrated, luminously original *The Ballad of Little Jo*. More spectacularly, virtual textbook pastiches recycled the heroic codes and violent rhetoric of Peckinpah and Leone to empower a black gunfighter in Mario Van Peebles' hip, rambunctious *Posse*, and Sharon Stone's avenging feminist angel in Sam Raimi's delirious *The Quick and The Dead*.

A parallel strategy, equally influential in re-positioning the form, was the radical reduction of the traditional hero, brilliantly orchestrated in Eastwood's hugely successful *Unforgiven*, and (anti)climaxing outrageously in Jim Jarmusch's extraordinary *Dead Man*. If the later films, too often voguishly condescended to as "shoot-outs at the PC corral," failed to strike the gold discovered by the Oscar-winning *Dances* and *Unforgiven*, success in an era of niche markets and multiple releases (theatrical, TV, Cable, video) may be seen to be a relative, complex phenomenon. If no longer dominant, the genre remains a strong competitor in the semiotic marketplace, de-centered but nevertheless accessible as a style and form, its iconography a rich resource. Apart from the Western *per se*, in an era where pluralism and hybridity reign, it comes as no surprise to encounter that iconography ironically inscribed repeatedly in other genres such as the road movie—another preferred form today—as in *Paris, Texas, Thelma and Louise, My Own Private Idaho*.

A major problem bedeviling discussion of the genre, and informing predictions of its death, has been the persistent and narrow identification of the Western with its traditional model, as if it were a monolith. In fact, as we well know, there have always been dissents, deviations, aberrations, revisions. Even in pre-classical silent days, before there was an established myth in the cinema to critique or subvert, there were pro-Indian films, films that championed women. Indeed, as Doug Williams shows in his genealogy of the Western, printed here for the first time, even in the genre's literary roots, its heroes could be critiqued and support periodically provided for minorities, alongside its more customary abuse or neglect of them.

The sound era shows many such pockets of dissent, ranging from the work of isolated misanthropic types such as director William Wellman and his *The Ox-Bow Incident* (1943) and *Yellow Sky* (1948) to enterprising individual set-pieces such as Henry King's *The Gunfighter* (1950), Nicholas Ray's *Johnny Guitar* (1954), and Sam Fuller's *Forty Guns* (1957). Indeed, as Richard Combs points out here in his retrospective overview, one of the most famous of all Westerns, Fred Zinneman's *High Noon*, has also been seen in such terms. And of course the 50s see a whole cycle of pro-Indian films, commencing with Anthony Mann's *Devil's Doorway* and Delmer Daves' *Broken Arrow*, both 1950, and culminating in the iconoclastic Fuller's *Run of the Arrow* (1957).

In retrospect, it is possible to see these movies as precursors to a counter-tradition that the Western tradition itself generates, a revisionist shadow, a parallel track to the imperial mainstream with all its ideological baggage. Accumulating in fragments and on the margins, this practice shifts gears radically in the 60s, wherein America loses her innocence, the result of traumatic change—the Vietnam war, civil rights, imperial assassinations, Watergate.

It is often possible to detect in discussions of "the end of the Western" a post-modern nostalgia, the desire to go back to the genre's Golden Age (usually the 50s, revealingly enough), a yearning which appears ironically to constitute a critical and scholarly parallel to the "elegiac Western," the Peckinpah text, so to speak. Blake Lucas' tribute to the ladies of the classical Western, also first printed here and set off by its location cheek by jowl with Pam Cook's feminist overview of women in the genre, can be said to communicate eloquently something of that spirit. But the Western cannot be dehistoricized anymore than America's psyche can.

"There have always been dissents, deviations, aberrations, revisions": Richard Widmark in William Wellman's Yellow Sky.

In fact, a strong strain of denial has been manifest in much discussion of the genre as it has darkened, evidence of a persistent, continuing, but ultimately doomed last stand against the encroachment of the revisionist films, often seen as doing violence to *the* Western—the classical model. It is perhaps a tribute to Ford's pre-eminence that the dream has been so persistently portrayed as the only content of the myth. If not reviled, revisionism has often been seen as unwelcome in its effects on the classical Western's world, disloyal, taking away, destructive, the antipathy hinted at in some of its labels—variously, the anti-Western, the modern Western, the gothic or "dirty" Western, the noir Western, the de-mythologizing, realist or "new wave" Western. Applied to the ambivalent, irreverent, critical, often hostile works that take center stage from the 60s on, such attempts to characterize them implicitly recognize an epochal turning point, the wave of revisionism driven by the period's counter-culture, a rupture marking an incipient post-modernism's impact as a cultural movement advancing the goals of pluralism and heterogeneity. A Hollywood map of this era locating landmark works would have to feature the Western's revisionist projects, some of the most interesting films of the period: most crucially, the hugely influential achievements of Peckinpah and Leone, key figures, Arthur Penn's work and especially *Little Big Man*, Robert Altman's *McCabe and Mrs. Miller*, Clint Eastwood and *The*

Outlaw Josey Wales in particular, Monte Hellman's existentialist low-budget efforts, *The Shooting* and *Ride the Whirlwind*, the popular comic attacks such as *Cat Ballou* and *Blazing Saddles*, and finally, Michael Cimino's *Heaven's Gate*—a disaster not because it silenced the form during the years of crimes and misdemeanors presided over by Ronald Reagan, the most prominent Western actor-auteur of them all, but because it failed to realize its epic, post-modern, revisionist vision.

Of course this deconstructive attack on the traditional in genre and myth extended far beyond the Western, the work of Penn, Kubrick and Altman across the spectrum of Hollywood's popular forms providing further evidence of a developing post-modern sensibility. Nonetheless, there now seems a strong argument for recognition of the revisionist Western as a discrete, dominant type. Indeed, films that in whole or part interrogate aspects of the genre such as its traditional representations of history and myth, heroism and violence, masculinity and minorities, can be seen now to make up the primary focus of the genre. Journalistic references to the type as a sub-genre are commonplace, the longstanding implication being that these attempts to reconstruct the Western's furniture, as it were, are exceptions to the classical rule. But even as the exceptions have begun to outnumber the rule, the idea that these films now constitute the creative mainstream of the genre has not truly registered.

Since it was published in 1988, before *Dances With Wolves* and the second wave of revisionist Westerns, perhaps it is understandable that the authoritative *BFI Companion to the Western* engages the concept neither in the short history by editor Edward Buscombe, nor in its culture and history listings.[2] However, I do not think it possible any longer to overlook the category, although attempts to avoid taxonomies in general are certainly understandable. Boundary lines are increasingly porous in post-modern times. Attempts to define genres usually involve a futile erection of fences, attempts to designate the ins and the outs. Increasingly, a notion of genre as an extended family of shared tendencies and resemblances, although inevitably at the mercy of normative models, family law, as it were, seems attractive.[3] Certainly, revisionism is just such a problematic model. Ford, the essence of the classical artist, meditated on revisionism as early as *Fort Apache* (1948), and became increasingly reflective and critical with later works. Is *The Searchers* revisionist? Is *Ride the High Country* the last classical Western? Or is it, like most of Peckinpah and Leone, on the boundary, overlapping and embracing, both recycling and going beyond earlier styles? Boundaries are unstable, and the art and culture always more layered and elusive than the paradigm. However, if post-modernism is hostile to separate, linear models, to categorization, it also dearly loves contradiction. Whatever the limitations of revisionism as a classification system, the need to point to an ongoing stream of works that play off the traditional, push against the past, and erect a counter-myth, is self-evident. America's official national ideology marking the millennium is multi-culturalism, itself a revision of the melting pot thesis that underlay and underwrote the nation in the 20th century. And it has been this massive shift in ideology toward pluralism and inclusion that has generated the second great wave of revisionist works, those of the 90s.

In a post-modern society determinedly bending and breaking genres, and genders and ideologies there inscribed, we can find dominants and respondants, myths and aberrations everywhere. However, no other form appears to have generated a

The Western in the 90s: Wes Studi as Geronimo: An American Legend; *Jeff Bridges as* Wild Bill; *Daniel Day-Lewis in* The Last of the Mohicans; *and Johnny Depp in* Dead Man.

counter-tradition on the Western's scale, and with good reason. Above all, revisionism is an attitude toward the past, an established practice and model in historical studies. And, of course, the Western *incarnates* history—both America's and its own.[4] The long, illustrious history of the traditional Western thus provides contemporary film-makers a readymade canvas for correcting the sins of our fathers, for inscribing other genders, other races, other sexualities. If the Western is no longer the grand narrative, central, totalizing, hegemonic, it has already shown its resiliency and value as a set of codes that can speak with authority to a new millennium. The totality of remarkable works corrective of America stretching back to the 60s has not eroded or diminished or killed off the Western, it now *is* the Western.

2

There are many histories and traditions of the Western that invite attention. It would be tempting to try to represent them all here. Archeology of the pre-classical era holds its own fascination, the tentative first Westerns of the new century that immediately seized the imagination of a world-wide audience. There is the emergence of the Western's own star system, the long iconic line that stretches from Bronco Billy and William S. Hart to Wayne and Fonda, Stewart and Eastwood. Other key beginnings in the silent era, as with epic works such as *The Covered Wagon* and *The Iron Horse*, are also overlooked here, as are later developments—the singing cowboy and the B-movie traditions. But no single volume can hope to address all the manifold achievements of the genre.[5]

Many may find the journey we construct here conservative, too "monumental." Indeed, we must plead guilty to having wanted to capture something of the main lines of the genre at its fullest stretch, to represent many of its key practitioners and works, and to chart how the dynamic critical practice it generated has established the genre as a pioneering site of influential formal and ideological studies. It will come as no surprise, then, that Ford is a dominant figure here, as he is in the genre itself. *The Searchers* is usually seen as Ford's authoritative text, privileged by challenging studies such as Peter Lehman's, which we are happy to reprint here. However, throughout this volume it is *My Darling Clementine* that emerges as a leitmotif and touchstone, a key film addressed by all the early foundational studies, and returned to in later analyses—of Monument Valley by Edward Buscombe, of Ford's visual style by Michael Budd, and of *Clementine* itself by Scott Simmon. In England it was Lindsay Anderson who had first championed the film in the 50s, eventually passing the torch to Paddy Whannel, the head of the British Film Institute's Education Department, who in turn ignited the passions of a whole community of colleagues and students for the film, and for the Western generally, many of them represented herein. For Whannel, one of the architects of the early film education movement, *Clementine* was an exemplary text of popular art, proof that within the very heart of the mass culture machine, it was possible to create unifying rituals, a populist poetry, good art—the kind that hopefully makes us better as people.[6]

It was Alan Lovell who thereafter advanced *Clementine* as the acme of the classical Western, in answer to Bazin's prior claims for *Stagecoach*. Lovell was at pains to challenge generalizations about Hollywood and genre as closed systems, the movies stereotyped products of a capitalist machine, a position that periodically finds wide acceptance, as in discussions of the "classic realist text" in the 70s, and in current post-modern neo-marxist critics. Lovell's essay is reprinted in the first volume of *Movies and Methods*, whose editor, Bill Nichols, also seized on *Clementine* in a culminating essay on film style, to foreground Ford's moody, contemplative tableaux as problematizing the accepted wisdom of the film, that it celebrates the integration of hero and community.[7]

*   *   *

"What kind of town is this?" Posed at the outset of the film, this question suggests an enigma, an ambiguity that is in fact largely absent in Ford's deliberate, loving portrait of the old West and its heroes. Echoing throughout *My Darling Clementine*, Wyatt Earp's thrice-uttered question is reinforced by other incredulous or awed remarks that we hear: "Marshalin'? In *Tombstone*?"; and, "Shakespeare . . . in Tombstone..."; and finally, "Church bells . . . in Tombstone." That such an untamed America should be able to accommodate law, culture and religion, it is suggested, is something of a miracle. But of course the movie enjoys a rich double-think, a "wide-awake wide-open" Tombstone just barbaric enough—once Indian Charlie has been kicked out of town and Wyatt installed as marshal—to settle immediately into sedate routines. The transitional moment is charmingly captured in the film's portrait of a schizoid community moved to applaud itself wildly on being addressed as ladies and gentlemen, and to a rough justice ("ride him round town on the rail") on being deprived of their Shakespeare.

Clementine's heart is the dance of Wyatt and Clem, its beat driving the whole film, a magical moment in the cinema, an icon that contends and codifies at the level of Gene Kelly's solo song and dance in *Singin' in the Rain* in its affirmation of America; we are talking serious semiotics here. That the scene can be easily detached from the whole film should not be held against it; *Singin' In the Rain* also achieves that high intensity saturation of codes, creating a wonderful world of plenitude, the American Dream.

But if the dance is an epiphany, a hymn to harmony, it is just the high point in an ideological operation which everywhere valorizes order and social regulation. A network of themes and codes comes together to create the image of an ideal community, where the meals ("Stowed away a whole skilletful of ham and eggs") are as regular as the orderly comings and goings of the stage that provides links to the nation, the occasionally infectious intruder—like the shady gambler resignedly moving on—a minor turbulence in the clear sky, the clear sailing. Ingeniously, wittily, the film constructs a persistent hat code signifying around the poles of civilization and culture, balance and restraint, or their lack, the frames often like still life compositions organized around huge cowboy hats, sombreros, flowery bonnets, stovepipes, military headgear, a chef's toque, etc. Prominent everywhere, but especially in the saloon, where they are removed only while eating, the hats help to create a formal world, giving the characters weight and personality. Both in individual close-ups and ensemble shots, chapeaux dominate the West, Ford's contemplative tableau style creating a signifying force field of sculptured images that rival the *mise en scène* of his exteriors, his land-scaping with buttes and mesas.

The various cultural and cinema codes lock into a synergistic construction that speaks the civilizing of America, a masterful marshaling of behavioral and iconic laws, of performance and choreography protocols, costume and body language, of visual, editing and musical systems, an orchestration of signs and meanings which reaches its peak in the formal deportment of Wyatt and Clem in their walk to the church. Ford's style has been described as "realism at its prettiest," an attempt, perhaps, to pin down its poetic swell of meanings. Here our perfumed hero—fresh from the bar-ber's chair, hat smartly squared in the mirror—carefully squires his lady fair from in front of the sun-drenched hotel, slowly along its boardwalk, up the hill to the church where under the open sky and fluttering flags, a "dad-blasted good dance" is about to commence. In the movie's glorious setpiece, Ford's own brother, Francis, is on the violin under the baton of Russell Simpson, *The Grapes of Wrath*'s family elder.

Given that Wyatt and Clem's union is so central in the film's network of codes and themes celebratory of a new community, it is understandable that their separation at the end has been seen as its enigma. In this, *My Darling Clementine* can be said to resemble the reverse of one of those family melodramas, *All That Heaven Allows* the *locus classicus*, where the narrative's odyssey of suffering is undercut, a happy ending materializing at the last minute. Here it is the powerful, positive thrust of the film's ener-gies toward a romantic union and closure that is displaced, with Earp and the final moment by the fence—"Ma'am, I sure like that name . . . *Clementine*!", then riding off.

But why not stay? Saving resort to some vague stereotype—the cowboy must go on, over the next hill—it must be granted that the action of the film, what Peter Wollen called Earp's "uncomplicated passage from nature to culture," is problema-tized, the theme of reconciliation broken.[8] Taking into account the great divide of dif-fering readings—the promise held out that Wyatt will be back, for instance (but, we must ask, how many children had lady Clementine?)—Scott Simmon clarifies the film's double personality now by positioning it on an appropriately ambiguous fron-tier. On the one hand, *Clementine* can be seen to be gazing off to the horizon like its hero, a classical celebration of America's bright future. However, on the other hand, Simmon's analysis also suggests the basis for a post-modern reading that might pos-ture its postwar audience recumbent, gazing back nostalgically at an earlier America where men could lay down the law, decorum, form and manners, a world of order and regulation, where "keeping the peace is no whit less important," and "the east-bound stage don't leave til noon on Sunday," where Shakespeare and regular meals are much more in evidence than violence, and where women and minorities knew their place, or could be exiled to it.

*   *   *

If the Western was the first genre to receive serious and sustained critical atten-tion, providing an early, productive site for critical analysis and methodological debate, it was in part because of Paddy Whannel's leadership in focusing critical issues in

London's dynamic, heady 60s, providing a spirit that still lives in this book. Indeed, a good many of the comrades-in-arms gathered together amicably in this collection were participant warriors in that period's critical wars. Centered around the BFI Education Department and *Movie* magazine, belligerent foes in those days, two Hawksian elites, the combat raged endlessly over the American cinema and Hollywood, art and popular culture, authorship and genre, Ford and Hawks. My own *Horizons West* can be said to have been shaped by, and given voice to, that discourse. Robin Wood, one of *Movie*'s top guns, here provides a basic text in his study of *Rio Bravo* that is fully representative of that group's distinguished authorial studies. Peter Wollen, represented in these pages by the auteur study of Budd Boetticher penned by his alter ego, Lee Russell, introduced cine/auteur-structuralism to the fray, while Raymond Durgnat's distinctive voice provided broad cultural and philosophical perspective, as in his analysis here (with Simmon) of the "Six Creeds That Won the Western."

If hostilities can rage within an era's critical ranks, generational insult and attack are also a norm. Each generation,

"Wyatt and Clem's union." Henry Fonda and Cathy Downs, with John Ford's brother, Francis, on the violin under the baton of Russell Simpson, The Grapes of Wrath's *family elder.*

following some immutable law legislating aggression, savages its predecessors. The earliest critics of the Western were of course men; a feminist critic taking up the Western will refer to these earlier scholars as "fans." Pioneering thematic critics are scalped, their remains used as platforms from which to champion *mise en scène* or ideology. Robert Warshow's magisterial piece on "The Westerner" has often been scolded for its prescriptive definition of the genre, its critique of the "super-Western." However, what was the critical landscape like when Warshow wrote? What sustained him in this ground-breaking study, at once formal, thematic, ideological, of a prime example of the period's "low culture?" Many of Warshow's insights remain unsurpassed, as in his view that the genre recognizes "the value of violence," later to emerge as an obsessive Peckinpah theme.

Although the Western may live on, no longer the favorite but one of the family, the death notices may also continue. Surely one reading of such predictions must accommodate the possibility of wish-fulfillment, of a not-so-latent hostility toward the form, of a positive desire that it bite the dust. Bazin's writings on the Western are typical of the early high regard for it abroad, the awareness of the special, privileged nature of the genre as a national language, with its landscape iconography so elegantly expressive of American doctrine and ideology. Like jazz and American literature, the Western was embraced in Europe even as it was being condescended to on its home turf. Bazin

Western itself, all the better to resurrect and re-affirm it. Exemplary post-modern texts, these films exist in the middle ground of contemporary post-modernism which Andreas Huyssen has defined as:

> . . . a field of tension between tradition and innovation, conservation and renewal, mass culture and high art, in which the second terms are no longer automatically privileged over the first; a field of tension which can no longer be grasped in categories such as progress vs reaction, Left vs Right, present vs past, modernism vs realism, abstraction vs representation, avant-garde vs Kitsch.[11]

Nothing testifies more to the continuing vitality and relevance of the Western than these two remarkable films, with *Dead Man* in a wonderfully post-modern irony providing the landmark (not a tombstone!) for the half-century's journey that the Western has described since 1946's *My Darling Clementine*. Finally, however, it is *Little Jo* that asks to be bookended with *Dead Man*. The two, after all, are a walking contradiction, a structural analysis waiting to happen—female and male, positive and negative, life and death, heaven and hell, transcendence and nihilism, tragedy and comedy, Bazin and Brecht, and so on. But as we know, binaries tend to hybridize into a "field of tension," as with Huyssen's categories, or as with the genre's classic garden/wilderness antinomies, and indeed, as with our two movies in their ying and yang. At first glance so opposed, our two texts are in fact more alike than dissimilar in their play of wit and *gravitas*. Little Jo's overcoming of tests and trials to have the last

"Exemplary post-modern texts." Suzy Amis in The Ballad of Little Jo *and Johnny Depp in* Dead Man.

Victor Mature and Linda Darnell in Clementine: *"The Queen is dead—long live the Queen!"*

laugh at the gender frontier is balanced by *Dead Man*'s Brechtian comedy, the self-canceling excess of death and despair, a West as pure hell—*not*! What we have here, finally, is an example of post-moderism's inclusiveness, the both/and rather than the either/or, two transcendental Westerns that take different trails to track the spiritual odyssey of a millennial America, on the move, guided by its people of color.

A cultural theory, an artistic movement, a social condition, a world-view, a complex of political and ideological discourses, post-modernism provides a critical lens which can help us re-see our myths, and discern new relationships in both contemporary and older works. Returning its focus to Ford's film, for instance, we might now want to dwell on a different moment than the luminous dance of Wyatt and Clem that hovers over the classical Western, an image with a different cast as well, providing a different boundary marker for the whereabouts of the Western in the post-modern era. Rather than follow the stately walk of Clem and Wyatt, arm-in-arm, a past America's marriage, we remain with a darker hero, Doc Holliday, damaged, hungover, dissolute, who the night before, racked with remorse and alcohol, had been unable to look on his own inglorious reflection in a doctor's framed degree, to face how far he had fallen. More sober now, in the light of a new day, Doc Holliday confirms a new path, bidding farewell to the embodiment of the dream, pure Clementine, America's Manifest Destiny, the path of honor and decorum, to embrace a more common figure, Linda Darnell's unchaste Chihuahua, a woman of color, a half-breed with roots south of the border. Given its historical moment, of course, the film itself cannot endorse this mixed marriage, Ford dooming the ignoble couple to the shadows of Doc's bedroom, Wyatt and Clem center-stage forever.[12]

Fifty years later, however, our own impulse must be to recuperate this lowly pair, however unseemly in their turbulence, sensuality and excess, against the grain of the film itself, but in keeping with our era. Admittedly, this is not a wholly disinterested intervention—for indeed, in some obvious respects the genre's own situation is parallel to this scenario, wherein our tarnished hero re-directs his gaze forward in greeting his new consort—"The Queen is dead—long live the Queen!" Surely we might echo this cry, in many ways so appropriate for the Western, but that it parades an unseemly invocation of royalty, hardly apropos in the downsizing atmosphere of post-modernism. No, in the interests of clarity and realism, we must finally abandon *My Darling Clementine* and John Ford, and turn to a later figure, more in tune with our own ethos—Sam Peckinpah, of course—and locate a marker for the new millennium's Western in the wry philosophy and laughter of Edmond O'Brien as *The Wild Bunch*'s sagacious, ancient Sykes. Recruiting his old comrade, Robert Ryan's Deke Thornton, to the work that remains to be done, the past's sins and self-interest set aside, allied now to people of color in a new mission, Sykes opines:

> It ain't like it used to be, but . . . it'll do.

NOTES

1. Charles Jenks, ed., *The Post-modern Reader* (New York: St. Martin's, 1992), pulls together all the major theorists, barring Jameson, and provides a strong overview of a burgeoning and diverse field, and its main issues. Fredric Jameson's *Postmodernism or, The Cultural Logic of Late Capitalism* (Durham: Duke University Press, 1995) greatly expands on Jameson's original *New Left Review* (no. 146) article, and is excerpted in Joseph Natoli and Linda Hutcheon, eds., *A Postmodern Reader* (Albany: State University of New York Press, 1993). Within this dynamic movement a post-modern respect for difference, for local rather than central authority, translates into such basic lack of agreement as how to spell the word. The hyphen is often omitted if reference is to the social condition, and used for the cultural movement, to underline the double-coding. But in this practice, as in the theory generally, there is little consensus.

2. Edward Buscombe, ed., *The BFI Companion to the Western* (New York: Da Capo Press, 1988).

3. I am indebted to Nanna Verhoeff for her paper, "Shooting Matters: Some Questions on the Limits of Genre," from the conference of July, 1997 held at Utrecht University, Holland: "Back in the Saddle Again: Critical Approaches to the Early Western Film."

4. When *Horizons West* was published in 1969 I was critiqued for arguing that "first of all the Western is American history." I remain unrepentant. Current accounts of the Western in English and belles-lettres studies appear dominated by ideological critics such as Jane Tomkins (*West of Everything*, New York: Oxford University Press, 1992) and Lee Clark Mitchell (*Westerns*, Chicago: The University of Chicago Press, 1995), who insist masculinity is what defines the Western. Tomkins is highly selective in fashioning her arguments that see the genre's manliness as hostile to language, the hero aspiring to be a kind of landscape, etc. The classical Western is a male-oriented genre undoubtedly, but this focus

is not unique to the Western, which cannot exist outside of its nationalist and historical base that provides the genre's framework and iconography.

5. See *The Book of Westerns*, Ian Cameron and Douglas Pye, eds. (New York: Continuum, 1996) for another anthology on the genre, a much broader coverage and a collection of largely new articles from *Movie* writers (available as *The Movie Book of The Western* in England).

6. Lindsay Anderson. *About John Ford . . .* (London: McGraw-Hill Book Company, 1981), pp. 13–5. Stuart Hall and Paddy Whannel, *The Popular Arts* (London: Hutchinson Educational, 1964), pp. 99–109.

7. Alan Lovell, "The Western," and Bill Nichols, "Style, Grammar and the Movies," in *Movies and Methods*, Nichols ed. (Berkeley: University of California Press, 1976). The site of successive beachheads and a cumulative analyis, *My Darling Clementine*'s critical history provides an index to the evolution of cinema studies approaches, from genre and popular culture studies to authorship, *mise en scene*, and structuralism to ideological and post-modern readings. Critiqued for its "aestheticizing" departure from the ordinary genre movie by both Warshow and Bazin, praised as populist poetry by both Anderson and Whannel, the film was seen by Lovell as effecting the ideal marriage of history, narrative and action. However, Nichols viewed its style as a "morbid delaying tactic," rebutting Peter Wollen who had positioned the film in his *Signs and Meaning in the Cinema*, as the initial stable leg in a triadic trajectory toward the indeterminacy of *The Searchers* and the despair of *The Man Who Shot Libery Valance*.

8. Peter Wollen, *Signs and Meanings in the Cinema* (London: Martin, Secker & Warburg, 1969), p. 96.

9. Pauline Kael, *I Lost It at The Movies* (Boston: Little, Brown & Company/Bantam, 1966), p. 287.

10. Andrew Sarris, *American Cinema: Directors and Directions* (New York: E.P. Dutton, 1968), p. 30.

11. Andres Huyssen, "Mapping the Postmodern," *The Post-modern Reader*, p.40.

12. "Chi-hua-hua *n.*—any of an ancient Mexican breed of very small dog with large, pointed ears." Chihuahua is also linked with Indian roots in Wyatt's casually racist threat to send her "back to the Apache reservation where you belong"; shortly thereafter he dunks her in the horse trough. Yet Linda Darnell's detailing humanizes the woman, sympathetic in her abject passion for Doc, even in her infidelity, gamely wiping her nose with her skirt. The script has Tombstone rallying round for her operation, but the film's ideology and symbolism—brazen Chihuahua sporting Cory Sue's cross, the dead James' "chingadera"—insist on her as an impurity that must be removed.

MOVIE CHRONICLE:
The Westerner

Robert Warshow (1954)

They that have power to hurt and will do none, That do not do the thing they most do show,
Who, moving others, are themselves as stone, Unmoved, cold, and to temptation slow;
They rightly do inherit heaven's graces,
And husband nature's riches from expense;
They are the lords and owners of their faces,
Others but stewards of their excellence.

The two most successful creations of American movies are the gangster and the Westerner: men with guns. Guns as physical objects, and the postures associated with their use, form the visual and emotional center of both types of films. I suppose this reflects the importance of guns in the fantasy life of Americans; but that is a less illuminating point than it appears to be.

The gangster movie, which no longer exists in its "classical" form, is a story of enterprise and success ending in precipitate failure. Success is conceived as an increasing power to work injury, it belongs to the city, and it is of course a form of evil (though the gangster's death, presented usually as "punishment," is perceived simply as defeat). The peculiarity of the gangster is his unceasing, nervous activity. The exact nature of his enterprises may remain vague, but his commitment to enterprise is always clear, and all the more clear because he operates outside the field of utility. He is without culture, without manners, without leisure, or at any rate his leisure is likely to be spent in debauchery so compulsively aggressive as to seem only another aspect of his "work." But he is graceful, moving like a dancer among the crowded dangers of the city.

Like other tycoons, the gangster is crude in conceiving his ends but by no means inarticulate; on the contrary, he is usually expansive and noisy (the introspective gangster is a fairly recent development), and can state definitely what he wants: to take over the North Side, to own a hundred suits, to be Number One. But new "frontiers" will present themselves infinitely, and by a rigid convention it is understood that as soon as he wishes to rest on his gains, he is on the way to destruction.

The gangster is lonely and melancholy, and can give the impression of a profound worldly wisdom. He appeals most to adolescents with their impatience and their feeling of being outsiders, but more generally he appeals to that side of all of us which refuses to believe in the "normal" possibilities of happiness and achievement; the gangster is the "no" to that great American "yes" which is stamped so big over our official culture and yet has so little to do with the way we really feel about our lives. But the gangster's loneliness and melancholy are not "authentic"; like everything else that belongs to him, they are not honestly come by: he is lonely and melancholy not because life ultimately demands such feelings but because he has put himself in a position where everybody wants to kill him and eventually somebody will. He is wide open and defenseless, incomplete because unable to accept any limits or come to terms with his own nature, fearful, loveless. And the story of his career is a nightmare inversion of the values of ambition and opportunity. From the window of Scarface's bulletproof apartment can be seen an electric sign proclaiming: "The World Is Yours," and, if I remember, this sign is the last thing we see after Scarface lies dead in the street. In the end it is the gangster's weakness as much as his power and freedom that appeals to us; the world is not ours, but it is not his either, and in his death he "pays" for our fantasies, releasing us momentarily both from the concept of success, which he denies by caricaturing it, and from the need to succeed, which he shows to be dangerous.

The Western hero, by contrast, is a figure of repose. He resembles the gangster in being lonely and to some degree melancholy. But his melancholy comes from the "simple" recognition that life is unavoidably serious, not from the disproportions of his own temperament. And his loneliness is organic, not imposed on him by his situation but belonging to him intimately and testifying to his completeness. The gangster must reject others violently or draw them violently to him. The Westerner is not thus compelled to seek love; he is prepared to accept it, perhaps, but he never asks of it more than it can give, and we see him constantly in situations where love is at best an irrelevance. If there is a woman he loves, she is usually unable to understand his motives; she is against killing and being killed, and he finds it impossible to explain to her that there is no point in being "against" these things: they belong to his world.

Very often this woman is from the East and her failure to understand represents a clash of cultures. In the American mind, refinement, virtue, civilization, Christianity itself, are seen as feminine, and therefore women are often portrayed as possessing some kind of deeper wisdom, while the men, for all their apparent self-assurance, are fundamentally childish. But the West, lacking the graces of civilization, is the place "where men are men"; in Western movies, men have the deeper wisdom and the women are children. Those women in the Western movies who share the hero's understanding of life are prostitutes (or, as they are usually presented, barroom entertainers)—women, that is, who have come to understand in the most practical way how love can be an irrelevance, and therefore "fallen" women. The gangster, too, associates with prostitutes, but for him the important things about a prostitute are her passive availability and her costliness: she is part of his winnings. In Western movies, the important thing about a prostitute is her quasi-masculine independence: nobody owns her, nothing has to be explained to her, and she is not, like a virtuous woman, a "value" that demands to be protected. When the Westerner leaves the prostitute for a virtuous woman—for love—he is in fact forsaking a way of life, though the point of the choice is often obscured by having the prostitute killed by getting into the line of fire.

The Westerner is *par excellence* a man of leisure. Even when he wears the badge of a marshal or, more rarely, owns a ranch, he appears to be unemployed. We see him standing at a bar, or playing poker—a game which expresses perfectly his talent for remaining relaxed in the midst of tension—or perhaps camping out on the plains on some extraordinary errand. If he does own a ranch, it is in the background; we are not actually aware that he owns anything except his horse. his guns, and the one worn suit of clothing which is likely to remain unchanged all through the movie. It comes as a surprise to see him take money from his pocket or an extra shirt from his saddlebags. As a rule we do not even know where he sleeps at night and don't think of asking. Yet it never occurs to us that he is a poor man; there is no poverty in Western movies, and really no wealth either: those great cattle domains and shipments of gold which figure so largely in the plots are moral and not material quantities, not the objects of contention but only its occasion. Possessions too are irrelevant.

Employment of some kind—usually unproductive—is always open to the Westerner, but when he accepts it, it is not because he needs to make a living, much less from any idea of "getting ahead." Where could he want to "get ahead" to? By the time we see him, he is already "there": he can ride a horse faultlessly, keep his countenance in the face of death, and draw his gun a little faster and shoot it a little straighter than anyone he is likely to meet. These are sharply defined acquirements, giving to the figure of the Westerner an apparent moral clarity which corresponds to the clarity of his physical image against his bare landscape; initially, at any rate, the Western movie presents itself as being without mystery, its whole universe comprehended in what we see on the screen.

Much of this apparent simplicity arises directly from those "cinematic" elements which have long been understood to give the Western theme its special appropriateness for the movies: the wide expanses of land, the free movement of men on horses. As guns constitute the visible moral center of the Western movie, suggesting continually the possibility of violence, so land and horses represent the movie's material basis, its sphere of action. But the land and the horses have also a moral significance: the physical freedom they represent belongs to the moral "openness" of the West—corresponding to the fact that guns are carried where they can be seen. (And, as we shall see, the character of land and horses changes as the Western film becomes more complex.)

The gangster's world is less open, and his arts not so easily identifiable as the Westerner's. Perhaps he too can keep his countenance, but the mask he wears is really no mask: its purpose is precisely to make evident the fact that he desperately wants to "get ahead" and will stop at nothing. Where the Westerner imposes himself by the appearance of unshakable control, the gangster's pre-eminence lies in the suggestion that he may at any moment lose control; his strength is not in being able to shoot faster or straighter than others, but in being more willing to shoot. "Do it first," says Scarface expounding his mode of operation, "and keep on doing it." With the Westerner, it is a crucial point of honor not to "do it first"; his gun remains in its holster until the moment of combat.

There is no suggestion, however, that he draws the gun reluctantly. The Westerner could not fulfill himself if the moment did not finally come when he can shoot his enemy down. But because that moment is so thoroughly the expression of his being, it must be kept pure. He will not violate the accepted forms of combat though by doing so he could save a city. And he can wait. "When you call me that— smile!"—the villain smiles weakly, soon he is laughing with horrible joviality, and the crisis is past. But it is allowed to pass because it must come again: sooner or later Trampas will "make his play," and the Virginian will be ready for him.

What does the Westerner fight for? We know he is on the side of justice and order, and of course it can be said he fights for these things. But such broad aims never correspond exactly to his real motives; they only offer him his opportunity. The Westerner himself, when an explanation is asked of him (usually by a woman), is likely to say that he does what he "has to do." If justice and order did not continually demand his protection, he would be without a calling. Indeed, we come upon him often in just that situation, as the reign of law settles over the West and he is forced to see that his day is over; those are the pictures which end with his death or with his departure for some more remote frontier. What he defends, at bottom, is the purity of his own image—in fact his honor. This is what makes him invulnerable. When the gangster is killed, his whole life is shown to have been a mistake, but the image the Westerner seeks to maintain can be presented as clearly in defeat as in victory: he fights not for advantage and not for the right, but to state what he is, and he must live in a world which permits that statement. The Westerner is the last gentleman, and the movies which over and over again tell his story are probably the last art form in which the concept of honor retains its strength.

Of course I do not mean to say that ideas of virtue and justice and courage have gone out of culture. Honor is more than these things: it is a style, concerned with harmonious appearances as much as with desirable consequences, and tending therefore toward the denial of life in favor of art. "Who hath it? he that died o' Wednesday." On the whole, a world that leans to Falstaff's view is a more civilized and even, finally, a more graceful world. It is just the march of civilization that forces the Westerner to move on; and if we actually had to confront the question it might turn out that the woman who refuses to understand him is right as often as she is wrong. But we do not confront the question. Where the Westerner lives it is always about 1870—not the real 1870, either, or the real West—and he is killed or goes away when his position becomes problematical. The fact that he continues to hold our attention is evidence enough that, in his proper frame, he presents an image of personal nobility that is still real for us.

Clearly, this image easily becomes ridiculous: we need only look at William S. Hart or Tom Mix, who in the wooden absoluteness of their virtue represented little that an adult could take seriously; and doubtless such figures as Gene Autry or Roy Rogers are no better, though I confess I have seen none of their movies. Some film enthusiasts claim to find in the early, unsophisticated Westerns a "cinematic purity" that has since been lost; this idea is as valid, and finally as misleading, as T. S. Eliot's statement that *Everyman* is the only play in English that stays within the limitations of art. The truth is that the Westerner comes into the field of serious art only when his moral code, without ceasing to be compelling, is seen also to be imperfect. The Westerner at his best exhibits a moral ambiguity which darkens his image and saves him from absurdity; this ambiguity arises from the fact that, whatever his justifications, he is a killer of men.

In *The Virginian*, which is an archetypal Western movie as *Scarface* or *Little*

William S. Hart in Tumbleweeds: *"The wooden absoluteness of ... virtue."*

Caesar are archetypal gangster movies, there is a lynching in which the hero (Gary Cooper), as leader of a posse, must supervise the hanging of his best friend for stealing cattle. With the growth of American "social consciousness," it is no longer possible to present a lynching in the movies unless the point is the illegality and injustice of the lynching itself; *The Ox-Bow Incident*, made in 1943, explicitly puts forward the newer point of view and can be regarded as a kind of "anti-Western." But in 1929, when *The Virginian* was made, the present inhibition about lynching was not yet in force; the justice, and therefore the necessity, of the hanging is never questioned—except by the schoolteacher from the East, whose refusal to understand serves as usual to set forth more sharply the deeper seriousness of the West. The Virginian is thus in a tragic dilemma where one moral absolute conflicts with another and the choice of either must leave a moral stain. If he had chosen to save his friend, he would have violated the image of himself that he had made essential to his existence, and the movie would have had to end with his death, for only by his death could the image have been restored. Having chosen instead to sacrifice his friend to the higher demands of the "code"—the only choice worthy of him, as even the friend understands—he is none the less stained by the killing, but what is needed now to set accounts straight is not his death but the death of the villain Trampas, the leader of the cattle thieves, who had escaped the posse and abandoned the Virginian's friend to his fate. Again the woman intervenes: Why must there be *more* killing? If the hero really loved her, he would leave town, refusing Trampas' challenge. What good will it be if Trampas should kill him? But the Virginian does once more what he "has to do," and in avenging his friend's death wipes out the stain on his own honor. Yet his victory cannot be complete: no death can be paid for and no stain truly wiped out; the movie is still a tragedy, for though the hero escapes with his life, he has been forced to confront the ultimate limits of his moral ideas.

This mature sense of limitation and unavoidable guilt is what gives the Westerner a "right" to his melancholy. It is true that the gangster's story is also a tragedy—in certain formal ways more clearly a tragedy than the Westerner's—but it is a romantic tragedy, based on a hero whose defeat springs with almost mechanical inevitability from the outrageous presumption of his demands: the gangster is bound to go on until he is killed. The Westerner is a more classical figure, self-contained and limited to begin with, seeking not to extend his dominion but only to assert his personal value, and his tragedy lies in the fact that even this circumscribed demand cannot be fully realized. Since the Westerner is not a murderer but (most of the time) a man of virtue, and since he is always prepared for defeat, he retains his inner invulnerability and his story need not end with his death (and usually does not); but what we finally respond to is not his victory but his defeat.

Up to a point, it is plain that the deeper seriousness of the good Western films comes from the introduction of a realism, both physical and psychological, that was missing with Tom Mix and William S. Hart. As lines of age have come into Gary Cooper's face since *The Virginian*, so the outlines of the Western movie in general have become less smooth, its background more drab. The sun still beats upon the town, but the camera is likely now to take advantage of this illumination to seek out more closely the shabbiness of buildings and furniture, the loose, worn hang of clothing, the wrinkles and dirt of the faces. Once it has been discovered that the true theme of the Western movie is not the freedom and expansiveness of frontier life, but its limitations, its material bareness, the pressures of obligation, then even the landscape itself ceases to be quite the arena of free movement it once was, but becomes instead a great empty waste, cutting down more often than it exaggerates the stature of the horseman who rides across it. We are more likely now to see the Westerner struggling against the obstacles of the physical world (as in the wonderful scenes on the desert and among the rocks in *The Last Posse)* than carelessly surmounting them. Even the horses, no longer the "friends" of man or the inspired chargers of knight-errantry, have lost much of the moral significance that once seemed to belong to them in their careering across the screen. It seems to me the horses grow tired and stumble more often than they did, and that we see them less frequently at the gallop.

In *The Gunfighter,* a remarkable film of a couple of years ago, the landscape has virtually disappeared. Most of the action takes place indoors, in a cheerless saloon where a tired "bad man" (Gregory Peck) contemplates the waste of his life, to be senselessly killed at the end by a vicious youngster setting off on the same futile path. The movie is done in cold, quiet tones of gray, and every object in it—faces, clothing, a table, the hero's heavy mustache—is given an air of uncompromising authenticity, suggesting those dim photographs of the nineteenth-century West in which Wyatt Earp, say, turns out to be a blank untidy figure posing awkwardly before some uninteresting building. This "authenticity," to be sure, is only aesthetic; the chief fact about nineteenth-century photographs, to my eyes at any rate, is how stonily they refuse to yield up the truth. But that limitation is just what is needed: by preserving some hint of the rigidity of archaic photography (only in tone and decor, never in composition), *The Gunfighter* can permit us to feel that we are looking at a more "real" West than the one the movies have accustomed us to—harder, duller, less "romantic"—and yet without forcing us outside the boundaries which give the Western movie its validity.

We come upon the hero of *The Gunfighter* at the end of a career in which he has never upheld justice and order, and has been at times, apparently, an actual criminal; in this case, it is clear that the hero has been wrong and the woman who has rejected his way of life has been right. He is thus without any of the larger justifications, and knows himself a ruined man. There can be no question of his "redeeming" himself in any socially constructive way. He is too much the victim of his own reputation to turn marshal as one of his old friends has done, and he is not offered the sentimental solution of a chance to give up his life for some good end; the whole point is that he exists outside the field of social value. Indeed, if we were once allowed to see him in the days of his "success," he might become a figure like the gangster, for his career has been aggressively "anti-social" and the practical problem he faces is the gangster's problem: there will always be somebody trying to kill him. Yet it is obviously absurd to speak of him as "anti-social," not only because we do not see him acting as a criminal, but more fundamentally because we do not see his milieu as a society. Of course it has its "social problems" and a kind of static history: civilization is always just at the point of driving out the old freedom; there are women and children to represent the possibility of a settled life; and there is the marshal, a bad man turned good, determined to keep at least his area of jurisdiction at peace. But these elements are not, in fact, a part of the film's "realism," even though they come out of the real history of the West; they belong to the conventions of the form, to that accepted framework which makes the film possible in the first place, and they exist not to provide a standard by which the gunfighter can be judged, but only to set him off. The true "civilization" of the Western movie is always embodied in an individual, good or bad is more a matter of personal bearing than of social consequences, and the conflict of good and bad is a duel between two men. Deeply troubled and obviously doomed, the gunfighter is the Western hero still, perhaps all the more because his value must express itself entirely in his own being—in his presence, the way he holds our eyes—and in contradiction to the facts. No matter what he has done, he looks right, and he remains invulnerable because, without acknowledging anyone else's right to judge him, he has judged his own failure and has already assimilated it, understanding—as no one else understands except the marshal and the barroom girl— that he can do nothing but play out the drama of the gun fight again and again until the time comes when it will be he who gets killed. What "redeems" him is that he no longer believes in this drama and nevertheless will continue to play his role perfectly: the pattern is all.

The proper function of realism in the Western movie can only be to deepen the lines of that pattern. It is an art form for connoisseurs, where the spectator derives his pleasure from the appreciation of minor variations within the working out of a pre-established order. One does not want too much novelty: it comes as a shock, for instance, when the hero is made to operate without a gun, as has been done in several pictures (e.g., *Destry Rides Again*), and our uneasiness is allayed only when he is finally compelled to put his "pacifism" aside. If the hero can be shown to be troubled, complex, fallible, even eccentric, or the villain given some psychological taint or, better, some evocative physical mannerism, to shade the colors of his villainy, that is all to the good. Indeed, that kind of variation is absolutely necessary to keep the type from becoming sterile; we do not want to see the same movie over and over again, only the same form. But when the impulse toward realism is extended into a "reinterpretation" of the West as a developed society, drawing our eyes away from the hero if only to the extent of showing him as the one dominant figure in a complex social order, then the pattern is broken and the West itself begins to be uninteresting. If the "social problems" of the frontier are to be the movie's chief concern, there is no longer any point in re-examining these problems twenty times a year; they have been solved, and the people for whom they once were real are dead. Moreover, the hero himself, still the film's central figure, now tends to become its one unassimilable element, since he is the most "unreal."

The Ox-Bow Incident, by denying the convention of the lynching, presents us with a modern "social drama" and evokes a corresponding response, but in doing so it almost makes the Western setting irrelevant, a mere backdrop of beautiful scenery. (It is significant that *The Ox-Bow Incident* has no hero; a hero would have to stop the lynching or be killed in trying to stop it, and then the "problem" of lynching would no longer be central.) Even in *The Gunfighter* the women and children are a little too much in evidence, threatening constantly to become a real focus of concern instead of simply part of the given framework; and the young tough who kills the hero has too much the air of juvenile criminality: the hero himself could never have been like that,

Gregory Peck as The Gunfighter: *"No longer interested in the drama of combat."*

and the idea of a cycle being repeated therefore loses its sharpness. But the most striking example of the confusion created by a too conscientious "social" realism is in the celebrated *High Noon*.

In *High Noon* we find Gary Cooper still the upholder of order that he was in *The Virginian*, but twenty-four years older, stooped, slower moving, awkward, his face lined, the flesh sagging, a less beautiful and weaker figure, but with the suggestion of greater depth that belongs almost automatically to age. Like the hero of *The Gunfighter*, he no longer has to assert his character and is no longer interested in the drama of combat; it is hard to imagine that he might once have been so youthful as to say, "When you call me that—smile!" In fact, when we come upon him he is hanging up his guns and his marshal's badge in order to begin a new, peaceful life with his bride, who is a Quaker. But then the news comes that a man he had sent to prison has been pardoned and will get to town on the noon train; three friends of this man have come to wait for him at the station, and when the freed convict arrives the four of them will come to kill the marshal. He is thus trapped; the bride will object, the hero himself will waver much more than he would have done twenty-four years ago, but in the end he will play out the drama because it is what he "has to do." All this belongs to the established form (there is even the "fallen woman" who understands the marshal's position as his wife does not). Leaving aside the crudity of building up suspense by means of the clock, the actual Western drama of *High Noon* is well handled and forms a good companion piece to *The Virginian*, showing in both conception and technique the ways in which the Western movie has naturally developed.

But there is a second drama along with the first. As the marshal sets out to find deputies to help him deal with the four gunmen, we are taken through the various social strata of the town, each group in turn refusing its assistance out of cowardice, malice, irresponsibility, or venality. With this we are in the field of "social drama"—of a very low order, incidentally, altogether unconvincing and displaying a vulgar anti-populism that has marred some other movies of Stanley Kramer's. But the falsity of the "social drama" is less important than the fact that it does not belong in the movie to begin with. The technical problem was to make it necessary for the marshal to face his enemies alone; to explain *why* the other townspeople are not at his side is to raise a question which does not exist in the proper frame of the Western movie, where the hero is "naturally" alone and it is only necessary to contrive the physical absence of those who might be his allies, if any contrivance is needed at all. In addition, though the hero of *High Noon* proves himself a better man than all around him, the actual effect of this contrast is to lessen his stature: he becomes only a rejected man of virtue. In our final glimpse of him, as he rides away through the town where he has spent most of his life without really imposing himself on it, he is a pathetic rather than a tragic figure. And his departure has another meaning as well; the "social drama" has no place for him.

But there is also a different way of violating the Western form. This is to yield entirely to its static quality as legend and to the "cinematic" temptations of its landscape, the horses, the quiet men. John Ford's famous *Stagecoach* (1939) had much of this unhappy preoccupation with style, and the same director's *My Darling Clementine* (1946), a soft and beautiful movie about Wyatt Earp, goes further along the same path, offering indeed a superficial accuracy of historical reconstruction, but so loving in execution as to destroy the outlines of the Western legend, assimilating it to the more sentimental legend of rural America and making the hero a more dangerous Mr. Deeds. *(Powder River*, a recent "routine" Western shamelessly copied from *My Darling Clementine*, is in most ways a better film; lacking the benefit of a serious director, it is necessarily more concerned with drama than with style.)

The highest expression of this aestheticizing tendency is in George Stevens' *Shane*, where the legend of the West is virtually reduced to its essentials and then fixed in the dreamy clarity of a fairy tale. There never was so broad and bare and lovely a landscape as Stevens puts before us, or so unimaginably comfortless a "town" as the little group of buildings on the prairie to which the settlers must come for their supplies and to buy a drink. The mere physical progress of the film, following the style of *A Place in the Sun*, is so deliberately graceful that everything seems to be happening at the bottom of a clear lake. The hero (Alan Ladd) is hardly a man at all, but something like the Spirit of the West, beautiful in fringed buckskins. He emerges mysteriously from the plains, breathing sweetness and a melancholy which is no longer simply the Westerner's natural response to experience but has taken on spirituality; and when he has accomplished his mission, meeting and destroying in the black figure of Jack Palance a Spirit of Evil just as metaphysical as his own embodiment of virtue, he fades away again into the more distant West, a man whose "day is over," leaving behind the wondering little boy who might have imagined the whole story. The choice of Alan Ladd to play the leading role is alone an indication of this film's tendency. Actors like Gary Cooper or Gregory Peck are in themselves, as material objects, "realistic," seeming to bear in their bodies and their faces mortality, limitation, the knowledge of good and evil. Ladd is a more "aesthetic" object, with some of the "universality" of a piece of sculpture; his special quality is in his physical smoothness and serenity, unworldly and yet not innocent, but suggesting that no experience can really touch him. Stevens has tried to freeze the Western myth once and for all in the immobility of Alan Ladd's countenance. If *Shane* were "right," and fully successful, it might be possible to say there was no point in making any more Western movies; once the hero is apotheosized, variation and development are closed off.

Alan Ladd in George Stevens' Shane: *"the dreamy clarity of a fairy tale."*

Shane is not "right," but it is still true that the possibilities of fruitful variation in the Western movie are limited. The form can keep its freshness through endless repetitions only because of the special character of the film medium, where the physical difference between one object and another—above all, between one actor and another—is of such enormous importance, serving the function that is served by the variety of language in the perpetuation of literary types. In this sense, the "vocabulary" of films is much larger than that of literature and falls more readily into pleasing and significant arrangements. (That may explain why the middle levels of excellence are more easily reached in the movies than in literary forms, and perhaps also why the status of the movies as art is constantly being called into question.) But the advantage of this almost automatic particularity belongs to all films alike. Why does the Western movie especially have such a hold on our imagination?

Chiefly, I think, because it offers a serious orientation to the problem of violence such as can be found almost nowhere else in our culture. One of the well-known peculiarities of modern civilized opinion is its refusal to acknowledge the value of violence. This refusal is a virtue, but like many virtues it involves a certain willful blindness and it encourages hypocrisy. We train ourselves to be shocked or bored by cultural images of violence, and our very concept of heroism tends to be a passive one: we are less drawn to the brave young men who kill large numbers of our enemies than to the heroic prisoners who endure torture without capitulating. In art, though we may still be able to understand and participate in the values of the Iliad, a modern writer like Ernest Hemingway we find somewhat embarrassing: there is no doubt that he stirs us, but we cannot help recognizing also that he is a little childish. And in the criticism of popular culture, where the educated observer is usually under the illusion that he has nothing at stake, the presence of images of violence is often assumed to be in itself a sufficient ground for condemnation.

These attitudes, however, have not reduced the element of violence in our culture but, if anything, have helped to free it from moral control by letting it take on the aura of "emancipation." The celebration of acts of violence is left more and more to the irresponsible: on the higher cultural levels to writers like Céline, and lower down to Mickey Spillane or Horace McCoy, or to the comic books, television, and the movies. The gangster movie, with its numerous variations, belongs to this cultural "underground" which sets forth the attractions of violence in the face of all our higher social attitudes. It is a more "modern" genre than the Western, perhaps even more profound, because it confronts industrial society on its own ground—the city—and because, like much of our advanced art, it gains its effects by a gross insistence on its own narrow logic. But it is anti-social, resting on fantasies of irresponsible freedom. If we are brought finally to acquiesce in the denial of these fantasies, it is only because they have been shown to be dangerous, not because they have given way to a better vision of behavior.[1]

In war movies, to be sure, it is possible to present the uses of violence within a framework of responsibility. But there is the disadvantage that modern war is a co-operative enterprise; its violence is largely impersonal, and heroism belongs to the group more than to the individual. The hero of a war movie is most often simply a leader, and his superiority is likely to be expressed in a denial of the heroic: you are not supposed to be brave, you are supposed to get the job done and stay alive (this too, of course, is a kind of heroic posture, but a new—and "practical"—one). At its best, the war movie may represent a more civilized point of view than the Western, and if it were not continually marred by ideological sentimentality we might hope to find it developing into a higher form of drama. But it cannot supply the values we seek in the Western.

Those values are in the image of a single man who wears a gun on his thigh. The gun tells us that he lives in a world of violence, and even that he "believes in violence." But the drama is one of self-restraint: the moment of violence must come in its own time and according to its special laws, or else it is valueless. There is little cruelty in Western movies, and little sentimentality; our eyes are not focused on the sufferings of the defeated but on the deportment of the hero. Really, it is not violence at all which is the "point" of the Western movie, but a certain image of man, a style, which expresses itself most clearly in violence. Watch a child with his toy guns and you will see: what most interests him is not (as we so much fear) the fantasy of hurting others, but to work out how a man might look when he shoots or is shot. A hero is one who looks like a hero.

Whatever the limitations of such an idea in experience, it has always been valid in art, and has a special validity in an art where appearances are everything. The Western hero is necessarily an archaic figure; we do not really believe in him and would not have him step out of his rigidly conventionalized background. But his archaicism does not take away from his power; on the contrary, it adds to it by keeping him just a little beyond the reach both of common sense and of absolutized emotion, the two usual impulses of our art. And he has, after all, his own kind of relevance. He is there to remind us of the possibility of style in an age which has put on itself the burden of pretending that style has no meaning, and, in the midst of our anxieties over the problem of violence, to suggest that even in killing or being killed we are not freed from the necessity of establishing satisfactory modes of behavior. Above all, the movies in which the Westerner plays out his role preserve for us the pleasures of a complete and self-contained drama—and one which still effortlessly crosses the boundaries which divide our culture—in a time when other, more consciously serious art forms are increasingly complex, uncertain, and ill-defined.

NOTE

1. I am not concerned here with the actual social consequences of gangster movies, though I suspect they could not have been so pernicious as they were thought to be. Some of the compromises introduced to avoid the supposed bad effects of the old gangster movies may be, if anything, more dangerous, for the sadistic violence that once belonged only to the gangster is now commonly enlisted on the side of the law and thus goes undefeated, allowing us (if we wish) to find in the movies a sort of "confirmation" of our fantasies.

Stagecoach: *"At the source of the western the ethics of the epic and even of tragedy."*
Below: Red River, *"a genuine western."*

THE EVOLUTION OF THE WESTERN

Andre Bazin (1955)

By the eve of the war the western had reached a definitive stage of perfection. The year 1940 marks a point beyond which some new development seemed inevitable, a development that the four years of war delayed, then modified, though without controlling it. *Stagecoach* (1939) is the ideal example of the maturity of a style brought to classic perfection. John Ford struck the ideal balance between social myth, historical reconstruction, psychological truth, and the traditional theme of the western *mise en scène*. None of these elements dominated any other. *Stagecoach* is like a wheel, so perfectly made that it remains in equilibrium on its axis in any position. Let us list some names and titles for 1939-1940: King Vidor: *Northwest Passage* (1940), Michael Curtiz: *The Santa Fe Trail* (1940), *Virginia City* (1940); Fritz Lang: The *Return of Frank James* (1940), *Western Union*, (1940); John Ford: *Drums Along the Mohawk* (1939); William Wyler: *The Westerner* (1940); George Marshall, *Destry Rides Again*, with Marlene Dietrich, (1939).[1]

This list is significant. It shows that the established directors, having perhaps begun their careers twenty years before with series westerns made almost anonymously, turn (or return) to the western at the peak of their careers—even Wyler whose gift seemed to be for anything but this genre.

This phenomenon can be explained by the widespread publicity given westerns between 1937 and 1940. Perhaps the sense of national awareness which preceded the war in the Roosevelt era contributed to this. We are disposed to think so, insofar as the western is rooted in the history of the American nation which it exalts directly or indirectly.

Eroticism in the super-western: Jennifer Jones in Duel in the Sun.

In any case, this period supports J.-L. Rieupeyrout's argument for the historical realism of the western.[2]

But by a paradox more apparent than real, the war years, properly so called, almost removed the western from Hollywood's repertoire. On reflection this is not surprising. For the same reason that the westerns were multiplied and admired at the expense of other adventure films, the war film was to exclude them, at least provisionally, from the market.

As soon as the war seemed virtually won and even before peace was definitely established, the western reappeared and was again made in large numbers, but this new phase of its history deserves a closer look.

The perfection, or the classic stage, which the genre had reached implied that it had to justify its survival by introducing new elements. I do not pretend to explain everything by the famous law of successive aesthetic periods but there is no rule against bringing it into play here. Take the new films of John Ford. *My Darling Clementine* (1946) and *Fort Apache* (1948) could well be examples of baroque embellishment of the classicism of *Stagecoach*. All the same, although this concept of the baroque may account for a certain technical formalism, or for the relative preciousness of this or that scenario, I do not feel that it can justify any further complex evolution. This evolution must be explained doubtless in relation to the level of perfection reached in 1940 but also in terms of the events of 1941 to 1945.

Let us call the ensemble of forms adopted by the postwar western the "superwestern." For the purposes of our exposé this word will bring together phenomena that are not always comparable. It can certainly be justified on negative grounds, in contrast to the classicism of the forties and to the tradition of which it is the outcome. The superwestern is a western that would be ashamed to be just itself, and looks for some additional interest to justify its existence—an aesthetic, sociological, moral, psychological, political, or erotic interest, in short some quality extrinsic to the genre and which is supposed to enrich it. We will come back later to these adjectives. But first we should indicate the influence of the war on the evolution of the western after 1944. The phenomenon of the superwestern would probably have emerged anyway, but its content would have been different. The real influence of the war made itself deeply felt when it was over. The major films inspired by it come, naturally, after 1945. But the world conflict not only provided Hollywood with spectacular scenes, it also provided and, indeed, forced upon it, some subjects to reflect upon, at least for a few years. History, which was formally only the material of the western, will often become its subject: this is particularly true of *Fort Apache* in which we see the beginning of political rehabilitation of the Indian, which was followed up by numerous westerns up to *Apache* and exemplified particularly in *Broken Arrow* by Delmer Daves (1950). But the profounder influence of the war is undoubtedly more indirect and one must look to find it wherever the film substitutes a social or moral theme for the traditional one. The origin of this goes back to 1943 with William Wellman's *Ox-Bow Incident*, of which *High Noon* is the distant relation. (However, in Zinnemann's film it is also a rampant McCarthyism that is under scrutiny.)

Eroticism also may be seen to be at least an indirect consequence of the war, so far as it derives from the triumph of the pin-up girl. This is true perhaps of Howard Hughes' *The Outlaw* (1943). Love is to all intents and purposes foreign to the western. (*Shane* will rightly exploit this conflict.) And eroticism all the more so, its appearance as a dramatic springboard implying that henceforth the genre is just being used as a foil the better to set off the sex appeal of the heroine. There is no doubt about what is intended in *Duel in the Sun* (King Vidor, 1946) whose spectacular luxury provides a further reason, albeit on formal grounds, to classify it as a superwestern.

Yet *High Noon* and *Shane* remain the two films that best illustrate the mutation in the western genre as an effect of the awareness it has gained of itself and its limits. In the former, Fred Zinnemann combines the effect of moral drama with the aestheticism of his framing. I am not one of those who turn up their noses at *High Noon*. I consider it a fine film and prefer it to Stevens' film. But the great skill exemplified in Foreman's adaptation was his ability to combine a story that might well have been developed in another genre with a traditional western theme. In other words, he treated the western as a form in need of a content. As for *Shane* this is the ultimate in "superwesternization." In fact, with it, George Stevens sets out to justify the western—by the western. The others do their ingenious best to extract explicit themes from implied myths but the theme of *Shane* is the myth. In it Stevens combines two or

Shane, the "superwestern." Alan Ladd, "the knight errant in search of his grail," finds it at the farm.

three basic western themes, the chief being the knight errant in search of his grail, and so that no one will miss the point, Stevens dresses him in white. White clothes and a white horse are taken for granted in the Manichean world of the western, but it is clear that the costume of Alan Ladd carries with it all the weighty significance of a symbol, while on Tom Mix it was simply the uniform of goodness and daring. So we have come full circle. The earth is round. The superwestern has gone so far beyond itself as to find itself back in the Rocky Mountains.

If the western was about to disappear, the superwestern would be the perfect expression of its decadence, of its final collapse. But the western is definitely made of quite other stuff than the American comedy or the crime film. Its ups and downs do not affect its existence very much. Its roots continue to spread under the Hollywood humus and one is amazed to see green and robust suckers spring up in the midst of the seductive but sterile hybrids that some would replace them by.

To begin with, the appearance of the superwestern has only affected the more out-of-the-ordinary productions: those of the A-film and of the superproduction. These surface tremors have not disturbed the commercial nucleus, the central block of the ultracommercial westerns, horseback or musical, which may even have found a second youth on television. (The success of Hopalong Cassidy is a witness to this and proves likewise the vitality of the myth even in its most elementary form.) Their acceptance by the new generation guarantees them several more cycles of years to come. But low-budget westerns never came to France and we have to be satisfied with an assurance of their survival from the personnel of American distribution companies. If their aesthetic interest, individually, is limited, their existence on the other hand is probably decisive for the general health of the genre. It is in these "lower" layers whose economic fertility has not diminished that the traditional western has continued to take root, Superwestern or no superwestern, we are never without the B-western that does not attempt to find refuge in intellectual or aesthetic alibis. Indeed, maybe the notion of the B-film is open to dispute since everything depends on how far up the scale you put the letter A. The productions I am talking about are frankly commercial, probably fairly costly, relying for their acceptance only on the reputation of their leading man and a solid story without any intellectual ambitions. *The Gunfighter*, directed by Henry King (1950) and starring Gregory Peck, is a splendid example of this attractive type of production, in which the classic theme of the killer, sick of being on the run and yet forced to kill again, is handled within a dramatic framework with great restraint. We might mention too *Across the Wide Missouri*, directed by William Wellman (1951), starring Clark Gable, and particularly *Westward the Women* (1951) by the same director.

In *Rio Grande* (1951), John Ford himself has clearly returned to the semiserial format, or at any rate to the commercial tradition—romance and all. So it is no surprise to find on this list an elderly survivor from the pioneer days of old, Allan Dwan, who for his part has never forsaken the old Triangle[3] style, even when the liquidation of McCarthyism gave him the chance to broaden the scope of the old-time themes (*Silver Lode*, 1954).

I have still a few more points to make. The classification I have followed up to now will turn out to be inadequate and I must no longer explain the evolution of the western genre by the western genre itself. Instead I must take the authors into greater account as a determining factor. It will doubtless have been observed that the list of relatively traditional productions that have been little influenced by the superwestern includes only names of established directors who even before the war specialized in fast-moving adventure films. It should come as no surprise that their work affirms the durability of the western and its laws. Howard Hawks, indeed, at the height of the vogue of the superwestern should be credited with having demonstrated that it had always been possible to turn out a genuine western based on the old dramatic and spectacle themes, without distracting our attention with some social thesis, or, what would amount to the same thing, by the form given the production. *Red River* (1948) and *The Big Sky* (1952) are western masterpieces but there is nothing baroque or decadent about them. The understanding and awareness of the means matches perfectly the sincerity of the story.

The same goes for Raoul Walsh, all due allowances being made, whose film *Saskatchewan* (1954) is a classical example of a borrowing from American history. But his other films provide me—and I am sorry if it is a little contrived—with the transition I was looking for: *Colorado Territory* (1949), *Pursued* (1947) and *Along the Great Divide* (1951) are, in a sense, perfect examples of westerns just above the B-level, made in a pleasantly traditional dramatic vein. Certainly there is no trace of a thesis. We are interested in the characters because of what happens to them and nothing happens that is not in perfect accord with the western theme. But there is something about them that, if we had no information about their date, would make us place them at once among more recent productions, and it is this "something" that I would like to define.

I have hesitated a great deal over what adjective best applies to these westerns of the fifties. At first I thought I ought to turn to words like "feeling," "sensibility," "lyricism." In any case I think that these words must not be dismissed and that they describe pretty well the character of the modem western as compared with the super-western, which is almost always intellectual at least to the degree that it requires the spectator to reflect before he can admire. All the titles I am about to list belong to films that are, if not less intelligent than *High Noon* at least without *arrière-pensée* and in which talent is always a servant of history and not of the meaning behind history. There is another word, maybe more suitable than those I have suggested or which provides a useful complement—the word "sincerity." I mean by this that the directors play fair with the genre even when they are conscious of "making a western." At the stage to which we have come in the history of the cinema naïveté is hardly conceivable, but although the superwestern replaces naïveté by preciousness or cynicism, we have proof that it is still possible to be sincere. Nicholas Ray, shooting *Johnny Guitar* (1954) to the undying fame of Joan Crawford, obviously knows what he is about. He is no less aware of the rhetoric of the genre than the George Stevens of *Shane*, and furthermore the script and the director are not without their humor; but not once does Ray adopt a condescending or paternalist attitude toward his film. He may have fun with it but he is not making fun of it. He does not feel restricted in what he has to say by the limits of the western even if what he has to say is decidedly more personal and more subtle than its unchanging mythology.

It is with an eye on the style of the narrative, rather than on the subjective attitude of the director to the genre, that I will finally choose my epithet. I say freely of the westerns I have yet to name—the best in my view—that they are "novelistic." By this I mean that without departing from the traditional themes they enrich them from within by the originality of their characters, their psychological flavor, an engaging individuality, which is what we expect from the hero of a novel. Clearly when one talks about the psychological richness of *Stagecoach*, one is talking about the way it is used and not about any particular character. For the latter we remain within the established casting categories of the western: the banker, the narrow-minded woman, the prostitute with a heart of gold, the elegant gambler, and so on. In *Run for Cover* (1955) it is something else again. The situation and characters are still just variations on the tradition, but what attracts our interest is their uniqueness rather than their generosity. We know also that Nicholas Ray always treats his pet subject, namely the violence and mystery of adolescence. The best example of this "novelization" of the western from within is provided by Edward Dmytryk in *Broken Lance* (1954), which we know is only a western remake of Mankewicz's *House of Strangers*. For the uninformed, *Broken Lance* is simply a western that is subtler than the others with more individualized characters and more complex relationships but which stays no less rigidly within the limits of two or three classic themes. In point of fact, Elia Kazan has treated a psychologically somewhat similar subject with great simplicity in his *Sea of Grass* (1947), also with Spencer Tracy. We can imagine many intermediate grades between the most dutiful B-western and the novelistic western, and my classification is inevitably arbitrary.

Nevertheless I offer the following idea. Just as Walsh is the most remarkable of the traditional veterans, Anthony Mann could be considered the most classical of the young novelistic directors. We owe the most beautifully true western of recent years to

Run for Cover. *"The novelization of the western."*

him. Indeed, the author of *The Naked Spur* is probably the one postwar American director who seems to have specialized in a field into which others have made only sporadic incursions. In any case, each of Mann's films reveals a touching frankness of attitude toward the western, an effortless sincerity to get inside its themes and there bring to life appealing characters and to invent captivating situations. Anyone who wants to know what a real western is, and the qualities it presupposes in a director, has to have seen *Devil's Doorway* (1950) with Robert Taylor, *Bend of the River* (1952) and *The Far Country* (1954) with James Stewart. Even if he does not know these three films, he simply has to know the finest of all, *The Naked Spur* (1953). Let us hope that CinemaScope will not rob Anthony Mann of his natural gift for direct and discreet use of the lyrical and above all his infallible sureness of touch in bringing together man and nature, that feeling of the open air, which in his films seems to be the very soul of the western and as a result of which he has recaptured—but at the level of the hero of the novel and no longer of the hero of the myth—the great lost secret of the Triangle days.

The above examples show that a new style and a new generation have come into existence simultaneously. It would be both going too far and naïve to pretend that the novelistic western is just something created by young men who came to film-making after the war. You could rightly refute this by pointing out that this quality is evident in *The Westerner*, for example, and there is something of it in *Red River* and *The Big Sky*. People assure me, although I am personally not aware of it, that there is much of it in Fritz Lang's *Rancho Notorious* (1952). At all events it is certain that King

Vidor's excellent *Man Without a Star* (1954) is to be placed in the same perspective, somewhere between Nicholas Ray and Anthony Mann. But we can certainly find three or four films made by the veterans to place alongside those that the younger men have made. In spite of everything, it is chiefly the newcomers who delight in the western that is both classic and novelistic: Robert Aldrich is the most recent and brilliant example of this with his *Apache* (1954) and especially his *Vera Cruz* (1954).

There remains now the problem of CinemaScope. This process was used for *Broken Lance, Garden of Evil* (1954) by Henry Hathaway (a good script at once classic and novelistic but treated without great inventiveness), and *The Kentuckian* (1955) with Burt Lancaster which bored the Venice Festival to tears. I only know one film in CinemaScope that added anything of importance to the *mise en scène*, namely Otto Preminger's *River of No Return* (1954), photographed by Joseph LaShelle. Yet how often have we not read or have even ourselves written that while enlarging of the screen is not called for elsewhere, the new format will renew the westerns whose wide-open spaces and hard riding call out for wide horizons. This deduction is too pat and likely sounding to be true. The most convincing examples of the use of CinemaScope have been in psychological films such as *East of Eden*. I would not go so far as to say that paradoxically the wide screen is unsuitable for westerns or that it adds nothing to them, but it seems to me already an accepted fact that CinemaScope will add nothing decisive to this field.[4]

The western, whether in its standard proportions, in Vistavision, or on a super-wide screen, will remain the western we hope our grandchildren will still be allowed to know.

NOTES

1. A disappointing remake of this film was shot in 1955 by the same George Marshall, with Audie Murphy.

2. *Le Western ou le cinéma américain par excellence*, Collection Septième Art, Editions du Cerf, Paris, 1953.

3. An amalgamation of three American film-production companies, Keystone, KayBee, and Fine Arts.

4. We have a reassuring example of this in *The Man from Laramie* (1955), in which Anthony Mann does not use CinemaScope as a new format but as an extension of the space around man.

AUTHORSHIP AND GENRE:
Notes on the Western

Jim Kitses (1969)

First of all, the western is American history. Needless to say, this does not mean that the films are historically accurate or that they cannot be made by Italians. More simply, the statement means that American frontier life provides the milieu and mores of the western, its wild bunch of cowboys, its straggling towns and mountain scenery. Of course westward expansion was to continue for over a century, the frontier throughout that period a constantly shifting belt of settlement. However, Hollywood's West has typically been, from about 1865 to 1890 or so, a brief final instant in the process. This twilight era was a momentous one: within just its span we can count a number of frontiers in the sudden rash of mining camps, the building of the railways, the Indian Wars, the cattle drives, the coming of the farmer. Together with the last days of the Civil War and the exploits of the badmen, here is the raw material of the western.

At the heart of this material, and crucial to an understanding of the gifts the form holds out to its practitioners, is an ambiguous, mercurial concept: the idea of the West. From time immemorial the West had beckoned to statesmen and poets, existing as both a direction and a place, an imperialist theme and a pastoral Utopia. Great empires developed ever westward: from Greece to Rome, from Rome to Britain, from Britain to America. It was in the West as well that the fabled lands lay, the Elysian fields, Atlantis, El Dorado. As every American schoolboy knows, it was in sailing on his passage to India, moving ever westward to realize the riches of the East, that Columbus chanced on the New World. Hand in hand with the hope of fragrant spices

57

and marvelous tapestries went the ever-beckoning dream of life eternal: surely some-where, there where the sun slept, was the fountain of youth.

As America began to be settled and moved into its expansionist phases, this apocalyptic and materialist vision found new expression. In his seminal study *Virgin Land*, Henry Nash Smith has traced how the West as symbol has functioned in America's history and consciousness. Is the West a Garden of natural dignity and innocence offering refuge from the decadence of civilization? Or is it a treacherous Desert stubbornly resisting the gradual sweep of agrarian progress and community values? Dominating America's intellectual life in the nineteenth century, these warring ideas were most clearly at work in attitudes surrounding figures like Daniel Boone, Kit Carson and Buffalo Bill Cody, who were variously seen as rough innocents ever in flight from society's artifice, and as enlightened pathfinders for the new nation. A folk-hero manufactured in his own time, Cody himself succumbed towards the end of his life to the play of these concepts that so gripped the imagination of his countrymen: "I stood between savagery and civilization most all my early days."

Refracted through and pervading the genre, this ideological tension has meant that a wide range of variation is possible in the basic elements of the form. The plains and mountains of western landscape can be an inspiring and civilizing environment, a moral universe productive of the western hero, a man with a code. But this view, popularized by Robert Warshow in his famous essay, "The Westerner", is one-sided.

Richard Widmark in John Ford's Cheyenne Autumn: *"First of all the Western is American history."*

Equally the terrain can be barren and savage, surroundings so demanding that men are rendered morally ambiguous, or wholly brutalized. In the same way, the community in the western can be seen as a positive force, a movement of refinement, order and local democracy into the wilds, or as a harbinger of corruption in the form of Eastern values which threaten frontier ways. This analysis over-simplifies in isolating the attitudes: a conceptually complex structure that draws on both images is the typical one. If Eastern figures such as bankers, lawyers and journalists are often either drunkards or corrupt, their female counterparts generally carry virtues and graces which the West clearly lacks. And if Nature's harmonies produce the upright hero, they also harbour the animalistic Indian. Thus central to the form we have a philosophical dialectic, an ambiguous cluster of meanings and attitudes that provide the traditional thematic structure of the genre. This shifting ideological play can be described through a series of antinomies, so:

THE WILDERNESS	CIVILIZATION
The Individual	*The Community*
freedom	restriction
honor	institutions
self-knowledge	illusion
integrity	compromise
self-interest	social responsibility
solipsism	democracy
Nature	*Culture*
purity	corruption
experience	knowledge
empiricism	legalism
pragmatism	idealism
brutalization	refinement
savagery	humanity
The West	*The East*
America	Europe
the frontier	America
equality	class
agrarianism	industrialism
tradition	change
the past	the future

In scanning this grid, if we compare the tops and tails of each sub-section, we can see the ambivalence at work at its outer limits: the West, for example, rapidly moves from being the spearhead of manifest destiny to the retreat of ritual. What we are dealing with here, of course, is no less than a national world-view: underlying the whole complex is the grave problem of identity that has special meaning for Americans. The isolation of a vast unexplored continent, the slow growth of social forms, the impact of an unremitting New England Puritanism obsessed with the cosmic struggle of good and evil, of the elect and the damned, the clash of allegiances to Mother Country and New World, these factors are the crucible in which American consciousness was formed. The thrust of contradictions, everywhere apparent in American life and culture, is clearest in the great literary heritage of the romantic novel that springs from Fenimore Cooper and moves through Hawthorne and Melville, Mark Twain and Henry James, Fitzgerald and Faulkner, Hemingway and Mailer. As Richard Chase has underlined in his *The American Novel and Its Tradition*, this form in American hands has always tended to explore rather than to order, to reflect on rather than to moralize about, the irreconcilables that it confronts; and where contradictions are resolved the mode is often that of melodrama or the pastoral. For failing to find a moral tone and a style of close social observation—in short, for failing to be *English*—the American novel has often had its knuckles rapped. As with literature, so with the film: the prejudice that even now persists in many quarters of criticism and education with reference to the Hollywood cinema (paramountly in America itself) flows from a similar lack of understanding.

The ideology that I have been discussing inevitably filters through many of Hollywood's genres: the western has no monopoly here. But what gives the form a particular thrust and centrality is its historical setting; its being placed at exactly that moment when options are still open, the dream of a primitivistic individualism, the ambivalence of at once beneficent and threatening horizons, still tenable. For the film-maker who is preoccupied with these motifs, the western has offered a remarkably expressive canvas. Nowhere, of course, is the freedom that it bestows for personal expression more evident than in the cinema of John Ford.

It would be presumptuous to do more than refer here to this distinguished body of work, the crucial silent period of which remains almost wholly inaccessible. Yet Ford's career, a full-scale scrutiny of which must be a priority, stands as unassailable proof of how the historical dimensions of the form can be orchestrated to produce the most personal kind of art. As Andrew Sarris has pointed out, "no American director has ranged so far across the landscape of the American past." But the journey has been a long and deeply private one through green valleys of hope on to bitter sands of despair. The peak comes in the forties where Ford's works are bright monuments to his vision of the trek of the faithful to the Promised Land, the populist hope of an ideal community, a dream affectionately etched in *The Grapes of Wrath, My Darling Clementine, Wagonmaster*. But as the years slip by the darker side of Ford's romanticism comes to the foreground, and twenty years after the war—in *The Man Who Shot Liberty Valance, Two Rode Together, Cheyenne Autumn*—we find a regret for the past, a bitterness at the larger role of Washington, and a desolation over the neglect of older values. The trooping of the colors has a different meaning now. As Peter Wollen has described in his chapter on *auteur* theory in *Signs and Meaning in the Cinema*, the progression can be traced in the transposition of civilized and savage elements. The Indians of *Drums Along the Mohawk* and *Stagecoach*, devilish marauders that threaten the hardy pioneers, suffer a sea-change as Ford's hopes wane, until with *Cheyenne Autumn* they are a civilized, tragic people at the mercy of a savage community. The ringing of the changes is discernible in the choice of star as well, the movement from the quiet idealism of the early Fonda through the rough pragmatism of the Wayne *persona* to the cynical self-interest of James Stewart. As Ford grows older the American dream sours, and we are left with nostalgia for the Desert.

Imperious as he is, Ford is not the western; nor is the western history. For if we stand back from the western, we are less aware of historical (or representational) elements than of form and *archetype*. This may sound platitudinous: for years critics have spoken confidently of the balletic movement of the genre, of pattern and variation, of myth. This last, ever in the air when the form is discussed, clouds the issues completely. We can speak of the genre's celebration of America, of the contrasting images of Garden and Desert, as national myth. We can speak of the parade of mythology that is mass culture, of which the western is clearly a part. We can invoke Greek and medieval myth, referring to the western hero as a latter-day knight, a contemporary Achilles. Or we can simply speak of the myth of the western, a journalistic usage which evidently implies that life is not like that. However, in strict classical terms of definition myth has to do with the activity of gods, and as such the western has no myth. Rather, it incorporates elements of *displaced* (or corrupted) myth on a scale that can render them considerably more prominent than in most art. It is not surprising that little advance is made upon the clichés, no analysis undertaken that interprets how these elements are at work within a particular film or director's career. What are the archetypal elements we sense within the genre and how do they function? As Northrop Frye has shown in his monumental *The Anatomy of Criticism*, for centuries this immensely tangled ground has remained almost wholly unexplored in literature itself. The primitive state of film criticism inevitably reveals a yawning abyss in this direction.

Certain facts are clear. Ultimately the western derives from the long and fertile tradition of Wild West literature that had dominated the mass taste of nineteenth-century America. Fenimore Cooper is again the germinal figure here: Nash Smith has traced how the roots of the formula, the adventures of an isolated, aged trapper/hunter (reminiscent of Daniel Boone) who rescues genteel heroines from the Indians, were in the *Leatherstocking Tales* which began to emerge in the 1820s. These works, fundamentally in the tradition of the sentimental novel, soon gave way to a rush of pulp literature in succeeding decades culminating in the famous series edited by Erastus Beadle which had astonishing sales for its time. Specialists in the adventure tale, the romance, the sea story, turned to the West for their setting to cash in on the huge market. As the appetite for violence and spectacle grew, variations followed, the younger hunter that had succeeded Cooper's hero losing his pristine nature and giving way to a morally ambiguous figure with a dark past, a Deadwood Dick who is finally redeemed by a woman's love. The genre, much of it sub-literary, became increasingly hungry for innovation as the century wore on, its Amazon heroines perhaps only the most spectacular sign of a desperation at its declining hold on the imagination. As the actual drama of the frontier finally came to a close, marked by Frederick J. Turner's historic address before the American Historical Association in 1893 where he advanced his thesis on free land and its continual recession westward as the key factor in America's development, the vogue for the dime novel waned, its hero now frozen in the figure of the American cowboy.

In 1900 the Wild Bunch held up and robbed a Union Pacific railway train in Wyoming; in 1903 Edwin S. Porter made *The Great Train Robbery* in New Jersey. The chronology of these events, often commented on, seems less important than their geography: it had been the East as well from which Beadle westerns such as *Seth Jones; or, The Captives of the Frontier* had flowed. The cinema was born, its novel visual apparatus at the ready, the heir to a venerable tradition of reworking history (the immediate past) in tune with ancient classical rhythms. In general, of course, the early silent cinema everywhere drew on and experimented with traditional and folkloric patterns for the forms it required. What seems remarkable about the western, however, is that the core of a formulaic lineage already existed. The heart of this legacy was romantic narrative, tales which insisted on the idealization of characters who wielded near-magical powers. Recurrent confrontations between the personified forces of good and evil, testimony to the grip of the New England Calvinist ethic, had soon focused the tales in the direction of morality play. However, in any case, the structure was an impure one which had interpolated melodramatic patterns of corruption and redemption, the revenge motif borrowed from the stage towards the end of the century, and humour in the Davy Crockett and Eastern cracker-barrel traditions. The physical action and spectacle of the Wild West shows, an offshoot of the penny-dreadful vogue, was to be another factor.

This complex inheritance meant that from the outset the western could be many things. In their anecdotal *The Western* George N. Fenin and William K. Everson have chronicled the proliferating, overlapping growth of early days: Bronco Billy Anderson's robust action melodramas, Thomas H. Ince's darker tales, W. S. Hart's more "authentic" romances, the antics of the virtuous Tom Mix, the Cruze and Ford epics of the twenties, the stunts and flamboyance of Ken Maynard and Hoot Gibson, the flood of "B" movies, revenge sagas, serials, and so on. Experiment seems always to have been varied and development dynamic, the pendulum swinging back and forth between opposing poles of emphasis on drama and history, plots and spectacle, romance and "realism," seriousness and comedy. At any point where audience response was felt the action could freeze, the industrial machine moving into high gear to produce a cycle and, in effect, establish a minor tradition within the form. Whatever "worked" was produced, the singing westerns of the thirties perhaps only the most prominent example of this policy of eclectic enterprise.

For many students of the western Gene Autry and Roy Rogers have seemed an embarrassing aberration. However, such a view presupposes that there is such an animal as *the* western, a precise model rather than a loose, shifting and variegated genre with many roots and branches. The word "genre" itself, although a helpful one, is a mixed blessing: for many the term carries literary overtones of technical *rules*. Nor is "form" any better; the western is many *forms*. Only a pluralist vision makes sense of

"The antics of the virtuous Tom Mix." Here with Fred Kohler and Muriel Evans in Riders of Death Valley *(1932).*

our experience of the genre and begins to explain its amazing vigour and adaptability, the way it moves closer and further from our own world, brightening or darkening with each succeeding decade. Yet over the years critics have ever tried to freeze the genre once and for all in a definitive model of the "classical" western. Certainly it must be admitted that works such as *Shane* and *My Darling Clementine* weld together in remarkable balance historical reconstruction and national themes with personal drama and archetypal elements. In his essay, "The Evolution of the Western," Bazin declared *Stagecoach* the summit of the form, an example of "classic maturity," before going on to see in Anthony Mann's early small westerns the path of further progress. Although there is a certain logic in searching for films at the center of the spectrum, I suspect it is a false one and can see little value in it. Wherever definitions of *the* genre movie have been advanced they have become the weapons of generalization. Insisting on the purity of his classical elements, Bazin dismisses "superwesterns" *(Shane, High Noon, Duel in the Sun)* because of their introduction of interests "not endemic." Warshow's position is similar, although his conception of the form is nar-rower, a particular kind of moral and physical texture embodied in his famous but inadequate view of the hero as "the last gentleman." Elsewhere Mann's films have been faulted for their neurotic qualities, strange and powerful works such as *Rancho Notorious* have been refused entry because they are somehow "not westerns." This impulse may well be informed by a fear that unless the form is defined precisely (which inevitably excludes) it will disappear, wraith-like, from under our eyes. The call has echoed out over the lonely landscape of critical endeavour: what is the western?

The model we must hold before us is of a varied and flexible structure, a the-matically fertile and ambiguous world of historical material shot through with arche-typal elements which are themselves ever in flux. In defining the five basic modes of literary fiction Northrop Frye has described myth as stories about gods; romance as a world in which men are superior both to other men and to their environment; high mimetic where the hero is a leader but subject to social criticism and natural law; low mimetic where the hero is one of us; and ironic where the hero is inferior to ourselves and we look down on the absurdity of his plight. If we borrow this scale, it quickly becomes apparent that if the western was originally rooted between romance and high mimetic (characteristic forms of which are epic and tragedy), it rapidly became open to inflection in any direction. Surely the only definition we can advance of the western hero, for example, is that he is both complete and incomplete, serene and growing, vulnerable and invulnerable, a man and a god. If at juvenile levels the action approaches the near-divine, for serious artists who understand the tensions within the genre the focus can be anywhere along the scale. . . . For example, in Anthony Mann there is a constant drive towards mythic quality in the hero; in Sam Peckinpah there is a rich creative play with the romantic potential; with Budd Boetticher it is the ironic mode that dominates.

The romantic mainstream that the western took on from pulp literature provided it with the stately ritual of displaced myth, the movement of a god-like figure into the demonic wasteland, the death and resurrection, the return to a paradisal garden. Within the form were to be found seminal archetypes common to all myth, the journey and the quest, the ceremonies of love and marriage, food and drink, the rhythms of waking and sleeping, life and death. But the incursions of melodrama and revenge had turned the form on its axis, the structure torn in the directions of both morality play and tragedy. Overlaying and interpenetrating the historical thematic there was an archetypal and metaphysical ideology as well. Manifest destiny was answered by divine providence, a Classical conception of fate brooding over the sins of man. Where history was localizing and authenticating archetype, archetype was stiffening and universalizing history.

The western thus was—and is—a complex variable, its peculiar alchemy allowing a wide range of intervention, choice and experiment by script-writer and director. History provides a source of epics, spectacle and action films, pictures sympathetic to the Indian, "realistic" films, even anti-westerns (Delmer Daves' *Cowboy*). From the archetypal base flow revenge films, fables, tragedies, pastorals, and a juvenile stream of product. But of course the dialectic is always at work and the elements are never pure. Much that is produced, the great bulk of it inevitably undistinguished, occupies a blurred middle ground. But for the artist of vision in *rapport* with the genre, it offers a great freedom for local concentration and imaginative play.

"My name is John Ford. I make westerns." Few film-makers can have been so serene about accepting such a label. After all, the industry must have ambivalent attitudes about the "horse-opera" which has been their bread and butter for so long. And of course the western has been at the heart of mass culture, the staple of television, its motifs decorating advertisements and politicians, the pulp fiction and comic books flowing endlessly as do the films themselves. But in fact its greatest strength has been this very pervasiveness and repetition. In this context, the western appears a huge iceberg the small tip of which has been the province of criticism, the great undifferentiated and submerged body below principally agitating the social critic, the student of

Joel McCrea and Virginia Mayo in Raoul Walsh's Colorado Territory. *"The Western's peculiar alchemy allows a wide range of intervention."*

mass media, the educationalist. This sharp division has been unfortunate: sociology and education have often taken up crude positions in their obliviousness to the highest achievements; criticism has failed to explore the dialectic that keeps the form vigorous. For if mass production at the base exploits the peak, the existence of that base allows refinement and reinvigoration. It is only because the western has been everywhere before us for so long that it "works." For over the years a highly sophisticated sub-language of the cinema has been created that is intuitively understood by the audience, a firm basis for art.

It is not just that in approaching the western a director has a structure that is saturated with conceptual significance: the core of meanings is in the imagery itself. Through usage and time, recurring elements anchored in the admixture of history and archetype and so central as to be termed *structural*—the hero, the antagonist, the community, landscape—have taken on an everpresent cluster of possible significances. To see a church in a movie—any film but a western—is to see a church; the camera records. By working carefully for it a film-maker can give that church meaning, through visual emphasis, context, repetitions, dialogue. But a church in a western has *a priori* a potential expressiveness rooted in the accretions of the past. In Ford's *My Darling Clementine* a half-built church appears in one brief scene: yet it embodies the spirit of pioneer America. Settlers dance vigorously on the rough planks in the open air, the flag fluttering above the frame of the church perched precariously on the edge of the desert. Marching ceremoniously up the incline towards them, the camera receding with an audacious stateliness, come Tombstone's knight and his "lady fair," Wyatt Earp and Clementine. The community are ordered aside by the elder as the couple move on to the floor, their robust dance marking the marriage ceremony that unites the best qualities of East and West. It is one of Ford's great moments.

"A defined symbolic field, a tradition." Above, John Wayne in John Ford's The Horse Soldiers; *below, James Coburn and Charlton Heston in Sam Peckinpah's* Major Dundee.

However, the scene is not magic, but flows from an exact understanding (or intuition) of how time-honored elements can have the resonance of an *icon*. This term, which I borrow from art history, should connote an image that both records and carries a conceptual and emotional weight drawn from a *defined* symbolic field, a tradition. Like Scripture, the western offers a world of metaphor, a range of latent content that can be made manifest depending on the film-maker's awareness and preoccupations. Thus in Boetticher's *Decision at Sundown* a marriage ceremony is completely violated by the hero who promises to kill the bridegroom by nightfall. Here the meaning flows completely from the players, in particular Randolph Scott's irrational behaviour; the church itself is devoid of meaning. In Anthony Mann churches rarely appear. In Peckinpah churches have been a saloon and a brothel, and religion in characters has masked a damaging repressiveness. If we turn to the Indian we find that, apart from the early *Seminole*, he functions in Boetticher as part of a hostile universe, no more and no less. In Mann, however, the Indian is part of the natural order and as such his slaughter stains the landscape; it is not surprising that at times he comes, like an avenging spirit, to redress the balance. In Peckinpah the Indian, ushering in the theme of savagery, brings us to the very center of the director's world.

Central to much that I have been saying is the principle of convention. I have refrained from using the term only because it is often loosely used and might have confused the issues. At times the term is used pejoratively, implying cliché; at others it is employed to invoke a set of mystical rules that the master of the form can juggle. In this light, a western is a western is a western. If we see the term more neutrally, as an area of agreement between audience and artist with reference to the form which his art will take, it might prove useful at this stage to recapitulate the argument by summarizing the interrelated aspects of the genre that I have tried to isolate, all of which are in some measure conventional.

> *(a) History:* The basic convention of the genre is that films in western guise are about America's past. This constant tension with history and the freedom it extends to script-writer and film-maker to choose their distance is a great strength.
>
> *(b) Themes:* The precise chronology of the genre and its inheritance of contradictions fundamental to the American mind dictate a rich range of themes expressed through a series of familiar character types and conflicts (e.g. law versus the gun, sheep versus cattle). These motifs, situations and characters can be the focus for a director's interests or can supply the ground from which he will quarry what concerns him.
>
> *(c) Archetype:* The inherent complexity and structural confusion (or the *decadence*) of the pulp literature tradition that the western drew on from the beginning meant that westerns could incorporate elements of romance, tragedy, comedy, morality play. By a process of natural commercial selection cycles emerged and began to establish a range of forms.
>
> *(d) Icons:* As a result of mass production, the accretions of time, and the dialectic of history and archetype, characters, situations and actions can have an emblematic power. Movement on the horizon, the erection of a community, the pursuit of Indians, these have a range of possible associations. Scenes such as passing on gun-lore, bathing or being barbered, playing poker, have a latent ritualistic meaning which can be brought

conscious—often pompously conscious—of representing America's essence. If it falsifies the "little" details of history, it's only to show more clearly the crucial and underlying truths. This national "essence" is a distillation of several political, philosophical, and religious ideologies. Through America's short history, they have been unified by the loosest of dialectics into a synthesis that is apparently monolithic, but really chemically unstable. Indeed, its continuing contradictions inspire most of the Western's dramatic conflicts, and often criss-cross them, or are blurred and buried by them.

We will excavate these creeds in more or less chronological order of their arrival in America. But in Westerns they synthesize in unexpected ways somewhat like the folded strata in the looming canyon walls the cowboy rides past. Although the creeds were first deposited in coherent layers, time and narrative demands have imposed these ideological strata onto each other in "recumbent folds," as a geologist would say. The best way to grab hold of a Western is neither as history nor as archetypal myth but through these cultural strata.

A Cowpoke's Covenant

Stetsons were scarce on the Mayflower, but tracking the cowboy character back to Puritanism is tenderfoot work: much of the American character itself hides out along that beaten path. What is curious is how the cowboy retains traits of the grimmest Puritanism, and embodies a reclusive inner-direction that was only an ideal for Puritans themselves. The cowboy's natural state is solitude, a necessity for the Puritan due to his scrutiny of every act and thought if his private council with God was not to be broken. Like the Puritan, the cowboy needs ultimately to make an antinomian rejection of the public world. His intensity forms a Puritan-like figure with spring-loaded inner awareness and an exterior calm, shunning emotionalism and casual intimacies.

In *The Man from Laramie*, Charley (Wallace Ford) opens up to Will Lockhart (James Stewart), staking out a friendship which classic Westerns usually leave as unspoken leaps of faith: "I'm a lonely man, Mister Lockhart. So are you. I don't suppose we spoke ten words coming down here. But I feel I know you, and I like what I know." William S. Hart's broomstick-backbone stiffness telegraphs moral posture through physical posture. Such iconographic interiority persists through John Wayne's homage to Harry Carey in the "lonely" (as Wayne put it) elbow-clutch in the last shot of *The Searchers*.

The cowboy rides through a Calvinist world fraught with moral and mortal danger. He survives because he expects the world to be as tough and evil as it proves, without him, to be. Man's measure for a Puritan is how he copes with this depraved world. And in the Western the Puritan's obsession with spiritual survival is extended by its secularized forms of physical survival.

Of course evil drapes itself in seductive forms, as Adam discovered. The most insidious danger for the cowboy or Puritan is the temptation to easy pleasures, particularly those brought by women. The stampede that crushes a man in *Red River* is started by a weak cowboy's desire for sugar. The tough Calvinist conclusion—pleasure causes death—is of a piece with the decision of Tom Dunson (John Wayne) to leave his woman behind when he pulls out of the wagon train to tackle the wilderness with

"A lonely man": Will Lockhart (James Stewart) in The Man from Laramie, *confronting Barbara Waggoman (Cathy O'Donnell).*

men. God "has made women weaker," Jonathan Edwards wrote with a succinctness matched by a title in *Tumbleweeds* (1925): "Women ain't reliable, cows are." Women hauled along are apt to find schoolmarmish excuses for the hero to shuck his manly, moral duties. Gary Cooper's girl in *The Virginian* (1929) whines over his shoot-out with Trampas and his hanging of a pal who's tread the primrose path to rustling. Twenty-three years later, Coop is sitting through the same spiel from his Quaker bride in *High Noon.* Cowboys and women are all but definitional antagonists: "Cowboys don't get married, unless they stop being cowboys," as Lee Marvin says in *Monte Walsh.*

The dread of feminized pleasures is the flip-side of the Puritan Ethic's defense of work as a moral yardstick. It saw success as a sign of salvation, of election. But the Ethic lays a heavy contradiction on the Puritan: he must be inner-directed while also driven to public demonstrations of his worth through successful work. One response—the frenzied hope of making it—runs through Poor Richard and Horatio Alger to Jay Gatsby and the gangster-as-hero. The cool, grim response ends in the strong, silent cowboy-gunman who flaunts the Puritan's calm, accepts the Ethic, and doesn't resort to the frenzy of the gangster because his public display need only be of his *self*. A man is his work, or his land. In a Western the nervous ones are either villains or those too raw and untouched by depravity to have worked through to the ideal of potent passivity—such as that least likely of Westerners, Anthony Perkins, who as a greenhorn in *The Tin Star* hops around with Norman Batesian twitches until Henry Fonda eases him through the standard shooting lesson. Always *squeeze* the trigger, son; only gangsters jerk the trigger.

The Western's merciless stance toward any defeat dramatizes the Calvinist belief that Failure = Moral Failure. In *Shane*, Torrey (Elisha Cook, Jr.) bites the dust because he hasn't grasped the rules of evil; Wilson (Jack Palance) guns him down while abiding by the letter of the Code of the West. Playing the fool is a crime punished by death. Conversely, a gunfighter's cool persona has to be validated by a show of inner-tension through hair-trigger reflexes. God's grace is shown through success, and success through reflexes.

Viewing Westerns through a filter of Puritanism makes them sound perversely harsh, since classic Hollywood films, including Westerns, never finally forbid pleasure or the love of a good woman. Especially on plot levels, the Western shuns the pieties of a raised-on-prunes-and-proverbs Puritanism, and a cowboy's rough-riding vitality can't stomach the anxious restraint of Calvinism. It's not surprising that, in Owen Wister's seminal novel, the Virginian is at his least forgiving after fidgeting through a Sinners-in-the-Hands-of-an-Angry-God sermon, and connives to send the traveling minister packing. Common sense gives the lie to the minister's rantings about evil. The Virginian's pals, hey, they good ol' boys.

The Nature of Nature

Just beyond the sagebrush, Thomas Hobbes and Jean-Jacques Rousseau wrangle for a grasp on the Western. In an American context, Hobbes sides up with the Puritans; his view of nature looks like secularized Calvinism. In nature, "all men have a desire and will to hurt" coming from the paradox of their first needs: liberty and power over others. Thus warfare is man's natural state and his life is "solitary, poore, nasty, brutish, and short." Gunfighters, even townsfolk, have come to live in a Hobbesian natural state since the Western backed down before films like Sergio Leone's *Once Upon a Time in the West* and Sam Peckinpah's *The Wild Bunch*.

But even in classic Westerns, when Hobbesian nature doesn't really define the world the Westerner has to live in, it is the world he has ultimately to defeat. The incursion of archaic, personal evil is the Mr. Hyde of the classic Western. John Ford rings shocking changes on the convention when *families* come on as vicious, pre-social units—*Wagon Master*'s Cleggs, *Stagecoach*'s Plummers, *My Darling Clementine*'s Clantons. The Clanton clan vilely mirrors the Earp family. Westerns are set in a world where a stolid social contact has either yet to rigidify or has just broken down. Then the gunfighter comes into his true milieu as a Hobbesian individualist fighting for self-preservation, the single right Hobbes allows is superior to the social contract. But the gunfighter is restrained by conflicting codes from taking up Hobbes's "two cardinal virtues" in nature: "force and fraud."

Hence the real Hobbesian individualists are outlaws. Most Westerns posit that somewhere back East is a civilization run under Enlightenment ideas, while the West stays Hobbesian turf. Thus in *The Man Who Shot Liberty Valance*, when Ranse Stoddard (James Stewart) is shoved around while his stagecoach from the East is robbed, he simply can't comprehend the brutality of Liberty Valance (Lee Marvin). He hardly even accepts the fact of the robbery itself. Liberty Valance's pre-social-contract state is underscored by the disgust with which he snarls "law books!" before flinging the ripped pages at Ranse—an inversion of the scene in *Young Mr. Lincoln* where Ford has Henry Fonda cradle the same words in a reverential hush when a family gives him the books.

But Westerns have their idyllic side, the wilderness turning to a Rousseauvian pastoral garden where men dwell in harmony. For Rousseau, conflict begins with inequality through the idea of private property. In the pure state of nature, man is self-reliant. The Western sees the open spaces of God's Green Earth as a moral force, a character-builder, as opposed to the East's suspect arts and frivolity. Rousseau's Nature, like Hobbes', is a logical but not historical conception. It's as imaginary as the Western's Trans-Mississippi plains—a blank natural slate where everyone's born free, at least free to grab up their equal share of homesteaded property.

Life, Liberty, and the Pursuit of Bad Guys

In its contrary religious and philosophical assumptions, the Western can acknowledge as possible and plausible the opposite poles of its own synthesis. There is less tension in its political stance: the classic Western always comes around to championing the Ur-democracy of the rural town. But Westerns do stage variants of democratic historical ideology, especially Jeffersonian and Jacksonian.

From Jeffersonian democracy the Western takes its exaltation of the yeoman farmer, the property owner. For Thomas Jefferson, "the small landowners are the most precious part of a state." The expansion of this national backbone would ensure that America could never know poverty. His idea, later made a cynically urban-serving slogan by Horace Greeley, was that city squatters would form up into wagon trains, go West, and prosper. The Louisiana Purchase was to give space for these small farms, as would Jefferson's sought-for push into Florida and Canada.

The Western leans heavily on this idolization of property. Plots hinge on land boundaries and settlement rights. The vilest taunt isn't "murderer" but "rustler" or, worse, "horse thief." You can get off with calling a cowboy a "son of a . . ." if you smile when you say that, as in *The Virginian*, but those words that label a man a thief of property are sure signs of impending death. "Any man says I'd rustle cattle's a liar!" Lockhart finally shouts after enduring the torching of his property in *The Man from Laramie* and, natch, the cattleman who says it is dead by the film's end.

Richard Hofstadter, whose catch-phrase for Jefferson is "the aristocrat as democrat," has it that "an element of gentle condescension is unmistakable in his democracy." So maybe the *loci classici* of Jeffersonian democracy in film are Ford's *My Darling Clementine* and *The Sun Shines Bright*. In the first, Wyatt Earp (Henry Fonda) mulls around whistling "Clementine," admiring himself in mirrors and windows, and honing his balancing act on the porch, while he waits like anti-Hamlet or a decent Ahab to circuit his private revenge into the civic spirit he parades at the dance. In staying above the townsfolk as a Calvinist loner and avenger, he forks away from Judge Priest in *The Sun Shines Bright*, who displays to the town the most tolerant of rural virtues, thus "saving" it from itself.

Both leaders come on as aristocratic Jeffersonian gentlemen: Judge Priest by class and Southern gentility, Wyatt Earp more elusively through his actions. The two films hint at a mashup between the (Jeffersonian) "leader who is *unlike* the led" and the (Jacksonian) "leader who is *like* the led," the latter closer to what one expects from Ford's democratic egalitarianism and anti-WASP elitism. America ousts the idea of class by the idea of a class of leaders risen from the led—what Jefferson meant by "natural aristocrats" coming from any class—as in *My Darling Clementine. The Sun Shines Bright* is Ford's tribute to a class of leaders unafraid to sink below the level of the led. It's such blurring of class lines that makes the Jeffersonian Western finally merge into the Jacksonian.

Gunmen sit as the labor aristocracy in the Western. Their freedom and straight-shooting skills form an escapist paraphrase of manual labor. Though they are carnivore consultants to a rat race, the dream remains that they are craftsmen who don't work, except for those split-seconds of well-timed death for the lumpen to gape at from behind the curtains and the saloon door.

The "Jacksonian revolution" also puffed itself as bringing democracy to "the common man." What it really managed was to extend *laissez-faire* self-interest to a rising middle class of businessmen, in opposition to large business and, particularly, large banking interests. Fighting the privately run U.S. Bank, Jackson told his successor, "The Bank is trying to kill me, but I will kill it." His frontier metaphor sets the black-hatted, cat-eyed Bank at the end of a deserted street while Old Hickory, the star-totin' gunslinger, paces easily toward the showdown. Jackson's rhetoric made stupendous claims for his "common man": "Never can the great body of citizens intend to do wrong."

Westerns accept this lofty evaluation of democracy with perfect morality. *The Ox-Bow Incident* is the tentative liberal exception: the great body of citizens manages to screw up when the majority votes for the hanging. And even that scene is much less unsettling than one in *Deliverance* where the Burt Reynolds character gets the others to conspire to hide the mountain man's murder by an ominous logic which begins, "You believe in democracy, don't you Drew?"

The public mask of Old Hickory (alias "The Wild Man of the West") didn't fit too snugly on Jackson himself. He was fond of a genteel brag that he'd never had a fist fight, only duels. Still, something of his popular persona winds its way to Westerns in premises about the feebleness of book-larnin' set against horse sense and the superiority of action to thought. An 1850 homage, starting up the no-frills mythologizing, tells us Jackson "had no such word as failure. Accordingly, there is no failure in his history." The Western hero too makes that absurdist logical-leap from denying the existence of failure to exorcising the fact of it. In *The Searchers* Martin (Jeffrey Hunter), positioned as "bait" while Ethan (John Wayne) guns down a would-be murderer, complains, "What if you'd missed?" "It never occurred to me," says Ethan. Every fastest gun-in-the-West hangs on to that most precarious of titles until *doubt* arises (blood-brother to nervousness). Only then is failure possible. And failure, in the Social Darwinist and Puritan world of the Western, means death.

*   *   *

Every Western stresses some creeds over others—as when Westerns by the mid-Sixties had opted for Hobbesian nature over Rousseauvian. A subtler sliding scale makes sense of the approaches to democracy in two Ford Westerns. *The Man Who Shot Liberty Valance* sets itself up as a Jeffersonian Western; *Stagecoach* can be read as a Jacksonian one.

The central story within *Liberty Valance*'s two-era frame-tale is itself hung on a pair of conflicts. The first pits Jeffersonian democracy, as lugged from the East by Ranse Stoddard, against the individualism incarnated in Tom Doniphon (John Wayne). The second sets the townsfolk and small farmers against the cattle barons. The film has many nuanced reservations about its conclusion. But finally it exalts Jeffersonian democracy over previously indispensable individualists like Doniphon, who must reluctantly be shunted aside for the greater good. And the cattlemen, as outmoded as the florid rhetoric that Major Starbuckle (John Carradine) uses in their defense, must move along to make way for Jefferson's "precious" agrarian settlers.

In the schoolroom scene the Jeffersonian thrust is explicit. The black Pompey (Woody Strode) recites what was "writ by Mister Thomas Jefferson" about men's unalienable rights. But Ranse, bringing civilization, pounces with a Jeffersonian "gentle condescension" on Pompey's grammar, and ignores all the larger historical ironies. Throughout, the film puts forward those aspects of democratic society that Jefferson did; hence the logic of Liberty Valance turning his sadism toward the "free press" after dispensing with law books. Democracy in *Liberty Valance* takes Puritan strictures and labels them politically necessary. Ranse brings a vague, "civilized" confinement of individual vitality with his law books (reinforced by the womenfolk). And at the barroom town-meeting Doniphon restates Ranse's specific prohibitions against drinking on election day: "No exceptions. He says that's one of the fundamental laws of democracy."

Stagecoach, on the other hand, supports a democracy based on a Jacksonian fighting spirit and love of the common man. The most unrelenting conflict within the coach sets a banker—the Jacksonian personification of evil—against the rest of the riders. Ford's treatment of the banker-as-skulking-thief is particularly pointed in light of his praise for the common folk—independent, self-sufficient travelers who can pull together when a baby is born or the Indians attack. The crowning touch of the banker's villainy is his incessant badmouthing of the cavalry—fine Jacksonian military men who ride split-second to his rescue anyway.

An evil capitalist is a standard convention in Westerns, taken over from the foreclosing landlord or banker of low melodrama and from that political reality as Populism's mainspring. The forces of money are embodied less often in bankers, however, than in heartless cattle ranchers (as in *Duel in the Sun* or *The Big Country*) with railroad men (as in *The Iron Horse* or *Union Pacific*), or gun and whiskey runners or Indians (as in *Fort Apache* or *Winchester '73*: "They all want repeaters after the Little Bighorn. Thought I'd clean up and get out").

Unlike *Liberty Valance*, *Stagecoach* ultimately endorses the fighting spirit of an individual, and sees him rewarded when personal vengeance coincides with community service. After apprehending the Ringo Kid (John Wayne), the sheriff turns his back long enough for the necessary extermination of the Plummers, and then allows Ringo a final escape with a send-off like Huck Finn lighting out for the territory: "Well, they're saved from the blessings of civilization." "One man of courage makes a majority" is the Jacksonian text for such an apparent exception to democratic law.

We're rotten glad, as Huck would say, to see Wayne's character get off in view of the constricting pettiness of many of those civilized blessings in *Liberty Valance* (silverware positioned correctly, hats removed indoors). If the later film is more disillusioned, it's hard to say whether it's because Ford is an older, sadder, and wiser man, or because the times are more cynical and Ford with them. Yet both agree that there's no place *within* the community for individual vitality—a sad conclusion for a democratic spirit. And this uneasiness about individualism turns Western heroes into melancholy wanderers. The curse of Cain lies on Shane, on Ethan Edwards, on all those ubiquitous who-was-that-masked-man sunset riders.

Looking Out for Number One

"The Man" who is *"from* Laramie" claims "I always feel I belong where I am"— but it's anguish over his lost property that first prompts his sticking around for revenge. Although the classic Western seems to celebrate the nomad, it never loses touch with possessions for long. It defines society as a series of market relations, with labor and skill as one's first salable possession, and thus reckons on "possessive individualism." A Westerner's possessive power comes from his survival of a Social Darwinist world through *laissez-faire* means. The two doctrines are tightly bound in the Western, where *laissez-faire* methods become a sub-tenet of Social Darwinism, where the economic jungle of ranching or farming renders judgment on who shall survive.

The family is the first economic unit of individualism in Westerns. And it antedates all society; it's even older than the individual. The lone gunman, like Shane, is humanized, and haunted, by his respect for the world of the family, or justified in his vengeance by the death of a family. This justification sets *Winchester '73*, that *La Ronde* of death, in motion. Its idealized rifle—"An Indian would sell his soul to own one"— passes from hand to successively fitter hand until it comes full circle back to Lin McAdam (James Stewart), who is both the fittest of the fit and the film's moral superior.

Social Darwinism is a useful creed for the Western because both take for granted an *advancing* world—evolutionary or expansionist. (It's not paradoxical that though the Western believes in the America which is to come, it's fraught with nostalgia for the West as the crucible of *becoming*.) The term "Social Darwinism" is seldom uttered aloud these days, since it calls up the racism of Darwin's subtitle to *The Origin of Species:* "The Preservation of Favored Races in the Struggle for Life." American ideology "covered" the brutality and pessimism, which is overt in Social Darwinism, through a belief in Progress, softening competition to modern sensibilities. Instead of "the final solution for the unfittest," the terms are "onward and upward." But Social Darwinism has been a dogged force in vernacular philosophy, from the bully racism of Teddy Roosevelt's draconian solutions to the "Indian Problem" to John Wayne's advice to snow-bound frontier families in *The Big Trail* (1930): "You fight, that's life. You stop fighting, that's death."

The classic Western hero is invariably both morally good and best at fighting— thus grabbing himself a spot right at the top of both Puritan and Social Darwinist hierarchies. It's hard to overstate the pervasiveness of this formula. It shows up even in the meek, one-armed hero played by an aging Spencer Tracy in the post-Western *Bad Day at Black Rock* who can still lick the town bully (Ernest Borgnine) when the going gets tough. Tying moral right to "supreme organic excellence" (Jack London's phrase) rules out almost everything but optimism and affirmation.

It also avoids that awkward question: What if the bad guy were the best gun-slinger? In *Broken Lance* Joe Deveraux (Robert Wagner) is asked if anyone still calls him "half-breed," and he responds with a tough grin, "not since my first day at school" (when, we gather, he beat his fellow pupils up). Here the avoidance is of some related, equally awkward questions that come up had he been only the second-best fighter. For then he would have been a harassed minority, lorded over by the bully and the crowd. Even in *McCabe and Mrs. Miller*, a consciously antimythic Western where the bad guys are equally good fighters and McCabe dies bleeding in the snow, there is still the feeling that McCabe wins by every moral and emotional measure.

Peckinpah's *The Ballad of Cable Hogue* stresses the Western's Social Darwinist and *laissez-faire* strata. Cable (Jason Robards) survives abandonment in the desert—by partners who reckon they've water enough only for two—through stumbling onto a water-hole which he celebrates with a manic cry of individualism: "Told you I was gonna live! Me! Cable Hogue! It's Cable Hogue talkin'! Me, Me, Me!" The film opens with an execution speech Cable delivers to a hissing lizard: "Sorry, old timer, but you're only part poison and I'm hungry for meat" (only to have the lizard shot from under him by one of his less scrupulous partners).

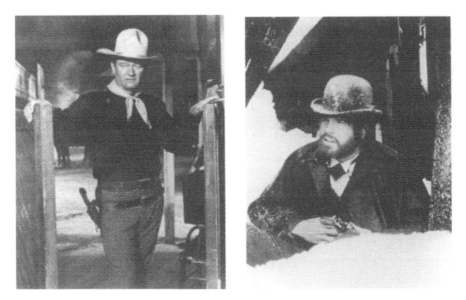

Men of the West: Tom Doniphon (John Wayne) "skirting self-destruction" in The Man Who Shot Liberty Valance; *McCabe (Warren Beatty) bleeding in the snow in* McCabe and Mrs. Miller. *"You fight, that's life. You stop fighting, that's death."*

Cable starts in figuring on a higher morality than survival-of-the-fittest, but he is soon disillusioned—as are, for instance, most of the heroes of Anthony Mann's Westerns. They become dead-eye purveyors of the Darwinist ethic, avengers of the Eastern ideal of accountability. Cable *claims* to be obsessed by such revenge, but the return of his partners turns out, even for him, to be anticlimactic. The survival theme is less prominent than we might expect in the classic Western, which is geared to the categorical imperative and to the feeling of an empire being built. We have to go to the fringe- or para-Western for the force of brutal survival subversive of man's nobility—to *The Savage Innocents*, the gold rush sections of *The New Land*, or the conclusion of *Greed*.

As in *Cable Hogue*, survival in Westerns often masks territoriality and possessive individualism. Cable's real worth is validated less by his survival in the wilderness than by his *laissez-faire* economics: financing conversion of the water-hole into "Cable Springs" and enforcing his ten-cent-a-drink price through a quick-draw skill that does away with any repeat business from his "first customer." Cable's entrepreneurial individualism ("My land, my water. Found it where it ain't") lets civilization advance. He dies, however, crushed by an automobile—a persistent motif in end-of-the-West Westerns (e.g., *Lonely Are the Brave*) and a bludgeon-image for *Liberty Valance's* judgment that at a certain historical point the vital individual is no longer fit to survive. But that's the point where the Western (and the West) is overtaken by Progress, and fades away into the modern world.

The Residue of Populism

The classic Western, thriving under contradictions, accepts the anti-*laissez-faire* and anti-Social Darwinist ideals of Populism. While celebrating Jefferson's agrarian utopia of small farmers, Populism extended Jackson in blaming farm troubles on monopolies and private banking. Hence the Populist platform called for an end to the gold standard (manipulated by oily Eastern moneymen) and the public ownership of utilities, including railroads.

The Western can glorify the virtues of the small farmer because it seldom lingers over the grit of farm life. We're like Joey (Brandon De Wilde) in *Shane*, obsessively sneaking from his noble farmer father to spy under swinging doors at the flashy world of gunfighters. Small farming exists in the Western, as it did for Jefferson and Populism, as an idealized moral center that vanishes if scrutinized. Shane carefully frames tedious homilies for Joey about Pa's virtues, just as in *The Magnificent Seven* O'Reilly (Charles Bronson) takes time out from bleeding to death to urge the wide-eyed farm urchins to follow their fathers who are "courageous because they have responsibilities." When cattle-baron Senator McCanles (Lionel Barrymore) in *Duel in the Sun* rails against "ignorant farmers . . . putting up fences," it's an early clue to how misguided is his power.

Anthony Mann's *Bend of the River* molds the Western into a Populist parable. Glyn McLyntock (James Stewart) guides a passel of Missouri sod-busters on a wagon train to Oregon. His dream is to win acceptance into this group of worthies, who embody all the humanitarian and familial virtues lacking in the miners and city-folk they meet up with. It's relatively simple for him to defend them from the Injuns that menace the wagon train, but less so from *laissez-faire* speculation in the price of their supplies brought on by a gold rush.

Bend of the River charts the collapse of traditional agrarian values when "mankind" is "crucified upon a cross of gold" (the single phrase left in popular memory from William Jennings Bryan's usurpation of the Populist monetary policy in his presidential campaign of 1896). Mann's film replaces the steady, grinding hardships of the small farmer by a vaster, but only temporary, inflation. Its cause is gold, and the monopolistic power of a town boss. The town boss (shifting from a drinks-on-the-house merchant to murderous money-changer) treats the settlers' paid-up supplies with a disregard somewhere between *caveat emptor* and fraud. Their barrels stay undelivered on the dock and scribbled over with successive prices, an awkward icon of inflation: "You see that price? That's what you bought it at. And *that's* what it's worth now." Monopolies and the gold standard result here in a lowly civilization going along with the high prices. Shiftless laborers lie around on the dock scoffing at work. And gold fever tempts Cole (Arthur Kennedy) to revert to the outlaw he (like McLyntock) once was.

The failure of Populism came not only through its incorporation into a badly defeated Democratic party, but from the fairy-tale species of "small farmer" it was ostensibly designed to aid. A reverie in *Bend of the River* by Jeremy (Jay C. Flippen), the farmers' leader, goes to the depths of the idealization: "It's what I've always dreamed of, Glyn—a new country where we can make things grow. We'll find a valley where the earth is rich, where the mountains shelter us from the north wind. We'll . . . cut a clearing in the wilderness. We'll put in roads, use the timber to bridge the streams where we have to. Then we'll build our houses, Glyn, build 'em strong to stand against the winter snow. There'll be a meeting house, a church, we'll have a school. Then we'll put down seedlings—apples, pears. In a few years we'll bring fruit to the world such as the eyes of man have never seen." *Bend of the River* thus parallels Populism's turn from a leftist movement (aid to agriculture through monetary restrictions and the socialization of monopolistic utilities) into a right-wing celebration of the classless, church-centered, rural small town.

The notion that the small town is the repository for the finest moral values is another creed the classic Western can't do without. The Western scene of a slew of townsfolk setting up their sheriff or mayor is both the essence of participatory democracy and an enactment of Rousseau's purest social contract, where men would come together in sparsely populated rural societies. The implicit claim for the small town is that it's made up of the *real*, pioneering Americans, as opposed to them swarthy, city melting-pot immigrants. The small town in the Western becomes an idealization of classless (i.e., white middle-class) harmony, but it takes as little as one outsider to rock the placidity.

The height of this ideal in the Thirties, Forties, and Fifties matches the years when the Western goes through its wildest massacres of Indians, the extreme versions of ethnic outcasts. The racism of Populism targeted the Jew (and his purported control over the "international gold ring"), a conveniently specific symbol of an otherwise vague distrust of urbanism. When Wyatt Earp in *My Darling Clementine* kicks a drunk Indian out of the bar—"Indian, get outta town and stay out!"—this is considered such an unprecedented act of civic virtue that the streets swell with folks shouting for him to be sheriff.

Union Pacific: *Driving the Golden Spike.*

thing, just as, for Ford, military discipline is good Social Darwinism. The wagons in *She Wore a Yellow Ribbon* can't be stopped for only one man: "He's a soldier, he'll have to take a soldier's risks." The Western shootout paraphrases cut-throat competition as a soot-and-whitewash melodrama that disguises its complex amorality.

The doubts about the Western myth that turned obvious in the films of the Sixties didn't pop from nowhere; they were there all the time. With so many creeds piled in "recumbent folds" on one another, the myth has to have strong internal tensions—which solemnized the Western in the Cold War years, yet finally let in the Spaghetti Western. The way classic Westerns choose to stress some creeds and downplay others creates sliding scales of tensions; when Social Darwinism and Hobbesian nature are elevated, and conflicting creeds (Populism, democracy) are shucked off as meaningless, we arrive at the Spaghetti Western.

The Western is notoriously able to hold together the greatest contradictions. Even on the simplest of plot levels there are films like *The Last Roundup* (1947), which seems set in the vague Western past until Gene Autry whips out his TV camera to convince the Indians by long-distance that there's been no land swindle. Westerns can turn insuperable ideological contradictions into dramatic conflicts which, although they can be resolved in a "non-controversial" way, don't always lose their sense of a paradox that is occasionally tragic. Sometimes the tragedy is seen as "the human condition"; sometimes it becomes social criticism; the spectator can take it whichever way he likes. As Claude Levi-Strauss said (and as we all knew), "the purpose of myth is to provide a logical model capable of overcoming a contradiction."

Since the Western "myth" has *always* been an unstable agglomeration, it shouldn't have taken much to upset it. Certainly Vietnam and Watergate were a double whammy more than enough to jinx its waning power. And it's questionable how seriously that myth was *ever* taken. For mass audiences, Western conventions probably never merged into quite the monolithic and archetypal myth that writers on film now like to make out they did.

In this context, it's curious how most of the eulogies for John Wayne came round to being paeans to a monolithic image of self-assured American individualism, and gave commentators (including that ol' Death Valley Rider, Ronald Reagan) a chance to praise the reactionary traits of the classic Western. But it's revealing how those eulogies for "John Wayne, American" (as his Congressional Medal reads) ignored the intriguing tensions in Wayne's persona that are necessarily the same as those in the Western myth itself. Each of Wayne's best roles—in *Red River*, *The Searchers*, and *The Man Who Shot Liberty Valance*—skirts a self-destruction that comes less from the paradox in the good-cowboy character (he fights for civilization's progress, but that progress destroys his free way of life) than from the rigidities of his Puritan individualism.

Maybe there are such tensions and contradictions in the Western myth because modern life (education, newspapers, etc.) doesn't let myths be as monolithic as "myth" suggests. Once audiences start suspecting that something may be seriously wrong with their culture, it becomes possible for popular forms like the Western to turn from myth to muckraking, to seek not continuity but novelties. The revisionist Western hints that inside every myth is a muckraker struggling to get out. The search for novelties will touch on cracks in the myth, but take care to hedge its bets by lucky chances and individual set-ups. Thus some films query and undermine (*Little Big Man*), some query and reinforce (*Cheyenne Autumn*), and some remain interestingly in between (*Run of the Arrow*).

At the moment American films have moved away from the Manifest Destiny of the wide open spaces toward the pole of purer urbanism, at least as found in the discontents of civilized love, gang rumbles of Wandering Warriors, and titanium jungles of space wars. If Westerns aren't quite the dream vision audiences are willing to shell out for, maybe that's because Westerns, at least in their "classic" form, suited a Fifties assumption of unlimited expansionist freedom that is becoming as nostalgic as the Old West once was.

But the current state doesn't mean Westerns have hit the trail for good. Death-of-the-Western prophecies are second only to death-of-the-novel ones, and the mistake with both death knells is believing a genre stuck into the rigid set of conventions. What *may* be gone for good is the fragile balance of ideas that rules the classic Western. But the undying notion of the West as a blank slate means it's always ready to interpret another set of creeds. And as we write, there are some promising Westerns right over that next rise....

"The demise of the genre": The Wild Bunch *and* The Good, the Bad, and the Ugly.

HOW THE WESTERN WAS LOST

J. Hoberman (1991)

They tell me everything isn't black and white. Well I say why the hell not?
—John Wayne, 1969

The buffalo are gone. The railroad is finished. The red men are in disarray. The sun sets on Monument Valley. Once the quintessential Hollywood genre, the Western, as we knew it, is virtually extinct.

The cowboy movie was typically the vehicle America used to explain itself to itself. Who makes the law? What is the order? Where is the frontier? Which ones are the good guys? Why is it that a man's gotta do what a man's gotta do—and how does he do it? Each Hollywood Western, no matter how trite, was a national ritual, a passion play dramatizing and redramatizing the triumph of civilization over "savage" Indians or outlaws. It is the Western that was our true Fourth of July celebration. As historian Richard Slotkin has pointed out, in the national imagination America's real founding fathers are less those celebrated gentlemen who composed a nation in the genteel city of Philadelphia than "the rogues, adventurers, and land-boomers, the Indian fighters, traders, missionaries, explorers, and hunters who killed and were killed until they had mastered the wilderness." Add to these the cavalrymen and demobilized soldiers, freed slaves and impoverished homesteaders, picturesque immigrants and miscellaneous riffraff who went west after the Civil War—as well as "the Indians themselves, both as they were and as they appeared to the settlers, for whom they were the special demonic personification of the American wilderness"—and you have the characters for what seemed the pageant that could not die.

Like baseball, the Western is a sacred part of America's post-Civil War national mythology—a shared language, a unifying set of symbols and metaphors, and a source of (mainly male) identity. But baseball is all form; the Western is heavy, heavy, heavy on content. That the national pastime was successfully integrated after World War II while the demographics of the Western remained overwhelmingly white up until the eve of the genre's demise—despite the fact that at least a quarter of the working cowboys in the late nineteenth century were of African descent—should alert us to the possibility that the Western was as concerned with concealing as enacting historical truth.

As a genre, the Western was most often confined to a relatively brief era of American history—the twenty-five-year-long mop-up operation between Lee's surrender at Appomattox and the defeat of the Sioux at Wounded Knee. The Hollywood Western enjoyed its Golden Age during a quarter-century Pax Americana that followed World War II, a mainstay of early television no less than of "grind" movie theaters. Between 1865 and 1890, individuals were armed and the violence was constant; between 1948 and 1973, the nation was mobilized and the fear of war endemic. By focusing on the distinction between legal and illegal killing, the Western supported American hypervigilance during an age when, it was feared, widespread affluence might lull the nation into decadent complacence. Not for nothing did John F. Kennedy name his program the New Frontier, or Stanley Kubrick choose cowboy icon Slim Pickens to ride a hydrogen bomb, in *Dr. Strangelove*, bareback to Armageddon.

The celebration of national expansion intrinsic to the Western implicitly supported the Cold War ethos of limitless growth and personal freedom. The Cinerama spectacular *How the West Was Won* (1962), which climaxed its epic saga with a vision of freeways, conveniently designates the high-water mark of this optimistic worldview. Thereafter, confidence in the Western began to ebb in response to the struggle for civil rights at home and the questioning of imperial ambition abroad. If the Eisenhower era represented the Western's high noon, an era in which the U.S. appointed itself global sheriff and the gunslinger supplanted the cowboy as the archetypal Western hero, shadows had lengthened by the time Kennedy reached the White House. The old stars and veteran directors were aging. Sam Peckinpah's *Ride the High Country* and John Ford's *The Man Who Shot Liberty Valance* (both 1962) introduced the crepuscular mood that deepened in Ford's *Cheyenne Autumn* (1964) and Howard Hawks's *El Dorado* (1967).

The sixties brought unprecedented domestic and foreign upheaval and, given its privileged place in American popular culture, the Western could hardly remain immune. In Italy, Sergio Leone made the genre more immediately relevant by raising the body count. At once more abstract and more violently naturalistic than Hollywood Westerns, Leone's *Dollars* trilogy not only unveiled the last Western hero, Clint Eastwood—the "dirty" icon who would preside over the end of the Western and the birth of the urban anti-Miranda *policier*—but invented a new mode. Excessive, operatic, thoroughly cynical in its representation of frontier heroism, the so-called spaghetti

Clint Eastwood in For a Few Dollars More: *the last western hero, the "dirty" icon.*

Western liberated the furies within Sam Peckinpah, inspiring Hollywood to new heights of carnage and a greater degree of naturalism.

By the mid sixties the Western had outgrown the screen. As many have observed, the men who fought in Vietnam were raised on Westerns—presented with cap-firing six-guns and Davy Crockett coonskin caps and deposited at Saturday matinees to watch the adventures of Hopalong Cassidy and Gene Autry. The average recruit had entered his teens at a time when eight of the top prime time TV shows were Westerns. Small wonder that John Wayne, the greatest of movie cowboys, became a talisman for a substantial number of American soldiers in Vietnam, or that he took the war as his personal crusade. Wayne's base in *The Green Berets* (1968) is called Dodge City. Meanwhile, in the actual Vietnam, where dangerous areas were known as "Indian country," Vietnamese scouts were termed "Kit Carsons" and Americans painted the slogan "The Only Good Gook Is a Dead Gook" on their flak jackets. There is a celebrated passage in Michael Herr's book *Dispatches* in which a combat reporter is invited out on a search-and-destroy mission against the Viet Cong: "'Come on,' the captain said, "we'll take you out to play Cowboys and Indians.'"

In the national dream life, Indochina was an extension of the Western frontier and Americans were once again settlers, cavalrymen, schoolmarms, gunslingers, and marshals on a mission of protection and progress. The metaphor was irresistible, but this time there was no consensus on who were the good guys and who were the bad guys. Lyndon Johnson called upon the U.S. Army to "nail the coonskin to the cabin door"; the counterculture opposing his war identified itself with outlaws or worse....

The Western mythology played itself out in Vietnam and vice versa. Peckinpah's *The Wild Bunch* and the William Goldman-George Roy Hill *Butch Cassidy and the Sundance Kid*—both key 1969 releases—embodied a striking inversion of values. At once cynical and romantic, both movies presented the unregenerate criminal

John Wayne and Aldo Ray in The Green Berets: *"They tell me everything isn't black and white. Well, I say why the hell not?"*

as a sympathetic figure and were regretful at his elimination by the agents of law and order. In the wake of *The Wild Bunch* and the My Lai massacre, the genre grew increasingly apocalyptic. *The Green Berets* aside, Hollywood produced no movies on the war while the war was being waged. Instead, there were such revisionist and counter-revisionist essays as *Little Big Man* (Arthur Penn, 1970), *The Cowboys* (Mark Rydell, 1971), *Bad Company* (Robert Benton, 1972), *Ulzana's Raid* (Robert Aldrich, 1972), and *High Plains Drifter* (Eastwood's first Western as a director, 1973), crypto-Vietnam films all. The Western split into radical right- and left-wing camps. Those starring John Wayne and, to a lesser extent, Clint Eastwood took up the cudgels against those directed by Arthur Penn and Robert Altman (*McCabe and Mrs. Miller*, 1971; *Buffalo Bill and the Indians*, 1976), while Peckinpah's Westerns were divided against themselves (*The Ballad of Cable Hogue*, 1970; *Junior Bonner*, 1972; *Pat Garrett*

"In the wake of The Wild Bunch *and the My Lai massacre, the genre grew increasingly apocalyptic."*

Cleavon Little as the Sheriff in Blazing Saddles.

and Billy the Kid, 1973). Common to all, however, was a sense of social breakdown, disillusionment, and the distrust of "liberal" mainstream values.

The most overtly ideological of revisionist Westerns concerned the Indian wars. The revelation of American atrocities in Vietnam only reinforced the argument that the slaughter of Native Americans was less the distortion than the essence of the white man's wars. *Little Big Man, Soldier Blue* (Ralph Nelson), and *A Man Called Horse* (Elliot Silverstein) identified with the Indians so strongly as to be the equivalent of marching against the war beneath a Viet Cong flag. Released in 1970 and coinciding with the publication of two influential histories, *Custer Died for Your Sins* and *Bury My Heart at Wounded Knee*, these films proposed that any and all Indian barbarities paled before the enormity of white genocide. Indeed, Sidney Poitier's *Buck and the Preacher* (1972) proposed an alliance of red and black men.

By the middle of Richard Nixon's first term, the quintessential Hollywood genre had clearly come unglued. But, in addition to widespread confusion, the extraordinary succession of revisionist and parody Westerns that appeared around the turn of the decade did embody a desire to acknowledge a multiplicity of perspectives on the winning (or losing) of the West. The ultimate desecration of the genre, Mel Brooks's *Blazing Saddles* (1974), the highest-grossing Western before *Dances With Wolves*, capped the assorted anti-, post-, spaghetti, revisionist, psychedelic, black, and burlesque Westerns of the early seventies. (It is appropriate that the concept for Michael Cimino's *Heaven's Gate*, blamed by some for the demise of the genre, also dates from this period.) By that time, *The Godfather* had emerged as a new sort of national epic and, as presaged by Eastwood's Western-lawman-in-New-York *Coogan's Bluff* (Donald Siegel, 1968), Fort Apache was relocated to the urban wilderness of the Bronx.

From 1910 through the end of the fifties, a quarter of all Hollywood films had been Westerns. As late as 1972, the high point of genre revisionism, the year of *Jeremiah Johnson* (Sydney Pollack) and *The Life and Times of Judge Roy Bean* (John Huston), *The Great Northfield Minnesota Raid* (Philip Kaufman) and *The Culpepper Cattle Company* (Dick Richards), *Buck and the Preacher* (Sidney Poitier) and *Greaser's Palace* (Robert Downey), Westerns still represented twelve percent of Hollywood's output. But the year that brought Nixon's triumphant reelection was the last in which Western releases would reach double figures. The subsequent falloff was dramatic: four Westerns were released in 1973, two in 1974, five in 1975, seven for the Bicentennial, two in 1977, three in 1978, and a total of three between 1979 and 1984, the year of TV Western host Ronald Reagan's even more spectacular reelection. As J. Fred MacDonald put it in his history of the television Western, "no form of mass entertainment has been so dominant and then so insignificant."

Though the Western has bequeathed such enduring American totems as Marlboros and blue jeans, its decline effectively redefined the masculine screen image. There were no new heroic cowboys after Eastwood. When Dustin Hoffman made a Western he impersonated an Indian. Robert Redford played a notorious outlaw; Warren Beatty, a failed pimp. The seventies gave us an entire generation of movie stars who have never donned Stetsons (De Niro, Stallone, Pacino, Dreyfuss). At the same time, the issues that preoccupied the Western have either been repressed or dispersed to other genres—including the Vietnam war film.

That the Western landscape still holds the promise of liberation and/or redemption, rebirth or reinvention, can be seen in such disparate nineties hits as *Thelma and Louise* and *City Slickers*, not to mention the phenomenal success of *Dances With Wolves* and the TV miniseries *Lonesome Dove*. That the Western itself, save for a handful of releases, has remained defunct since the fall of Saigon suggests that the spectacle by which America came to be America has proved resistant to the reillusionment of the past dozen years. The rhetoric that supported Desert Storm and the celebrations that followed were notable for a paucity of Western imagery, despite the leadership of our first Texan president since Lyndon Johnson. (It's striking that the yellow ribbon, symbol of Americans held hostage overseas, is habitually located in a 1973 Tony Orlando song rather than a 1949 John Ford cavalry Western.)

Yet the popularity of Kevin Costner's *Dances With Wolves* (1990), a softer version of the Indian Westerns of 1970, demonstrates our enduring fascination with the classic Western situation—the confrontation in the wilderness between the European and the native American. It will be more difficult, I suspect, to make so "universal" a movie on the subject of the Alamo or the Mexican War. Although acknowledging the presence of blacks and Asians and thus grudgingly "urbanizing" the West, the two most ambitious Reagan-era Westerns, Clint Eastwood's *Pale Rider* (1985) and Lawrence Kasdan's *Silverado* (1985), were noticeably uncomplicated by the presence of Indians or Hispanics. Indeed, *Dances With Wolves* is itself so antiseptic and well regulated as to reduce our national dark-and-bloody ground to campsite proportions.

If nothing else, the hysterical response to the Smithsonian's recent exhibition "The West as America"—centering, for the most part, on the unremarkable curatorial suggestion that the Western art of the nineteenth and early twentieth centuries may have had its own ideological agenda—shows how contested and problematic this territory is. In that sense, the Western is still at the impasse it reached twenty years ago. Bloody and confused, the iconoclastic last Westerns took moviegoers to the end of a long and winding trail and found a thicket of ambiguities. It remains to be seen whether the first post-Western generation has any pathfinders with the nerve to push deeper still into that wilderness and reignite a genre that once epitomized America to itself and to the world.

PILGRIMS AND THE PROMISED LAND:
A Genealogy of the Western

Doug Williams (1998)

> The main point stems from the fact that I've always acted alone. Americans admire that enormously. Americans admire the cowboy leading the caravan alone astride his horse. Without even a pistol, maybe, because he doesn't go in for the shooting. He acts, that's all: aiming at the right spot at the right time. A wild West tale, if you like.
>
> —Henry Kissinger[1]

> Where is my John Wayne?
> Where is my prairie son?
> Where is my happy ending?
> Where have all the cowboys gone?
> —Paula Cole, "Where Have All The Cowboys Gone?" (1996)

W hat is the Western? What do cowboys and the West mean to us today? Aspects of the Western—attitudes, behaviors, and character types—seem to permeate other genres in American cinema; the Western is more than horses, guns, Indians, and Monument Valley. The core that underlies the surface is important to understand, in that the Western is the American Epic. If one were to ask, "what is an American," the image that comes to most people's minds is the frontier, and the self-reliant, masterful figure for whom the unknown holds no terrors. No personage illustrates this more than John Wayne, the actor most associated with the Western genre. Wayne is an icon of American identity, just as Odysseus once was for the Hellenes. It is understandable that Kissinger, a foreign-born Secretary of State, would associate himself with a typical American image. But even presidents require the Wayne mantle, and seek to be associated with his image. Garry Wills notes that Ronald Reagan made a pilgrimage to John Wayne's birthplace during his reelection campaign in 1984. "Wayne understood what the American spirit was all about," he said to a group of visitors to the White House in 1988. "The way to be an American," Wills concludes, "was to be Wayne...."[2]

Wayne's identity is a personification of a myth through which the collective desires and understandings of the United States evolved in relation to the world. In his *Politica*, Aristotle advises his students to "consider things in their first growth and origin," in order to obtain the clearest view of them.[3] Accordingly, I will turn to the period when the myths were made. This was not on the American plains of the 19th century, but in the forests at the edge of the sea in the 17th century, the first "Western" frontier. Wayne's Tom Doniphon calls Ransom Stoddard (James Stewart) a "pilgrim" in John Ford's *The Man Who Shot Liberty Valance* (1962), in reference to the first European settlers. If Wayne's character represents the American ideal, "pilgrim" evokes a range of associated meanings, both of virtue and ineptness, that Ford relies on his audience to understand about Stoddard.

The word specifically refers to travellers who journey "to some sacred place, as an act of religious devotion."[4] The Pilgrims who founded Plymouth in 1620, as well as the other Puritan settlers of the early 17th century, came to a continent that had sprung up on European maps without history or explanation. Confronted with this inexplicable (and for Christians who believed in a world foretold by Biblical prophecy, monstrous) void, Europeans of all nationalities imposed their own dreams and desires on the "new world." For the Puritans, an oppressed minority who felt themselves to be the Elect of God in a corrupted world, the answer to the mystery of North America was clear—the New Continent was the Promised Land for God's Chosen People, providentially revealed. Here they literally could fulfil the Pauline injunction: "[C]ome out from among them, and be ye separate, saith the Lord, and touch not the unclean thing; and I will receive you. And will be a Father unto you, and ye shall be my sons and daughters, saith the Lord Almighty."[5]

The Promised Land myth arose as an implication of the Puritan metaphorical identity as the new Israel:

> [T]he Puritans easily discovered numerous similarities between themselves and the Israelis. They...viewed England as their Egypt, James I as their Pharaoh, the Atlantic as their Red Sea. They were also an embattled people obviously chosen to carry out divine plans for the world's redemption. They too had been driven out from their homes, not as punishment, but to build a promised land. The only significant difference they could see between ancient Israel and themselves was that they were expected to convert the very wilderness to a promised land.[6]

As Henry Nash Smith noted, the metaphor implies an agricultural Chosen People, with both a material and allegorical interpretation of cultivated land.[7] The

Puritan elect would cultivate a wilderness waste into a garden, just as missionaries would christianize the Fallen World in time, and be redeemed by Jesus' sacrifice. For the Puritan, the very difficulty of the task to bring order out of the wilderness chaos would prove their status as anointed Saints, to the greater glory of God. John Winthrop, the first leader of the Massachusetts Bay Colony, told his colonists: "We shall find that the God of Israel is among us, when ten of us shall be able to resist a thousand of our enemies; when He shall make of us a praise and glory that men shall say of succeeding plantations, 'the Lord make it like that of New England.'"[8]

The mythic accession of God's Community to the Promised Land is a fulfillment of prophecy. That accession requires not just strength, but faith—an act of defiance against the material world. In *The Man Who Shot Liberty Valance*, Ransom Stoddard refuses to yield to force or reason. It is his faith in the triumph of law that makes him noble, rather than a fool. Because of this act of will and faith, as Winthrop and others assured the early colonists, the means by which the wilderness becomes transformed become available. Stoddard is a deliberate stretching of the type, as I will discuss below. Frequently it is a religious woman, the voice of her materially weak but spiritually indomitable community, who is the symbol of this faith. More typical examples are Jane-Ellen Mathews and her father Caliphet in *The Westerner* (1940), or Penelope Worth (Gail Russell) and her Quaker family and community in *Angel and the Badman* (1947). Faith is rewarded by the displacement of cattle with farms; water flows in the dry land.

In Ford's *Wagon Master* (1950), Mormon pilgrims are on a journey to "a valley that's been reserved for us by the Lord," as Elder Wiggs (Ward Bond) reverently tells Travis (Ben Johnson): "Been reserved for His people." Travis and his friend Sandy (Harry Carey, Jr.) are horsetraders. They are amused—and a little flattered—to hear that Elder Wiggs believes them to be the answer to the Mormons' prayers to be "shown the way" across the desert to their promised land. When the traders refuse— with the implication that the wagon-train must then become lost—Wiggs leads his pilgrims into the desert anyway. Ford invokes the enduring mother of his *The Grapes of Wrath* by casting Jane Darwell as Sister Ledyard; she embodies this spirit of unquestioning faith in the film. She is the old woman who blows the horn, which seems to be a longhorn, but is evocative of the ram's horn of Jewish rituals, sounded on solemn occasions. After Wiggs announces his decision, she comes up and says to him, "we'll get there, Elder—with the Lord's help!" Wiggs agrees, though his reason troubles him. "Sister Ledyard, supposin' you blow that horn again." She blows loudly and long; and it is the sound of that horn, of the willingness to abandon reason to music, mourning to celebration, dread to the anticipation which that sound represents, that reassures the party at this point, and at every point of crisis in the film.

In echo of this opposition of reason to music, the horse-traders Travis and Sandy watch the wagon-train roll into the desert. They ride up to a fence—a John Ford fence, meaning a dividing point between possible life-paths. They watch the wagon-train, each wanting to join, each knowing it is a foolish thing to do, and that there are "a lot easier ways to make a living." But then Sandy breaks into song: "I left my gal in old Virginny..." "Fell in 'hind the wagon-train," Travis replies. They sing a few bars, and obey the song and their feelings, not their reason. Once they join, Ford has the Sons of the Pioneers sing the complementary song, "Wagons West are Rolling"—which, as with

Wagonmaster: *Sister Ledyard blows the horn; the wagon train rolls; Travis and Sandy on "a John Ford fence."*

all biblical prophecy, celebrates the journey we see being made as an already historical event. The song, in counterpoint to the struggling wagon-train, is one of the means that Ford uses to engage the audience's feelings; like Travis and Sandy, the audience-chorus for whom the "Sons" speak is meant to vicariously join the wagon-train as it rolls into the desert. Ford's sentimentalism underlines that this is one of those acts of faith that Winthrop speaks of; the song—sung by the "sons" of those whom we see—positions the film as an act of homage to that faith.

The presence of an implied posterity in *Wagon Master* is not by accident. The land takes its meaning in the Puritan romance myth as the restored Garden of Eden, in which the faithful remnant comes out of a fallen society to restore the land, and to recreate the linkage between God and the world. Whether stated explicitly or not, the Western is always a battle over the land's future: Whose posterity will inherit the land? What will be made of the land's potential? Does history progress, or retrogress? Every one of Cooper's Leatherstocking Tales takes up this theme—most famously, *The Last of the Mohicans*, in which Tamenund, the ancient chief of the Delaware, mournfully observes that "the pale-faces are masters of the earth," and that he has lived to see "the last warrior of the wise race of the Mohicans."[9] Indians may be noble in Cooper, but land requires a specific type of settler—one with "white gifts," in Natty Bumppo's phrase, to transform the land from a wasteland to the garden that prefigures the millennial kingdom. The attention Ford pays to the land is not so much an innovation as it is a recapitulation of the core meaning of land in the Western.

Patriarchy, as a mystery-ritual, has also been a core element. The Western draws its symbols from European culture, in which the woman represents land, immanent fecundity, awaiting the male's animating spirit and will to awaken her power of life.[10] God is male; the church of the faithful is female. The spirit of civilization is masculine, Apollonian, rational; the spirit of nature is feminine, Dionysian, irrational. In the Western, the cultural agent of civilization is the woman who is faithful to God and Civilization, while the cultural agent of wilderness is the Indian, the son of Nature. The civilized woman is nature transformed by the paternal spirit, while the uncivilized man is the phallic projection of the untamed maternal spirit.

In the Western, the civilized woman enters the wilderness already pregnant with civilization, the spirit of reason; she requires the material intermediary to bring this spiritual pregnancy into being. The uncivilized man, as embodied in the Indian, is immanently in communion with Unconsciousness, the Ishtar/Artemis/Kali goddess of frenzy and desire. The wilderness' transformation requires the right male, the man who mediates between the paternal spiritual and the maternal natural worlds, and their manifestation in a physical reality. In accordance with the romance hero myth, this man is one who has gone beyond the frontier to the wilderness and gained knowledge of it without himself degenerating into wildness. He then returns to the frontier, no longer a part of civilization, but rather its gateway. The Western is a narrative of a successful Pentheus, who violates the Bacchic rituals of the natural world. Unlike Euripides' Pentheus of *The Bacchae*, the Leatherstocking Western hero is a puritan, and so his self-denial allows him to survive the experience of unmediated experience of nature. Yet to violate the barrier between Culture and Nature is not done without cost. The pure type of the Western hero, like Pentheus, is torn, damaged, a castrated hero, denied progeny. He is Pathfinder, not patriarch, a sacrifice, like Moses or Jesus, by which the world becomes transformed.

In Cooper's *The Pioneers*, which initiated the pattern, Oliver is a dispossessed gentleman become forester. He is part of the monastic fraternity of Natty Bumppo and Chingachgook. Unlike Natty, however, he is not fully initiated in the rites of the wilderness, and thus is reclaimable. Elizabeth Temple, the daughter of the man whom he thinks has taken his property, softens his harshness, and lures him back to civilization. "I have been driven to the woods in despair; but your society has tamed the lion within me.... If I have forgotten my wrongs, 'twas you that taught me charity," Oliver tells Elizabeth. She turns down a Frenchman's offer of marriage—the obligatory decadent man of excessive culture—and accepts the tamed lion's. The pure Western hero, like Natty, cannot return to civilization. Far more common however is the Oliver type, a tamed Leatherstocking, recalled from communion with savagery. Cole Hardin in *The Westerner*, Wyatt Earp in My *Darling Clementine*, and Howard Kemp in *The Naked Spur*, to name just a few, are all examples of the Pentheus-hero, recalled from the edge of Dionysian self-destruction by the Apollonian woman.

The classic film Western drew from the basic myth Cooper outlined, incorporating the alterations that dime-novel variants and different ideological movements appended to it. One particular element that became more articulated in the Western was Social Darwinism, the doctrine elaborated by Herbert Spencer that equated social class with natural selection. John D. Rockefeller said that "the growth of a large business is merely survival of the fittest."[11] Speaking of social reformers who denounced the exploitation of immigrants and the concentration of wealth in the hands of a few, Andrew Carnegie commented:

> We might as well urge the destruction of the highest existing type of man because he failed to reach our ideal as to favor the destruction of Individualism, Private Property, the Law of Accumulation of Wealth, and the Law of Competition; for these are the highest result of human experience, the soil in which society so far has produced the best fruit.[12]

Westerns began to develop this idea more consciously in relation to immigrants. The West was a Darwinian trial, in which the natural laws that had created social classes were reproduced in individual struggles in the West. City life had always been inferior to country life in American mythology,[13] but the sense of alienation and fear produced in existing residents by the realization that immigrants from different cultures were changing America crystallized in the City, the center of this change. Cities took the place Europe had held in the imaginations of the Puritans, and in the writings of Cooper. They were Egypt: unnatural, decadent, corrupt and corrupting.

Probably the most influential narrative at the time the film Westerns began was Owen Wister's *The Virginian*. *The Virginian*'s title character and the Eastern Schoolmarm Molly reiterated Cooper's basic pattern, transposing it to the prairie. The Virginian's antagonist is not an Indian, however, but "Trampas," a foreign name. Wister dedicated his book to his friend and ideological associate, Theodore Roosevelt, whose seven-volume history *The Winning of the West* (1885-94) propounded the argument that the frontier was the catalyst for the emergence (or restoration) of an undegenerated Anglo-Saxon natural aristocracy, and a refuge from the alleged pollution of European decadence and undesirable immigrants.[14] Roosevelt, Wister, and the managerial class whom they represented mythologized the frontier as a location that validated class and race barriers. On Wister and Roosevelt's frontier, "rainbows of men,—Chinese, Indian chiefs, Africans, General Miles, younger sons, Austrian nobility, wide females in pink...drained prismatically" to the frontier, but the Anglo-Saxon aristocracy naturally rose to the top.[15]

The film Western inherited this sensibility, but as both the producers and the audience of early cinema were predominantly themselves immigrants, or children of immigrants, the Western emphasized spectacle and struggle on the frontier rather than class conflict. When the Western was revitalized by James Cruze's *The Covered Wagon* (1923) and John Ford's *The Iron Horse* (1924), it was as an epic narrative of immigration. The struggle between classes that gradually emerged in the sound era was not of classes so much as it was of newcomers against established residents. A Southern background—like Judge Roy Bean's (Walter Brennan) in *The Westerner*, or the gambler Hatfield (John Carradine) in *Stagecoach*—developed as a signifier of a character who disliked or exploited immigrants, or defended entrenched privilege. Cattle barons vs. Farmers was another means of representing the same conflict. The idea of the West as an evolutionary testing ground remained, but stripped of its racial or cultural significance. In a forward to one of his collections of short stories, Louis L'Amour states that his Western heroes "have nothing to do with race, creed, or nationality." On the other hand, "the frontier was itself selective" of a certain type of

The Virginian (Gary Cooper), the Eastern Schoolmarm (Mary Brian) and cowpokes in The Virginian *(1929)—one of several film versions of Owen Wister's novel.*

hero; the Western hero is an individualist, a Darwinian artifact of a war of all against all. "Group thinking and peer behavior had only a limited application."[16]

Wagon Master shows the heritage both of religious and Social Darwinist themes in the Western. Prudence (Kathleen O'Malley), Elder Perkins' daughter, marries Sandy instead of the religiously dogmatic Jackson (Chuck Hayward), whom her father prefers. *Wagon Master* resolves the conflict between wilderness and civilization through a marriage between a "prudent" pilgrim and a man of the west—Sandy, a man emerging from the desert itself. This contrast of the unfit Easterner with the Westerner is the translation of Cooper's contrast between his heroines' potential marriages to decadent Europeans, or Westerners like Paul Hover of *The Prairie*. In the Darwinist translation, the proper marriage ensures a fit posterity—a pretty compliment, to us, as that implied posterity is the audience. The Frontiersman acquires a purpose for his competence, and the Eastern Woman acquires the practical agent through which her imminent civilization can flower. The marriage between opposites is the *heiros gamos*, the holy marriage which awakens the desert, and allows it to become a garden. Once this union of opposites is accomplished, as the wild cattleman Cole Hardin (Gary Cooper) tells Jane-Ellen (Doris Davenport) in *The Westerner*, after he has been tamed, Hardin can see and speak the phrase that, immanent, awaited him to speak it: "This is the promised land."

This frontier-civilization marriage story has a historical basis on which the myth was constructed. If the continent was the promised land to the Puritans, it did not mean that it was on their arrival a new eden, innocent of sin. Over time, the Puritans increasingly believed that, like Christian's journey through cities and the wilderness to the Celestial Country in Bunyan's *Pilgrim's Progress*, the landscape itself was both a physical and spiritual test of their election. Although there was some initial speculation that the virtues of Indians were due to their lineage from the lost tribes of Israel, the predominant attitude of Puritan leaders toward the Native Americans were that their differing customs were proof of their allegiance to the devil. "The New Englanders are a people of God settled in those, which were once the devil's territories," Cotton Mather advised his readers in his history *Magnalia Christi Americana* (1693).[17] In time, the Puritans became more settlers, and less soldiers at war with Satan. They developed more of a sensitivity to the land and to the reasons for Indian ways. Particularly after the French and Indian War (1755-64), with its battles against Indians, and more objective (as opposed to the Puritan hellish) captivity narratives, new types of heroes emerged, at home in the wilderness. These types' attitude toward Indians were not necessarily favorable, as I will discuss later, but at the very least, they learned from them. The Indians' powers in the wilderness became their own. Robert Rogers of Roger's Rangers, Daniel Boone, and the young George Washington (with whom Cooper begins *Last of the Mohicans)*, were exemplars of the type. They were the direct precursors of Fenimore Cooper's Natty Bumppo.

A consequence of the Western hero's emergence was that the Puritan who fears the wilderness changed from a positive to a negative character. The obtuse doctrinaire religious type, who misunderstands or despises the frontier, became comically ineffectual or evilly degenerate stock characters in the evolving Western myth. Elder Adam Perkins in *Wagon Master* suggests the range of the type, from comic irrelevance to unChristian vindictiveness. Elder Wiggs contends with hostile townspeople and the sharp horse-trading of the romantic leads Sandy and Travis, in order to outfit his wagon train. In addition to this, Wiggs also has to endure Perkins' comically unhelpful reminders not to offend the Lord with "words of wrath," no matter the provocation. He seems relatively harmless, until the wagon-train comes across Doctor Hall's Medicine Wagon Show, with its dying party of "gentiles," intoxicated on the "Lightning Elixir" they drank to stay alive. At this point, Sam Jackson, Sandy's competitor for Prudence's hand, appears in the frame. He is young but equally priggish, symbolic of dogmatic religion, as Sandy is of the pragmatic Westerner. Wiggs tells the Mormons that the showpeople were driven out into the wilderness, like them, that their horses have run away, and that they had no choice but to drink elixir to survive. Perkins, and his spiritual son, Jackson, stare at them with righteous disgust. As Zane Gray phrased a similar expression in *Riders of the Purple Sage*, "as his religious mood was fanatical and inexorable, so would his physical hate be merciless."[18] Ford shows that this is not necessarily a correct religious response by contrasting Perkins and Jackson with Sister Ledyard. She is immediately sympathetic to the showpeople, and at the end of the sequence forms a musical partnership with the Medicine Show drummer, Mr. Peachtree.

Perkins and Jackson take turns making hostile comments, as the other nods, and demand that Wiggs give them a few supplies and abandon them in the desert. Travis replies that they are too weak to survive on their own, and that they should be allowed to join the wagon-train until they can be shown the California trail, in three days. True to the Pauline injunction, Perkins refuses. "Don't think we ought to take up with their kind of people." Better that they die in the wilderness, as Travis implies they will, than allow the chosen people to be corrupted. Ford's casting makes Perkins and Jackson's resistance more believable; Ben Johnson and Harry Carey, Jr., do not have the iconic resonance of implacable will John Wayne would have carried to this scene. Sandy and Travis can lose. Through his casting, Ford underscores his intent in this scene: Moral choices are hard, and heroes are not predestined, but rather made as a result of choices and actions. Perkins and Jackson see themselves as already saved, and the rest of the world as something less than human. This cruel version of religion emerges in many Westerns, though rarely so explicitly in film Westerns. More commonly, the effects of the dogmatically religious are seen more in evocative images, like those of the Ladies Law and Order League, in John Ford's *Stagecoach* (1939). Ringo (John Wayne) describes them as "worse than Indians," and it is they who truly threaten characters like Dallas (Claire Trevor).

The antipode of religious zealots are the barbarians, or anti-pilgrims. Natty Bumppo himself rails against another group worse than Indians in *The Pioneers*, whites who have lived on the frontier and become creatures of the wilderness: fallen pilgrims without mission. Sometimes the characters whose role is to personify law and civilization themselves degenerate; the Rev. Hendley in Hart's *Hell's Hinges* (1915) is an early film example. Natty calls them "Yankee Indians...who belong to none of God's creatur's, to my seeming, being, as it were, neither fish nor flesh—neither white man nor savage."[19] The "Yankee Indian" has a tribal identity, rather than a religious membership, and no law other than "an eye for an eye." Cooper's Ishmael Bush and clan, in *The Prairie* (1827) was the first sustained characterization of this type. As the name implies, the Yankee Indian, confronted with the lack of social structure on the frontier, degenerates to a creature "of the bush," with all the usual connotations of Ishmael, the child left out of the covenant.

At best, the Yankee Indian is loyal only to clan interests, and neutral to all else. At worst, the Yankee Indian actively preys on all those not of the clan. He represents a cultural primitiveness beneath both Indian and white societies. This again is a carry-over from the Puritan period; at each step of the way on the pilgrim's path to Zion, before s/he gathers with the saints at the river below the City on the Hill of *Pilgrim's Progress*, pilgrims were in danger of becoming confused about what was right, and lost in the wilderness.[20] The conflicting values of Christian and Indian societies, combined with the removal of almost all social and institutional supports on the frontier, could create moral confusion. To Cotton Mather, the result of such a meeting was witchcraft, yet another attack by the Devil on the Chosen People.[21] To the more secular age which followed, the result was madness, or a particularly obtuse self-interest.

Increasingly, the Yankee Indian has come to occupy the central place as the Western villain. There are two reasons for this. One is that the Otherness of Native-Americans, and indeed, of the wilderness itself, has become remote and irrelevant to the Western's audience. The wilderness is now no longer a place where the devil rules, but is now wholly the promised land, in which the repressed can become themselves. The unboundedness that wilderness represents is not so much a threat to audiences today as are those who use that openness to harm others. Where Indians are central, as in revisionist Westerns like *Devil's Doorway* (1950), *Broken Arrow* (1950), *Apache* (1954), *Run of the Arrow* (1957), *Little Big Man* (1970), *Soldier Blue* (1970), *Buffalo Bill and the Indians* (1976), or *Dances With Wolves* (1990), they are a moral vantage-point from which the Western argues that the dominant culture is controlled by Yankee Indians.

Second, white America became ashamed of the genocidal policies against Indians and their culture, and, more broadly, of the casual equation in the Western of whiteness as an indicator of civilization. In the 1950s, as Brian Henderson notes, the context of the Western was often the Civil Rights movement.[22] Mel Brooks' *Blazing Saddles* (1974) mocked the stereotype of the white Western hero with a frontier town's dumbfounded reaction to an African-American sheriff. Since the late 1960s, Indian culture has been a vehicle for counterculture critiques of the dominant society. The implicit racism in Westerns toward people of color is disappearing; racial types as a justification for Manifest Destiny are neither relevant nor acceptable to a contemporary audience. The implied miscegenation of "Yankee Indian" is becoming meaningless, but its core meanings of false pilgrim and barbarian remain, capable of continuing variations.

Run of the Arrow: *Where Indians are central, a moral vantage point.*

The Cleggs in *Wagon Master* are particularly good instances of the Yankee Indian, as the characters show something of the type's range. Uncle Shiloh is crafty, but utterly lacking in empathy for anyone other than his sons. As a false pilgrim, he speaks the phrases of the true pilgrim, but interprets their meaning in accordance to his own desires; unlike the pilgrims, a people of the Book, the anti-pilgrim is not bound by words. Of his sons, two especially stand out. Luke, whom Shiloh says is "not quite right in the head," smiles vacantly in anticipation equally of killing Navajos or Mormons. Sister Ledyard, along with the showpeople's Mr. Peachtree, also seems "simple," but where Luke is incapable of any goodness, and smiles at the prospect of killing, Ledyard and Mr. Peachtree are only capable of seeing and doing good. Similarly, Reese and Jackson are antipodes. Jackson only understands religion, law, and the abstract; his violence is the violence of the law, as the sequence introducing the Medicine Show people shows. Reese's violence is expressed in his assault on a Navajo woman; he is illiterate, ungoverned, and physical. Where the pilgrim is insensible to the land, and the Western hero in balance with it, the Yankee Indian is the Puritan image of the bewitched pilgrim, no longer human, degenerated into a creature of the devil. After Travis and Sandy have shot the Cleggs, Wiggs says, "I thought you never drew on a man." "That's right, sir," Travis replies, echoing Cotton Mather's denunciation of the "serpent" of hell, "only on snakes."

Travis and Sandy are model Western heroes, personifications of civilization on the frontier. They are also, like Natty Bumppo, characters who know of Indian ways, and are responsive to the land. Indeed, in many early Westerns, Wayne's early Lone Star Westerns among them, the hero's status is marked by his having an Indian companion. Tonto, the Lone Ranger's companion, is the most famous of these figures. How the Western hero could learn Indian ways was at first a difficult problem. In the Puritan Promised Land myth, the Native Americans had been a spiritual threat, even though their knowledge of the land was desirable. To be taken captive by the Indians was an acceptable way of acquiring that knowledge, as Richard Slotkin has observed:

> The Puritan was no longer sure of his ability to conquer the wilderness in a righteous manner; instead he felt himself weak enough to be debased by the wilderness to the level of the depraved natural man, the Indian. The safest way of discovering the wilderness, therefore, was as the unwilling captive of the wilderness's familiar demons. One could then justify the gaining of intimate knowledge of the Indian life as a result of divine agency.[23]

In accordance with romance structure, the hero is taken out of society, acquires valuable knowledge through undergoing trials, and returns to bring the benefits of that knowledge back to society.

As religious intolerance declined, however, and as Enlightenment theories began to inform colonial perceptions, the captives began to see virtues in the Indian way of life. "They appeared to be fulfilling the scriptures beyond those who profess to believe them, in that of taking no thought for tomorrow; and also in living in love, peace and friendship together," wrote James Smith, a captive of the Iroquois for five years during the French and Indian War.[24] Fear of Indians as the anti-civilization did not disappear, but became blended with respect and even admiration. Colonial heroes changed, from wilderness-haters like Winthrop and Mather, to mediators between the wilderness and civilization, like George Washington and Daniel Boone. Captivity became displaced by friendship, or even (as in the Lone Ranger's case) an unspoken, mystic bond. Like Merlin in the Arthurian legends, who mediated between the fairy and human world, the Men who Spoke with Indians and Knew Their Ways had both the power of the wilderness, as signified by their Indian familiars, and the desire to extend civilization through that power's use.

The Western hero lives at the edge of the envelope, to borrow a phrase from another "frontier"; he has the right stuff. The test pilot's "right stuff" is, as Tom Wolfe noted, the direct secular descendant of Puritan election.[25] The very ideal of Test Pilot and Astronaut is drawn directly from the Western myth; the one illuminates the other. Where Puritans proved their elect status by their adherence to the moral code, and the strength of their faith in trials, Western heroes prove their status through the exercise of their "gifts," as Natty calls it, of their ability to express the best traits of civilization and nature—and in so doing, exalt both themselves, and by reflection, the society for whom they act. Natty Bumppo set the standard for Chuck Yeager: become alert, not afraid, at moments of danger.[26] In the Western, the gun serves as the principal medium to illustrate the hero's status, as the test flight does for pilots. As the Western hero is a master of horses, so the test pilot is the master of machines. The Lone Ranger exhibits an extraordinary mastery of firearms when called upon, but it is in his constant understanding and command of Silver, the horse no other can ride, through which the reader/listener/viewer is constantly reminded that the Lone Ranger is no ordinary man.[27]

This mastery manifests itself in instantaneous action, through which is shown the hero's nature, frontier training, and technical mastery. It is not simply bravery, or desire. It is, rather, a pure harmony sustained in the hero's actions—a blend of wilderness and civilization mediated through the hero's will in a perfect moment. *The Pioneers* establishes this theme in the opening scene of the book, in which Natty is shown in old age. Three men fire at a deer, at almost the same instant. Judge Temple misses the deer and hits Natty's protege Oliver. Natty hits the deer's neck. Oliver, in spite of being wounded an instant before he fires, kills the deer with a shot through the heart, as Natty would have done in his youth. You have it, or you do not; you are of the elect or you are not. In Owen Wister's *The Virginian*, the narrator and the Virginian talk about an outlaw, significantly named "Shorty," whose mistake led to the capture of part of the gang. The Virginian observes that

> [B]ack East you can be middling and get along. But if you go to try a thing on in this Western country, you've got to do it *well*. You've got to deal cyards (sic) *well*; you've got to steal *well*; and if you claim to be quick with your gun, you must be quick, for you're a public temptation, and some man will not resist trying to prove he is the quicker. You must break all the commandments *well* in this Western country, and Shorty should have stayed in Brooklyn, for he will be a novice all his livelong days.[28]

The narrator extends this Western ethic of Right Stuff by commenting to the Virginian that the true novice was not Shorty, but Trampas, the gang leader villain in *The Virginian*. Trampas claimed that he was a better man than the Virginian, but he is proven wrong. He took a weak man into his gang.

As the implicit comparison between Trampas and the Virginian suggests, the Puritan anxiety about proving one's elect status underlies one of the Western's fundamental plot elements, the test between villain and hero over who really has the "right stuff." In his essay "The Dandy," Stanley Cavell quotes Oscar Wilde's definition of the dandy as one who used personal appearance and elegance as symbols of aristocratic superiority; one who preserved his/her composure at all times; the dandy, Cavell summarized, had a "passive potency" whose realization, as Wilde conceived it, was in the production of art.[29] In the Western, as in the test flight, the realization is in survival when confronted with the fatal moment. That consummate dandy, the Lone Ranger, with his black mask and silver bullets, is the exaggerated acme of the type. But all Western heroes have some distinguishing style, of appearance or behavior. Wayne brought a subtle physical grace to his character, for instance, as Garry Wills notes, that served to set his characters off from the ungainly movements of other men; Wayne's appearance of balance and ease is his art.

Pretenders aspire to the prestige that the dandy receives. They may be skilful, perhaps, but fail the test. The false dandy tries to look and act like the true dandy, just as the false Puritan might attend church. The false dandy abuses his presumed possession of mastery to take over water rights, or to bully farmers from their land. In ambiguous characters like Clint Eastwood's loners in Leone's Spaghetti Westerns, or Pike and Dutch in *The Wild Bunch*, what helps to define them as heroes is their almost physical revulsion at the crude selfishness of false dandies. But when the clock strikes the hour, as clocks so often strike in Westerns to call the gunfighters to their doom and final judgment, it is the true dandy who lives, or dies (as in *The Wild Bunch)* in an apotheosis of mastery, and the false dandy who is flung, his glory shattered, on boot hill.

The false dandy often distinguishes himself by his visual grandeur, and usually—though not always—by his overt unsuitability within civilization. He is a churl posing as a gentleman. In *The Man Who Shot Liberty Valance*, Liberty (Lee Marvin) seems almost a complete brute. Yet he takes a conscious pride in his prowess as "the toughest man south of the Picket-wire—next to me," as Tom describes him. Liberty aspires to aristocracy. He wears a filigreed vest, and sports a silver-embellished quirt. He does not merely hurt people; he must look stylish as he hurts. He shouts, bullies and preens his way through his scenes. Wilson (Jack Palance), the cattle baron's gunman in *Shane* (1953), is a more typical false dandy. He does not bluster like Liberty, yet each shines in their predominantly black outfits, and struts slowly, self-consciously, apart from the tasteless commoners who watch them.

There is a narcissistic, blasphemous selfishness to the false dandy; in accordance with the Western's Puritan roots, the false dandy is an imitator of Satan, as the dandy is an imitator of Christ. Overreaching is part of the false dandy's identity. Frank (Henry Fonda), the gunslinger whom railroad baron Mr. Morton has hired to "clear small obstructions from the roadway" in *Once Upon a Time in the West* (1968), is a distillation of the false dandy's desires and manners. He lives for the moment of power behind the gun, yet he also wants to have the abstract power of his boss, Mr. Morton, the man

False dandies: Liberty (Lee Marvin) in The Man Who Shot Liberty Valance, *Frank (Henry Fonda) in* Once Upon a Time in the West, *and "English Bob" (Richard Harris) in* Unforgiven.

behind the desk. He desires to be a force of nature, something inhuman, unstoppable: a self-made gentleman/gunman. In contrast, the true dandy (in the Western, at least) seems to pay attention to matters of dress and action as an extension of his "calling"; an audience is less desired than suffered. The true dandy is *the* gentleman/gunman, a medium through which divine forces express themselves. Like the Lone Ranger, the true Western hero does what he cannot help but do, and rides off to new challenges before the townspeople, farmers or ranchers are quite sure he was there.

Unforgiven (1992) takes place in a Western version of Bunyan's Vanity Fair, and is a virtual parade of falsity. To force the dandy's skill in order to see it proven is to suffer it, and so the threat of being one of the Elect is enough. Tough Westerners on a train yield, once they realize they are challenging a "true" gunman, English Bob (Richard Harris). English Bob the "Duke of death," becomes transformed to the "duck of death" when confronted by Little Bill, who is not awed by his act. In his surprise at seeing Little Bill, augmented by his deputies, English Bob's cultivated act slips. "Little Bill! Why, I thought you was—Well, I thought that you were dead." Little Bill is what the false dandy fears most—a bad audience. The Schofield Kid keeps trying to impress Ned Logan and William Munny, especially Munny. But the true dandy does not seek an audience. He compels it by his nature. The Kid's desperate longing for applause is proof of his incompetence.

Unforgiven underscores something that *Shane*, and other glamorized dandy films, only hint at: the dandy's calling is inherently savage. To be a dandy is to risk corruption. It is not by chance that, after shooting the Cleggses, Travis tosses his gun into a canyon. The Western hero cannot cross over the river to gather with the Saints in Zion in possession of a gun. For a dandy to be one of the saints requires a renunciation of power, a dual admission both that reliance on personal power is wrong, and that to the extent that it was good, it was an expression of divine law.[30] This contradiction of divine power in mortal hands results in two kinds of Western hero. One is the Cooper Leatherstocking hero, the self-aware mediator between Dionysian and Apollonian, Indian and white cultures. As the character evolved, reaching its current form in Cooper's *The Oak Opening* (1848) and its more influential descendent, Wister's *The Virginian* (1902), the hero metamorphizes from an agent of civilization's advance to a member of civilization, marked by the hero's marriage to a woman who brings pilgrim values to the wilderness. The other, more sinister hero developed concurrently, in books like James McHenry's *The Spectre of the Forest* (1823), and Robert Montgomery Bird's *Nick of the Woods* (1837). This type is an avenger. He is angry, irrational, implacable—a visitation of divine wrath. He bears a resemblance to the Yankee Indian, but his vengeance is in the cause of civilization.

Natty Bumppo is "without a cross," which as Leslie Fiedler noted, has the dual meaning that he has neither Indian ancestry, nor is a conventional Christian.[31] He is a holy monster: exiled between the Indian and European worlds, valued by each but part of neither. He partakes of the Dionysian communion with nature, yet retains the Apollonian knowledge of civilization. His punishment for this violation is that he is the agency through which the nature he loves is destroyed. Most characters who live beyond law and society degenerate in Cooper.[32] Natty's virtues emerge under the stress of freedom. As a Pentheus hero, Natty cannot marry. Cooper intuited this, and had already written of his bachelorhood and death, in extreme old age, before he turned to books on Natty's youth to explain his bachelorhood. But characters similar to Natty, in *The Prairie, The Pathfinder* and *The Pioneers*, who could become like him, give up the communion of the wilderness's freedom for the restrictions of civilized identity, responsibility, and domesticity that the Cooper heroine offers.

Wagon Master, as I have outlined it above, is a pure example of this story. *The Man Who Shot Liberty Valance* is a tragic variant whose contrasts underline the myth's core themes. In *Wagon Master*, Jackson, the man of stubborn faith, does not survive. In *The Man Who Shot Liberty Valance*, Ransom, the stubborn idealistic Eastern lawyer, marries Hallie. But Hallie is a Western woman. She can become cultivated, just as the territory can become a state, but civilization is not immanent in her. Hallie, not Ransom, is the one who needs to be instructed in all points of civilization: the journalist, Mr. Peabody, must instruct her in the placement of cutlery, and Ransom must teach her to read. Similarly, Ransom is not a dandy. Ransom's "gifts," as Ford shows by placing him in an apron, and by having him teach school, are those of the Eastern heroine, Wister's Schoolmarm of *The Virginian*. He is pure Apollonian, without the experience to perform the ritual Dionysian murder the Western hero must be capable of to transform the land. When the degenerative power of wilderness must be fought, in the form of the villain, Liberty Valance, Hallie turns to Tom.

Tom Doniphon, the John Wayne Western hero, has the mastery and knowledge of the wilderness. But neither Tom nor Hallie are carriers of civilization; for them to marry is not progress, but stagnation. Tom and Ransom would be the ideal Western couple—but while the frontier in the Western has a tradition of same-sex couples, as Fiedler noted, to found a civilization on such a couple was not part of the myth in the early Sixties.[33] Ransom could become Tom's protege, as Oliver became Natty's in *The Pioneers*. Tom establishes this by noting that Ransom "throws a good punch" at the statehood convention, and offers him a grudging respect for his will, if not his abilities. But there is no time for Ransom to learn how to be a Westerner, and to combine the best of the West with the East. The Western's roles are so clearly defined, that there is no solution except in deception: Tom kills Liberty Valance, in order to make it possible for Hallie to become civilized, and assigns the credit to Ransom so that civilization can come. Like Natty, he is pathfinder, not patriarch. But because Ransom, in terms of the myth, has not fled but challenged the Dionysian order, he emerges a broken, compromised man, haunted by the lie that anyone can fully master both the Dionysian and the Apollonian.[34] He, too, is a pathfinder rather than a patriarch, a man whose actions transform the desert into the garden, yet is incapable of children. Only Hallie attains the Western hero's state, at the end of the film, as the mediator between Nature and Culture—but too late for fruitful union.

The second Western hero type is the Avenger. Where the pathfinder is a monster who may transform into a settler, the avenger is a settler transformed into a monster. In the Avenger myth's original form, Indians murder a boy or a young man's family. Spiritually, the civilized boy or man dies in that instant; all that is left is a murderous rage against Indians, and indeed, wilderness itself. This is the direct contrast to Natty Bumppo's love for his constant friend Chingachgook, and of his love of nature. The Avenger combines the Puritan's hatred of the wilderness with the Leatherstocking hero's knowledge of it, to become a monster whose evil serves to advance the good of civilization. In *The Confidence-Man* (1857), Herman Melville describes the characteristics of what was already a stereotype:

> An intenser Hannibal, he makes a vow, the hate of which is a vortex from whose suction scarce the remotest chip of the guilty race may reasonably feel secure. Next, he declares himself and settles his temporal affairs. With the solemnity of a Spaniard turned monk, he takes leave of his next of kin; or rather, these leave-takings have something of the still more impressive finality of death-bed adieus. Last, he commits himself to the forest primeval; there so long as life shall be his, to act upon a calm, cloistered scheme of strategical, implacable, and lonesome vengeance. Ever on the noiseless trail; cool, collected, patient; less seen than felt; snuffing, smelling—a Leather-stocking Nemesis.[35]

There are many instances of this type—Harmonica (Charles Bronson) in *Once Upon a Time in the West*, and Munny (Clint Eastwood) in *Unforgiven* are two excellent examples—but Wayne's Ethan Edwards, in John Ford's *The Searchers* (1956) is the most influential example. True to his calling as an avenger-dandy, he cannot surrender his sword at the end of the Civil War. The Edwards family is killed after Ethan is introduced, but he has the characteristics of the Avenger from the beginning. "Fella could mistake you for a half-breed," he instantly growls at Martin Pawley when he first sees him, snuffing out his partial Indian heritage.

We are never told much about Ethan, but he is a master of Indian religions, movements and practices. Even Scar, the Indian avenger-chief who has captured Debbie Edwards, comments to Ethan, "you speak good Comanch'—someone teach you?" After the cavalry attack Scar's camp in the Winter, Ethan and Marty look over white captives the cavalry recover to see if one is Debbie. There are only two quick dolly-ins in *The Searchers*, the shot reserved in classic Hollywood cinema to signify fear or another strong emotion. One of them is on Lucy Edwards, Ethan's niece, as she realizes that Indians are about to attack. She fears—correctly—that she will die. The other is on Ethan, as he looks at captives the U.S. Cavalry has recovered from defeated Indian tribes. Ford shows the children—fearful, gibbering, staring preternaturally—and then shows Ethan in that quick dolly. Ethan is lit by a low key light. He looks afraid, for the only time in the film. Here is Cotton Mather's image of the West made manifest, and Ethan sees and fears it, and fears it could be him. This is why Ethan hates the Indians: their presence reminds him of the mythical Indian within him, of the human monster without God or community.

This fear of becoming lost directly motivates the protagonists of many interesting Westerns. Anthony Mann's Western heroes are all pilgrims in the wilderness; all travel the thin edge between the Elect and the Lost. When Lena Patch (Janet Leigh) stops Jimmy Stewart's Howard Kemp from carrying Ben's body back for the bounty in *The Naked Spur*, it is the fear of losing his own true self that she opens before his eyes that stops him. Another example is Wayne's Quirt Evans in *Angel and the Bad Man*. He sees himself reflected in Penelope Worth and the Quakers' eyes, and can no longer be content with material comforts and fallen women. Clint Eastwood's Munny in *Unforgiven* is a post-marriage Quirt Evans. The money that draws him is exactly one of those traps to which the pilgrim is exposed. Munny seems fearless. But when his identity is discovered; when his friend Ned is killed; when it becomes apparent that the money he sought is not a shortcut to his pilgrimage, but a trap; when the extent of his degeneration from where his Wife had led him is undeniable, then the sleeping Avenger becomes fully awake. Munny's terrible competence and wrath emerge directly from his hatred, not of Little Bill, but of that savagery in himself that Little Bill shares, and so freely and sinfully indulges in his pretense of civility.[36]

I have outlined the Western's core character types, their history and the myth they serve. But as the West is a living genre, it continues to evolve variations on these basic themes. It must, if it is to continue to hold its place in the American imagination. The frontier is gone. Although *Once Upon A Time in the West* ends with the pyrrhic victory of people against the corporation, and Westerns like Wayne's *The Star-Packer* (1934) and *Rio Bravo* (1959) with the overcoming of cattle-empire bosses, we all know that we live in a corporate, enclosed world. Films like *Greed* (1925), which begins significantly in a hard-rock mine, *The Man Who Shot Liberty Valance*, and *The Wild Bunch* (1969), take as their starting point the closure of possibilities for the individual, the displacement of human agency with bureaucracy, and nobility with pettiness. Paula Cole's song, "Where Have All the Cowboys Gone," is of this departed West, in which farmers become factory workers, and freedom replaced with a mortgage-payment. Were the Western simply to celebrate victories over corporatism, its falseness would repel the audience, its delusive fantasy sicken.

Ethan Edwards and the captives: "Cotton Mather's image of the West made manifest."
The Searchers.

But the Western has survived by progressively broadening its identity of the chosen people, and redefining the evils of contemporary America in the structural identity of false pilgrims. The mythic frontier remains a place where utopian versions of the City on a Hill can be re-imagined to incorporate those who are left out or repressed in the current social order. In this century, Western authors and filmmakers have begun to accommodate its themes of a chosen people to more ethnically diverse audiences. Increasingly, the frontiers of race and sex largely unexplored in the past are the subject of new work in the genre. More often than not now, it is women and Native-Americans, Asians and African-Americans, who seek to build a city on a hill in an intolerant wilderness.

From the beginning of European settlement of North America to the present, America's cultural identity has been created out of the myth of the frontier. I have outlined the structure of this myth, but the forms in which these structures are expressed will continue to change. The Chosen People and Promised Land remain constant, but what once was an exclusive promise for a sect of a few hundreds of pilgrims has become a myth of identity through which a multicultural nation helps to create a unified sense of itself. The Western periodically dies, as the needs it served fade, and then is rediscovered in a new form, more responsive to the needs of its time. These changes are never without some struggle. The West is the ritual altar of American identity, and the form in which it is manifested is an affirmation of particular visions of American society. Elitists and egalitarians, Social Darwinists and Progressives, the Establishment and the Radicals: in every age, social conflict takes shape and communicates itself through the Western.

NOTES

1. Henry Kissinger, "An Interview with Oriana Fallaci," *The New Republic* (Dec. 16, 1972), p. 21, quoted in Ralph Brauer and Donna Brauer, *The Horse, The Gun, and the Piece of Property: Changing Images in the TV Western* (Bowling Green, Ohio: Bowling Green University Press, 1975), p. 1.

2. Garry Wills, "John Wayne's Body," *New Yorker* Vol. LXXII, No. 24 (Aug. 19, 1996), p. 39.

3. Aristotle, *Politica*, in Richard McKeon, *Introduction to Aristotle* 2nd ed. (Chicago: University of Chicago Press, 1973), p. 596.

4. William Little, et al, *The Oxford Universal Dictionary Illustrated* (Oxford: Clarendon Press, 1974), p. 1584.

5. II Cor 6: 17-18; see also Vernon L. Parrington, *Main Currents in American Thought* (New York: Harcourt, Brace and World, Inc., 1958), pp. 8-9, for its background in Puritan thought.

6. Joseph Gair and Ben Siegel, *The Puritan Heritage, America's Roots in the Bible* (New York: Mentor Books, 1964), p. 26.

7. Henry Nash Smith, *Virgin Land* (Cambridge, MA: Harvard University Press, 1978 [1950]), pp. 123-132.

8. John Winthrop, "A Model of Christian Charity," in Ronald Gottesman, et al, *The Norton Anthology of American Literature* Vol. 1 (New York: W. W. Norton, 1979), pp. 11-24.

9. James Fenimore Cooper, *The Last of the Mohicans* (New York: Charles Scribner's Sons, 1947), p. 370.

10. See Simone de Beauvoir, *The Second Sex* (New York: Bantam Books, 1970 [1953]), pp. 134-138.

11. Quoted in Richard Hofstadter, *The American Political Tradition* (New York: Vintage Books, 1948), p. 168.

12. Andrew Carnegie, "Wealth," in Richard Hofstadter, ed., *Great Issues in American History* Vol. 2 (New York: Vintage Books 1958), p. 88.

13. See Richard Hofstadter, "The Agrarian Myth and Commercial Reality," in *The Age of Reform* (New York: Vintage Books, 1955).

14. See Richard Slotkin, *Gunfighter Nation* (New York: Atheneum, 1992), pp. 34-54.

15. Wister, pp. 81-82. Note the paragraphs immediately preceding the quote. Compare also Shorty's complaints about the Virginian's luck and the Virginian's response, p. 149.

16. Louis L'Amour, *The Strong Shall Live* (New York: Bantam Books, 1980), pp. xi-x.

17. Cotton Mather, "A People of God in the Devil's Territories," *Magnalia Christi Americana*, in Gottesman, et al, *The Norton Anthology of American Literature*, p. 119.

18. Zane Gray, *Riders of the Purple Sage* (Roslyn, NY: Walter J. Black, Inc., 1940 [1912]).

19. James Fenimore Cooper, *The Pioneers*, p. 420.

20. See John Bunyan, *Pilgrim's Progress* (New York: P. F. Collier and Company, 1937), p. 161, for a description of this final "gathering at the river."

21. See Richard Slotkin, *Regeneration through Violence* (Middletown, CT: Wesleyan University Press, 1973), p. 132.

22. See Brian Henderson, "*The Searchers*: An American Dilemma," in Bill Nichols, ed., *Movies and Methods* Vol. 2 (Berkeley: University of California Press, 1985), pp. 29-449.

23. Richard Slotkin, *Regeneration through Violence*, pp. 99-100.

24. James Smith, *Account of the Remarkable Occurrences in the Life and Travels of Col. James Smith* (1799), in Archibald Loudon, *A Selection* (New York: Arno Press, 1971), p. 159.

25. Tom Wolfe, *The Right Stuff* (New York: Bantam Books, 1980), pp. 111-112.

26. Phillip Kaufman, director of *The Right Stuff* (1983), understood this. He cast playwright Sam Shepard as Yeager, a playwright whose screen persona and works are centered on the Western myth.

27. Ralph Brauer and Donna Brauer, in *The Horse, The Gun, and the Piece of Property: Changing*

Images in the TV Western, discusses the horse's role in certifying the Western hero's status in detail.

28. Wister, *The Virginian*, p. 219.

29. Stanley Cavell, *The World Viewed*, Enlarged Edition (Cambridge, Mass.: Harvard University Press, 1979), pp. 55-60.

30. This is the point of Stephen Crane's "The Bride Comes to Yellow Sky."

31. See, for instance, Natty and Cooper's discussion of religion in *Last of the Mohicans*, Chapter 12. See Leslie Fiedler, "Come Back to the Raft Agin', Huck Honey," in *An End to Innocence* (Boston: Beacon Press, 1955).

32. Ishmael Bush's clan in *The Prairie*, and indeed, all the white characters in *The Deerslayer* except Hetty and Natty, are some of the more notable examples.

33. This *has* been done, in the television show *Northern Exposure*'s origin episode "Cecily." A lesbian couple, one a Westerner, the other the Woman of Culture, transform a frontier town into the civilized "Paris of the North."

34. See Tag Gallagher, *John Ford: The Man and His Films* (Berkeley: University of California Press, 1986), pp. 404-413, in which Gallagher discusses the depth of Ransom's compromises.

35. Herman Melville, *The Confidence-Man* (San Francisco: Chandler Publishing Company, 1968 [1857]), pp. 233-234.

36. Interestingly enough, Little Bill also seems to have his roots in Cooper. In *The Pioneers*, Judge Temple's attempted humane exercise of law is thwarted by its agent, Sheriff Hiram Doolittle. Like Little Bill, Doolittle exercises his power not by his own abilities, but by the threat of his deputies assembled. Like Little Bill, Doolittle is a terrible carpenter, who mis-builds Judge Temple's house. See James Fenimore Cooper, *The Pioneers* (New York: Washington Square Press, 1962), pp. 27-30; 394-404.

John Wayne in John Ford's She Wore a Yellow Ribbon: *"A constructed, not a found, landscape."*

INVENTING MONUMENT VALLEY:
Nineteenth Century Landscape
Photography and the Western Film

Edward Buscombe (1995)

> This mesa plain had an appearance of great antiquity, and of incompleteness; as if, with all the materials for world-making assembled, the Creator had desisted, gone away and left everything on the point of being brought together, on the eve of being arranged into mountain, plain, plateau. The country was still waiting to be made into a landscape.
>
> —Willa Cather

I

"**C**owboys, Indians and Mexicans must be seen in proper scenic backgrounds to convey any impression of reality." So wrote a critic in the *New York Dramatic Mirror* on 5 June 1909 (Robert Anderson 24). Conventional film history, including my own, has generally dated the Western from the appearance of *The Great Train Robbery* in 1903. But recently, scholars have doubted whether this film may properly be called a Western at all (Neale 52). Certainly it was not made in the West, the location sequences being shot on the Delaware and Lackawanna Railroad in New Jersey. The first recognizably Western films to be shot in a recognizably western landscape did not appear until 1907, when the Selig company ventured to Colorado. The company went out of its way to publicize the "magnificent scenic effects" of its productions. *Western Justice* was advertised in *Moving Picture World* as set "in the wildest and most beautiful scenery of the Western country" (Robert Anderson 23).

The next year, 1908, Selig was followed to Colorado by Essanay. So successful were the resulting films that many of the established film companies such as Biograph, Edison, Lubin, Vitagraph, and Kalem attempted to exploit the popularity of the emergent genre by producing their own Westerns back east. But these eastern Westerns could not compare in authenticity with the productions of Selig and Essanay. The critics roundly condemned their lack of true local color. In a mere two years the response of the *New York Dramatic Mirror* makes clear, western locations had gone from being a novelty to a necessity. By 1911, D. W. Griffith and the Biograph company had followed suit and gone west. Griffith's *The Heart of a Savage* was advertized in the *New York Dramatic Mirror* as featuring "the most beautiful Californian mountain scenery ever photographed" (Robert Anderson 26).

Robert Anderson, who has traced these developments in the formation of the Western genre, argues that its rapid rise to popularity—by 1910 20 percent of American pictures were Westerns—was a major factor in the successful battle of American producers against foreign imports. Attempts at this time by European companies to make their own Westerns in France, England, Denmark, and elsewhere testified to the box office success of this type of film, but the results appeared only to confirm that the appeal depended crucially on an authentically western look. American producers had found a type of film they could call their own, a truly national genre which proved a continuing hit with the public and for which foreign imports could not substitute. Not for another fifty years, until the rise of the Italian Western in the 1960s, were American producers challenged in their monopoly of the cinema's most popular genre.

But if Westerns needed western scenery to be authentic, what exactly were "the proper scenic backgrounds" which the critics demanded and which the companies were eager to provide? What ought Western landscapes to look like? The West, after all, was a big place. It offered a wide variety of potential locations for the filmmaker. Which was the most apt for Western subjects? And if there was an accepted type of landscape, how had the canon of taste been formed?

Visual representations of landscapes west of the Mississippi begin to appear in the 1830s, when professional artists first journeyed west to see for themselves. Though there are pictures of the Great Plains dating from this era, it was the Rocky Mountains which first captured the imagination both of painters trained in the European traditions of high art and of those working in a more popular idiom. By the 1860s, mountains in general and the Rockies in particular had become established as what western landscape was all about. A popular chromolithograph by Fanny Palmer issued by the Currier and Ives company in 1866 is entitled *The Rocky Mountains/Emigrants Crossing the Plains*. It depicts a wagon train making progress through a vista of verdant meadows which Constable would not have disdained. In the background, white-capped mountains rise to dizzying heights. The scene owes everything to European models, mixing the pastoral and the romantic in equal parts.

The foremost painter of western landscapes at this time, Albert Bierstadt, had trained in Düsseldorf, home of German romanticism. He found the Rockies "very fine. As seen from the plains they resemble very much the Bernese Alps; they are of granite formation, the same as the Swiss mountains . . . the colours are like those of Italy" (Goetzmann 225). He proceeded to paint them so, dramatizing his pictures with thrilling effects of light and cloud. The pictures were themselves on a physical scale to

Carleton E. Watkins, "Yosemite Valley" (1886). From the American Geographical Society Collection, University of Wisconsin-Milwaukee Library.

match their subjects—six feet by ten feet. They were wildly successful with the public and, despite Bierstadt's European training, were hailed as representative of a genuinely American art. The critic Henry T. Tuckerman, writing in 1870, thought Bierstadt's *The Rocky Mountains* "eminently national . . . a grand and gracious epitome and reflection of nature on this Continent" (qtd. in Baigell 11).

Bierstadt's pictures of the California Sierras were equally spectacular. The pearl of the Sierras was the valley of Yosemite. From the beginning of the 1860s it had attracted the attention of both painters and photographers, whose images were influential in the decision by President Lincoln in 1864 to decree Yosemite a natural preserve. The San Francisco photographers Carleton Watkins and Eadweard Muybridge vied with each other in producing ever more sumptuous views of the Yosemite landscape on the huge (18" X 22") glass plates of their specially constructed cameras. The principles of composition which the photographers adopted were drawn directly from the traditions of landscape painting. The rules governing the respective proportions of landscape and sky, the framing of a distant view by foliage artfully arranged in the foreground, the frequent use of an expanse of water to reflect and so enhance the beauty of the view, all are transposed directly into the new medium of photography—and back again, for Bierstadt in turn used the photographs of Watkins and Muybridge to assist him in his painting of Yosemite (Baigell 13).

The growth in production of photographs of beauty spots such as Yosemite was both the cause and the effect of tourism. Photography increased the visibility of such places, stimulating the desire to travel to them, and it provided a means whereby the landscape could be rendered into a consumable form and carried away at an afford-able price. This kind of art photography, with its painterly qualities, based on the representation of landscapes validated by a European tradition and reflecting the taste of the comfortable middle classes who consumed it, passed easily into the cinema. From the earliest Westerns located in the Rockies of Colorado to the classics of the 1950s and 1960s, mountain scenery has been used to authenticate "Westernness." André Bazin identified what he called the "superwestern": the Western "that would be ashamed to be just itself, and looks for some additional interest to justify its existence—an aesthetic, sociological, moral, psychological, political or erotic interest, in short some quality extrinsic to the genre and which is supposed to enrich it" (151). The opening sequence of *Shane*, a self-conscious attempt to create a summation of the genre, an instant "classic," is indeed "enriched" by the combination of distant mountains, framing foliage and reflecting water as the young Joey observes from behind the trees the approach of Shane. The director George Stevens' use of landscape derives from the tradition which Bierstadt was instrumental in creating. And one may even suspect a more direct borrowing from one painting in particular, for in the opening sequence is there not in the watchful deer posed against the backdrop of the Tetons an echo of Bierstadt's painting *Estes Park, Colorado: Whyte's Lake*?

Landscape in this tradition is an aesthetic object. Its function is to be gazed at, in an act of reverential contemplation. Roderick Nash has placed the sources of this attitude to landscape within the romantic movement: "The concept of the sublime and picturesque led the way by enlisting aesthetics in wild country's behalf while deism associated nature and religion. Combined with the primitivistic idealization of a life close to nature, these ideas fed the Romantic movement which had far-reaching implications for wilderness" (Nash 44). Nature is conceived of as essentially unspoiled. Human beings appear in these pictures only rarely. Indians are allowable because they are assumed to be part of the natural world, and humans may also function as markers of scale, serving to play up the vastness of the panoramas displayed. Besides conforming to the aesthetic rules of landscape art, photographers of western scenes also followed the practice of painters by including the viewing subject in the scene, inscribing into the image the correct way of reading it. The spectator within the frame, in a position of static, usually sedentary relaxation, gazes in awe at the wonders in the distance. Mountain scenery in this tradition seems inescapably bound to a kind of spiritual uplift, as if the verticality of the mountains were in some way a metaphor of their effect upon the observer. In Hollywood cinema, and in the Western in particular, mountain scenery could be said to function as a substitute for religion, a way of introducing a secular spiritual dimension.

II

Yet today when we think of the West and Westerns, it's not mountains, trees, and lakes that first come to mind, but more often the deserts and canyon lands of Arizona and Utah. Since the 1860s the center of gravity of the Western landscape has moved southwest. As we have seen in the case of *Shane*, deserts and canyons never managed a monopoly of Western scenery. But they did achieve a certain domination, such that Anthony Mann, famed for his use of mountain scenery, was moved to protest: "I have never understood why people make almost all Westerns in desert country. John Ford, for example, adores Monument Valley, but Monument Valley, which I know well, is not the whole of the west. In fact the desert represents only a part of the American west" (qtd. in Mauduy and Henriet 69). In *Géographers du Western*, a map shows that for a total of 411 films surveyed the setting of the diegesis was heavily weighted toward the Southwest, including New Mexico and Texas. A second map shows the actual locations in which films were shot. Here, for a total of 191 films surveyed, the preponderance of southwest setting is even more pronounced (Mauduy and Henriet 23). Particularly striking is the fact that despite the large number of films set in New Mexico and Texas, very few were actually shot there. In many cases Utah and Arizona are doubling for these two states, presumably on the grounds that they correspond more to what Texas and New Mexico "ought" to look like. John Ford's *The Searchers*, set in Texas but largely shot in Monument Valley in Arizona, is a notable example.

Over the past hundred years or so, two topographical features of the Southwest landscape have achieved special status, though via somewhat different routes. The Grand Canyon and Monument Valley have come to signify, in contemporary usage, not just the Western, but America itself. In a recent British Airways commercial, the Grand Canyon stands as a symbol of the access to the exciting places in the world which the airline claims to provide, even though there are no scheduled British Airways services to the Grand Canyon itself. In the last few years, the silhouette of Monument Valley has become an even more readily identifiable icon of the West of America, and of the West as America. In a Burger King commercial, a couple of Indiana Jones-type flyers in a World War II Dakota touch down in the valley for fast food. In a recent campaign for Rebel Yell bourbon, Monument Valley appears in a bizarre collage of icons—a bucking bronco, the Confederate flag on a guitar, the Statue of Liberty—designed to communicate the essence of America.

Monument Valley was placed on the cultural map by John Ford, who first went there in 1938 to make *Stagecoach* and subsequently shot seven more Westerns there. Over a period of about ten or fifteen years that one location became almost exclusively identified with Ford's films. Other filmmakers have on occasion ventured to the same spot, but they have been very few, and often, as in the case of Sergio Leone's *Once Upon a time in the West*, a deliberate reference to Ford has been intended. As a result of this close identification between Ford, the Western, and southwestern scenery, critics sometimes assume that any film showing canyons and desert must have been shot in Monument Valley. In *The BFI Companion to the Western*, Paul Willemen's entry on Raoul Walsh's *Pursued* mistakenly refers to "the towering rocks of Monument Valley" (Buscombe 290). I myself, in an entry on Monument Valley, mistakenly claim that Ford's *Wagon Master* and *3 Godfathers* were shot there (Buscombe 191). More recently, Leo Braudy writes in a review of *Thelma and Louise:*

> As they escape, when the film truly hits the road, the promise of space and freedom lures them on. But the camera still continues to stress the choking inevitability of

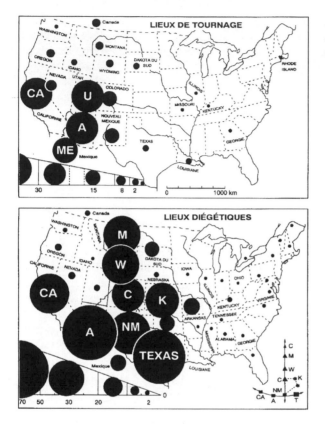

Diagrams from J. Mauduy and G. Henriet, Geographies du Western.

the world they are trying to escape, not just the massive machinery, oil drilling equipment, and trucks that constantly threaten to squeeze them out of our vision, but even the seemingly more benevolent spaces and spires of John Ford's Monument Valley.(28)

As the closing credits to the film tell us, the western scenes of *Thelma and Louise* were actually shot in Arches and Canyonlands National Parks. But Monument Valley has now come to signify Ford, Ford has come to be synonymous with the Western, the Western signifies Hollywood cinema, and Hollywood stands for America. Thus, through a kind of metonymic chain, Monument Valley has come to represent America itself.

Ford's genius for framing and camera placement drew from this one location an astonishingly rich and evocative variety of meanings. But before he could exploit its resources, the landscape had first to be invested with meaning. The process whereby its unique arrangements of rock and space accreted aesthetic value had taken place much earlier, in the last part of the nineteenth century when the shift in public taste occurred through which deserts and canyons replaced mountains as the most beautiful and authentic American landscape.

As we have seen in the case of Bierstadt, the celebration of America's natural wonders was held to be an eminently patriotic activity. But inevitably there was something imitative about the depiction of the Rockies and Sierras. Other countries too had beautiful mountains; had, in a sense, had them for longer than America. What was needed was something different, something unique. That something was first revealed during the 1870s as the Southwest of the United States was opened up by systematic exploration and a new kind of landscape was discovered, one which could not easily be understood within the categories of the sublime or the picturesque which had previously valorized the mountains.

The largest feature in the landscape of the Southwest was of course the Grand Canyon. The first white men to see it were part of the Coronado expedition of 1540, but, strange though it now seems, it made little impression on them. It was as if they literally could not see it, because they could not fit it into the visual framework of the time. The first proper exploration came with the Ives expedition by the Army Corps of Topographical Engineers in 1858, whose report was published in 1861. Ten years later, at the beginning of the 1870s, two separate government expeditions brought back the first photographs of the canyon. Under the sponsorship of the Smithsonian Institution, Major John Wesley Powell, a one-armed Civil War veteran, made an extensive survey of the entire canyon by boat. Powell had made a previous river passage in 1869; this time he had a photographer, Jack Hillers.

Also exploring the Grand Canyon area in 1871 was an army expedition led by Lieutenant George Wheeler. The photographer with Wheeler's party was Timothy O'Sullivan, who had learned his trade while a member of Matthew Brady's Photographic Corps in the Civil War. In 1873 O'Sullivan returned to the Southwest with Clarence King's geological survey, making pictures of the Canyon de Chelly and elsewhere in Arizona. Many of his photographs were destroyed when a reporter carrying them back east was killed by Apaches in the Wickenberg Stagecoach Massacre of 1873—a case perhaps of nature imitating art—but fortunately some survive. . . .

The philosophical impact of the scientific explorations set in motion by nineteenth century geological explorations can scarcely be overestimated. The Grand Canyon was by far the most visually spectacular demonstration of the revolution that geology demanded in the conception of historical time. If, as geologists argued, the gorge of the Colorado had been caused by fluvial erosion, then vast eons must have elapsed while the river cut its way deep into the earth. "The growing realization, confirmed by Darwin's success, that the earth was not merely older than previously thought but immensely and indescribably older found expression in the erosional forms of the Colorado Plateau" (Pyne 21). The photographs brought back by Hillers and O'Sullivan provided stunning views of the canyon's wonders. The visual evidence they provided of the almost unimaginable antiquity of the earth surely endowed the pictures with an added dimension, a philosophical frission. Just as the astronomical revelations of Galileo removed the earth from its presumed position at the center of the universe, so geology decentered humanity from its position of occupying the whole of history. Human beings were now seen to be late arrivals on a planet whose physical shape had been carved out over periods of time virtually "measureless to

Timothy O'Sullivan, "Canyon de Chelly" (1873). Library of Congress, Washington, D.C.

man." If the sight of mountains aroused the spectator to a quasi-religious awe, raised him or her up, almost literally, to a contemplation of what was most noble in human nature, the vision down into the earth, peering back into countless millions of years, produced a no less awesome sense of humility in the face of the immensity of time....

It would be hard to overestimate the influence of Hillers and his peers on the popular taste in landscape pictures:

> Because he worked solely for organizations dedicated to conveying information to various publics, Hillers's works probably were more widely disseminated, and seen by more people in the nineteenth century and since, than any of his peers'. First his photographs were used as the basis for engravings or woodcut illustrations, and later (as printing technology improved) for half tones, in many publications of the Bureau of American Ethnology and the Geological Survey. No actual count has been made of the number of Hillers's images used in those publications during his active career, but it would likely run to over four hundred examples. Bureau of Ethnology and Geological Survey publications were widely distributed. Often as many as 10,000 copies were ordered printed.... Thousands of copies of the stereographs that Hillers made from 1872 through at least 1879 were duplicated by the Jarvis Company of Washington D.C.... Finally, Hillers's prints and transparencies were shown at several international expositions from 1876 to 1904. (Fowler 155)

The demand in the later part of the nineteenth century for landscape photography, for pictures of mountains and canyons alike, was immense. In 1902, its peak year, the Detroit Photographic Company, which had eventually purchased most of Jackson's negatives, sold over 7 million photographs, a large number of them landscapes, ranging from postcards and stereographs to panoramas 20 x 150". Stereographs were especially popular. They had created a sensation when shown at the Crystal Palace Exhibition in London in 1851. All the important photographers of the West, including Muybridge, Watkins, Jackson, and O'Sullivan, made stereographs for sale to the public. From the Powell survey, about 650 different stereographs were made by Hillers and others for commercial sale....

III

By the turn of the century, tourism to the Grand Canyon was in full swing, so much so that it became itself the actual subject of the picture in Oscar Berninghaus' 1915 painting *A Showery Day, Grand Canyon*, which depicts visitors enjoying the view. The 1899 edition of Baedecker's guide to the United States included a map and instructions on how to reach it by stagecoach. When the Santa Fe Railroad built its spur to the south rim, the Fred Harvey company put up the El Tovar hotel at the terminus. In 1903 Teddy Roosevelt, that great booster of the West, came and pronounced: "In the Grand Canyon Arizona has a natural wonder which, as far as I know, is in kind absolutely unparalleled throughout the rest of the world.... You cannot improve on it. The ages have been at work on it, and man can only mar it.... Keep it for your children, your children's children, and for all who come after you, as the one great sight which every American . . . should see" (qtd. in Pyne 29).

Once the Southwest had been opened to the traveling public there was a concerted attempt to populate the landscape and to recreate Indian life specifically for the purposes of tourism. In 1903 the Santa Fe published *Indians of the Southwest* by George Dorsey with illustrations by the great photographer Edward Curtis. In 1904 Fred Harvey, who had made a fortune out of the restaurant concession on the Santa Fe, commissioned the Detroit Photographic Company to produce a large number of views of the country through which the railroad traveled, for sale at his restaurants and hotels:

> At a time when the Southwest remained one of the few regions tourists still insisted they'd rather travel through at night than during the daytime, Harvey's decision to use the Detroit Photographic Company and the postcard medium as a means of generating a new and more positive image, was brilliant.... Harvey's commissions presented the Southwest as a place of romance rather than Romanticism. Focusing first on the most obvious points of tourist interest, the earlier sets "worked up" the Grand Canyon, revitalized the Indian as a creature of interest to visitors, and began to market a new Western sublime of the desert.... Harvey's set showed Kit Carson's house, Navajo medicine men, an "Apache War Party," Indians on horseback, Indians in ceremonial garb, Indians in all possible poses designed to suggest to the viewer the possibility of reenacting a mythological Western past without danger to self or property. And this presentation dovetailed with the campaign to present the dry Southwest as a place with an exciting past and a picturesque present. (Hales 266)[1]

Besides Harvey's postcards, the Santa Fe produced hundreds of lantern slides which were exhibited in Lecture Lounges in Harvey hotels during illustrated talks for tourists, as well as in schools and places of business.[2] Each year the Santa Fe published a calendar featuring paintings of Indian life by such well-known artists as E. Irving Couse, a founder of the Taos School. The railroad named cars on its famous *Super Chief* train after famous Indians such as Satanta and Geronimo (McLuhan 194). On the way from Chicago to Los Angeles passengers could take an Indian Detour at Albuquerque, where they would embark on a luxury motor bus and visit Indian pueblos and the Canyon de Chelly. Famous detourists included European royalty and Albert Einstein.

This safely romanticized and humanized version of the Southwest finds appropriate and accurate cinematic expression in *The Harvey Girls*, MGM's musical tribute to the Harvey restaurant chain. The film opens with Judy Garland singing from the back of a Santa Fe car as it speeds through Monument Valley on its way to the town where Judy will be employed in a Harvey's restaurant and will thus play a full part in the civilizing of the West. The sequence calls attention to the role of the railroad in the aestheticization of the desert and in making it available for mass consumption. In the course of her song, Judy retires into the interior of the car, from where the landscape can be seen rolling past the windows, thus giving us a taste of the effect of Hale's Tours, that curious contraption from the early years of cinema in which a paying audi-

W. H. Jackson, "Chalk Creek Canyon" (c. 1887). Courtesy Amon Carter Museum, Fort Worth, Texas.

Judy Garland in The Harvey Girls (MGM, 1945).

ence was accommodated in a mock-up of a railway car while filmed travel scenes were projected outside. The relation between the railroad, tourism, the aesthetics of landscape, and the cinema could not be more concisely communicated.

IV

How far can we see in the films of John Ford traces of these historical discourses which produced such a shift in the aesthetics of the western landscape? Despite the attentions of Ford and other filmmakers, Monument Valley has never become a tourist mecca like the Grand Canyon. It was, when John Ford first went there, the furthest point in the continental United States from a railroad—180 miles, in fact. Even today tourism is little developed. The valley lies in an empty quarter on the way to nowhere in particular, and few visitors make the detour. It has, unlike the Grand Canyon, essentially no existence in the popular mind except as a movie set. Its later iconographic status seems entirely due to the influence of Ford's work. Nevertheless, what Ford manages to make the landscape mean owes much to what artistic and photographic discourses had previously inscribed upon it. First, Ford's framing of the landscape to exert the maximum contrast between its vast distances and the small-ness of the figures that populate it is a clear echo of nineteenth-century photographic practice. Just as the photographers of that time played on the vastness of both space and time, so in looking at the vistas which Ford puts before us it is impossible not to register the relative puniness of humanity measured against his towering mesas. And just as the Grand Canyon excited the imaginations of nineteenth-century geologists, dramatizing the huge forces and vast eons that had carved such a chasm, so the thou-sand-feet-high outcrops of de Chelly sandstone rising starkly from the valley floor of Monument Valley surely call to mind an equally awesome sense of time etched into the rock by millions of years of erosion.

Monument Valley in Stagecoach *(United Artists, 1939).*

However, landscape in the cinema is never, or never for long, an object merely of contemplation. Narrative is all. In a film, landscape becomes scenery in another, theatrical sense, a backdrop against which the action is played. In the Western, that action frequently takes the form of a journey; landscape then becomes an obstacle which has to be overcome. Its beauty is incidental to its function as a test of the protagonists' characters. At the end of *Wagon Master* the emigrants gird themselves for one last haul up the jagged cliff face. When finally the journey is successfully achieved, and the terrain, with its physical obstacles, has been traversed, then the sense of accomplishment is akin to that in the railroad photographs of chasms bridged and mountains tunneled. The conquest of the terrain is emblematic of the achievement of the individual in overcoming personal trials and is analogous to the wider victory of capital in subjugating nature. Ford's epic Western of the 1920s, *The Iron Horse*, celebrates just such a personal and social conquest of the mountains in the construction of the first transcontinental railroad.

IV

The vision of a picturesque Southwest constructed in the promotional publications of the Santa Fe railroad and Fred Harvey appears to have jumped straight off the page and into MGM's movie about Harvey's business venture. When the train arrives in the town there is a lavish musical number ("The Atchison, Topeka and the Santa Fe") in which colorfully dressed cowboys join with Indians in southwest-style garb in an exuberant celebration of a tourist paradise. There are moments in Ford's Westerns when the mannered way in which Indians are posed against a landscape seems designed to trigger a not dissimilar response, as for example toward the end of *She Wore a Yellow Ribbon*, when John Wayne as Captain Brittles rides into the Indian camp to meet his friend Chief Big Tree, and in a series of shots warriors are positioned picturesquely against the skyline. Usually, however, the view of the Southwest which found its way into Ford's films was a trifle more robust, more "manly" than the feminized world of the MGM musical. Though visually it undoubtedly owed something to tourist postcards, it was also refracted through other media of popular culture, most notably the stories of Zane Grey. In 1907 Grey, by profession a dentist and an aspiring but as yet unsuccessful writer, was taken on a trip to Flagstaff, Arizona, and then by horseback to the Grand Canyon. The effect on him of the desert scenery was momentous. His first bestseller, *The Heritage of the Desert*, was written under its spell. Not only was Grey the most popular Western novelist of the time, but his tales were to become the most filmed. The first film made from a Grey novel, *The Last Trail*, was produced by Fox in 1918; over the next thirty years scores of others followed, many with a southwest setting and with titles such as *Call of the Canyon, Wanderer of the Wasteland, Drums of the Desert, Under the Tonto Rim*. In 1913 Grey had visited Monument Valley and written about it in *Tales of Lonely Trails* (Gaberscek 144). Paramount's film version of Grey's novel *The Vanishing American* (1925) has some of its initial scenes set in Monument Valley. In his most famous work, *Riders of the Purple Sage* (1912), there is a description of canyon country:

Edward S. Curtis, "Saguaro Gatherers" (1907). Library of Congress, Washington, D.C.

All about him was ridgy roll of wind-smoothed, rain-washed rock. Not a tuft of grass or a bunch of sage colored the dull rust-yellow. He saw where, to the right, this uneven flow of stone ended in a blunt wall. Leftward, from the hollow that lay at his feet, mounted a gradual slow-swelling slope to a great height topped by leaning, cracked, and ruined crags. Not for some time did he grasp the wonder of that acclivity. It was no less than a mountain-side, glistening in the sun like polished granite, with cedar-trees springing as if by magic out of the denuded surface. Wind had swept it clear of weathered shale, and rain had washed it free of dust. Far up the curved slope its beautiful lines broke to meet the vertical rimwall, to lose its grace in a different order and color of rock, a stained yellow cliff of cracks and caves and seamed crags . . . The canyon opened fan-shaped into a great oval of green and gray growths. It was the hub of an oblong wheel, and from it, at regular distances, like spokes, ran the outgoing canyons. Here a dull red color predominated over the fading yellow. The corners of wall bluntly rose, scarred and scrawled, to taper into towers and serrated peaks and pinnacled domes. (Grey 44-45)

Unlike *The Harvey Girls*, the trajectory of *Riders of the Purple Sage* is one of retreat from the softness of civilization into the stoicism of the wilderness. At the end, the hero takes the heroine into a remote and secret canyon guarded by a huge stone. He then rolls the stone across the entrance to keep them immured forever. Ironically, though, that very celebration of the distance of the Southwest from civilization which Grey's novels achieved was already bringing civilization, in the form of tourists, into the region.

My Darling Clementine: *"the question of the cactus."*

VI

In case there should be any doubt that Ford's Monument Valley is a constructed, not a found, landscape, consider finally the question of the cactus. At some point in the process of popularizing the scenery of the desert, cactus became a key iconographical feature. So recognizable did one distinctive species, the organ-pipe or saguaro cactus, become that it virtually came in itself to signify the West. It appears in a photograph by Edward Curtis in 1907; by the middle of the century it had achieved synecdochic status, a commonplace in advertising of all kinds, on the label for a tape of songs by the Sons of the Pioneers (a group Ford used in his films), on the covers of countless paperback novels, and of course in the movies. We may choose to read Ford's landscape as the expression of his personal sensibility, but it is formed of just such popular elements. The saguaro cactus is not, one would hazard, native to Monument Valley itself. But as Henry Fonda leans lazily back in his chair while surveying the main street of Tombstone in *My Darling Clementine*, what do we see in the distance, along with those familiar mesas, but cactus?

NOTES

1. I have collected some of these postcards. They mostly show Hopi or Navajo engaged in everyday tasks such as carrying water or weaving baskets. However one shows a white lady in a flowered hat and carrying a parasol sitting overlooking a canyon through which a train is rushing. The legend reads: "Crozier Canyon is but one of the many picturesque gorges, out in Arizona, penetrated by Santa Fe rails en route to California. It is several

miles long and lies between Peach Springs and Hackberry stations. In this canyon is a U.S. Government Indian school where the Hualapai and Havasupai Indians are made over into educated citizens. The scenery here is typical of western Arizona—bare red rock, sand and cactus, with sparse vegetation: the coloring is beautiful."

2. Many of these slides are reproduced in *Dream Tracks: The Railroad and the American Indian 1890–1930* by T. C. McLuhan.

WORKS CITED

Anderson, Nancy K. "The Kiss of Enterprise." *The West as America: Reinterpreting Images of the Frontier 1820–1920*. William Truettner, ed. Washington: Smithsonian Institution, 1991. 237–83.

Anderson, Robert. "The Role of the Western Film Genre in Industry Competition 1907–1911." *Journal of the University Film Association* 31.2 (1979): 19–27.

Baigell, Matthew. *Albert Bierstadt*. New York: Watson-Guptill, 1981.

Bazin, André. "The Evolution of the Western." *What Is Cinema?* Vol. 2 Trans. Hugh Gray. Berkeley: U of Calfornia P. 1971.

Braudy, Leo. "Thelma and Louise." *Film Quarterly* 45.2 (1991–92): 28–29.

Buscombe, Edward. *The BFI Companion to the Western*. London: Deutsch, 1988.

Fowler, Don D. *Myself in the Water: The Western Photographs of John K. Hillers*. Washington: Smithsonian Institution, 1989.

Gaberscek, Carlo. "*The Vanishing American:* In Monument Valley before Ford." *Griffithiana* 35–36 (1989): 127–49.

Goetzmann, William H. *Exploration and Empire*. New York: Vintage, 1972.

_____, and William N. Goetzmann. *The West of the Imagination*. New York: Norton, 1986.

Grey, Zane. *Riders of the Purple Sage*. New York: Pocket, 1980.

Hales, Peter B. *William Henry Jackson and the Transformation of the American Landscape*. Philadelphia: Temple UP, 1988.

McLuhan, Teri C. *Dream Tracks: The Raildoad and the American Indian 1890–1930*. New York: Abrams, 1985.

Mauduy, Jacques, and Gérard Henriet. *Géographies du Western*. Paris: Nathan, 1989.

Nash, Roderick. *Wilderness and the American Mind*. 3rd ed. New Haven: Yale UP, 1982.

Neale, Steve. "Questions of Genre." *Screen* 31.1 (1990): 45–66.

Pyne, Stephen J. *Dutton's Point: An Intellectual History of the Grand Canyon*. Grand Canyon Natural History Association, 1982.

II
THE
CLASSIC
WESTERN

A HOME IN THE WILDERNESS:
Visual Imagery in John Ford's Westerns

Michael Budd (1976)

I t has frequently been noted that the Western genre as a tradition in film and literature is based on a series of related oppositions—civilization and savagery, culture and nature, East and West, settlement and wilderness. These abstract themes and concepts are given definite form in individual films. Every director who has constructed a distinctive Western world in his films has made images with which to visualize and particularize the meanings latent in these abstract elements. In many of the films of Budd Boetticher, for example, towns and settlements are virtually absent, fertile oases in the desert providing the only resting places for travelers. In the Westerns of Sam Peckinpah the walled-in squares of Mexican villages are transformed from places of peace and refuge into traps, locations for the most extreme outbursts of violence. And Sergio Leone makes his sleepy little towns into labyrinths, every door and window potentially hiding a gunman. The cinematic world of each of these directors is delineated by recurrent images, images which make visual a particular version of the general Western oppositions, which select from and inflect the range of possibilities present in the genre.

In the Westerns of John Ford, civilization is embodied primarily in the family and the community, and characteristically located in homes, cavalry forts, stagecoaches, covered wagons, or other shelters. This study examines a visual tradition in which home and shelter is juxtaposed with its opposite, the desert wilderness, within single images. The tradition is a recurrent complex of images which, in various ways, relates home space to wilderness space, bringing them into visual confrontation within the frame. The encounter of home and wilderness is more than a theme in Ford's Westerns: it is a central, formative viewpoint, a way of looking at the world.

The viewpoint is communicated visually by a *frame* within the larger frame. Shots looking through doors, through windows, gates, porches, and canopies bring indoors and outdoors into juxtaposition. Such images are sufficiently pervasive to suggest a structuring vision of the nature of the frontier itself. Images using a frame are a central aspect of the visual organization which complements the narrative in every film. Despite differences in many elements, the visual encounter of inside and outside, home and desert, refuge and danger appears throughout, and helps to define each film as a part of the whole group. Virtually every film has its distinctive variation *of* the frame-within-a-frame configuration, but every film also contains variations found in other films. The complex of home-wilderness images seems central to the similarities among Ford's Westerns: not only does it bring together the underlying elements of the genre, connecting the dynamics of the Western to the specific concerns of the director, but it also permeates the formal pattern and texture of the films. The meeting of home and wilderness, the edge of the frontier, is constituted in the design of the images themselves.

As early as 1917, 22 years before *Stagecoach* and 47 years before *Cheyenne Autumn*, Ford's first feature-length film, *Straight Shooting*, contains several doorway images; the doorway becomes the predominant version of the home-wilderness image in the sound Westerns. From inside a dark cabin, the camera repeatedly frames the bright outdoors through the front door, so that characters moving in and outside of the cabin are always visible. In *Three Bad Men* (1926), Ford uses this doorway imagery in at least three different situations. As riders pull up in front of a burning house, they are framed from inside, between the flaming boards; a shot from inside a covered wagon frames the "three bad men" in the canopy of darkness, anticipating similar shots in *Fort Apache* and *Three Godfathers* (both 1948); a man waits for his pursuers in a little shack, watching the trail outside through a window. In these two silent Westerns the door and window imagery is neither as frequent nor as contextually significant as in the later films. The imagery of the silent films initiates a visual motif which gradually gains distinctive connotations in the 12 sound Westerns.

Stagecoach marks the journey from Tonto to Lordsburg with images of gates and fences which spatially separate the relative safety of the towns and way stations from the open desert where the stagecoach is vulnerable to Indian attack. These gates and fences do not provide the same secure shelter that covered doorways do: the passengers are only safe from Indians in the towns at the beginning and end of the journey. As the stagecoach first moves out of Tonto into the desert, it is seen from behind a wooden fence as it travels into the distance toward a single spire-like monument on the horizon. At the first two of the three way stations, the stagecoach comes through the gate seen from inside, visibly finding a place of protection. Then at the third station, the arrival appears similar, with the stagecoach seen through a wooden fence as it approaches. But suddenly the camera tracks back and to the side as it follows the vehicle into the station, revealing that the station house and fence are burning. The connotations of the flimsy wooden fence as protection are illusory, and the open space inside the compound, which seems safe at the Dry Fork and Apache Wells stations, is now exposed to the desert.

Doorways: Harry Carey in Straight Shooting.

From the security of the town of Tonto to the destroyed shelter at the Lee's Ferry station, the boundaries separating civilization's outposts from the surrounding wilderness are less and less substantial. Fittingly, then, the climactic Indian attack is visualized in images of gradual encirclement and the subsequent cavalry rescue creates a new demarcation in the featureless landscape, behind which the stagecoach is finally safe again. As the Apaches close in around the speeding vehicle, the cavalry charges in a broad line stretching from foreground almost to horizon. Then the charge is seen from behind, as the stagecoach comes forward into a "gate" opening in the cavalry line and slows to a stop, while a cloud of dust separates the vehicle from the battle in the background. The line of cavalrymen facing outward against Indian attackers will be a recurring image in Ford's Westerns, briefly and tenuously extending the doorway configuration into the wilderness, away from homes and other places of cover.

But *Stagecoach*'s unique variation on the imagery of home and wilderness is its juxtaposition of the cramped space inside the stagecoach with the vast open spaces outside. Throughout the trip, characters are continually seen talking and moving through its windows and doors, with the desert and finally the attacking Apaches framed in the windows outside. The characters first make the interior into a microcosm of the towns they travel between, the respectable people shunning the social outcasts who sit next to them. They try to separate their tiny space from the frontier environment around them. But the pressure of spatial proximity transforms the little group into a unit: social distance and prejudice virtually collapse when the space is invaded by an Indian arrow and the attack begins. Through the journey, the increasing intimacy of the passengers helps make the interior of the coach a safe, familiar place, its spatial form thoroughly explored, its changing social atmosphere well delineated. But the repeated shots through the windows from inside to outside or vice versa are reminders of the constant presence of the unfamiliar beyond the fragile enclosed space, and during one moment of particular familiarity the camera suddenly pans to reveal an arrow stuck in Mr. Peacock's shoulder. During the attack, defenders inside the coach are recurrently framed with Indians seen behind them through the windows in the background. The chase is a visual encroachment of one space on another, and the cavalry line reestablishes an area of civilization against the desert.

In *My Darling Clementine* (1946) the wilderness is a more benign presence. Though it harbors the murderous Clantons, its openness and freedom are more emphasized; the bright sky dominates. Thus the relation between two kinds of space connoted by the frame image is a kind of balance, a counterpoising, rather than a threat or invasion by the wilderness as in *Stagecoach*. The earlier film takes a vulnerable society out of the safety of its towns and exposes it to the transforming effects of the frontier through the gradual dissolution of its protective frames, its fences, walls, and gates. *My Darling Clementine* places the town of Tombstone at the moment of taming, with the newborn community in visual equilibrium with its ancient surroundings.

Thus the film's distinctive variation on the frame image is its extensive exploration of the long porch, the meeting point between shelter and wilderness. The town's single street has buildings on only one side, and so is open to the desert. The porch extends the shelter of the buildings, yet is penetrated by the outdoors and the

The long porch in My Darling Clementine: *Wyatt and Clem.*

slanting sunlight which so often brings the outdoors inside in these films. Under the porch, at the juncture of sunlight and shadow, Wyatt takes his place as protector. The combination of spaces is continually framed from just under or outside the porch roof: the edge of the frontier is not a hard line drawn by civilization as in *Stagecoach*, but a beneficent interpenetration of the expansive wilderness with the refuge of human cover, which results in the birth of a new community.

Placed between enclosure and vast space, porches are a characteristic location for mediating heroes, whether defenders like Wyatt Earp or outsiders like Ethan Edwards in *The Searchers*. Rocking chairs, reminders of rest in old age, appear frequently on porches, and the churchgoers in *My Darling Clementine* are briefly seen rocking on the hotel porch after Sunday dinner. Just as old people sit on a porch to look outward from home, young lovers find it a place to be alone together, to escape temporarily the community's presence. Michael and Philadelphia in *Fort Apache*, Brad and Lucy in *The Searchers*, Tom and Mary in *Sergeant Rutledge*, Jim and Marty in *Two Rode Together*—for all these pairs the porch is an appropriate setting for courtship. And where there is no sheltering porch, a couple moves naturally to the edge of settlement for privacy, as do Dallas and Ringo in *Stagecoach*, and Olivia and Flint in *She Wore a Yellow Ribbon*. In both these cases the periphery is at once a place of danger and of new closeness between man and woman.

In *My Darling Clementine*, the imagery of porches and of Tombstone's boundaries culminates in the famous Sunday morning sequence when Clementine joins Wyatt for the church dance. The sequence brings together the many connotations of intermingled home and wilderness space in the film. It begins by evoking the porch as a *place* as never before. The narrative slows almost to a halt; as Wyatt walks casually out of the barbershop and down the long porch to take his accustomed spot, the flow of pioneers and their wagons past him toward the church is a continuous presence in image and sound; immersion in setting replaces action. Actually, a new momentum, a sea change is beginning: the events surrounding Wyatt, Doc, and Clementine are poised for resolution, and the movement of the churchgoers provides the impetus. Barbershop, hotel lobby, porch, street, and desert—the acute sense of the continuity of these spaces seems in itself to draw Clementine and Wyatt from one to the other, on and on. Countering the associations of the desert with the murderous Clantons, the pioneers converge on the town from outside, pass through its center and on to the half-built church on the outskirts. They seem to bear the townspeople with them, as if to join the two areas at a meeting point.

Clementine and Wyatt complete this movement in their walk from the town's center to its edge, extending the frontier by establishing a new center. They leave the shelter of frames and porches for a church without walls. Appropriately, the dance is being held to raise money to put up a roof: it is the precise moment when wilderness becomes home. The two kinds of space seem to merge, as the pioneers celebrate the integration of natural and human order. The frame of the church steeple is open to the sky; virtually every shot places the dancers against horizon and sky; the sequence builds and builds.

The church dance sequence forms a crescendo to the measured tempo of Sunday morning in Tombstone and is divided into five smaller sequences, each part a minor crescendo carrying toward the larger climax. The various elements of the scene—the couple, the town, the church and its people, the surrounding buttes—are analyzed and synthesized in a new unification of spaces and forces.

In the first part, Wyatt and Clementine move away from Tombstone's enclosures, and the camera marks a growing sense of spaciousness. The church is shown only in extreme long shot, and the congregation is an undifferentiated mass, the ringing bell and the hymn heard from afar. The couple is separated spatially from their destination, and they recede at the end of this first part toward the faraway gathering at the edge of town.

The second part explores the church scene itself, isolating its elements and bringing us closer into its spirit. Elder Simpson celebrates the transition from hymn to dance music, the musicians are seen in individual medium shots, and the dancers whirl between rows of clapping participants. And closer long shots of the entire church make the mass now a group of individual people. The music comes up as the dancers become animated; we watch the community being created.

The third part of the sequence intercuts Wyatt and Clementine, standing to the side, with the increasingly ebullient dancers. Couple and community are in separate shots; the dance continues to build, while Wyatt and Clementine, not yet participants, are more and more attracted to it The parallel actions culminate in the final three shots of this part. The dancers begin a movement of both lines through the center, a climactic affirmation of communal unity. Only then, in the next shot, are the town and the far-off monuments added to the church scene, all elements in the film accumulating in one synoptic image in preparation for the couple's inclusion. And so when Wyatt subsequently asks Clementine to dance, and they start to join the community, the action carries a tremendous charge of assimilation and consummation. Separate spaces, sounds, and forces are joined; the community finds a center; from bell to hymn to dance, the rising music draws everything together.

In the fourth part, Wyatt and Clementine join the celebration, and the parallel lines of dancers in previous shots become a circle around them as they dance, a circle of people who are the church's only walls. The marshal and his lady fair dance in their "Promised Land" as the Mormons in *Wagon Master* do not, because their arrival at the church celebrates a journey like the Mormons', a civilizing act. The church is not a destination but a process.

Finally, in the fifth and final part of the sequence, Morgan and Virgil drive up in the wagon to watch, surprised, as Wyatt dances enthusiastically with Clementine. Now the pattern of part three is varied: Wyatt has acquired a new family and community, his older loyalties left behind (temporarily), his brothers separated spatially as he was earlier. And in accordance with the progression throughout the entire sequence, the shots get closer and closer. The camera tilts up as the couple dances toward it, and records their smiling faces as they whirl by. The five-part sequence moves from the porch shelters of Tombstone to the open air of the church, accumulating the town and surrounding desert, and placing the civilizing couple at the community's center. In this prolonged moment of frontier, the landscape is ambiguously harsh and beautiful, and pioneers need no shelter: at the leading edge of civilization, home and wilderness are united.

At the end of the film, Wyatt's approach to the gunfire at the OK Corral is structured like the couple's earlier approach to the church dance. Why? The Clantons bring their violence through town and out again to its edges, just as the pioneers earlier brought a pacific community through town and out to its edges. The pioneers' movement to the church unified Tombstone and made it more secure; Wyatt's second walk to the town's frontier defends the meaning of the first. So Wyatt stands under a roof and Old Man Clanton outside it as Wyatt curses him away after the gunfight: the marshal makes a shelter of the corral just as he and Clementine completed the open church.

At the end, Wyatt and Morgan ride away in a shot almost identical to the one at the beginning of *Stagecoach* in which the coach and cavalry escort begin the journey. Again the travelers pass the wooden fence signifying the edge of civilization; the road leads straight toward the same spire-like monument on the horizon. In *Stagecoach,* the open fence comes to suggest the pioneers' flimsy defenses. In *My Darling Clementine* the same fence is like the frame of the church steeple, connoting the freedom at the juncture of home and wilderness. Wyatt may begin a new *Stagecoach* adventure at the end of *My Darling Clementine*, but whereas the earlier film is one of barriers broken and reinforced, Wyatt's world is morally and spatially continuous.

Porches are also explored in *Fort Apache*, but because they are within the safe walls of the fort, they are not a junction of home and wilderness. Instead, their domestic functions are emphasized: Michael and Philadelphia carry on various stages of courtship there; the Collingwoods and their guests come out onto the porch to listen to the serenade; and the porch links the homes, offices, and ballroom with a common frontage space.

In *Fort Apache*, the confrontation between home and wilderness occurs in the desert, away from sanctuary. When the sergeants pick up the two troopers tortured and killed by Diablo's band, the action is framed from inside the covered wagon, civilization's refuge extended into the desert to receive its dead. And the linear configuration of the cavalry charge is repeated from *Stagecoach* a moment later, as again the wagon comes to safety through a "gate" opening in the cavalry's demarcation. But the reversal as the massacre is marked afterward by a new, defensive version of the cavalry line. As York's remaining men wait behind their wagons for the Indian attack which does not come, the camera looks past them to the buttes, the desert, and the dust which hides the Apaches. Now the cavalry's line of refuge is threatened, thrown back, and the only secure place is the cover of the fort itself.

In *Three Godfathers* Indians do not appear, and the sun and wind and sand of the desert are the bandits' primary antagonists. There is no refuge for them outside the towns, and the film's unique variations in imagery center around the frail protections from the sun provided by the wagon, and by the men for each other.

At Apache Wells, Miss Florie's cabin and porch cast a prominent shadow across the ground, the darkness a shelter from the killing sun. But the similar shadow from the wagon in which the mother dies has connotations of mortality, since the darkness within the wagon is associated with the sacredness of death as well as of birth. The wagon and its shadow bring the men in contact with an unearthly refuge. Pedro, then Perley, are framed in the canopy of the covered wagon from inside, like the dead men and the sergeants in *Fort Apache*. Here, though, the inside of the wagon is completely dark, signifying its otherworldliness. The Kid's death is portended when, holding and singing to his godson, he walks in the lengthening shadow of the wagon. And the meanings of shadow are extended to the men's shading of one another: the Kid holds his hat over Bob's head, briefly protecting Bob and the baby from the sun, and then as the Kid dies, Bob does the same for him, shading him until death. With no home or cover, the outlaws' only refuge is the immaterial shadow of death. Darkness is a refuge in death for the mother, the Kid, and Pedro, yet Bob must escape it, since he must live to protect his godson. The saloon in New Jerusalem into which Bob stumbles at the end is, appropriately, a bright haven against the night which surrounds him as he struggles to keep going. *Three Godfathers* transforms the frame imagery associated with the frontier into a light-shade dichotomy associated with material and spiritual worlds.

She Wore a Yellow Ribbon (1949) returns to the frontier of a cavalry post and its environs, and Monument Valley is a recurrent presence surrounding Fort Stark as it is not in *Fort Apache*. The two cavalry films are indirectly linked by the massacre in *Fort Apache*, which is like Custer's last stand; *She Wore a Yellow Ribbon* begins with the news of the Custer massacre. Thus the menace and beauty of the wilderness are closer now, Indian nations united all across the frontier. The shelter of the fort is constantly juxtaposed with the monuments rising just outside its walls. Seen usually in the clear, slanting light of early morning, these buttes and spires are as tangible as anywhere in the Monument Valley films: their agelessness challenges the man-made walls below, the flimsy cloth tents of the cavalry.

She Wore a Yellow Ribbon, like *Rio Grande* a year later, adapts the gate imagery of *Stagecoach* to the army fort, repeatedly framing the gate from inside as a doorway to the wilderness. The beginning and end of Brittles' last patrol are placed in this frame, enclosed in the protective darkness of surrounding walls. At the beginning the men and horses are fresh, and a ceremonial color guard flanks their exit, while at the end the ground is muddy, Brittles and his column trudging on foot back inside, tired and dispirited. And Brittles is framed again through this doorway as he leaves alone the next morning. More than in any previous Ford Western, and in anticipation of *The Searchers, She Wore a Yellow Ribbon* forms the encounter of home and wilderness as a doorway, the sunlit desert circumscribed by sheltering darkness. More often than in earlier films, too, the point of view is that of the human confronting the wilderness from within his own home.

In *Wagon Master* (1950) the Mormons are trying to reach home, their San Juan Valley, and not even the wagons form any shelter from the Cleggs, who hide inside them from the sheriff's posse. The wagon train is as open to the desert as is the town of Tombstone in *My Darling Clementine:* in the earlier film new places are secured at the frontier of civilization's expansion, while in *Wagon Master* the constantly moving pioneers make small, precarious camps in different places each night.

As in *Stagecoach* and *My Darling Clementine*, a wooden fence delimits town and wilderness. Travis and Sandy sit on it as they watch the wagons moving out, the pioneers hugging the boundary as if in protection against the expanse of barren dryness beyond. When Travis crosses the fence to join the train, he heads the wagons directly into the desert.

Without real cover or shelter, the Mormon party has only the light of its camp-fires and lamps as refuge against the surrounding darkness, and a recurrent nighttime image places the characters around the bright center of the frame, while darkness fills the outer edges of the scene. This imagery is educed most fully in the riverside dance, whose illuminated core appears first; succeeding shots then include more and more of the darkness outside the circle of wagons, until the light and movement are seen from outside, encircled by darkness, and the Cleggs intrude. In images like these, the risk and uncertainty of the pioneers' journey is formed visually.

Rio Grande continues the tradition of the cavalry films, both in adapting the porch imagery from *Fort Apache*, and in elaborating the door imagery from *She Wore a Yellow Ribbon*. The film begins and ends with the troop entering the gate; at the end, Kathleen Yorke is waiting. Her gradual assimilation is traced in the changing viewpoint on her in relation to the open-ended tent, a tent which replaces the porches of *Fort Apache*. At first the camera looks from the darkness into the bright interior at the couple, as with the serenade and York's return to the dance in *Fort Apache*. Later, though, in preparation for the ending, the point of view shifts inside, and Kathleen stands under the tent's roof watching the troop ride out. The change in the camera's placement corresponds with her acceptance of her husband's tent as home. Visually, the tent does not represent home and shelter (the inside-to-outside door image) until Kathleen is within it.

In addition to establishing the Yorkes' new home in the safety of the fort, *Rio Grande*, like *Stagecoach* and *Fort Apache*, extends home-wilderness imagery beyond the limits of permanent settlement as the cavalry finds and makes new refuges. The defensive line of cavalrymen behind their wagons is repeated from *Fort Apache*, with the women behind, the Apaches in front. And the frame-within-a-frame image finds an extravagant variation in the cross-shaped hole in the door of the church where the children are imprisoned by the Apaches. Tyree, Boone, and Jeff sneak into the church from

The troop at the gate:
Rio Grande.

the back to protect the children, and they look through the cross to the Indians dancing below. When attacked, Boone and Tyree shoot through the cross, the Indians outside falling as if before an unseen force as they approach the symbol of armed Christianity. The old church, with its cross-shaped view of savagery, becomes a sanctuary instead of a prison, traditions of home and religion united in the image of the cross-as-door.

The Searchers (1956) is both a culmination and an innovation in the imagery of home and wilderness. The film not only recapitulates a large part of the complex of images described above—ways in which two kinds of space are juxtaposed—but it also expands and elaborates on that tradition, integrating it into the structure and texture of the film. The door image in *The Searchers* not only links home to wilderness; it also links more and less private spaces within the home, and assumes a new shape, the cave entrance, away from home. The doorway becomes the controlling image of the film.

The Searchers begins with Martha opening the door of the Edwards home to Ethan and the wilderness, as the camera tracks forward out of the darkness and onto the porch behind her. The film ends with a symmetrical reversal of this movement, as the camera tracks backward into the dark frame of the Jorgenson home with Debbie and Mrs. Jorgenson, Lars, then Laurie and Martin coming inside, leaving Ethan alone in the doorway to return to the desert as the door closes on him. Between these two images, between the first encounter with the wilderness and the final withdrawal from it, the film is in large part a meditation on homes—their various forms, the threats to them, the possibilities for replacing them. Martin and Debbie find a new home; Ethan cannot. Scar and Ethan defile each other's homes; Look is killed in hers; caves replace homes as a last refuge. Central to the film, and unique in Ford's Westerns, are the changes in the contextual meaning of the doorway: its connotations are deepened, intensified, and multiplied. The familiar associations of the home-to-wilderness, dark-to-light point of view, brought from earlier films and evoked again at the beginning, are inverted, tested against their opposites, simultaneously modified and reaffirmed in the course of the film.

The after-dinner scene at the Edwards home begins with Martin sitting on the porch, a shaft of warm yellow light shining out from the door as he goes inside. The scene ends with Ethan on the porch looking into the dark house, the shadows now tinged with cold blue. Through the front door, Ethan sees his brother Aaron closing the bedroom door—a door through which Ethan earlier watches Martha, and from which Clayton turns away when he sees Martha caressing Ethan's coat. The doorway of Aaron and Martha's bedroom links a private place to the larger home. Though the bedroom doorway is analogous to the front doorway in relating two kinds of space, the camera is never placed inside it as at the front door. The bedroom is given the same aura of privacy by characters and camera that the "birth room" in *Stagecoach* has; even more than in the earlier film, the door image is doubled within the home. Ethan is twice outside the family; the sense of an intimate home-within-a-home makes the massacre even more terrible; already, too, in a link to the private horror of the massacre, the open front doorway is paired with another not to be entered, from which to avert one's eyes.

Exteriors and interiors in Ford's films are often related with lamplight shining out onto a dark porch, or sunlight slanting across a dark room from a door or win-

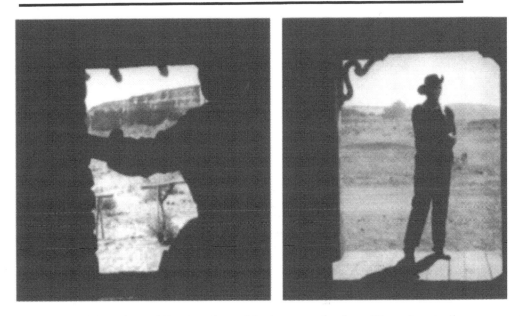

The first and last shots of The Searchers: *Martha opens the door, Ethan alone in the doorway.*

dow. In *The Searchers* the impending massacre is indicated by the bright red-orange "sunset" light which suffuses the front of the Edwards cabin. The usually friendly sunlight, now harsh and ominous, seems to invade the home and set it afire, in anticipation of the Comanche attackers.

A more important change—a reversal—in the meaning of the door image comes after the massacre in Ethan's realization of Martha's rape and murder. As he picks up her bloody dress outside the burning house, he looks toward the black hole that is the doorway to the low smoke house. Then he is framed in the darkness from inside as he walks to the doorway, looks inside, and slumps to the ground in horror and dismay at what he sees. The entrance frame is no longer the home from which we look out on danger, but one of those dark, unshown places in Ford's Westerns where mutilation and death occur. The sacred darkness of the wagon canopy in *Three Godfathers* is now ugly and ominous. And just as the Edwards' bedroom is not to be entered, neither is this place of horror; privacy has a different meaning now, and Ethan instead of Clayton protects it. Previously the dark frame is a protective separation from the wilderness outside; here it is a protective separation from the barbarity inside, that only Ethan sees.

The Edwards' family enclosure has been broken, and the tentative quality of Ethan and Martin's new relationship to the Jorgenson family is expressed in their first arrival at the Jorgenson home. Whereas Ethan's homecoming at the Edwards' in the beginning is seen from the viewpoint of home, from the porch and doorway, this viewpoint is modified at the Jorgensons', with shots outside the house, looking toward it, as the two men ride up, are greeted, and go inside. The two are not framed in the shelter of the porch as Ethan is at the beginning; it is not yet their home. Ethan sits briefly in a rocking chair and talks to the Jorgensons as he does earlier at the Edwards', but this time it is on the porch instead of in front of the fireplace.

The door image is reversed in a second way: it is shifted to the teepee homes of the Comanche enemies, who now are within, invaded by Ethan and the cavalry. When the two searchers find Look dead in the Comanche village devastated by cavalry, they are framed at the doorway of the teepee as they look down at her body inside. And much of the meeting in Scar's teepee is shown from the back of the shelter, outward through the doorway, looking past Ethan and Scar who are faced off defiantly. Scar tells how his wives replace dead sons in the home, how fiercely he defends and avenges his own, and the point of view, both verbal and visual, is the Indian's. The endless, obsessive cycle of revenge that drives the story forward is built into the succession of door images, as the private refuge of the Edwards' home is linked to its counterparts in the opposing culture. Comanche homes are violated, too; home and wilderness spaces are transposable; similar pictorial configurations are set against one another.

Finally, the doorway image is changed in another way: it becomes a cave, a natural refuge for Indian and white alike, a last desperate shelter not made by humans, within the earth. Ethan and Martin take cover from Scar's attacking band in a narrow cave among the rocks; afterward Martin catches water dripping off the high walls of the weird cleft hideout. They are driven to make the strange high places in the land their only shelters. Thus appropriately, the climax of the film is located at a cave, the earlier chase by Scar reversed as Ethan pursues Debbie to the cave entrance, to take her away to her own door. The doorway as shelter is taken to its extreme, for Debbie, like Martin and Ethan earlier, finds an alien doorway, not a home. The comforting intimacy and familiarity of the dark frame have been stripped

Caves in The Searchers: *"the universal human need for refuge against the wilderness."*

away during the film, from pioneer home to pioneer massacre to Comanche home to cave hideout. The frame's symbolic associations, no longer simple, trace a confrontation with savagery and a concurrent exploration of the universal human need for refuge against the wilderness. From Ethan's homecoming at the beginning to Debbie's flight in fear at the climax, the repetition of the door image in different contexts reduces its meaning to essentials, from family home to primitive shelter.

The ending is like a mirror image of the beginning, a similar sequence of shots arranged in reverse order. Seen down the length of the porch, the family members look out toward their returning "kinfolk"; moving head-on to the camera, Ethan brings Debbie to the threshold of the Jorgenson home; the camera recedes imposingly into the doorway in precise synchronization with the movement of mother and daughter. Five years of pioneer progress are measured between the first and last door images, too: in place of the rough logs across the Edwards' porch roof, a gothic ornament decorates the porch post of the two-story Jorgenson home. The desert is still the same, though.

The visual scheme at the end of *The Searchers* confirms the film as a pivotal moment in the development of Ford's Westerns. The complex and contradictory associations which the door image assumes through the film are subsumed in the profound ambivalence of the ending, the hero separated from the home he restores. The original meaning of the door image has been reestablished, while its new associations are not lost. In elegant simplicity, the basic elements of the Fordian Western—home, desert, and hero—are isolated, as the hero advances, then retreats within the doorway.

In the home-wilderness complex of images generally, and in the door image specifically, there exists a tension between the two spaces, between the home enclosure, which separates us from the wilderness, and the doorway opening, which links us to the wilderness. The tension is focused at the end of *The Searchers*: the happiness of the family's reunification is juxtaposed with the sadness of Ethan's departure, and the reestablished security of the home is balanced against its cost implied in the retreat of the desert and the closing door. The dark enclosure around the desert and its prisoner removes them twice from our world, mediates them doubly in a framed frame. Already in the darkness of home in *The Searchers* there is the intimation of a prison and a trap, suggested in the blackness of the smoke house, the violated teepees, the harshness and bleakness of the caves. In the late Ford films, frames will often connote imprisonment, those inside separated from the wilderness as Ethan is captive within it.

Sergeant Rutledge (1960) and *Two Rode Together* (1961) both adopt the archway as their characteristic frame images. In neither film, though, is there any strong sense of home as a place opposed to wilderness, and the archway merely notes the presence of settlement and shelter, largely devoid of the emotional overtones of the doorway image in *The Searchers* and before. At the beginning of *Sergeant Rutledge*, Rutledge, as a prisoner, marches through an arched porch to his court-martial; at the end he leads his men back the same way to their desert patrol, as Tom and Mary embrace under the arch, which has now become a marriage canopy.

In *Two Rode Together* a high Spanish arch introduces the Tascosa scenes at the beginning and end. The fort, too, has an arched entrance, with the tents and wagons of the civilians close outside it. But the familiar framed door images are deceptive: the light shines cheerfully out into the darkness from the doorways of the Frazer home and the ballroom, but inside Elena is rejected, shut off alone. She returns to the darkness outside, just as she (with McCabe) escapes Tascosa at the end. And the shelter of civilization is a prison for the Indian boy Running Wolf, too. The barred windows of his cell are shown from inside as he hangs on them, yelling and struggling to escape from the frame.

The Man Who Shot Liberty Valance (1962) is characterized by bright interiors against the dark streets of Shinbone—Hallie's second-story light, as Tom calls her to help Ranse, the doors of the saloon and kitchen, the large front window of the newspaper office. The darkness that hides Indians in *Sergeant Rutledge* and *Two Rode Together* is predominant here, and it is Liberty Valance's natural habitat, as he constantly emerges from, then fades into it again. The lights are usually small and feeble, surrounded by blackness. When confronted with the night outside, the lively activity of the interiors is endangered. In comparison to Clementine in *My Darling Clementine*, for example, Hallie seems trapped in the small enclosed world of the kitchen and the dining room. As she stands at the door of the kitchen watching Tom walk into the dark street she is alone in the communal home. In retrospect, the very intimacy of that home will seem paradoxically imprisoning, since it brings her closer to Ranse and isolates her from Tom. The separation of home and wilderness, reaffirmed at the end of *The Searchers*, is now ironic, because Tom is part of the wilderness.

Thus Tom's despair at losing Hallie is visualized in relation to his own home and its doorways. As he stumbles drunkenly inside, the completed extra room is shown from outside for the first time, its porch and rocking chair linking this home to others in *My Darling Clementine, She Wore a Yellow Ribbon, The Searchers*, and elsewhere. Framed in the doorway from the new room to the old—from his hoped-for future to his present and past—he lights a lamp, hurls it into a corner of the new room, then sits back to watch through the door as the flames engulf the symbol of his future. Like Ethan in *The Searchers*, whom he greatly resembles in this scene, Tom cannot enter that door to the family home; unlike Ethan, he deteriorates and dies outside it (he would die in the fire if not saved by Pompey). The bright flames ironically reverse the heartening atmosphere of other interiors, as Tom is left finally in the darkness once again. In *The Searchers* light often threatens enclosing darkness, and in *The Man Who Shot Liberty Valance* enclosing darkness threatens light; the second film continues the symbolic separation of the two, but with a new sadness.

Sadness pervades *Cheyenne Autumn* (1964) as it does the framed story in *The Man Who Shot Liberty Valance*, since home and wilderness have virtually inverted meanings in relation to the early films. Now the Cheyenne are surrounded by savage whites, every enclosure a trap for them. Familiar images separating home and wilderness are transmuted: the defensive line of cavalrymen now fire confusedly in all directions as they are attacked from the side; the doorway of a deserted schoolhouse looks out on the desert; hungry Cheyenne stand all day across a large open space from an empty table set for white congressmen. And the frame of the church steeple in *My Darling Clementine* is echoed visually by the empty teepee frames against the sky after the Cheyenne leave the reservation. The earlier image celebrates the pioneer community's oneness with its environment; here, though, a white man's windmill frame stands among the hollow skeletons to indicate the Cheyenne's misplacement.

The film follows a pattern of imprisonment and escape. At the fort where they are locked in the freezing warehouse, the Cheyenne are framed in the frost-lined windows of their jail, searchlights playing across their faces. The fort is as much a prison for their jailer, Captain Wessels, as for them; after they escape with terrible casualties, Wessels stumbles out the front gate past the bodies in the snow, to "start wandering." And the Cheyenne refuge and rendezvous in Victory Cave almost becomes their grave, as Schurz stops the army from massacring them.

For Ethan, Martin, and Debbie in *The Searchers*, caves are a barren last refuge from pursuers; the cave in *Cheyenne Autumn* is a national home. Within *The Searchers*, and from *The Searchers* to *Cheyenne Autumn*, the home established in the early films is extended into the wilderness, and the human enclosure acquires connotations of imprisonment. From the early silent films to *Cheyenne Autumn*, Ford's Westerns trace a changing view of the pioneer home in the desert wilderness, a kind of reversal of the connotations of door imagery: security is increasingly threatened, shelter is as often a trap as a refuge, and the desert itself becomes home. The world delineated by these films changes from one of bright hopes and certainties into a more precarious one, of doubts, regrets, and apprehensions.

That "world" is not a collection of themes, or a gallery of familiar characters, though these elements are important. It is primarily a visual imagination of the West, in which theme is inseparable from *mise en scène, what* inseparable from *how*. Behind the films is Ford's profound, life-long response to the elements and assumptions of the Western genre, but it is the films themselves that matter. And crucial to the visual organization of Ford's Westerns, central to their construction and existence *as* Westerns, is the complex of frame images I have described. Interestingly, such images are relatively rare in Ford's non-Western films, and are certainly less significant contextually. Frame and doorway imagery constitutes an implicit choice, a development of particular possibilities in the generic structure. Most important, this imagery is multifarious, evoking a shifting variety of meanings over time, making a tradition both diverse and unified. Ford's Westerns don't illustrate themes or make statements; an imagined West forms their very texture, their visual surface.

Wyatt Earp (Henry Fonda) in one of "his many self-reflections."

CONCERNING THE WEARY LEGS OF WYATT EARP:
The Classic Western According to Shakespeare

Scott Simmon (1996)

"Shakespeare, huh? He musta been from Texas."
> —John Wayne, in *Dark Command* (1940, Republic Pictures)

"People talk about classic Westerns. The classic thing has always been the space, the emptiness. The lines are drawn for us. All we have to do is insert the figures, men in dusty boots, certain faces. Figures in open space have always been what film is all about. American film. This is the situation. People in a wilderness, a wild and barren space. The space is the desert, the movie screen, the strip of film, however you see it. What are the people doing here? This is their existence. They're here to work out their existence. This space, this emptiness is what they have to confront."
> —Don DeLillo, *The Names*[1]

"**S**hakespeare? In Tombstone?": the astonishment from gunslinger and gambler Doc Holliday within John Ford's *My Darling Clementine* probably anticipates moviegoers' reactions. But notwithstanding its curious borrowings from *Hamlet*, Ford's 1946 rendition of the Wyatt Earp legend has been seen as "the perfect example of the classic Western" (Lovell 169). Historically, performances from Shakespeare would have been common enough in Tombstone, as they were throughout the mining towns of the West.[2] What's surprising is less Shakespeare in the

149

Tombstone of 1882 than Shakespeare in the Hollywood of 1946, by which time the cultural division between the two sorts of "classics" was all but complete, with low-art moviemaking split off from high-art Shakespeare.[3] The scene that opens *The Arizonian* (1935, RKO; directed by Charles Vidor) projects a twentieth-century "highbrow/lowbrow" hierarchy back onto the nineteenth-century frontier: *Hamlet* so bores the audience of miners that they shoot the ghost of Hamlet's father off the stage.

Hamlet also bores the Clanton gang in *My Darling Clementine*, but the reaction from the other gunfighters—and from the film itself—is rather more complex. Ford's film uses Shakespeare's words in a thoroughly contradictory way to further an almost exclusively visual argument. We will come around to this, and to the way that this transformation away from dialogue toward what *Hamlet* would call "dumb show" may help to get at the core of Ford's elusive cinematic genius. But it is probably helpful first to recall the outline of the film's rather predictable story:

On the harsh desert outside of Tombstone, Arizona, Wyatt Earp (Henry Fonda) meets Old Man Clanton (Walter Brennan) and turns down his purchase offer for cattle the four Earp brothers are herding west. That evening, the three eldest brothers ride back from the "wide-awake, wide-open town" to find eighteen-year-old James Earp murdered and the cattle rustled. Wyatt accepts the job as Tombstone's marshal and, through a barroom confrontation, reaches an accommodation with Doc Holliday (Victor Mature) that leaves Doc in charge of the gambling. Arriving by stagecoach is Clementine Carter (Cathy Downs), a genteel Boston beauty, Holliday's abandoned fiancée and nurse from his days as a practicing doctor. She incites distant admiration from Wyatt and quick jealousy from Chihuahua (Linda Darnell), the saloon singer who calls herself, with reason, "Doc's girl." Clementine cannot persuade the apparently tubercular Doc to return east with her and makes plans to return alone.

Wyatt spots Chihuahua wearing the silver pendant stolen from James Earp at his murder. She claims it to have been a present from Doc, but, when confronted by him, admits it was a gift from one of Clanton's four sons, Billy—who shoots her at the moment of her confession and is himself mortally wounded as he gallops from town. Pursuing Billy, Virgil Earp arrives at the Clanton ranch, where he is shot in the back by Old Man Clanton. Meanwhile, Doc returns to his surgical skills to operate on Chihuahua. Later that evening, Virgil's body is dumped onto the main street by the Clantons, and Chihuahua dies of her wounds. At sunup, Doc joins the two surviving Earps for a showdown with the four surviving Clantons at the O.K. Corral. When the dust clears, Doc Holliday and all of the Clantons are dead. Wyatt bids farewell to Clementine—who remains as town schoolmarm—and rides down the long trail to the distant mountains, further west.

Into this carnage comes *Hamlet*, brought to town by a touring theatrical company. Before we proceed, this Shakespearean intrusion into Ford's film also requires a closer description:

Wyatt and Doc are sitting in box-seats of Tombstone's Bird Cage Theater [see figure 1] above an audience grown rowdy over the disappearance of the actors. Wyatt averts their plan to ride the theater manager round town on a rail by going himself in search of the missing players. Dissolve to a smoky saloon, where the lead actor, a certain Granville Thorndyke (Alan Mowbray), is amidst a table-top performance for the four

Clanton boys [figure 2]. The Clantons are unimpressed with the performance thus far and shoot at Thorndyke's feet: "Look Yorick, can't you give us nothin' but them poems?"[4] Puffing himself up to buffoonish dignity, Thorndyke responds in his best drunken British accent, "I have a very large repertoire, sir," and, swigging from a whiskey bottle—soon shot by a Clanton—begins Hamlet's soliloquy, for which he is ideally dressed by nineteenth-century convention (in black, with cape, pendant, and sheathed dagger [figure 3]). Doc and Wyatt arrive, unnoticed, outside the swinging doors and are silhouetted in the night [figure 4], but Doc softly holds Wyatt back, "Wait, I want to hear this." Thorndyke recites faultlessly, if bombastically, as Doc and Wyatt move silently closer [figure 5]:

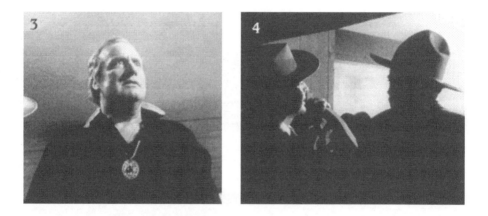

"To be, or not to be—that is the question:
Whether 'tis nobler in the mind to suffer
The slings and arrows of outrageous fortune,
Or to take arms against a sea of troubles,
And by opposing end them? To die, to sleep—
No more; and by that sleep to say we end
The heartache and the thousand natural shocks
That flesh is heir to—'tis a consummation
Devoutly to be wished: to die, to sleep.
To sleep, perchance to dream. Ay, there's the rub;
For in that sleep of death what dreams may come,
When we have shuffled off this mortal coil,..."

"That's enough!" shouts a Clanton, at the end of patience with such speechify-
ing. "Leave him alone," says Doc with undisturbed intensity—as the Clantons whirl
around to notice him—"Please go on, Mr. Thorndyke."

"Thank you sir.
Must give us pause. There's the respect
That makes calamity of so long life.
For who would bear the whips and scorns of time,
The law's delay,
The insolence of office, and the spurns
That patient merit of the unworthy takes,
When he himself might his quietus make
With a bare bodkin? Who would fardels bear,
To grunt and sweat under a weary life...life...."

Thorndyke, lost, finds a prompter in Doc ("But that the dread of something
after death...."); however, it is no use, and Thorndyke begs Doc to carry on for him.
Doc continues, as Wyatt watches [figures 6 & 7]:

"The undiscovered country, from whose borne
No traveller returns, puzzles the will,
And makes us rather bear those ills we have
Than fly to others that we know not of?
Thus conscience does make cowards of us all..."[5]

One of Doc's fits of tubercular coughing interrupts him and he escapes into the
night. As Wyatt helps Thorndyke off the table, the Clantons pull guns to make him stay.
Wyatt swiftly clubs one with his gun and shoots the hand of another, at which demonstration the two others raise their hands. With the commotion, Old Man Clanton
appears from among shrieking Mexican women in the back room ("Qué pasa! Qué
pasa! Parece que hay banditos!") and apologizes to the marshal for his boys having "had
a little whiskey" [figure 8]. As soon as Wyatt is out of earshot, Clanton whips his cowering sons [figure 9], bringing home his moral: "When you pull a gun, kill a man."

*   *   *

Shakespeare's plays may have been frequent visitors to the actual mining towns of the old West, but that still doesn't explain what this scene is doing in *My Darling Clementine*, a film which in any case thoroughly ignores the history of the region (especially in rewriting the lives of the Earps). No doubt *Hamlet* and *My Darling Clementine* are alike family revenge tragedies, even Oedipal ones—as Wyatt too comes round, the long way, to killing an evil father-figure (Old Man Clanton calls Wyatt "son" at their first meeting out among the cattle). But, in plot terms, it's easy enough to find other Westerns closer to *Hamlet:* take *The Phantom Bullet* (1926, Universal) in which Hoot Gibson's father is murdered while Gibson is away. Returning, he puts on foppish clothes (short pants and argyle socks) and Hamlet's "antic disposition," bringing guffaws to the ranchhands and anxiety to his girl (whose genre label for the goings-on is "tragic farce") until he maneuvers the murderer to reveal himself. The *Hamlet* connection to *My Darling Clementine* is looser but deeper. Doc chokes on the line "Thus conscience does makes cowards of us all."[6] And that becomes the text for one argument in the film. Will Wyatt be so rigorous in applying the letter of the law that he will let the Clantons escape? Will he lose his way in the details of bickering with Doc Holliday, who is really his blood brother (as Hamlet loses Laertes)? Will Wyatt, like Hamlet, let his disgust at corruption paralyze action? And will he take his vengeance in a way so roundabout and relaxed, so "lapsed in time and passion," that the Clantons will get the better of him? Thus will revenge itself—for some, the defining trait of the classic Western—be lost in "the law's delay"?[7] Even as Thorndyke recites Hamlet's prevarication, the actor's large silver pendant reminds us of the silver pendant stolen at the time of his murder from Wyatt's still-unavenged brother.

My Darling Clementine's shooting script drove home the relevance of *Hamlet* more heavily than in the finished film. In a scene which would have followed the one described above, Wyatt sends Thorndyke to the theater and goes in search of Doc, finding him in the Oriental Saloon. After Doc's recital of more lines from *Hamlet*, Wyatt responds, "First time I heard it. Parts I could understand make a powerful lot of sense—especially that last about conscience makin' cowards out of all of us." And in a

later scene also found only in the shooting script, Clementine continues her argument with Doc about his refusal to return East, "You've become a coward, John....A silly notion of self-sacrifice—of not wanting to hurt the people who love you—salves your conscience—and makes you think what you're doing is right" (Lyons 116–17). Though it is no longer possible to determine if these scenes were cut by Ford or by producer Darryl Zanuck, evidence of their other films suggests Ford's hand. To what the shooting script calls this "quietly emotional" tirade of Clementine's, Doc would have responded, "Quite a speech." And it does sound like exactly the sort of windy dialogue that Ford made no secret of despising.

What seems to have happened was this, and it is one key to the film's spirit: Hamlet's ethical and intellectual dilemma was transformed—between the script and the finished cut—from a *dramatic* dilemma (explored through dialogue) to a *lyrical* one (argued visually). Such a transformation, I would suggest, comes close to the essence of John Ford's genius, which is always so difficult to pinpoint. *Hamlet* hangs over the film as a mood that is never quite argued out dramatically.

My Darling Clementine has a *double* hero, a doubled Hamlet—Wyatt *and* Doc—as would have been dramatized by those two omitted scenes, with their dual "conscience/coward" refrains. In place of them, Ford offers up the double hero with visual economy: as in the two-shots of Wyatt and Doc as they listen to the soliloquy, and then the almost-matching intercut close-ups [figures 5, 6 & 7]. It's not exactly that parts of the soliloquy reflect Wyatt ("...to take arms against a sea of troubles,/And by opposing end them") while others reflect the self-destructive Doc ("'tis a consummation/Devoutly to be wished: to die, to sleep"); rather it's that the soliloquy presents a *choice*, which the film will illustrate doubly. Ultimately Wyatt will take one option, Doc the other.

If Wyatt seems more immediately Hamlet-like, it's partly because of his evident need to set right a political world turned dishonest, a world whose nature has been revealed by a family murder. Ford's familiar graveside soliloquies have their place here in expanding Wyatt's burden beyond mere family revenge ("Maybe when we leave this country, young kids like you will be able to grow up and live safe"); but more resonant are certain essentially silent sequences. Repeatedly, Fonda's Earp walks slowly from the camera, into darkness, down covered porches or along bar-rails, carrying his burden and ours.

But in many ways Doc is the clearer Hamlet figure, dressed in solemn black (though without the evening clothes and cloak given him by the shooting script). He's the supercivilized one, the champagne drinker, the intellectual who brings up—and perhaps thinks too deeply upon—the subject of "evil." Doc has "something in his soul/O'er which his melancholy sits on brood," evidentially a guilt-turned-deathwish, but we never learn why. On paper, he sounds like an extension of the Thomas Mitchell character in *Stagecoach*, another heavy-drinking frontier surgeon, but Doc is the darker figure, a noir Hamlet (by dress and by Victor Mature's persona[8])—a doctor turned gambler (intellect gone irresponsible), a doctor turned consumptive (a "city disease" in the West), a doctor who fails when his skills are tested (surely the only such instance in Ford). His cough cuts off his recitation of the next line of Hamlet's soliloquy, with its illness metaphor for intellectualized delay ("And thus the native hue of resolution/Is sicklied o'er with the pale cast of thought"). The excised dialogue between Doc and Clementine about cowardice-and-conscience derives from a 1939 Allan Dwan film for Zanuck, *Frontier Marshal*, where the parallel figures discuss how she used to read Shakespeare's *Julius Caesar* to him. "Cowards die many times before their deaths, the brave but once." "I'm a coward?," this Doc had asked. "You've become one, John. You're afraid of living and afraid of dying." While such an explanation seems true enough of *Clementine*'s Doc, it is discussed only visually. His equivalent to Wyatt's measured walks are his periodical frantic gallops off into Mexico, for reasons never explained. Although he remains a dramatically underexplored expression of one way of failing in the West, it takes only a little wilful distortion to call him (in John Baxter's words) "the true hero of the film" (101).

What is so central to Ford's method is the ways that the film argues out explicitly Shakespearean dilemmas without expressing them through dialogue. Exactly how Ford accomplishes this shift toward "dumb show" is difficult to explain, since here as elsewhere in Ford's body of work it so often centers on questions of physiognomy, of gesture, of the placement of figures in landscape, of the pace of a stride or a ride. But in *My Darling Clementine*, we can hazard a few observations about this lyrical argument by looking at the shifts in Henry Fonda's *posture*.

At each moment of crisis, when by classic-Western convention one anticipates active vengeance, we find Wyatt *recumbent*. This little purely visual argument, or subplot, is set up in the first scene in Tombstone, when Wyatt stops into the barbershop after time on the trail. He sits upright in the barber chair, but, with a small surprise to both him and us, falls backwards into a full horizontal ("I don't know how to work it so good," apologizes the barber), belying Wyatt's statement that he's "just passin' through here"—before gunshots burst the windows. The film's single most distinctive image comes in Wyatt's feet-up posture on the covered walkway, as when he does the strange little balancing/bicycling act that infuriates Chihuahua [figure 10]. Here, Wyatt's laid-back posture is set against surrounding verticals (the porch pillars, the cacti[9]) [figure 11]. At each moment that calls for classic gunfighting, Wyatt is seen leaning precariously back in chairs—at the poker table with the card cheat; during the evening after the body of his second murdered brother, Virgil, has been dumped in

the street [figure 12]. Is Wyatt waiting? weary? bored? lonely? self-absorbed? It is difficult to say, even alongside a similar pattern two years later in Laurence Olivier's *noir*-
ish film *Hamlet* of 1948, in which each visitation of his father's ghost knocks him onto
his back, from which contradictory posture he begins subsequent avowals of action
and revenge. If in *My Darling Clementine* one thinks of these postures as small character puzzles or as questions needing an answer, then they find one when Clementine
invites Wyatt to the inauguration of the half-completed church, and he dances with an
upright style, stiff-backboned, legs flung outward. It's gawky but somehow touching, a
perfect escape from recumbency and into, perhaps, community.

What *My Darling Clementine* may be arguing through this pattern of postures is
in many ways made clearer by looking back at Ford's (also Henry Fonda's and Darryl
Zanuck's) *Young Mr. Lincoln* (1939). Lincoln (Henry Fonda) is introduced, as yet
unseen, through flowery electioneering rhetoric "on behalf of the great and incorrupt-
ible Whig Party, God bless it," but when the camera cuts down the porch, Lincoln is
discovered leaning back in a chair, feet up on a barrel, and only slowly ambles over
for a self-effacing stump speech ("I presume you all know who I am. I'm plain
Abraham Lincoln"). When his first love, Ann Rutledge, initially comes across him in
the film, she expresses surprise at finding him recumbent—lying on the ground with

his feet up against a tree ("Aren't you afraid you'll put your eyes out, reading like that upside down?"). Later in his law office, he typically extends his feet out the window or props them on his desk, while leaning back in his rocking chair. The temptation, or taint, of recumbency remains a threat within Lincoln's character too. And these arguments via posture are all aspects of his own Hamlet temptation. ("You've read poetry and Shakespeare," Ann reminds him.) How will Lincoln, the legalist and idealist, avoid the temptation of paralysis, of inaction, of excessive contemplation? Indeed, *Young Mr. Lincoln* virtually builds its structure around this suspense. *How* will Lincoln square this temptation to passive recumbency with standing up for himself in a rough, cynical and cheating frontier world? And how will he be not only an idealist but an active politician, with all the moral compromises that entails? Recumbency looms as threat to Lincoln and Wyatt Earp both, if ultimately we suspect that their passivity is a *consequence* of admirable scruples of conscience.

The recumbency in Wyatt's posture suggests something additional as well, which arises from *My Darling Clementine*'s oblique but self-conscious position as a "postwar" narrative. The film isn't as blunt about that status as, say, *Dakota* (1945, Republic), with its title-crawl reminding audiences that "Those days were postwar too." Wyatt's fame as fighter on behalf of frontier civilization has proceeded him to Tombstone, but he initially corrects the town mayor as to his profession: "*Ex*-marshall." In William Wyler's essential postwar film, *The Best Years of Our Lives* (released the same month as *Clementine*), the Fredric March character returns from the war, props up his feet on his coffee table, and sighs, "Last year it was 'kill Japs,' this year it's 'make money.'" March is weary, and the film admires his presumption of a well-earned rest, feet up, taking time off for contemplation between wartime and postwar modes of action. Has Wyatt "sicklied o'er with the pale cast of thought" and lost "the name of action"; or has he perhaps earned such a "postwar" rest after taming those other frontier towns further east? (*Clementine* was the first film after war service for most of its principals: Ford, Fonda, Victor Mature, screenwriter Winston Miller).[10] Wyatt's posture *could* lead him to be mistaken for a member of the group of World War II veterans mocked in 1946 as "The Rocking Chair Club"—the eight-and-a-half million unemployed or semi-employed veterans who opted for a year of twenty-dollar-a-week "readjustment allowance," and who were paid (according to one who refused the money) for "sitting around on their dead asses" (Goulden 50–51). Wyatt's passivity would thus be close to that of Henry Fonda's veteran in Otto Preminger's *Daisy Kenyon* (1947), a convincing portrait of war weariness in which Fonda's lazy lingering under Joan Crawford's mothering love in her Greenwich Village apartment turns out to be necessary healing—a return to self-confidence. One of the tension points in Henry Fonda's persona does emerge in the postwar years: the threat within his heroism of disengagement, of stubbornness, of inflexibility (all of which become key to Ford's use of Fonda in their 1948 *Fort Apache*).

My Darling Clementine is ostensibly based on Stuart Lake's fitfully amusing but factually discredited 1931 biography, *Wyatt Earp, Frontier Marshal*. But Lake's governing image—"Wyatt Earp was a man of action"—could hardly be further from Fonda's Earp (p. vii). At the poker table, as Wyatt leans back precariously in his chair, Chihuahua is tauntingly explicit in her saloon song:

"Ten thousand cattle gone astray
Left my range and wandered away,
And the sons of guns, I'm here to say,
Have left me dead broke today.
In gamblin' halls delayin',
Ten thousand cattle strayin'. . . ."

The oddity of Wyatt's resting his feet in town comes less in his failure to take speedy revenge (after all, like Hamlet, he needs evidence, only strongly suspecting the murderer's identity) and more in his failure to track down his rustled cattle (even though Virgil Earp has determined that the Clantons are moving cattle). Scriptwriter Winston Miller looked on this doubly unmotivated lingering as the construction flaw he was unable to solve.[11] But lingering, roundabout vengeance is common enough to be nearly a genre trait of the classic Western. Even though Gary Cooper in *The Virginian* (1929) makes his own Shakespearean critique of inaction (by locating the source of Romeo's tragedy in his delays), when his own testing comes, he too delays in trusting his eyes' evidence that his pal is a rustler.

My Darling Clementine has ambivalence about Wyatt's delayed vengeance. On the one hand, he *should* brave the Eastern effeteness symbolized by the perfume sprayed on him by the town barber and by his many self-reflections in mirrors and windows, if he is to cease being too *farouche* for Clementine. On the other hand, Bill Nichols has a point in saying that "town-lingering is a somewhat morbid state for Earp" (617). One could complete Nichols' thought in three ways: (1) on a historical level (towns were often dangerous for cowboys, who had been weeks in the saddle and were paid in lump sums; they could be fleeced by the Chihuahuas, the Doc Hollidays), (2) on a contemporary sociological level (Wyatt could abandon himself to post-World War II comforts, become a "Rocking Chair Club" veteran like Gary Cooper's pajama-lounging brother-in-law in Leo McCarey's *Good Sam* [1948]), and (3) on an auteurist level (a hazard for Ford's sailors in their Long Voyage Home—in his 1940 film of that name—is the English city, with its bars and shanghaiers). Still, if we're never too worried that Wyatt will succumb to these threats, it's because his aloofness is itself a defense mechanism against them—to the point that Ford seems to make a tragic identification with his hero, never a criticism of him. Indeed, it's as if hero and director *alike* blank out various temptations, and accept as the price of both the hero's *and* the film's passivity a sort of stoic, melancholy non-analysis. In that sense, *My Darling Clementine* is just the opposite of *Young Mr. Lincoln*, which is specific and ingenious in its plotting and dialogue, a symbiosis of expressionist lyricism with "the well-made play."

If *My Darling Clementine* is both so minor (in its plot and moral issues) and yet so important in its visual argument, it's because its underdramatized tensions result in a focus on moods, on atmosphere, on faces like mesas and mesas like faces. Land lost and family lost unite in Ford's gravesite scenes and his acute topographical sense (mountains and cacti, wind and dust). Wagons and cattle moving across the empty spaces counterpoint Ford's epic energy with a mourning for the loss of stable families on their own land, as evoked here in the Earps' Sunday-morning memories of their mother and earlier by Ford in *The Grapes of Wrath* and *Tobacco Road*.

A tension between energy and melancholy is also one of *Hamlet*'s great tricks, both within Hamlet's character and over the drama as a whole. This tension also suggests why it's so satisfyingly dissonant and sad that *My Darling Clementine* should *end* as it does. Wyatt parts from Clementine and rides down the long road, further west. The film's way of evoking-without-explaining has tempted various critics into reading this ending, with equal certainty, in diametrically opposite ways. On one side, John Baxter, for instance, makes explicit what Peter Wollen implies: Wyatt is leaving "only for a short time" so as to explain the deaths to his "Pa" and will return to settle down as a "married" man with his schoolmarm Clementine (Baxter 105; Wollen 96). On the other side, Tag Gallagher can speak for J.A. Place and others who presume that Wyatt is "destined to wander forever toward some mountainous fate as Clementine waits forever" (Gallagher 230; Place 65).

My own sense is that the ending perfectly sums up the film's paradoxical power of blankness, its ability to specify almost nothing *without* disappointing its spectators—indeed suggesting much to critics who take the bait of the ending and run with it in either of two directions.

Those (like Gallager and Place) who envision Wyatt wandering forever in the wilderness are imposing onto *My Darling Clementine*'s blankness a literary pattern established in James Fenimore Cooper's Leatherstocking novels (explicitly in *The Pathfinder*, and hinted in *The Last of the Mohicans* and *The Deerslayer*), in which the hero, idealized though he may be, has internalized too much of the wildness of the West ever to find common ground with any Eastern bride. The wages of his righteousness are solitude. On the other hand, critics who see Wyatt happily settled and married are imposing onto *Clementine* a literary pattern first widely popularized in Owen Wister's *The Virginian* (1902), which marries its cowboy-gunfighter with its Eastern, Shakespeare-quoting schoolmarm, a match which, as the Virginian twice tells her, is "better than my dreams."[12] That latter option certainly *seems* to be the model toward which *Clementine* is heading: Wyatt will come in from the cold of his shattered cattleman family to be rewarded by the beautiful Clementine, the civilized/feminine East which has gone West to meet and complement him. In the twentieth century, the Cooper pattern generally lost out to the Wister one,[13] and *The Virginian* became the endemic model for pulp novels and the thirties B-Westerns. *The Dawn Rider* (1935), to take one film instance fairly close to *Clementine*, concludes with John Wayne and a friend facing a pair of bad brothers; the friend (like Doc Holliday) dies in a showdown. Cut to the perfunctory coda: Wayne "hitched up " with his dead pal's girl.

But *My Darling Clementine* uses the Wister pattern as a bluff. Wyatt returns to the wilds—for how long is anybody's guess. Does his refusal to settle down come from guilt about slaughtering the Claytons? Were the deaths of Chihuahua, Doc, and Wyatt's second brother an additional weight that he could not bear? Is he a loaner because he's a judge-figure, like Ford's Lincoln and Judge Priest? Or does he personify celibate, late marrying Irish habits beloved by Ford? Is he a scapegoat savior, like Shane? Or a tragic savior, like Hamlet? None of these explanations is inconsistent, but all are projections onto the landscape, the space, the emptiness.

After World War II, the melancholy middle ground, this ambiguous half-refusal to settle into the earned comforts of home and hearth recurs again and again at the end of Westerns—from Alan Ladd in *Whispering Smith* (1948) through James Stewart in *The Man from Laramie* (1955). But these films may suggest less the return of James Fenimore Cooper's spirit than the influence of *My Darling Clementine* itself. Too, a little postwar sociology of the movies puts Clementine's dilemma in perspective. As Martha Wolfenstein and Nathan Lectes determined in their 1950 study, only 15 percent of Hollywood heroines reveal evidence of ever having loved before (47). Clementine can hardly remain idealized and grab at Wyatt before her true love's body is cold. It is not just from lingering echoes of *Hamlet* that marriage to Clementine would seem "most wicked speed."

Perhaps the key is only that *My Darling Clementine* is so clearly set up in the Wister pattern to end happily that it cries out for dissonance. It's tempting just to say that Ford, being Ford, chose melancholy.[14] Although it has been called a "wholeheartedly militarist Western" (McBride and Wilmington 85–86), *My Darling Clementine* seems instead part of a cycle of Westerns resting on something more like postwar triste, with a new brooding quality and with heroes who move beyond demonstrations of heroics—a post World War II but essential pre-Cold-War cycle. Among its highlights would be *Along Came Jones* (1945), *Pursued* (1947) and *Angel and the Badman* (1947). Although the plotlines and dialogue of those three Westerns also reinforce the sense that heroes are finding enemies difficult to locate, it's again primarily acting styles and physical postures that convey a lingering confusion about how to take action. In *Along Came Jones*, Gary Cooper is the cowboy as postmodernist, comically deconstructing the mythic gunslinger: mistaken for a wanted outlaw, he learns that he can impose fear on the town by replacing his common-man geniality and cheerful singing with a measured, "unsmiling" dignity and an odd, stiff-necked posture. Raoul Walsh and Niven Busch's *Pursued* brings its hero back to New Mexico from the Spanish-American War with medals, wounds, and nightmares. The film rests on Robert Mitchum's deeply weary way of moving, his passive way of waiting for mysteries to unravel around him, as put to such good use in so many later noirs. His physical posture itself makes it impossible to imagine Mitchum as a star of prewar Hollywood. Similarly, one explanation for John Wayne's having to sit out the thirties in eighty forgettable B-Westerns is that his stardom had to wait for an era that treasured his oddly halting speech patterns and the considered weariness of his feline walk. Like *Pursued* and *My Darling Clementine* itself, Wayne's *Angel and the Badman* (his first independent production) is another superior Western that finds its overall visual pattern in an escape from film noir. Curiously, Wayne's character in *Angel and the Badman* is said to have taken part in the Tombstone gunfight against the Clantons, alongside Wyatt Earp. Thus, within the Western genre's ongoing debates, he must be seen as a Doc Holliday-figure who takes the other, active option offered by Hamlet's soliloquy, a Doc Holliday who succumbs to the efforts of *his* nurse (a Quaker daughter) to see him into health and pacifism. "Only a man who carries a gun ever needs one," Wayne concludes, astonishingly.

Henry Fonda's physical style in *My Darling Clementine* is of a piece with this pre-Cold-War argument, with its surprisingly complex qualms about militarism. Ultimately, Wyatt proves to be no Hamlet in inaction—any more than was Ford's Lincoln. *Young Mr. Lincoln* holds a knowing little joke about Lincoln's "passivity": in apparent indecision, he walks out to Ann Rutledge's grave to ask her spirit to choose his future vocation via the direction a twig will fall. But a line of dialogue keeps the door open to his own active willpower: "I wonder if I could have tipped it your way just a little?" It's a scrupulous worry, and of course he did tip the twig: he isn't recumbent in the end. Ultimately neither he nor Wyatt resemble the postwar Hamlet of Laurence Olivier, "the man who could not make up his mind." The Hamlet-soliloquy scene in *Clementine*, remember, ends with Clanton's advice to his boys, brought home with his whip: "When you pull a gun, kill a man." In the context of Hamlet's scrupulous worry over action and mortality, the line earns an audience laugh every time it cuts Hamlet's Gordian knot. But, of course, in having a figure of evil do so, it legitimizes Hamlet's scruples. Wyatt's style of lingering even when confronted with evil thus moves beyond the tradition of hair-trigger action, as represented, say, through another meeting of John Ford and Shakespeare in *The Man Who Shot Liberty Valance*. Drunken newspaper editor Edmund O'Brien fractures Henry V in anticipating the routing of outlaw Liberty Valance:

> But those in England now asleep
> Shall think themselves accursed they were not here
> Whiles any lives
> That fought with us upon Saint Crispin's day.
> But when the blast, the blast of war blows in our ears,
> Then we summon up, Liberty Valance.[15]

This sort of Shakespearean relish for testing in battle is missing from Wyatt. In its place is a certain regret and a risky nonviolence. Responding to Doc's leveled gun for the first time, he smoothly flips open his coat to reveal himself weaponless.

It's natural to accept Bill Nichols' characterization of Wyatt's stance as "town-lingering." Nevertheless, watched carefully, the film specifies the time from Wyatt's and Doc's meeting to the latter's death at the OK Corral as less than three days—from late on Friday night to Monday dawn. Still, *Clementine* is hardly of the *High Noon* or *3:10 to Yuma* clock-watching school. Even to notice that it is a weekend story is to violate its spirit. *Clementine*'s style—including acting style—suggests something more akin to Jean Renoir's philosophical sense of time, as in *The River* (1951), where "Captain John" comes to savor his slow recovery from war wounds in an Anglo-Indian garden. In neither case is the lingering "morbid" exactly: it is more a sad sense of *temps-morts*, a sense of life flowing by as you observe it from a well-situated chair, a Proustian more than a Shakespearean sense of time.

And this is the deeper, nearly indefinable trick of *My Darling Clementine*: its replacement of the confines of historical time with the expanses of space. Owen Wister once rhapsodized on a Turner-thesis pioneering theme in imagining that in journeying westward through frontier towns and primordial landscape Americans could experience time regained through a sense of "the various centuries jostled together. . . . We have taken the ages out of their processional arrangement and set them marching disorderly abreast in our wide territory"("Preface" vi: Bold p. 65). The B-Western too regularly jumbled time through its surreal convention by which one has only to step just beyond the reach of automobiles and telephones to be plunged into a Wild West of horses and six guns. Ford's transformation of time is more complex. Unlike the historical Tombstone, Arizona, or almost any frontier town known from photographs, Ford's Tombstone is built entirely on one side of its main street. No bastion, it's open to the landscape. Wyatt, feet up and leaning back in his chair, gazes out at the blank grandeur of the Monument Valley monoliths; in doing so, he exemplifies the inward/outward gaze of Hollywood's historical figures generally: looking, one might say, simultaneously forward and backward in time. Particularly, but not exclusively in Ford, this gaze outward at the landscape implies a hero's knowledge that adds to *our* past, hence a foreknowledge of his own future. It is that nearly Biblical burden of knowledge that adds to the *gravity* of Ford heroes, particularly those like Wyatt Earp and Abraham Lincoln whose very names reveal to us their mythic fate. If they too seem not unaware of their historical responsibility to overcome evil, it's with a touch of Hamlet's self-dramatization ("heaven hath minister"). In Ford, such self-dramatization, free of dialogue, is starkest at the end of *Young Mr. Lincoln*, where Lincoln's slow walk to the top of a hill signifies (partly via the "Battle hymn of the Republic" music) Lincoln's recognition of the burden of the Civil War to come; but Ford's Henry Fonda also conveys that knowledge of the American future in his heavy walks and in his unblinking gaze at the horizon at the end of *Drums Along the Mohawk* and *The Grapes of Wrath*, just as Ford's John Wayne has it at the ends of *They Were Expendable* and *Fort Apache*. We leave Ford's horizon-gazing historical heroes in the middle of their story, with their burden still heavy, their tasks still to complete: "the readiness is all."[16]

NOTES

1. Don DeLillo, *The Names* (New York: Vintage Books, 1983), p. 198.

2. See Clair Eugene Willson, *"Mimes and Miners: A Historical Study of the Theater in Tombstone,"* University of Arizona Bulletin, vol. 6, no 1 (Tucson, 1935), p. 128. In 1863, the actor Frank Mayo resisted requests that he play Hamlet for the miners of Virginia City, fearing that "audiences were so familiar with the play that nearly the complete text and action of the actor would be anticipated with 'preconceived ideas of correctness'"; Margaret G. Watson, *Silver Theater: Amusements of the Mining Frontier in Early Nevada. 1850-1864* (Glendale, Calif.: Arthur H. Clark Co., 1964), pp. 164-65.

3. For analysis of this evolution in perceptions of Shakespeare, see Lawrence W. Levine, *High-brow/Low-brow: The Emergence of Cultural Hierarchy in America* (Cambridge, Mass: Harvard University Press, 1988), pp. 13-81.

4. The Clantons' name for Thorndyke is a vestige of an earlier comic sequence, apparently cut by producer Darryl Zanuck, in which Thorndyke drunkenly misplaced his "Yorick's" skull prop for *Hamlet*. The omitted sequence also explains why Thorndyke performs alone: he has lost not only Yorick's skull but his entire acting company, who have run out on him. See Robert Lyons, *My Darling Clementine* (New Brunswick, N.J.: Rutgers University Press, 1984), pp. 115-16.

5. Doc as Shakespeare-reciting-gambler is not entirely a movie creation. One curious episode

in mining-town *Hamlet*s came in 1861 when a wager was made in Denver's *Rocky Mountain News* that no one could play the part of Hamlet on less than three days study. The "notorious gambler," C.B. Cooke took up the challenge and received a satisfactory review: "Mr. Cooke has not a strong voice, but his reading was most capital and his *action* graceful, artistic, and impressive....With practice and study Mr. Cooke would make a most capital actor, but we suppose he prefers to watch and prey" *(Daily Rocky Mountain News,* July 29, 1861); Melvin Schoberlin, *From Candles to Footlights: A Biography of the Pike's Peak Theater 1859-1876* (Denver: Old West Publishing Co., 1941), pp. 61-62. Granville Thorndyke has forgotten, or the scriptwriters have cut, a line-and-a-half: "...and scorns of time,/The oppressor's wrong, the proud man's contumely,/The pangs of disprized love, the law's delay...." [Punctuation and spelling follow G.R. Hibbard, ed., *Hamlet* (New York: Oxford University Press, 1987)].

6. Notwithstanding some *Hamlet* editors' annotations of "conscience" as meaning "consciousness," Shakespeare here and elsewhere seems to use "conscience" in our modern— and Western film—meaning of moral scruples (as in "thy conscience/Is so possessed with guilt"; *The Tempest,* I.ii. pp. 471-72).

7. For revenge as essential to the "complete classical form" of the Western, see Lovell, "Western," p. 169.

8. This was Victor Mature's first film in four years, but even in his brief career between 1939 and war service in 1942, he is memorably dark and languid, as in the early noir *I Wake Up Screaming* (where his style makes him the likeliest murder suspect) and von Sternberg's *The Shanghai Gesture* (where he is a "Doctor of Nothing," an ultimately appropriate degree for Holliday as well).

9. The saguaro cacti, not native to Monument Valley, are part of the purposeful set decoration.

10. Ford was still in uniform when he made the Navy story *They Were Expendable* in 1945.

11. "Actually, if you analyze that picture, there were a lot of flaws in the construction. Earp stays in town to get his brother's killer, and we vamp around for about sixty pages with what we hope are interesting scenes." "Interview with Winston Miller," in Lyons, *Clementine,* p. 148.

12. Wister 296, 297. The Virginian too finds Shakespeare a cowboy's ideal companion: he's seen several Shakespeare plays and borrows the schoolmarm's complete Shakespeare until he is able to buy one for himself.

13. For a discussion of this battle and of Frederic Remington's unpopular attempts to write fiction extending the Cooper pattern, see Bold, 37-75.

14. The problem with this reasoning is that Ford, much later, claimed he *had* wanted Earp to settle down in Tombstone with Clementine, and that the ending was forced on him, presumably by Darryl Zanuck (see Andrew Sinclair, *John Ford* [New York: Dial Press, 1979], p. 130). One must say "claimed" because neither the shooting script nor the screenwriter's recollections bear Ford out (see "Interview with Winston Miller," in Lyons, *Clementine,* pp. 148-49). My guess is that Ford, a notoriously grumpy and "revisionist"

interview subject, and never one to forget a grudge, was directing at the ending a general displeasure with a film Zanuck recut—and in particular left shorn of most of Ford's usual very broad comic relief ("And let those that play your clowns speak no more than is set down for them" seems to have been Zanuck's text). Ford was particularly annoyed at a clearly intrusive close-up *added* to the final scene: Wyatt and Clementine's kiss, an addition justified by Zanuck on the grounds that a preview audience had laughed at their handshake (see Gallagher, *Ford,* p. 233). Zanuck, at least by Hollywood standards, was something of a foe of the happy ending—among his memorable rewritings were the final lines for *I Am a Fugitive from a Chain Gang* (see Leonard Mosley, *Zanuck: The Rise and Fall of Hollywood's Last Tycoon* [Boston: Little, Brown & Co., 1984], pp. 112-13). Thus one might look to "the studio" too for the source of *Clementine*'s ending. *My Darling Clementine* was always notably absent from Ford's changing lists of "favorites" among his own films.

15.   For the unfractured version, see *Henry V,* III.i and IV.iii, and Sonnet p. 30.

16.   My particular thanks to Raymond Durgnat, whose ideas were fundamental to this essay.

WORKS CITED

Baxter, John. *The Cinema of John Ford.* New York: A.S. Barnes & Co, 1971.

Bold, Christine. *Selling the Wild West: Popular Western Fiction. 1860–1960.* Bloomington: Indiana UP. 1987.

Gallagher, Tag. *John Ford: The Man and His Films.* Berkeley: U of California P. 1986.

Goulden, Joseph C. *The Best Years: 1949–1950.* New York: Atheneum, 1976.

Lake, Stuart N. *Wyatt Earp, Frontier Marshal.* Boston: Houghton Mifflin Co., 1931, vii.

Lovell, Alan. "The Western." *Movies and Methods* vol. 1 Bill Nichols, ed. Berkeley: U of California P. 1976.

Lyons, Robert. *My Darling Clementine.* New Brunswick, NJ: Rutgers UP. 1984.

McBride, Joseph and Michael Wilmington. *John Ford.* New York: Da Capo P. 1975.

Nichols, Bill. "Style, Grammar and the Movies." *Movies and Methods* vol.1 Bill Nichols, ed. Berkeley: U of California P. 1976.

Place, J. A. *The Western Films of John Ford.* Secaucus. NJ: Citadel P. 1974.

Sinclair, Andrew. *John Ford.* New York: Dial P. 1979.

Wister, Owen. Preface. *Red Men and White.* New York: Grosset & Dunlap. 1895.

_____ . *The Virginian, A Horseman of the Plains* [1902]. Boston: Houghton Mifflin. 1968.

Wolfenstein, Martha and Nathan Leites. *Movies: A Psychological Study.* Glencoe, IL: The Free Press. 1950.

Wollen, Peter. *Signs and Meaning in the Cinema.* Bloomington: Indiana UP. 1972.

RETROSPECTIVE:
High Noon

Richard Combs (1986)

I s *High Noon* a classic Western, a realist Western, an ultimate Western, or an anti-Western? Its thirty-four-year critical history contains all these possibilities, various combinations and blurrings of them, and even the arguments of one position put forward in support of another. At this point, a historical assessment of *High Noon* would produce a rather *Rashomon*-like text (not inappropriate, given one Western trail which subsequently goes via Kurosawa), and it is interesting that reviewers recently presented with Cannon's revival, in a brand-new print struck from the original negative, reacted to it almost "clean," as something elemental and monumental, as if it had been tempered by its disputatious critical history and, in coming through, had proved it was made of the right stuff. (*The Financial Times* mockingly invoked "A man's gotta do what a man's gotta do," but the *Time Out* critic agreed to its "anatomy of what it took to make a man before the myth turned sour.")

Part of that reaction was to ignore the center of the dispute—*High Noon*'s integrity as a Western vs. its pretensions as a social document—and to concentrate, with some justice, on its star. The recent, dying stage of the Western has accustomed us to the spectacle of its stars dying before our eyes—William Holden in *The Wild Bunch*, John Wayne in *The Shootist*—and a whole other category of Western can now be read into *High Noon* by reading it through the ravaged, anxious physiognomy of Gary Cooper. There's an irony here—the beginning of one shift in the continental plates of critical attitudes—in that what was once claimed as the film's realism, its documentary treatment of its subject, now looks like internal documentary, a record of the history of the Western genre itself. The impact of a middle-aged Cooper was clearly intended to add to the moral seriousness of the story, but what is interesting is the beginning here of a second, self-conscious history of the Western (Ford, of course, always looking for an excuse for elegy, had begun artificially ageing the genre three years before by prematurely ageing John Wayne in *She Wore a Yellow Ribbon)*. It's this second history, a different kind of maturing, that develops in secret tandem with the eagerness in the 50s to develop something called the "adult Western."

In this perspective, *High Noon* may look more estimable now than when it was first released. To read the reviews of 1952 is to be struck by how little it was respected as a classic, realist or any other kind of Western; the tone is best summed up by one heading, "Western But Different." Most of the positive reviews begin with the sheepish acknowledgment that this is the Western as seen umpteen times before, but somehow elevated, not by ambitious social allegory but by the classiness of its execution: "It is a sheriff-versus-the-bad-man picture that is above the average because tense, hairspring direction quivers behind its straightforward story." (The negative reviews take the line that it is no more than the sum of its absolutely standard, generic elements.) The problem in which this argument bogs down is whether that "difference" is something imported to the Western, or simply an intensification of it; as the *Saturday Review* critic of the day perceptively put it: "You're on swampy ground when

"The failure of the citizens of Hadleyville."

you argue in favor of one Western over another; the good ones somehow have an even more ritualistic nature than the mediocre and bad." From this it's not too far to a review last year in *The Village Voice* (on the occasion of *High Noon*'s revival, along with *Shane*), which suggests that the makers were "not so much rethinking Western conventions as streamlining the format in order to point it in self-destructive directions." A developing sense of its own ritual is one of the things that defines the "classic" Western, but also leads it to outstrip itself (as perhaps all classicisms must), and finally to dissolve itself.

If *High Noon* still looks impressive (and inevitable) today, if it is possible to approach it "clean," it is because the film falls absolutely into this line of development: that shadow history which leads to the self-conscious Western, the "post-Western," of the 60s and 70s. Its inevitability now renders rather redundant the attacks on it for being anti-Western: first by Robert Warshow, who felt the need to protect some essential, unchanging Western, and ever since by auteurist critics, who felt the genre really belonged to its regular practitioners (Ford, Hawks) and not to visitors like Messers Zinnemann, Foreman and Kramer, who seemed to be trying to haul it into middlebrow respectability. The continuing hostility to *High Noon* is based on a confusion as to whether it is intensifying the Western or importing something alien to it—namely, scenarist Carl Foreman's notion of a political allegory about McCarthyism in the failure of the citizens of Hadleyville to support their sheriff in his hour of need. Actually the allegory is just about invisible; one might ignore it or reshape its meaning at will: the recent *Listener* review talked of an "anti-pacifist tract," an "aggression-in-the-name-of-self-defence role we've just seen President Reagan rehearse in the Libyan gulf and Honduras"; this could be the proto-*Death Wish* fable, and Marshal Kane's actions, up to his famous ditching of his badge, also parallel those of Dirty Harry Callahan.

It's this final act of disgust on Kane's part which has created more confusion about the film than anything else. John Wayne disapproved of it, thus lending credence to the belief that the film was strong left-wing material; but critics as diverse as Warshow and Andrew Sarris have also picked up on it to label the film "anti-populist," as if it had not only set itself against the Western but also against the popular audience. Since then, of course, this novel (though by no means unprecedented) emphasis on the veniality and cowardice of the townsfolk has entered the Western mainstream, via its Jacobean efflorescence in the Italian Western and then through films like *High Plains Drifter*. Signs of the "late" Western in fact proliferate in *High Noon*, one of the most interesting being Katy Jurado's role as the Latin element in the typically Anglo-Saxon West, a businesswoman who seems to own a good part of the town she despises (though covertly, through a network of fronts, except for the saloon which bears her name), and a woman no better than she should be, who is, or has been, involved with three of the main male characters in the film (sexual partners are referred to by everyone, even the outlaws, as "friends," which strangely suggests that Grace Kelly's Quaker also has the town sewn up). As Kane goes about his hopeless quest, children are already enacting the shoot-out, *à la* Peckinpah, and Lon Chaney's embittered ex-lawman, arthritic, impoverished, living with an Indian woman, rejecting the community that has discarded him, has his apotheosis in *Pat Garrett and Billy the Kid*.

What is disconcerting about *High Noon* is the way its starkly compressed and stylized storyline goes with a psychological realism that simultaneously diffuses and complicates the plot. There's an "everybody has his reasons" quality to the way the townspeople are presented, and their different excuses for backing out on Kane. Even more, the town of Hadleyville itself is a site of contradictions, from the way the fleeing circuit judge talks about it ("This is just a dirty little village in the middle of nowhere. Nothing that happens here is of any importance") to the peroration of Thomas Mitchell's selectman, who imagines armies of eager investors up north with their eyes on Hadleyville, waiting for it to prove itself more than just a "wide-open town." The ambiguity extends as well to matters of fact: the dating of the film's action has ranged in various accounts from 1865 to 1875, and there is a corresponding vagueness about its own range of reference (mention of the "North" often seems to involve Southern resentment, as if the men who freed Frank Miller were some amalgam of anti-slavery abolitionists, interfering carpetbaggers and bleeding-heart liberals).

If this ambivalence—shades of *Rashomon* indeed—is "realism," it is very different from the realism for which *High Noon* has usually been praised, which has to do with a documentary attention to "dusty lacklustre buildings and the white textureless skies" (*Film Criticism*, Winter 1976/77) and, particularly, its rigorous clockwatching (see below). On the contrary, the film's race against time, its compressed, over-driven narrative, creates a strangely hallucinatory air with great fluctuations in the sense of time and reality. The result is not unlike a horror film—again a link with the Gothic mood of Peckinpah—and as such *High Noon* is much more a drama of place than it is of time. The deep-focus photography of Floyd Crosby emphasizes boxed-in spaces rather than documentary flatness, the "contemporary newsreel" look director Fred Zinnemann is said to have wanted. The town itself, with its permanently empty main street and sharply etched shadows, is one big old dark house, and the plot of course forbids Kane to escape. Nothing outside Hadleyville seems to exist—certainly not the mythical other town where the hero plans to become a storekeeper with his Quaker bride. As for the conflict with Frank Miller, and the movie-long wait for the villain to arrive, there's a foretaste here of Polanski's intellectualized horror film, *Cul de Sac*—a resemblance now heightened by a final trick of time, which has made Miller's three loitering sidekicks such familiar Western faces, while the much-heralded appearance of their satanic leader finally produces only a cypher.

Postscript: Seven Ambiguities of Time

In the waxing and waning of critical enthusiasm for *High Noon*, the one thing that has been taken at face value is the film's timekeeping. The fact that its action takes place within a strictly delineated period of time, and that the film quite carefully observes this dramatic unity, has always been accepted as a defining feature, for good or ill, off its sense of reality, of its attempt to do something different with the Western. It has become, in fact, the central myth of *High Noon*'s realism, from contemporary reviews through subsequent reassessments ("The amount of time that expires in the movie is identical with the film's literal duration": *Film Criticism*, Winter 1976/77) up to the present revival ("[Zinnemann] was able to keep the on-screen clocks moving

precisely in step with the mounting tension in a masterly piece of pre-planning":
Evening Standard, April 2, 1986). But, although the ticking away of the minutes until
twelve certainly heightens the film's tension, there are many ways in which its sense
of time could be said to be quite out of joint . . .

1 The first clock seen in the film, in the office of the justice of the peace where Will
Kane and Amy Fowler are being married, gives the time as 10.35 A.M.. This is after
approximately five minutes of credits introduction as Miller's three men ride into
town. After the noon train arrives with Frank Miller, the film continues for approximately another fifteen minutes of showdown and shoot-out; giving 105 minutes of
action covered in 85 minutes of screen time.

*Gary Cooper and Grace
Kelly at* High Noon.

2   The abbreviation and condensation of action, the ellipsis of time, is even more dras-
     tic than this would suggest. Even considering Marshal Kane alone, the film covers
     very much more action, incident, conversation and confrontation than any mortal
     could encompass in 105 minutes; screen "real time" (even as Hitchcock tried to pin
     it down in *Rope*, only four years before) can never be more than the merest conven-
     tion for time as it really is. According to the film's own clocks, the scene near the
     beginning where Kane sets out from Hadleyville with Amy, changes his mind and
     drives back, takes less than five minutes.

3   The time recorded on Hadleyville's clocks proceeds in sudden fits and starts. The
     film quite carefully establishes that the marshal's wedding at the beginning is tak-
     ing place at the same time as Miller's men arrive at the train station to inquire
     about the noon train. It is several minutes in the film's running time, in fact, before
     the on-screen time seems to get beyond 10:35. Thereafter, the film's on-screen
     time tends to move ahead much more quickly than its actual running time.

4   Considering how much plot the film generally manages to pack into very few
     minutes, there is one stretch of strangely unaccounted time, between 10:47
     (approx.), when Judge Mettrick takes his leave of Kane, and the latter has his first
     argument with his deputy Harvey, and 11:03 (approx.). It takes only some four
     minutes of screen time to get between these two points.

5   The film largely makes no allowance for what must be overlapping or simultaneous
     scenes with different characters. But once it does "reverse" its clocks, to show
     Harvey entering the saloon after quitting his job at 11:10, subsequent to a scene in
     which Kane is shown leaving the hotel, having gone to warn Helen Ramirez of
     Miller's arrival, at 11:15. As the urgency only applies to Kane, scenes without him
     usually can't be placed in any time frame at all.

6   In one scene, Kane goes to the saloon to recruit deputies. He knocks down the
     bartender, whom he overhears betting that he won't survive the gunfight, then
     makes his unsuccessful pitch to his hostile audience. There are two clocks visible
     during this scene, at either end of the bar. They both show 11:20 when Kane
     enters and 11:20 when he leaves.

7   The film exploits its plethora of clocks, and its hero glancing nervously in their
     direction, to heighten mood. It uses them arbitrarily, as elements in a design, and
     one might say that they become part of the film's sense of threatening space—at
     times almost expressionist in what they are made to signify visually. During the
     montage sequence that precedes the train's final arrival, Kane is shown writing
     his will while a pendulum swings in massive close-up on his functional office
     clock. There is a slight frisson when this is cut against Grace Kelly's Amy looking
     up at a different clock, one whose face—prettily rounded, with decorative
     Romanesque numerals—seems to have been chosen to match hers.

RIO BRAVO & RETROSPECT

Robin Wood (1968, 1981)

The genesis of *Rio Bravo* was Hawks' reaction against *High Noon:* the hero of *High Noon* spends the whole film asking for help and in the end he doesn't need it. Hawks decided to reverse the process: the hero of *Rio Bravo* never asks for help and often rejects it; and he needs it at every crisis. The relationship between the two films is not quite as simple as that; the two exceptions to this general reversal-pattern are interesting, as they may both have suggested to Hawks, whether he was aware of it or not, aspects of *Rio Bravo:* (1) The Marshal (Gary Cooper) in *High Noon* does once reject the help of a one-eyed drunken cripple who sees in his offer of assistance the possibility of regaining his self-respect: "I used to be good," he tells Cooper, a line doubtless as common in Westerns as certain musical phrases were common in late eighteenth-century music, yet one which Hawks (like Mozart with his contemporary clichés) can fill with intensity. Are we to see in this the genesis of Dude and Stumpy? In one way obviously not, because both these characters, and their relation to the film's main hero-figure, have their ancestry in Hawks' own work, notably Eddie in *To Have and Have Not.* Yet, given the admitted relationship of *Rio Bravo* to *High Noon,* and the complexity of influence and reminiscence that can underlie any great work of art, it may not be far-fetched to feel some significance in this passing resemblance. (2) Grace Kelly's final intervention (shooting a man in the back to save her husband, against her Quaker principles) is one point where Cooper *does* need help, and may point forward to *Rio Bravo's* celebrated flower-pot scene and Angie Dickinson's subsequent distress at having been responsible for the deaths of four men.

Rio Bravo: *Stumpy (Walter Brennan) and Chance (John Wayne); Dude (Dean Martin), the hero's fallible friend.*

The reputation of *High Noon*—it is still widely regarded as one of the best Westerns, a film that confers dignity on a low genre by infusing into it a seriousness of moral purpose—is very revealing, as regards current attitudes to the Western and to film in general. This reputation is my only reason for undertaking a brief comparison of the two films: *High Noon* in itself doesn't offer anything that the critic who regards the cinema as, in its potentialities and to some extent its achievements, the equal of the other arts is likely to find worth serious consideration. It strikes me as the archetypal "Oscar" film, product of the combined talents of the archetypal "Oscar" director (Zinnemann), the archetypal "Oscar" writer (Carl Foreman), and the archetypal "Oscar" producer (Stanley Kramer): three gentlemen whose work has been characterized by those Good Intentions with which we understand the road to hell to be paved. *Mental* intentions, not emotional or intuitive intentions: intentions of the conscious, willing mind, not of the whole man. The film reeks of contrivance. Every sequence is constructed to lead up to, and make, a simple moral point, character, action, and dialogue being painstakingly manipulated to this end. Nowhere is there that sense of inner logic, of *organic* development, of the working-out of natural processes through the interaction of the characters, that one finds in the best films of Hawks. This characteristic is not only in the script. Zinnemann's direction, external and shallow, matches it perfectly. His handling of the actors is almost uniformly abominable, cliché-gesture following cliché-gesture (see, for instance, poor Thomas Mitchell, whose Kid in *Only Angels Have Wings* is among the American cinema's great supporting performances, in the church scene), just as cliché-set-up follows cliché-set-up in the camera positioning.

Quite fundamental issues are involved here, including the question of what constitutes cliché. But in *High Noon* not a single character or situation is spontaneously-intuitively felt—everything is in the head, a painstaking application of carefully learnt lessons. One could attack Carl Foreman's script for its contrivance, but, ultimately, to understand why *High Noon* is a bad film is to understand that the cinema is a director's art. There are situations, such as the scene between Katy Jurado and Lloyd Bridges where her contempt for him finally erupts after long suppression, which are perfectly valid emotionally, but which Zinnemann relentlessly turns into cliché-melo-drama with his academically conceived jumps into close-up at the most obvious moments, his insistence on acting that is conventional in the worst sense (it isn't the actors' fault), the obviousness of gesture and expression exactly corresponding to the obviousness of the editing.

Judgments of this kind are notoriously difficult to enforce when dealing with the cinema (how great an advantage the literary critic has in being able to quote!): one has to appeal not only to the reader's common experience, but to his memory of that experience. One can, however, in the case of *High Noon*, point to several obvious major inadequacies which are symptomatic of the quality of the film as a whole—its quality as a work of art, as a record of lived and felt experience (however indirectly expressed). There is the entire church sequence, where the cliché-treatment both of the congregation *en masse* and of individuals reaches risible extremes. There is the handling of the Cooper-Kelly relationship. It is presumably of importance that the audience feel this as meaningful, that a sense of frustrated mutual needs and resulting tensions is communicated. Yet if we look at what Zinnemann actually offers us we find, apart from one or two tentative attempts at inwardness from Grace Kelly in the early stages of the film, nothing at all convincing. The wife remains a mere puppet, manipulated according to the requirements of the plot: no understanding of her reactions is communicated, beyond the explicit statement of her Quakerism, which is then merely taken for granted. Everything important, in fact, is taken for granted: Cooper's need for her, the importance of the marriage to him, is reduced to a bit of data, never *felt* as real. Someone, indeed, seems to have felt that there was something missing there, that the marriage-theme needed a bit of artificial bolstering; hence the tiresome repetition on the sound-track of the lines from the theme-song, "I'm not afraid of death but Oh! what will I do if you leave me?"—the importance of the marriage is only there in the song, an explicit statement of intentions that remain quite unrealized.

But most interesting of all, in relation to Hawks and *Rio Bravo*, is the motivation of the hero's actions. It is clear, I think, that for the Marshal, as for Hawks' heroes, the essential motivation is the preservation of self-respect—he goes back to face Frank Miller because a failure to do so would be, for him, a failure to live up to his own conception of manhood. One may reflect that this is a theme that lends itself readily to (could even be said to be implicit in) the Western genre. It is not its theme that makes *Rio Bravo* great, but the intensity and emotional maturity with which it is felt. The level on which the theme is handled in *High Noon* can be, I think, fairly represented by the scene where Grace Kelly confronts Katy Jurado and asks her *why* Cooper is determined to stay. Cut to close-up of Jurado, who says, with heavy emphasis, "If you don't know, I can't explain it to you." The reader who doesn't see what I mean by cliché (in terms of acting, editing, camera-position) couldn't do better than study that moment. The reputation of *High Noon* rests, in fact, on two things, both quite superficial in relation to what the film actually is: its strict observation of the unities (which it never lets us forget), and its "Message." Its message is really its whole *raison d'être*.

Rio Bravo is the most traditional of films. The whole of Hawks is immediately behind it, and the whole tradition of the Western, and behind that is Hollywood itself. If I were asked to choose a film that would justify the existence of Hollywood, I think it would be *Rio Bravo*. Hawks is at his most completely personal and individual when his work is most firmly traditional: the more established the foundations, the freer he feels to be himself. Everything in *Rio Bravo* can be traced back to the Western tradition, yet everything in it is essential Hawks—every character, every situation, every sequence expresses him as surely as every detail in an Antonioni film expresses Antonioni.

List the stock types of Western convention, and your list will almost certainly include the following:

1. Hero: strong, silent, infallible.
2. Hero's friend: flawed, fallible, may let him down or betray him (through cowardice, avarice, etc.).
3. Woman of doubtful virtue, works or sings in saloon, gambles; will probably die saving hero's life.

4. Nice girl, schoolteacher or farmer's daughter, open-air type, public-spirited; will marry hero when he settles down.
5. Hero's comic assistant, talks too much, drinks.
6. Singing cowboy, plays guitar.
7. Comic Mexican, cowardly, talks too much, gesticulates.

In six of these seven stock types we can recognize the basis of the six leading characters of *Rio Bravo*; only the clean-living farmer's daughter is missing. These stock figures are used without the slightest self-consciousness or condescension. Hawks builds on these traditional foundations; he also builds on his actors, exploring and using their particular resources and limitations creatively. Just as *To Have and Have Not* gave us the fullest expression of Bogart, so here John Wayne, Dean Martin, Walter Brennan, and others are able to realize themselves, to fulfil the potentialities of their familiar screen *personae*. The extraordinary thing is that, while they can all be referred back to traditional Western types and to the personalities of the actors, the characters of *Rio Bravo* are at the same time entirely and quintessentially Hawksian, unmistakable in their behavior, their attitudes, their dialogue. The film offers, I think, the most complete expression we have had of Hawks himself, the completest statement of his position. There are no clichés in *Rio Bravo*.

The complex flavor of the film can be partly defined in terms of apparent contradictions: it is strongly traditional yet absolutely personal; it is the most natural of Westerns, all the action and interrelationships developing organically from thematic germs that are themselves expressed as actions, yet it is also stylized; if one looks at it dispassionately, one becomes aware of an extreme austerity—a few characters, the barest of settings, no concessions to spectacle (with the exception of the dynamite at the end) or prettiness, yet if one submits to the atmosphere and "feel" of the film one is chiefly aware of great richness and warmth. These characteristics are all very closely interconnected. It is the traditional qualities of the Western that allow Hawks to make a film so stylized in which we are so little aware, until we stand back and think about it, of stylization; the stylization and the austerity are but two ways of naming the same thing; the richness and warmth emanate from Hawks's personality, which pervades the whole; and it is the traditional and stylized form that sets him free to express himself with the minimum of constraint or interference.

The term "traditional," applied to the Western, can mean two things, and two very different kinds of Western. The genre gives great scope to the director with a feeling for America's past, for the borderline of history and myth, the early stages of civilization, primitive, precarious, and touching. But the genre also offers a collection of convenient conventions which allow the director to escape from the trammels of contemporary surface reality and the demand for verisimilitude, and express certain fundamental human urges or explore themes personal to him. If the classic Westerns of John Ford, with their loving and nostalgic evocation of the past, are the supreme examples of the first kind, *Rio Bravo* is the supreme example of the second. The distinction, obvious enough yet very important, can be exemplified by comparing the town in Ford's *My Darling Clementine* with the town in *Rio Bravo*. Ford's Tombstone is created in loving detail to convey precisely that sense of primitive civilization against the vastness and impersonality of nature, the profound respect for human endeavour and human achievement exemplified in even the simplest of men that is so characteristic of this director: on the one hand the Bon Ton Tonsorial Parlour and the honeysuckle-scented hair-spray, the tables in rows neatly laid with cloths in the dim hotel dining-room; on the other, the vast expanses of wilderness from which strange-shaped rocky projections grandly rise. Ford places his community against the wilderness, the wooden hotel, the skeletal wooden church tower, the dancers on the uncovered church floor unselfconsciously enjoying themselves under the sky, surrounded on all sides by the vast emptiness of desert.

There is nothing like this in *Rio Bravo*. Here the whole Ford theme of the defense of civilized order and civilized values against destructive elements is compressed into the single strong reaction evoked so powerfully by the murder, brutal, gratuitous, stupid, that precipitates the entire action. Hawks' town consists of jail, hotel, saloons, and rows of unadorned and inconspicuous house-fronts; inhabitants appear only when the narrative demands their presence, and there is never the least attempt to evoke that sense of community that is one of the finest and most characteristic features of the work of Ford. If a barn contains agricultural implements, they are there to provide cover in a gun-fight, not to suggest a background of agricultural activity; if the barn is littered with dust and straw, this is not to create atmosphere or a sense of place, but simply to use to blind a character momentarily. Every item of decor is strictly functional to the action. The social background is kept to the barest minimum below which we would be *aware* of stylization. Even the jail and hotel which are the two main centres of the action are not felt as having any real social function (no one seems to stay in the hotel unless the plot requires them: mainly only Angie Dickinson); but there is a certain unobtrusive symbolic opposition between them (women tend to dominate in the hotel, and are excluded from the jail, where a miniature all-male society develops in isolation). The bar in which the action begins is so neutral in atmosphere that it scarcely registers on the spectator as a "presence": Hawks uses it neither to suggest any potential fineness of civilization (however primitive) nor to create a background of incipient violence and disorder: it is just a bar. Neither is there any attempt at "period" evocation: the costumes, while not obtrusively stylized, are quite neutral in effect.

The result of all this is twofold. It frees Hawks from all obligation to fulfil the demands of surface naturalism, the accumulated convention of the Western tradition allowing him the simplest of frameworks which can be taken on trust; and this enables him to concentrate attention on the characters and their relationships, and the characteristic attitudes and themes developed through those relationships, to an extent impossible in an outdoor Western: we feel far more intimate with the characters of *Rio Bravo* than with those of *Red River*, let alone *The Big Sky*. The neutral background of the opening scene throws the initial confrontation between Wayne and Martin into forceful relief. But it would be a mistake to see the stark simplicity of setting in this film as *merely* a convenience. It has also, and more importantly, an expressive function, providing a perfect environment for the stoicism that characterizes Hawks' attitude to life. The action of *Rio Bravo* is played out against a background hard and bare, with nothing to distract the individual from working out his essential relationship to life. The virtual removal of a social framework—the relegating of society to the function of a *pretext*—throws all the emphasis on the characters' sense of *self*: on their need to find a sense of purpose and meaning not through allegiance to any developing order, but within themselves, in their own instinctual needs.

The value of existing conventions is that they not only give you a firm basis to build on but arouse expectations in the spectator which can be creatively cheated. We can study this principle in any art form in any period where a highly developed tradition is available to the artist. One can see it very clearly in Mozart: much of the freshness of his music, its ability continually to surprise and stimulate the listener into new awareness, derives from his use of the "conventional" language of the age in order to arouse and then cheat expectations—from a constant tension between the conventional background and the actual notes written. The effect depends very much on our awareness of the background, which needn't necessarily be a *conscious* awareness. This tension between foreground and background, between the conventions of the Western and what Hawks actually does with them, is everywhere apparent in *Rio Bravo*. It will be immediately evident, for anyone who has seen the film, in the relationship of the actual characters on whom the film is built to the stereotypes I listed above. Consider, for example, how Hawks uses John Wayne—both his qualities and his limitations. He is the archetypal Western hero, strong, silent, infallible. His taciturnity becomes the occasion for humour (especially in the scenes with Angie Dickinson) which is dependent partly on our awareness of John T. Chance as a genre-character; at the same time, the concept of stoical heroism Wayne embodies provides the film with one of its major touchstones for behaviour. For all the sophistication and the unobtrusive but extreme virtuosity, Hawks' art here has affinities, in its unselfconsciousness, its tendency to deal directly with basic human needs, its spontaneous-intuitive freshness, with folk-song: consider, for instance, the refusal to identify most of the characters with anything beyond descriptive-evocative nicknames: Dude, Feathers, Stumpy, Colorado . . . even Chance *sounds* like a nickname. Colorado has a surname somewhere, but who remembers it? One feels the characters as coming from a folk-ballad rather than from any actual social context: they have that kind of relationship to reality.

Feathers is the product of the union of her basic "type"—the saloon girl—and the Hawks woman, sturdy and independent yet sensitive and vulnerable, the equal of any man yet not in the least masculine. The tension between background (convention) and foreground (actual character) is nowhere more evident. We are very far here from the brash "entertainer" with a heart of gold who dies (more often than not) stopping a bullet intended for the hero. Angie Dickinson's marvelous performance gives us the perfect embodiment of the Hawksian woman, intelligent, resilient, and responsive. There is a continual sense of a woman who really grasps what is important to her. One is struck by the beauty of the character, the beauty of a living individual responding spontaneously to every situation from a secure centre of self. It is not so much a matter of characterization as the communication of a life-quality (a much rarer thing). What one most loves about Hawks, finally, is the aliveness of so many of his people.

Stumpy (Walter Brennan) and Carlos (Pedro Gonzalez-Gonzalez) are brilliant variants on the Western's traditional "comic relief" stock types. Both are so completely integrated, not only in the action, but in the overall moral pattern, that the term "comic relief" is ludicrously inadequate to describe their function. With Stumpy, as with Chance Wayne, the traditional figure merges indistinguishably into the personality of the actor. Brennan's *persona* of garrulous and toothless old cripple has been built up in numerous other films (some of them Hawks'—*To Have and Have Not, Red River*). Hawks' method with Brennan/ Stumpy is the same as with Wayne/Chance: the character is pushed to an extreme that verges on parody. With Chance this has the effect of testing the validity of the values the *persona* embodies by exposing them to the possibility of ridicule. With Stumpy the effect is dual: on the one hand we have Brennan's funniest and richest, most completely realized impersonation; on the other, the character's position in the film ceases to be marginal (as "comic relief" suggests). His garrulity gradually reveals itself as a cover for fear and a sense of inadequacy; it plays an essential part in the development of the action, contributing to Dude's breakdown. With Stumpy, humor and pathos are inseparable. The response the characterization evokes is remarkably complex: he is funny, pathetic, maddening, often all at the same time; yet, fully aware of his limitations, we never cease to respect him.

Carlos raises a more general problem: what some critics have described as Hawks's racialist tendencies. I feel myself that Hawks is entirely free of racial feeling; with Carlos, with the Dutchman in *Only Angels Have Wings*, with the French-Canadians in *The Big Sky*, he is simply taking over genre-figures (and often the character-actors associated with them) and building on them. One can say that the very existence of such stock figures is itself insulting, and this is fair enough; one can, I suppose, go on from that to complain that Hawks is unthinkingly helping to perpetuate the insult; but that is rather different from finding actual racial malice in his attitude. He is simply—and very characteristically—making use of the conventions (and the actors) that are to hand, and not questioning their initial validity. He takes the stock figure of the comic, cowardly, gesticulating, garrulous Mexican and, by eliminating the cowardliness while playing up the excitability, builds up a character whose dauntlessness and determination win our sympathy and respect even as we laugh at him. Hawks's handling not only revivifies and humanizes the stock type, but greatly increases his dignity and (moral!) stature.

But it is the figure of the Hero's Fallible Friend that is most fully worked on and transformed in *Rio Bravo*. Significantly, perhaps, this is the least stereotyped, the most uncertain and unpredictable, of the traditional Western ingredients. What I have in mind, however, is a character the variations on which the reader will have little difficulty in recognizing, whose function is usually to act as a foil to the hero, to set off his integrity and incorruptibility. Usually, he falls from grace either through weakness, personal inadequacy, or (more often perhaps) his betrayal of the hero, and gets killed. The characters played by Arthur Kennedy in two of Anthony Mann's excellent Westerns, *Bend of the River* and *The Man from Laramie*, are interesting variants on the basic type; Lloyd Bridges in *High Noon* is another example. A part of this function—a foil to set off the hero's moral infallibility—is still clearly operative in *Rio Bravo*; but Dude takes on such importance in the film that it becomes a question at times who is a foil for whom. Hawks says *Rio Bravo* is really Dean Martin's picture; and if one disagrees, it's not because it's John Wayne's, but because what gives *Rio Bravo* its beauty is above all the interaction of all the parts, the sense that its significance arises from the ensemble, not from any individual character in isolation. Otherwise Hawks (who said of the ending of *Red River* that he couldn't see the sense of killing people off unnecessarily) exactly reverses the Fallible Friend's usual progress: instead of decline and betrayal, we have a movement (despite setbacks) towards salvation. And it is very important that the first step in that salvation is the mainspring of the film's whole action: it is typical of Hawks that everything should hang, ultimately, on a matter of *personal* responsibility, not social duty.

Rio Bravo, then, is firmly rooted in a certain Hollywood tradition, and awareness of the tradition and its conventions can help to enrich our response to it. Nevertheless, it is equally true to say that the film can be understood without reference to "the Western" at all. It is as firmly rooted in Hawks' own past. Hawks has never rejected his past, and never really left it behind. In a sense, *Rio Bravo* subsumes almost everything he had done previously (without, of course, making the other films redundant). The expository first few minutes, where the situation from which all the action develops, and the film's central relationship, are established without a word being spoken, constitute, whether intentionally or not, a homage to the silent cinema that takes us right back to Hawks' roots. The whole pattern of relationships in the film will be familiar to those who have seen *Only Angels Have Wings* and *To Have and Have Not*. Consider the following parallels between the three films: the three heroes (Grant, Bogart, Wayne) are all variations on a basic concept; the women (Arthur, Bacall, Dickinson) all share a strong family resemblance, and there are clear similarities in their relationships with the films' respective heroes. Stumpy, obviously, can be traced back to Eddie in *To Have and Have Not*: the fact that both are played by Walter Brennan makes the similarity very conspicuous. But Dude can be traced back to Eddie too, and also to Bat in *Only Angels Have Wings* (one would not readily have connected Bat and Eddie without this sense that they are both partly subsumed in Dude). Stumpy is also related to Kid in *Only Angels Have Wings*—there is the same fear of growing old and no longer being of any use. Carlos has something in common with the Dutchman in *Only Angels Have Wings* and with Frenchy in *To Have and Have Not*; further, the "responsibility" he is given of putting Feathers on the stagecoach recalls the task of putting Slim on the plane entrusted to Crickett (Hoagy Carmichael). Both fail.

What is important to note are the differences that such juxtapositions force on the attention. The quite different "feel" of the three films is largely determined by the differences between their heroes. Grant in *Only Angels Have Wings* is much younger than the other two men, and strikes one as essentially more vulnerable (he is I think the only Hawks hero who ever cries), less finally formed by experience, his maturity and balance less secure. Hence the more extreme and drastic—almost exhibitionistic—nature of his rejection of sentimentality: it almost becomes the rejection of feeling itself, a trait criticized and qualified during the film. With the other two, especially Wayne, we are made aware of limitations rather than imperfections. Also, while Wayne and Bogart are both confronted with the *possibility* of their associates' death or collapse, Grant is the only one confronted with death itself. The possibility of desperation, which seems always, almost invisibly, to underlie the good-humored surface of the adventure films, is much more apparent in *Only Angels Have Wings* than in the later works, and it is largely the nature of the protagonist that makes this possible.

Bogart, on the other hand, of the three is the one most completely in command of the situations he finds himself in. Wayne appears to be in command; but a leading point of *Rio Bravo*—it amounts almost to a "running gag"—is that he isn't: his safety and success depend at every crisis on the timely intervention of others. *To Have and Have Not* and *Rio Bravo* are probably the two Hawks films which are closest to each other (if one excepts *Ball of Fire* and its inferior remake *A Song is Born*): the likeness of *El Dorado* to *Rio Bravo* may be more immediately obvious, but it proves on closer acquaintance also more superficial. *Rio Bravo* and *To Have and Have Not* give us closely parallel patterns of character-relationships, and even stretches (in the Bogart/Bacall and Wayne/Dickinson exchanges) of almost identical dialogue. The real difference between them rests not on obvious differences of location and plot-twists, but on the different relationship of the hero to the total work. In fact, the more one thinks about the three films, the more different they seem.

The wordless first minutes of the film are a good example of Hawks' use of actions to speak for themselves. Why does Dude strike Chance down? Why does Chance, despite his injury, so rashly—on the face of it hopelessly—follow and try to arrest Joe Burdett? Why does Dude help him? We feel we know the answers to all these questions, though they are never spelt out. All are essential to the film, and to what Hawks stands for.

The flooring of Chance establishes the basis on which Dude's whole development is built—his reluctance to be dragged up from his gutter when it is so much easier to sink further; and the resentment of the fallen man for the apparently infallible. Chance's single-handed attempt at arresting Joe Burdett in a saloon full of Joe's friends gives us a perfect image of the Hawks hero. There is no element of showing-off nor of self-willed martyrdom: Chance's attitude is rooted in a personal need for self-respect, which demands that an action that must be done be done unquestioningly, without fuss, and alone, even in the teeth of hopeless odds. Dude's intervention sets the pattern for the whole film, where at every crisis Chance is saved by assistance he hasn't asked for or has rejected; but its motivation is equally fundamental to the spirit of the film. When Chance prevented Dude from taking the coin from the spittoon, Dude was made conscious of his degradation; his beating-up by Joe intensifies this consciousness. Above all, he is confronted by two opposite examples: the moral disintegration of Joe, the moral integrity of Chance. On his choice between them depends his salvation as a human being: his decision to help Chance (physically) commits him to an attempt to save himself (morally and spiritually). To express all this purely through simple physical actions is profoundly characteristic of Hawks; so is the immediately established positive trend of the character development. There is nothing glib or sentimental about Hawks' treatment of his characters, but if he can possibly steer them towards salvation, he does. This spirit of generosity, the most creative human characteristic, vivifies all his best films. Even Tony Camonte, in *Scarface*, obviously an exception to any general rule one could make about Hawks' protagonists, becomes most interesting when self-awareness begins, belatedly, to break on him. It is consistently a moral rather than a psychological interest: the cure is always therapeutic, never psychoanalytical (though what happens to Dunson in *Red River* has certain affinities with the process of psychoanalysis).

If in *Rio Bravo* the traditional Western theme of the defense of civilized values is reduced to little more than a pretext, where, then, does Hawks put the emphasis? On values below the social level, but on which social values, if valid, must necessarily be built: man's innate need for self-respect or self-definition. As a motif, it will be easily seen that this pervades the film, as a unifying principle of composition. It is stated through virtually every character, usually on his first appearance, like the subject of a fugue, and developed throughout contrapuntally with fugal rigor. The film's first actions constitute a negative statement (Dude grovelling for the coin in the spittoon) and a positive one (Chance's intervention, and the ensuing arrest of Joe Burdett). The first words of Colorado (Ricky Nelson) insist on his rights as an individual: when Chance questions Pat Wheeler (Ward Bond) about him in his presence, he interrupts with, "I speak English, Sheriff, you wanna ask me." Pat, too old and unsteady to be of direct use, risking (and giving) his life to get others to help Chance; Stumpy asserting his independence by disobeying Chance's orders and standing in the jail doorway; Feathers refusing to stop gambling and wearing feathers as a way of escaping a suspect past ("That's what I'd do if I were the kind of girl that you think I am"); Carlos insisting with sudden touching dig-

Rio Bravo: *"Everything in it is essential Hawks."* Director and cast.

nity on his right to arrange matters as he pleases in his own hotel: all these constitute variants on the theme. *Variants*, not repetitions: the statements range from broad humor (Stumpy) to near tragedy (Dude): each is distinct from the others in tone and in moral weight. Examples could be multiplied throughout the film. There is a continual sense of the contrapuntal interaction of the various levels of seriousness and humor, so that great complexity of tone often results. Consider for example the way in which Stumpy's comic need to emphasize his alertness and mastery to offset his sense of disability ("Old cripples ain't wanted") precipitates Dude's breakdown when Stumpy shoots, as ordered, the moment someone fails to give the word on entering the jail (Dude, bathed and shaved, was unrecognizable). Everything in the film can be referred back to this unifying motif, yet, as always, it is nowhere given explicit statement. The density of the thematic development is increased by the element of parody introduced through the villains. Nathan Burdett (John Russell) goes to such lengths to get his brother out of jail not from motives of affection but from pride in his position: his actions are dictated, that is to say, by the desire not to lose face, a caricature of the motives for which the heroes act, rendered further invalid by the fact that he is defending a morally indefensible action. When Nathan tells Dude that everyone should have a taste of power before he dies, we are made strongly aware of the distinction between the kind of power Dude is experiencing in overcoming his tendency to disintegration, and the sort of power Burdett experiences.

By shifting the emphasis from man's responsibility to society (still there as a starting-point but no more than that) to his responsibility to himself, Hawks strips everything down to a basic stoic principle. From this follows his conception of friendship as a relationship based on mutual respect and mutual independence. Throughout the film we see Chance training Dude for the independence and self-respect that constitutes true manhood—for a relationship based on a balance of equality between free men. There are those who can see no more to this theme of close friendship between men in Hawks' films than the endorsement of a hearty, superficial matiness: nothing could be further from the truth. These relationships in Hawks almost invariably embody something strong, positive, and fruitful: at the least *(The Thing)* a warmth of mutual response; at the most *(Rio Bravo)* the veritable salvation of a human being.

Here, too, the essential things are conveyed through—or more accurately perhaps *grow out of*—physical actions. It is worth quoting Hawks here—a passage from the earlier of the two interviews he gave Peter Bogdanovich which throws much light on his methods:

> . . . we have to feel our way as we go along and we can add to a character or get a piece of business between two people and start some relationship going and then further it. In *Rio Bravo* Dean Martin had a bit in which he was required to roll a cigarette. His fingers weren't equal to it and Wayne kept passing him cigarettes. All of a sudden you realize that they are awfully good friends or he wouldn't be doing it. That grew out of Martin's asking me one day "Well, if my fingers are shaky, how can I roll this thing?" So Wayne said, "Here, I'll hand you one," and suddenly we had something going. . . .

There is a beautiful example in *Only Angels Have Wings* of the establishment of a relationship purely through actions: the scene where Cary Grant and Thomas Mitchell try to guide Joe down through the fog. Hawks builds the scene on a sense of instinctive awareness between the two men, Mitchell using his ears and Grant his voice as if they were two aspects of the same human being; at the end, when Joe has crashed, Mitchell holds out a cigarette he has rolled and Grant takes it, as if he knew it would be exactly there at exactly that moment, without looking. One moment in *Rio Bravo*, in itself very small, beautifully defines the relationship between Chance and Dude. Chance takes Dude out to patrol the streets, mainly to help him overcome the strain he is under from his need for alcohol, pauses by the paid gunman who has been appointed by Burdett to watch the jail, says "Good evening" to him and stands there till the man shuffles uneasily and moves away. We see Dude watching from the other side of the street, and from his face the impact on him of this expression of moral force, the authority that comes from integrity.

But for Hawks there comes a point where these friendships, valuable and creative as they are, reach the limit of their power to influence and affect, beyond which point the individual is alone with his own resources or sheer chance to fall back on. We saw this in the treatment of Kid's death in *Only Angels Have Wings*; in *Rio Bravo* Dude's salvation rests ultimately, not on Chance, but on chance. At the climax of his relapse, when he has failed in his responsibilities and decided to hand in his badge, he clumsily pours out a glass of whisky, nerves gone, hands trembling helplessly: it is his moment of defeat, from which it seems likely that he will never recover. Chance's example, combined with his stoic refusal to indulge him, no longer reaches him. Then, as he raises the glass, the "Alamo" music starts up again from the saloon across the street, and we see its immediate implications ("No quarter!"—it is being played on Burdett's orders) and its heroic associations strike him. He pauses, then pours the whisky back into the thin-necked bottle unfalteringly—"Didn't spill a drop." It is his moment of victory, and one of the great moments of the cinema. Its power to move derives partly from its context (it is, after all, one of the central moments in a film single-mindedly concerned with self-respect), partly from the irony (the tune played to undermine courage in fact has the opposite effect), and partly on our sense of the precariousness of everything.

One of the concerns common to *Red River* and *Rio Bravo*—though it takes very different forms in the two films—is a preoccupation with heroism, the conditions necessary to it, and the human limitations that accompany those conditions. This will be obvious enough in the earlier film, with its examination of the limits of the acceptability of Dunson's ruthlessness. The concept of the hero in *Rio Bravo*—of Hawks' attitude to him—may at first sight appear less complex, in that Chance is presented throughout as morally infallible. Yet Hawks' conception here is subtler. Without qualifying our sense of moral infallibility, Hawks defines in the course of the action the limitations that not only accompany it but are to some extent the conditions for its existence. Consider, for example, the song sequence, one of the film's focal points (it is often regarded as an irrelevance, forced into the action to give Ricky Nelson something to sing). It occurs just after Dude's triumph over his weakness, which in its turn was preceded by Colorado's intervention, his ceasing to "mind his own business," in the

The song sequence: "A bond of fellow-feeling through the shared experience of the music."

flower-pot scene. Earlier, his refusal to commit himself helped to make possible the murder of his boss, Pat Wheeler: Colorado, like Dude, was guilty of a failure of responsibility. In the song sequence he, Dude, and Stumpy sit in a circle in the jail, Stumpy accompanying on the harmonica while the other two sing. It is perhaps the best expression in Hawks' work of the spontaneous-intuitive sympathy which he makes so important as the basis of human relations. The compositions and the editing (by making us aware of the exchange of glances) as well as the acting contribute gradually to link the three men in a bond of fellow-feeling through the shared experience of the music. Throughout it, Chance stands outside the circle looking on, a paternally approving smile on his face, but none the less excluded from the common experience. The three physically or morally fallible men—cripple, reformed drunk, boy who failed once in his responsibility—are able to achieve a communion which the infallible man is denied, excluded by his very infallibility.

More obviously, Chance's limitations are revealed in his relationship with Feathers. For, if *Rio Bravo* as a whole is a summing-up of Hawks' adventure films, its love relationship, with the repeated discomfiture of the hero, succinctly recapitulates Hawksian comedy, and the film is enormously enriched by the interaction of the two. It is the first time in Hawks' work that this kind of relationship, so basic to the comedies, appears in an adventure film. Certainly the Grant/Arthur and Bogart/Bacall relationships in *Only Angels Have Wings* and *To Have and Have Not* have points in common with it; but Grant and Bogart, while they may have *resisted* their women for a time, were always able to handle them. *Rio Bravo* marks the beginning of a tendency (here kept beautifully under control and in balance) to satirize the hero—a tendency carried further with Wayne in *Hatari!*, and taking different forms in the parodistic "Wildcat Jones" song of *Red Line 7000* and in *El Dorado*, where the challenge comes not from women but from age.

Feathers' first appearance constitutes a humorous inversion of the fugue theme—Chance, the seemingly invulnerable, almost mythic figure of the "strong, silent man," finding his dignity abruptly undermined when the scarlet bloomers ordered for Carlos' wife are held up against him for Carlos' approval, and the woman greets him with, "Those things have great possibilities, Sheriff, but not on you." She has to take the initiative throughout their relationship; but—and this is what makes it so different from the man-woman relationship in, say, *I Was a Male War Bride*—its development is repeatedly given impetus by her attempts to drive him to establish authority over her, thereby completing his mastery of his world. Feathers, in fact, trains Chance rather as Chance trains Dude—trains him for a relationship of spiritual equals, for it is always clear that the establishment of male authority will be a matter of voluntary surrender on her part. It is true that Hawks never shows his man-woman relationships developing beyond a certain point; nevertheless, the relationship reached at the end of *Rio Bravo* carries a beautiful and satisfying sense of maturity, with both partners strong enough to preserve a certain independence and to come together on terms of equality. Again, it is a relationship of free people, each existing from an established centre of self-respect. The final scene between them, where Chance "tells her he loves her" by ordering her not to go down to the saloon to sing in the very revealing "entertainer's" costume which she wore before she knew him, far from seeming an anti-climax after the gun-and-dynamite showdown with Burdett and his men, is the true climax of the film. The lightly humorous treatment shouldn't blind us to its underlying seriousness and beauty.

There is a sense in which Chance's independence and self-sufficiency is illusory. He goes through the film systematically rejecting the help of others; yet every crisis without exception, from the arrest of Joe Burdett on, would end in disaster were it not for the unsolicited intervention of others. Without the cripple, the drunk, the comic Mexican, the teenage boy, a girl on hand to fling a well-timed flower-pot, the superman would be defeated before he had the chance to perform a single decisive action. Yet if the others are physically indispensable to him, it is never in doubt that Chance is spiritually indispensable to them. Remove him from the film, and you would be left largely with human wreckage; for it is abundantly clear that it is Chance, partly by direct influence, partly by example, by the very fact of his existence, who gives meaning, coherence, and integrity to the lives of those around him. As a concrete embodiment of the Hawksian values, he is the nucleus round which the others can organize themselves, without which there would be no possibility of order.

I am aware that this account of *Rio Bravo* is open to one serious objection: anyone reading it, with its talk of fugues, of stylistic and structural rigour, of moral seriousness, will be totally unprepared for the consistently relaxed, delightful, utterly unpretentious film that *Rio Bravo* is. In fact, when it first came out, almost nobody noticed that it was in any sense a serious work of art. Furthermore, it would be a great mistake to assume that there is any split here between the relaxed tone and the serious content—that Hawks has "something to say," a "message," and has deliberately (and compromisingly) made it "entertaining," sugaring the moral pill, so to speak, for the masses. One can feel confident that *Rio Bravo* is precisely the film he wanted to make. The immense good humor is, in fact, essential to the moral tone, and, together with the leisurely tempo, manifests an achieved serenity of mind; the relaxed mood of the film as a whole is never incompatible with the consistent tension in the relationships that shows the intensity of Hawks' involvement in his work.

The source of *Rio Bravo*'s richness is threefold: there is the sense of it as the product of a whole vital tradition, acting as a fruitful soil in which the film is rooted, nourishing it invisibly from beneath; and there is the sense of the film's working on many levels and for different sorts of spectator, the strength derived from its being the product and the representative of a popular art form, appealing to "groundlings" and intellectuals alike, and with no sense of discrepancy or conflict between these levels of appeal. But above all the richness derives from Hawks himself, from the warmth and generosity of his personality, pervading every scene of the film; from the essentially positive and creative nature of all the film's leading relationships; from the good humor and sanity that color every sequence. Everything in *Rio Bravo* ends happily; not a hero dies, the final battle becomes a kind of joyous celebration party for Dude's regeneration. Yet always one is aware of the extreme precariousness of everything. In the background, never very far away, is the eternal darkness surrounding human existence, against which the Hawksian stoicism shines; over everything, coloring each scene, is the marvellous good-natured humor and balance of Hawks when he is at his best.

RETROSPECT (1981)

···**M**y own work, and the position underlying it, have evolved considerably since the mid-60s when the book [*Howard Hawks*] was written—a development provoked partly by professional challenges (notably the work of *Screen* and the wider critical movement of which *Screen* is one representative), partly by changes in my personal life (notably my "coming out" as gay). I now see Hawks' films from a different perspective (in which Gay Liberation and Feminism have major roles); accordingly, the films change, reveal new aspects, new implications, new uses. This is not, I think, to distort the films, to twist them to particular ends. In a sense, *any* interpretation distorts, since no reading can escape particular personal/cultural emphasis. But semiology has confirmed what the more intelligent traditional criticism has always observed: that a given work of art, or a given artist, does not have a single, finite meaning that can be fixed for all time, but is the point of intersection of a multiplicity of interacting codes, hence capable of surrendering a range of meanings, the choice of which will be determined by the requirements of the situation within which work or artist is perceived.

Hawks and Hollywood Ideology

By the term "Hollywood ideology" I wish to convey the set of assumptions which classical Hollywood cinema tends *overall* to reproduce and reinforce. I do not mean to suggest that it corresponds closely to the ways in which individual Americans live and think or to the ways in which individual films actually work (if the latter were true, one would not need to bother oneself with Hollywood beyond the sort of cursory blanket dismissal favoured by intellectuals prior to the 50s). But it is clear enough that Hollywood has part-created, and done much to perpetuate, a body of myth (in the sense in which Barthes uses the term in *Mythologies*) which one must feel has played a dominant role in our culture, shaping our values, assumptions and aspirations.

The simplest embodiment of this ideology is the Hays Office Code, a set of rules explicitly elaborated to protect the American Way of Life. The *need* for such a code itself testifies eloquently to the continual conflict in the Hollywood cinema between the dominant ideology and the powerful impulses driving to its subversion, which go far beyond the attempts to get away with being "naughty" to which conventional film historians and *aficionados* of Mae West tend to reduce them. The basic principles can be put quite simply: capitalism, the right to ownership; the home, the family, the monogamous couple; patriarchy, with man as adventurer/pioneer/builder/breadwinner, woman as wife/mother/educator/center of civilization (the "feminine" sensibility); the "decent" containment of sexuality/love within its structure, its permitted manifestations governed by the foregoing principles and deviation from them punished; the general sense that all problems can be resolved within the system—that, although it may be in need of a bit of reform and improvement here and there, the system is fundamentally good (natural, true) and radical change inappropriate. (Indeed, one of the main functions of this ideology is, by "naturalizing" cultural assumptions, to render alternatives literally unthinkable.)

This ideology is challenged implicitly across the whole spectrum of the Hollywood cinema, most obviously in certain genres (for example, film noir) or in the work of certain directors (for example, Sirk); though it must be said that this obviousness was not apparent to audiences when the films were made. Crucial here is the concept of "entertainment," that extraordinary two-edged weapon of the capitalist establishment. Entertainment is the means whereby the exploited are kept happy and unaware; it is also (because, by definition, not taken seriously—"it's only entertainment" is a phrase commonly used to render any further discussion superfluous and even foolish) the means whereby in disguised forms, like Freudian dreams evading the "censor" in sleep, the most subversive impulses can find expression in an apparently harmless or insignificant form.

The interest of Hawks' work—from the general ideas and attitudes abstractable from it, down to the vivid detail of performance that gives his best films their inexhaustible freshness—derives from its ambiguous relationship to the dominant Hollywood ideology. Safely contained within the "entertainment" format, and invariably discussed by their director in terms of character and action with very little thematic (let alone ideological) awareness, the films maintain this ambiguity on every level. Consider the relationship of the male groups of the adventure films to established capitalist society. Dependent upon, and supportive of, that society, the groups actually embody values which are either irrelevant or antagonistic to it. The mail-plane fliers of *Only Angels Have Wings*, the sheriff and deputies of *Rio Bravo*, the animal catchers of *Hatari!*, all nominally serve the interests of society, yet are never motivated by that aim, which is relegated to the status of pretext. The values the films celebrate—a sort of primitive existentialism rooted in notions of self-respect, personal integrity, intuitive recognition and loyalty between individuals (the account expounded in this book seems to me still to stand up)—render irrelevant the accumulation of wealth and the development of civilization.

Most striking—and so much commented on that it is unnecessary to do more than glance at it here—is the films' treatment of the whole monogamy/family/home syndrome, conspicuous mainly for its absence. Almost no Hawks film is centred on a stable marriage relationship; the one obvious exception *(Monkey Business)* is concerned, characteristically, with the release of all the impulses which "stability" represses. Children in the Hawks world are wizened little grotesques (George Winslow in *Monkey Business* and *Gentlemen Prefer Blondes* is the definitive embodiment) who seem to have sprung from nowhere: one scarcely imagines them having parents or family backgrounds. Hawks was always content to work within the established genres, and the narrative structures of the films are therefore determined overall by the ideological system the genres variously embody: they move inevitably towards the establishment of the monogamous heterosexual couple. The strength and conviction of such generic resolutions, however, are everywhere undermined by the pervasive sense of impermanence that characterizes Hawks' world. This conflict sometimes produces flaws in the films' narrative coherence, a danger that even *Rio Bravo* (still in my opinion Hawks's masterpiece, the definitive elaboration of his "world') does not escape. The final John Wayne/Angie Dickinson scene in that film is curiously redundant: the tension it appears to be resolving was resolved much earlier in the film. What the logic of the narrative demands is a further *development* of the relationship; Hawks, unable to imagine this, produces only repetition. Interestingly, the corresponding scene in *El Dorado*, resolving the Wayne/Charlene Holt relationship, is simply absent, a curious and troubling hiatus in the narrative (troubling, that is, in terms of the expectations Hollywood narrative traditionally satisfies). In the Hawks universe there is no past (except as an unfortunate experience to be got over and forgotten) and no future (everyone may be dead by tomorrow); life is lived, spontaneously and exhilaratingly, in the present....

With Hawks' women, the principle of ambiguity again operates. The clearest way to establish this is to extend the now standard comparison with women in the films of Ford. The Fordian world view provides Woman with an entirely logical and central role: she is wife and mother, at once the validation for the man's building of civilization and the guarantee of its continuance; she is essential to the transmission of values from past to future. A sequence of scenes early in *Young Mr. Lincoln* exemplifies this precisely. Lincoln, still a humble shopkeeper, encounters a family who want to trade with him: the image of the covered wagon led by the father, with the two sons inside presided over by the mother, is itself an archetypal Fordian image of order and family. The mother mentions an old barrel which "might be worth fifty cents"; the father recalls that it's full of books, which belonged to his grandfather. From this Lincoln inherits the book of the

Law (Blackstone's *Commentaries*)—the Law of patriarchy which the mother, significant-ly, is debarred from reading; *her* function has been to preserve the books in perfect con-dition, not to understand them. There follows the scene with Ann Rutledge, a scene rich in the myths of our culture. Before Ann appears, Lincoln, amid the multitudinous signi-fiers of natural fertility, has translated the legal rights and wrongs of Blackstone (the basis of Western capitalism, in effect) into universal Right and Wrong: a marvellously concise example of the naturalization of ideological assumptions. It is Ann's function not to teach but to inspire: she exemplifies the myth of the "great woman behind every great man," urging Lincoln (who alone possesses knowledge) to "make something of himself." Abruptly, Ann is dead, but ice is breaking up on the swift-flowing river and Lincoln brings the first spring flowers to her grave. It is her continuing influence that drives Lincoln on, his allegiance to her memory (as also to the memory of his mother, who is "resurrected" in Mrs Clay) being crucially important.

Hawks' attitude to women, like Ford's, cannot be separated from his attitude to death, to society, to tradition. With the Fordian address to the grave (repeated in *My Darling Clementine* and *She Wore a Yellow Ribbon*) compare the famous steak scene of *Only Angels Have Wings* ("Who's Joe?"). With Ford's insistence on the future developing out of the past, a past which must always be revered, commemorated in transmitted rit-ual, compare the Hawksian insistence on life in the present. One might, I think, claim that Ford's work embodies the traditional concept of the woman's role under patriarchy at its noblest, finest, most respectable. In Hawks' world that role has no possible place: woman is unnecessary, either as a pretext for the building of civilization or as its pre-server and transmitter. Hawks' male groups are clearly patriarchal (the leader is actually addressed as "Poppa" in, for example, *Only Angels Have Wings* and *Rio Bravo*), but they lack a crucial constituent of traditional (or Fordian) patriarchy, the notion of inheritance which gives woman her function. There lies the enormous interest of Hawks' women: they are anomalous and threatening, but *there*. The much-noted attempt to turn them into men never quite works: they remain, obstinately, men/women, demanding a recognition somewhat different from that exchanged between the males; they are a per-manent problem, as they scarcely are in Ford.

Hawks' cinema, in other words, if it never offers any positive approach towards establishing a new female consciousness, raises the problem of the woman's role as it is raised nowhere else in classical cinema, by removing or rendering irrelevant the role which the woman traditionally fills. I think it is this, as much as the desire on Hawks' part to provide male fantasy-figures, which may account for the remarkable and (whatever ideological uneasiness one may feel) perpetually fresh aliveness of so many actresses' performances in his films: the assertion of life, the refusal to be con-fined in the traditional role, repeatedly undermines the generic patterns of resolution.

Male Relationships

The interest which Hawks' work can be argued to have for Feminism is exactly paralleled by its interest for Gay Liberation. Again, there is no question whatever of the films producing a clear-cut positive image of gay relationships that could be felt to have direct political force; again, the operative word must be "ambiguity"; yet again, within the classical Hollywood context, the films raise questions, open up possibilities.

Many critics have sensed the presence of a gay subtext running right through Hawks' output. Its presence would, of course, have been vehemently denied by Hawks himself, though he was able to describe two of his films *(A Girl in Every Port, The Big Sky)* as "a love story between two men." A practice common to so many recent "male bonding" films (e.g. *California Split, Midnight Cowboy, Scarecrow*) whereby the possible homosexual implications of the heroes' relationships are disowned by being projected on to an effeminate, ridiculous or vicious minor character, is fully anticipated in *Fig Leaves. A Girl in Every Port* stands out as the one film in which a close male relationship is finally confirmed, the girl (Louise Brooks) being dismissed from the film. Elsewhere, the progress is towards a heterosexual resolution *(The Big Sky, Red River, Rio Bravo, El Dorado)* or the death of one of the men *(Dawn Patrol,* Thomas Mitchell in *Only Angels Have Wings).* There are numerous striking examples of homosexual symbolism in Hawks' films, of which the most overt is perhaps the Montgomery Clift/John Ireland shooting contest in *Red River* (a scene unfortunately cut from the British release prints), for which the men exchange guns, with clear mutual admiration (Ireland subsequently gives as his reason for joining the cattle drive the hope that he may get Clift's gun some day). The way Hawks plays with, then rejects, homosexual attraction is neatly epitomized in a tiny, characteristic moment in *The Thing,* difficult to convey in words because it depends entirely on the way two men look at, and smile at, each other: the moment where the sergeant (Dewey Martin) manueuvres the captain (Kenneth Tobey) into shortening the watches over the monster in the ice and says, "I think you're right, Captain." The looks exchanged and the smile of mutual affection are both intimate and held; then the captain looks across at the woman Nicky (who has a male name and wears trousers), and crosses the room to join her.

One also notes the procession of young men (particularly in Hawks's later work) who have the appearance of gay male icons and whose role invariably involves a close intimacy with the hero, carrying the constant (if constantly submerged) impression of being a potential alternative to the woman: Montgomery Clift in *Red River*, Dewey Martin in *The Big Sky* and *The Thing*, Ricky Nelson in *Rio Bravo*, James Caan in *El Dorado*.

Reversals

The sexual relationship in Hawks' work have finally to be seen in the context of its most curious and consistent phenomenon, the obsession with reversal patterns.

...The master reversal-pattern, and surely the key to this phenomenon in Hawks, is of course that of male and female. In *Fig Leaves* there is a mock-courtship scene in which one of the men plays the woman's role. Men wear women's clothes in *Bringing Up Baby, I Was a Male War Bride, Monkey Business, Gentlemen Prefer Blondes* and, almost, *Rio Bravo* (the red bloomers held up against John Wayne). In *The Big Sky* a huge Frenchman pretends to be a woman in a dance on the ship's deck. In *His Girl Friday* Rosalind Russell literally plays the "man's role." Women wear masculine clothes in *I Was a Male War Bride*, *The Thing* and *Hatari!*; according to Hawks (*Wide Angle*, Summer 1976), he gave von Sternberg the idea of dressing Dietrich in men's clothes for her first stage appearance in *Morocco*, including embryonically, the exchange with a woman in the audience—a scene rich in bisexual connotations. A distinction needs to be made here. Consistently in the films it is funny for men to dress as woman, but attractive and enhancing for women to dress as men; the men are in drag, the women in work-clothes or uniform. Nevertheless, the implication of the interchangeability or role reversal is clearly there.

One less obvious but highly suggestive example is worth registering in detail: the interchangeability of Angie Dickinson in *Rio Bravo* and James Caan in *El Dorado*. Both are travelling people, and gamblers; both are given the same little bit of business with a pack of cards; both are identified by idiosyncratic clothing (Caan's hat, Dickinson's feathers); both stay on (in the long-standing tradition of Hawks heroines—cf. *Only Angels Have Wings* and *To Have and Have Not*) after Wayne has dismissed them; both simultaneously attract and exasperate him; both have the same line, "I always make you mad, don't I?" That Caan, rather than Charlene Holt, is the film's replacement for Dickinson and *almost* becomes the love-interest may help to account for the absence of the expected, really obligatory, John Wayne/Charlene Holt resolution at the end, especially as the Caan character's heterosexual relationship is also left unconfirmed. One has the sense that Hawks was simply unable to close the film; he pulls back on the "safe" buddy-relationship of Wayne and Mitchum.

In Hawks' world everything is potentially reversible or interchangeable; that is the real meaning of the chaos so ambivalently viewed, through the dual perspective of the adventure films and the comedies. The central, though always suppressed or disguised, drive of his work overall is towards the ultimate in interchangeability, bisexuality—the final breakdown of the established social order, the release, at once terrifying and exhilarating, of what society most fundamentally represses.

James Caan in El Dorado: *"Almost the love interest."*

Classicism and Containment

There is a brief sequence in *The Thing*, showing the flight back to base from the location where the flying saucer has been inadvertently destroyed and the monster dug out of the ice. A shot establishing the situation—a general view of the plane's interior—is followed by a sequence of five shots which is perfectly symmetrical in structure. Shots 1 and 5 show the captain and navigator in the cockpit, the camera filming them from the front; shots 2 and 4 are the reverse of these, looking from inside the plane into the cockpit, as the men discuss the nature and significance of the creature in the ice. The central, pivotal, shot shows the block of ice, the husky dogs uneasy around it. The sequence begins with light banter between the men, and ends with a joke involving the repetition of the long number of a bulletin. The banter and the joke *contain* the brief, central moment of terror, providing a means of either denying or distancing the threat of the unknown ("chaos").

The sequence can be taken as the epitome of Hawks' classicism, which is both the classicism of Hollywood (invisible technique, symmetry, orderly and logical narrative, economy of means) and an attitude to life. Classicism is Hawks' means of containing the chaos to which his work points, and which the comedies ambivalently celebrate.

The *Rio Bravo* song sequence can stand as the perfect enactment of the working of this classicism/containment in relation to male love or attraction in Hawks' work. The first song ("My rifle, my pony and me") opens with a close-up of Dean Martin, singing unaccompanied, as if he were alone; when the camera draws back to reveal the presence of the other men, the song develops into a "love duet" for Martin and Ricky Nelson. The editing excludes both Walter Brennan and Wayne during this, concentrating attention on the intimate exchange of looks between the two—those looks of mutual admiration and affection that recur throughout Hawks' work. When the song ends, Stumpy/Brennan demands ". . . something I can join in," and we have the folk song "Cindy" with its communal refrain: the potentially "dangerous" love-relationship is contained, and redefined, by the integration of the couple in the group, the sequence moving to a final group shot that unites the three men and Wayne, paternally looking on.

What I have called "containment" Andrew Britton calls "repression": one's final attitude to Hawks may well depend on the distinction between the two terms. I don't think one has any right to demand that an artist's work reflect or reinforce one's own ideology; one wants rather to define the relationship between them. Hawks' work is *both* progressive and conservative, at once opening up possibilities of "chaos" and formally containing them. It cannot be claimed that Hawks' work embodies a viable alternative to established Western culture, but it would be quite unreasonable to demand that it should: such a project has never been a necessary function of art. What it represents is an inexhaustibly fascinating and suggestive *intervention*, which raises the most fundamental questions about the nature of our culture and the ideological assumptions that structure it. Apparently safely contained within Hollywood Classicism and the "entertainment" syndrome, its implications throw everything open, put everything into question.

This essay owes much to the influence of Andrew Britton and Richard Dyer, though both would probably disagree with its conclusions.

BUDD BOETTICHER

Lee Russell (1965)

Budd Boetticher is not a well-known director; indeed, even such a knowledgeable critic as Andrew Sarris ranks him among "esoterica." Most critics would be inclined to dismiss him as responsible for no more than a few run-of-the-mill Westerns, hardly distinguishable from his equally anonymous fellows—a typical Hollywood technician, a name which flashes past on the credits and is soon forgotten. This would be to misjudge Boetticher. His works are, in fact, distinctive, homogeneous in theme and treatment, and of more than usual interest. He is an author and well aware of it himself; he is lucid about his own films. It is high time critics were equally lucid.

Budd Boetticher's first contact with the movies was in 1941, when Mamoulian went to Mexico to make *Blood and Sand*. Boetticher had already been in Mexico for some years—he went there to recuperate after an American football season—and while there had taken up bull-fighting, eventually becoming a professional. Mamoulian hired him, as an American and a torero, as the technical advisor on bull-fighting for his film. Boetticher became as enthusiastic about movies as he had about bull-fighting and, after three years as messenger boy and assistant director, made his first film, *One Mysterious Night*, in 1944. For a number of years he made ephemeral quickies; his *prise de conscience* as an author in his own right did not come till 1951, when he made *The Bullfighter and The Lady*. For this film, he changed his signature from Oscar Boetticher Jr. to Budd Boetticher; he himself has recognized it as the turning point in his career. Even then, it was another five years before Boetticher found the conditions which really suited him. The breakthrough came in 1956 with *Seven Men from Now*; his first film for Ranown productions, *The Tall T*, came the next year. During these two films the team was assembled with which Boetticher was to make his most characteristic work; Randolph Scott as star, Harry Joe Brown as producer, Burt Kennedy as script-writer. *Seven Men from Now* was also Boetticher's first film to get critical acknowledgement: Andre Bazin reviewed it in *Cahiers du Cinema* under the head, "An Exemplary Western." Boetticher made five Westerns with Ranown; they are the core of his achievement. Finally in 1960, he made his most celebrated work, *The Rise and Fall of Legs Diamond* for Warner. To make this film, he had to tear up a Philip Yordan script in Yordan's face and shoot in such a way that the producer could not puzzle out how to do the montage. Exasperated, he left Hollywood, determined, in future, to work under conditions of his own choice. Since then he has made only the unreleased *Arruza* in Mexico, after considerable difficulties. He now has numerous projects but uncertain prospects.

The typical Boetticher-Ranown Western may seem very unsophisticated. It begins with the hero (Randolph Scott) riding leisurely through a labyrinth of huge rounded rocks, classic badlands terrain, and emerging to approach an isolated swing-station. Then, gradually, further characters are made known; usually, the hero proves to be on a mission of vengeance. He and his small group of travelling companions, thrown together by accident, have to contend with various hazards: bandits, Indians, etc. The films develop, in Andrew Sarris' words, into floating poker games, where every character takes turns at bluffing about his hand until the final showdown. The hero expresses a "weary serenity," has a constant patient grin and willingness to brew up a pot of coffee, which disarms each adversary in turn as he is prised away from the others. Finally, after the showdown, the hero rides off again through the same rounded rocks, still alone, certainly with no exaltation after his victory.

At first sight, these Westerns are no more than extremely conservative exercizes in a kind of Western which has been outdated. This impression is strengthened by Randolph Scott's resemblance to William Hart, noted immediately by Bazin. The Westerns of Ince and Hart were simple moral confrontations, in which good vanquished evil; since then, the Western has been enriched by more complex sociological and psychological themes. John Ford's *The Iron Horse* (1924) already presaged new developments, which he himself was to carry through: the Western became the key genre for the creation of a popular myth of American society and history. Today, Westerns as diverse as Penn's *The Left-Handed Gun*, almost a psychological study of delinquency, or Fuller's *Run of The Arrow* have completely transformed the genre. Bazin saw, in Boetticher and Anthony Mann, a parallel tendency towards the increasingly subtle refinement of the pristine form of the genre; it cannot be denied that there was a strain of nostalgia for innocence in his attitude. In fact, Boetticher's works are something more than Bazin's expressions of classicism, the "essence" of a tradition, undistracted by intellectualism, symbolism, baroque formalism, etc. The classical form which he chooses is the form which best fits his themes: it presents an a-historical world in which each man is master of his own individual destiny. And it is the historic crisis of individualism which is crucial to Boetticher's preoccupations and his vision of the world.

"I am not interested in making films about mass feelings. I am for the individual." The central problem in Boetticher's films is the problem of the individual in an age—increasingly collectivized—in which individualism is no longer at all self-evident, in which individual action is increasingly problematic and the individual no longer conceived as a value per se. This problem is also central, as has often been pointed out, to the work of such writers as Hemingway and Malraux (Boetticher has himself expressed his sympathy for aspects of Hemingway). This crisis in individualism has led, as Lucien Goldmann has shown, to two principal problems: the problem of death and the problem of action. For individualism, death is an absolute limit which cannot be transcended; it renders the life which precedes it absurd. How then can there be any meaningful individual action during life? How can individual action have any value, if it cannot have transcendent value because of the absolutely devaluing limit of death? These problems are to be found in Boetticher's films. Indeed, Boetticher insists on putting them very starkly; he permits no compromise with any kind of collectivism, any kind of transcendence of the individual. Two examples will show this.

Boetticher has made only one war film, *Red Ball Express*, with which he was extremely dissatisfied. He later contrasted the Western in which individuals (the story must be kept very personal) accept to face dangers in which they risk death, in order to achieve a definite goal, with the war film "in which armies are flung into danger and destruction by destiny and at the command of the countries involved in the war."

"In other words, I prefer my films to be based on heroes who want to do what they are doing, despite the danger and the risk of death....In war, nobody wants to die and I hate making films about people who are forced to do such and such a thing." Courage in war is not authentic courage, because it is not authentically chosen: it is in desperate reaction. The same point comes out in *The Man From The Alamo*, about a Texan who leaves the Alamo just before the famous battle; he is branded a coward and a deserter. But for Boetticher he shows more courage than those who stayed; he made an individual choice to leave, to try and save his family in their border farmstead. He risked his life—and his repute—for a precise, personal goal rather than stay, under the pressure of mass feeling, to fight for a collective cause. He is a typical Boetticher hero. "He did his duty, which was as difficult and dangerous for him as for those who stayed." (In the same vein, Boetticher speaks of Shakespeare's *Henry V* and of the scene in which the king goes round the camp the night before the battle, when Shakespeare raises the whole issue of the personal involvement of the soldiers in the king's war.)

The risk of death is essential to any action in Boetticher's films. It is both the guarantee for the seriousness of the hero's action and the final mockery which makes that action absurd. Meaningful action is both dependent on the risk of death and made meaningless by it. Goldmann has described how, in the early novels of Malraux, a solution to this paradox is found by the total immersion of the hero in historical, collective action (the Chinese revolution) until the moment of death, not for the values of the revolution itself, quite foreign to a hero who is neither Chinese nor revolutionary by conviction, but for the opportunity it offers of authentically meaningful action. Boetticher, as we have seen, rejects this solution; he cannot identify himself, in any circumstances, with a historic cause or a collective action. He takes refuge, therefore, in an a-historical world, in which individuals can still act authentically as individuals, can still be masters of their own destiny. The goal of vengeance for a murdered wife which Boetticher's heroes have so often set themselves offers, in a society in which justice is not collectivized, the opportunity of meaningful personal action. Of course this significance is still retroactively destroyed at the moment of death. The full absurdity of death is quite ruthlessly shown in *The Tall T* in which bodies are thrown down a well—"Pretty soon, that well's going to be chock-a-block"—and in which the killer (Henry Silva) invites a victim to run for the well and see if he can get there before he is shot, "to kind of make it more interesting." The removal of an individual exactly amounts to the removal of all meaning from his life.

Of course, it is quite clear that the moral structure of Boetticher's world is utterly different from the simple moralism of Ince and Hart. There is no clear dividing line between bad and good in Boetticher's films. "All my films with Randy Scott have pretty much the same story, with variants. A man whose wife has been killed is searching out her murderer. In this way I can show quite subtle relations between a hero, wrongly bent on vengeance, and outlaws who, in contrast, want to break with their past." And, about the "bad men" in his Westerns: "They've made mistakes like everybody; but they are human beings, sometimes more human than Scott."

Randolph Scott and the hang tree from Ride Lonesome: *"an a-historical world, in which individuals can still act authentically as individuals."*

The question of good and evil is not for Boetticher a question of abstract and eternal moral principles; it is a question of individual choice in a given situation. The important thing, moreover, is the value which resides in action of a certain kind; not action to realize values of a certain kind. Evidently, this is a kind of existentialist ethic, which by its nature is impure and imperfect, but which recognizes this. Hence the irony which marks Boetticher's films and particularly his attitude to his heroes. The characters played by Randolph Scott are always fallible and vulnerable; they make their way inch by inch, not at all with the sublime confidence of crusaders. Yet it is possible for Andrew Sarris to talk of the "moral certitude" of Boetticher's heroes; in fact he is confusing the philosophical integrity which structures the films with what he takes to be the absolute moral endorsement of the hero. Boetticher sympathizes with almost all his characters; they are all in the same predicament in which the prime faults are inauthenticity and self-deception, rather than infringement of any collectively recognized code. The fact that some end up dead and some alive does not necessarily indicate any moral judgment, but an underlying tragedy which Boetticher prefers to treat with irony.

Something ought to be said about the heroes' style of action; this is not emphasized for its style in itself but as the most effective way of carrying out the action needed to achieve the goal chosen. Boetticher's heroes act by dissolving groups and collectivities of any kind into their constituent individuals. Thus, in *Seven Men From Now* and *The Tall T* the hero picks off the outlaws one by one, separating off each member of the band in turn. And in *Buchanan Rides Alone* the same method is applied to the three Agry brothers who run Agry Town, who at first grouped together against Buchanan (Randolph Scott), end up, after his prodding and prising, in conflict with each other. Similarly, in the same film, when Buchanan is about to be shot he manages to ally himself with one of the gunmen against the other, by confiding to Lafe from East Texas that all he wants is to head out and get himself a spread by the Pecos River. Buchanan's technique is, by his personal approach to Lafe, to reveal his own individuality to him so that he is no longer willing to act as an agent for somebody else or for the collectivity at large, enforced and enforcing.

Evidently, the themes and problems which I have discussed have a close connection to the ethos of bullfighting, about which Boetticher has made three films, and which is personally of great importance to him. The ethos of bullfighting also contains obvious traps and pitfalls; around it has crystallized an extremely repugnant elitism, quick to degenerate into a cult of violence, tradition, and super-humanity. Boetticher does not escape these traps. It is impossible to separate the personal encounter between the bullfighter and bull, the individual drama of action and death, from the society and social context which surrounds and exploits it. Thus, in *The Bullfighter and the Lady*, the role of the crowd, incapable itself of action, is to provoke the bullfighter into action, even when he is wounded. In this respect, the crowd in Boetticher's bullfighting movies is similar to the women in his westerns—phantoms, with no authentic significance.

"What counts is what the heroine provokes, or rather what she represents. She is the one, or rather the love or fear she inspires in the hero, or else the concern he feels for her, who makes him act the way he does. In herself, the woman has not the

"A close connection to the ethos of bullfighting." Randolph Scott, Maureen O'Sullivan, and Richard Boone in The Tall T.

slightest importance." The crowd, like the heroine, represents passivity in contrast with the hero, the bullfighter, who is the man of action. The danger is clear; it is not so unlikely that Boetticher could follow Malraux into an elitism, in which men of action are thought of as creating values.

There is much else which could be said—about Boetticher's attitude to his favorite country Mexico, for instance. But the important thing is to recognize the nature of his achievement up til now. In many ways, he is a miniaturist—he does not have great imaginative vigour or panoramic sweep or painful self-consciousness, but works on a much smaller scale and in a much lower key. In many ways, his concern with individualism is anachronistic, though less so, perhaps, in America, where old myths die hard. But it would be quite wrong to assume that, because his movies are not about the sociological and psychological problems to which we are more attuned, they are without theme or content. I realize that in this review I have committed the cardinal sin of talking about Westerns and philosophy in the same breath; I am quite unrepentant. Andre Bazin described *Seven Men From Now* as "one of the most intelligent westerns I know, but also one of the least intellectual." Boetticher, himself always a man of action (bull-fighter, horseman, etc.), does not give his movies an openly intellectual dimension; nevertheless, he has always insisted that the Western is more than cowboys and Indians, it is an expression of moral attitudes. He has always, since at least *The Bullfighter and the Lady*, taken filmmaking seriously, to the point of jeopardizing his career. And he has consistently made intelligent movies, treating—however intuitively—fundamental themes with great lucidity.

INTERVIEW WITH ANTHONY MANN

Christopher Wicking and Barrie Pattison (1969)

CW: Do you have any ideas formulated about the Western?

AM: Well, I think the reason why it's the most popular and long-lasting genre is that it gives you more freedom of action, in landscape, in passion. It's a primitive form. It's not governed by rule; you can do anything with it. It has the essential pictorial qualities; has the guts of any character you want; the violence of anything you need; the sweep of anything you feel; the joy of sheer exercise, of outdoorness. It is legend—and legend makes the very best cinema. It excites the imagination more—it's something audiences love. They don't have to say: "Oh I know about that"; they just need to feel it and be with it, because legend is a concept of characters greater than life. It releases you from inhibitions, rules. Because—how does an Indian act? How does he ride over the plains? How does a man come into a bar and shoot somebody? This doesn't happen any more. It isn't going on now, but it is a spirit, a kind of freedom of action and movement which instills itself into the minds of the audience. They say: "Oh, I wish I were in that time—isn't it fantastic what they accomplished in those days, what their dreams were, what their actions were?"

There are of course many other types of movie to be made. There are the new schools of motion pictures being made, but they limit you—for instance, Joe Losey's very good. *The Servant* is very effective, very well done—for its subject, extra-ordinarily well done and it broke new ground and many new barriers in terms of morals and so on; but it left you small and mean and petty; it didn't release you from anything; it drove home the oppression and weight of its theme rather than bursting you out of it. And this is what the Western does—it releases you, you can ride on the plains; you can capture the windswept skies; you can release your audiences and take them out to places which they never would have dreamt of.

And, more important—it releases the characters. They can be more primitive; they can be more Greek, like *Oedipus Rex* or *Antigone*, you see, because you are dealing again in a sweeping legend. This is what I love in picture making, and really what I stand for. Because *El Cid* is really a Spanish Western, and it's legend again. *Roman Empire* is even more than that. I spent a great deal of time in the snow-country, shot a whole funeral in the snow, and it's all tremendously pictorial. but it's bound by history and certain rules, because certain things have to happen. It wasn't completely a legend though it has a legendary quality.

BP: As you mentioned *Oedipus*, there's this element which starts with *Furies:* this business of the father-killer. It's in *Winchester '73, Man of the West, Man from Laramie* and Borden Chase uses it in *Backlash*. This is a thread that runs through the fifties' Westerns—tough grim subjects. Can you tell us why this should be?

AM: Well—it's also in *Roman Empire*. There he tries to kill his father's image, because this image is greater than his own. This is the story underneath the Oedipus drama. I don't know of any great man who ever had a great son. This must have been a terrible thing for the son to live with the image of his father, for although this is a love-image, it can also be a hate-image. This theme is recurrent, because it is a very strong one and, consequently, I like it—it reaches to heights and depths beyond more mundane stories.

BP: It seems that through the fifties you, John Sturges and Delmer Daves have a sort of unity of thought—setups, ideas, actors, cameramen crop up in each of your films—was there any kind of community where you all got together and talked over ideas and so on?

AM: No—actually I know them both. But we haven't spent any time together, even in a discussion of ideas. No, they are similar, but they came out very unconsciously.

CW: Back to your Westerns—from the very pure *Bend of the River*, they seem to get tougher, more cynical until in *Cimarron* the Hero, Glenn Ford, disappears and the film concentrates on Maria Schell. This is a little bit like the death of the West. If you had had your way, would you have concentrated more on the Ford character?

AM: Well, actually that whole picture was a mistake. Originally I had a wonderful idea for it, and the Metro executives agreed with me. After I had been shooting for twelve days, they decided to take the whole company indoors, so it became an economic disaster and a fiasco and the whole project was destroyed.

I wanted to show a huge plain out in the West with nothing on it, and how a

Mann directs Gary Cooper and Jack Lord in Man of the West.

group of men and women gathered at a line, and tore out across this plain and set up their stakes as claim for the land. And how a town, a city and finally a metropolis grew, all on this one piece of land. It would have been, I think, a tremendous experience for the world to see. This is how America was built. But the executives panicked. We had a couple of storms—which I shot in anyway—but they thought we'd have floods and so on, so they dragged us in and everything had to be duplicated on the set. The story had to be changed, because we couldn't do the things we wanted to. So I don't consider it a film. I just consider it a disaster.

CW: How can you have Glenn Ford die the most ignoble death of all—dying off-screen?

AM: Well, it wasn't shot that way, I promise you—there was a huge oil sequence and oil wells were blowing up and he was saving people and being very heroic. Why they ever changed it I'll never know—this was Mr. Sol Siegel, he did it behind my back, I didn't ever see it. If I'd screamed they wouldn't have bothered anyway; so I just let them destroy it at will.

CW: Do you think going out and shooting on location, doing it all physically, is the only way you can work?

AM: Yes, I think it's the only way to work anyway with films. I find by going out on location—like on *Heroes of Telemark*—that having gone up there and seen the ice lakes and the snow and so on, I can do things that I would not have done otherwise. I thought about it all, and utilized the very things that are indigenous to a country. Locations give you all sorts of ideas, if you look for them.

BP: In *Bend of the River, Man from Laramie* and *El Cid* again, you have scenes staged on the snowline—was this a way of getting more interesting shots?

AM: No, no—it shows a battling of the elements which I think is always good. You push actors and the whole company into something that is tough—if it really is tough, it can show itself on the screen much better. Certainly snow and so on is very pictorial, and you can produce all sorts of effects by it—horses breathing, the actors breathing, the difficulty of the terrain, the actual struggle one has to put forth in just doing the physical things, like climbing a mountain, say. It all adds a reality that is difficult to achieve in a studio. Things become so much more phoney indoors.

The studio isn't on your neck, nobody can control you, so you are at least able to do what you want to do—and this is wonderful, because it does give you a much greater freedom of movement and expression. They don't dare come up and see you because it would be too much hardship for them. In that sense, the more you can be left alone, the better you can make a picture.

CW: The *Winchester '73* climax is staged in the rocks, and turns up at least twice more in your films—is this adding to the drama, the idea of the elements again?

AM: Well, again there, I went out hunting for locations and, in looking over the terrain, this area excited me, because I saw all these rocks and caverns, holes and whatnot. I thought it would make a wonderful battleground between the two guys. You couldn't have a battle between two experts out in the open—they could both shoot each other like that (*snap fingers*). So you have to make it almost impossible for either of them to shoot the other, so that their expertness is doubly in use—now they also have to flush each other out, by maneuvering and cunning.

CW: You mentioned that you were able to achieve a sense of period here. Now, obviously, this is important for this kind of subject, and, in thrillers, period is inherent, because they are contemporary. But it's interesting that in your Westerns, again, one senses a period; they are set in time—towns change and grow up although it is never any explicit time. Why is this so?

AM: Well, of course, you always do try to get a feel of the period, if only because it enhances the characters and enhances the picture—in fact period can work for you. The very nature of the period can be the thing that gives you the key to the very things that you do and use to make it different. The huge six-foot blades I use in *El Cid* were of that period. So these weapons became great things for me to use. They hadn't been used before; I don't know why—maybe because once you start swinging you can't stop, and the actors have to be very careful and need to be rehearsed like in a ballet. But because you are using such a weapon, it becomes much more honest in terms of that period.

CW: Suppose somebody came to you with a script—what would be the factors to make you want or not want to do it?

AM: Well, first of all it would depend on its theme and its content. I would have to be interested in its subject matter. Now, of course, as I feel I don't *have* to make them, I want as much freedom as I can have and as much time to work on the script with the writers as I can. I want as much freedom of creativity as possible—it's not that I want it because I feel I'm the only guy that can do it, but because it's the only way to work. Every time I've had "supervision" the film has suffered. Therefore, no longer do I want it; no longer would I tolerate it; no longer would I accept it. But one has to learn the hard way.

CW: On which of your films did you have the greatest freedom?

AM: Well, let's see—I had a great deal of freedom with *Men in War* and *God's Little Acre*, *Winchester '73* and *Bend of the River*. I would say I had *no* freedom with *Cimarron* and *less* freedom (because Metro started to impose its will) with films like *Devil's Doorway* and *Tall Target*. The first one I had more freedom with was *Border Incident*, because they didn't even know what kind of animal I was.

CW: Was Fritz Lang in any way involved with *Winchester '73*?

AM: Absolutely not! At one time Fritz Lang was interested in a project written by Stuart Lake which was an historical compilation of the story of the Winchester rifle. This was at Universal, and two or three years afterwards he had not one foot of film shot, not one idea. In fact I threw everything out that he had even remotely thought about. It wasn't the kind of film I wanted to make anyway.

CW:So there's nothing of Lang's in it at all?

AM: No. Nothing. I absolutely, positively guarantee it . . . .

CW: You presumably prefer to work with a film "actor" like James Stewart, for instance, as opposed to a film personality like Victor Mature?

AM: Well, Stewart is a man who's devoted his whole life to acting and who's quite brilliant in what he does. He's very skillful and, once you start going with him, he's marvelous to work with, because he's always there; he's always anxious; he wants to be great; and this is not true of the other gentleman in question.

CW: Stewart's great moments of wild and desperate emotion in your films—being dragged through the fire in *Laramie*; shot to pieces and thrown in the river in *Far Country*; the blind anger in the saloon fight in *Winchester '73*—is this deep passion completely natural to him or do you have to dig for it?

AM: Natural to him? Within himself he has something much more burning and exciting than when you meet him personally. And he'll say: "Look, Tony, if you want me to be pulled through the fire, then I'll do it. If you want me to fight under the horses' hooves, I'll do it." This is the kind of guy he is; he likes to have to do these things. And a lot of actors don't. Mature can't get near a horse. It's a curse when they don't learn; when they're not adept at the art of riding, fencing, swimming and the other things that are necessary, which they must learn, if they don't know.

CW: How do you mold an actor to fit your requirements. How do you get Stewart to do it the first time, or Mature, or Cooper?

AM: Well, Jimmy Stewart was in a summer company I had at the Red Barn theater in Locust Valley when he'd just come out of college, so I had known him and had directed him in a couple of plays. He had seen *The Furies* and had asked for me, actually, and that's how the relationship got going again. I didn't like the property; I didn't like *Winchester* at all. This was Lang's version. I was working at Metro and everybody was pressuring me to make the fiim and I said: "I'd like to make the film, if you let me rewrite it completely. I want a new writer, new everything; I don't want the property the way it is." Finally, after a lot of haranguing, they agreed that I could do that and I brought in Borden Chase and we started from scratch on the script and it developed day by day. This is how all films are made, at least as far as I'm concerned.

Anthony Mann and James Stewart on location for The Man from Laramie.

But about actors. Naturally you have to utilize their greatest abilities and qualities, and you strengthen them if you can. You push them against something that's maybe foreign to them, but which, therefore, becomes more exciting, because you still have the same guy, but now you have him doing something that's more against his nature, so already you have a conflict of character against personality. This is good. So you have two dimensions to start with. Now, if you take him outdoors and put him into locations, you have three dimensions, because now you have all the elements fighting him. Then you pit him against some very violent pieces of action and you have a fourth dimension. Thus you build the character and situation.

CW: As you made so many films with Stewart, can it be assumed that he is your archetypal "hero"?

AM: Well no, because each film is an entirely different entity. I'd love to use him again, but I haven't had a script. I couldn't use him in *El Cid*; I couldn't use him in *God's Little Acre*, *Roman Empire*; couldn't have used him in lots of films. It has nothing to do with him; it's just the *films* are entirely out of his element.

CW: But regarding the Westerns . . . .

AM: Well, with the Westerns, he had a great quality. Gary Cooper certainly did, too. He is magnificent walking down a street with a Winchester rifle cradled in his arm, and so is Jimmy *firing* the Winchester. He studied hard at it, you know? He worked so hard his knuckles were raw with practicing, so that he could be right. And we had an expert from the Winchester Arms Company who taught him how to really *uniquely* use the gun. These are the things that give it a sense of tremendous reality. . . .

CW: How do you arrive at these tangible evocations of the mood and theme?
AM: Well, you do many things. You dramatize it by the juxtaposition of characters, putting them into situations that can drive them into that kind of a place. You know, you *look* for these places; you *look* for these things. Take *Man From Lamarie*. Out in the middle of a plain, a man is grabbed and his two arms are held and the gunmen are going to shoot his hand off. Well, it could have been done in many places, but, in the middle of this plain, it was frightening, because there was this beautiful expanse of country with all this evil going on in it. It's the juxtaposition of the very nature of the land, the very mountains, the very rivers, the very dust. All these you use to heighten the drama.

(This interview combines two interviews, the first conducted in March 1964 by the authors and the second in March 1965 by Wicking.—eds.)

The Man from Laramie: *"Contorted, 'neurotic' landscapes."*

ANTHONY MANN:
Looking at the Male

Paul Willemen (1981)

O ne reason why Mann's work has had to wait until now to be viewed as a retrospective whole is that auteurism always concentrated on thematic analysis, the challenge of deciphering an author's so-called "world view." Mann's Westerns *(Winchester '73, The Man from Laramie, The Far Country, The Last Frontier, Bend of the River, The Furies, Man of the West* and *The Naked Spur)* form a glaringly coherent thematic unity. As one American critic put it recently: "The characteristic love/hate rapport of charming "villain" and near-psychotic "hero" indicates that the greater danger for the Mann protagonist is the possibility of becoming completely what he so closely resembles, the Mann villain." Moreover, hero and villain are usually blood relatives. When asked for a definition of his Western hero (usually played by James Stewart, cast against type) Mann replied: "A man who could kill his own brother."

This very coherence, however, had the effect of relegating Mann's other films to passing mentions. As Phil Hardy puts it in his introduction to [a Mann] retrospective, "The grandeur of Mann's achievements in the Western has blinded critics to his not inconsiderable achievements outside that genre." The happy choice of the word "blinded" puts us on to a more important clue to the problem with Mann's work: the visual aspects of his films, as opposed to the moral profundities about the human condition so dear to auteurist critics of the 60s.

Trained in the theatre in the 20s and 30s (where he met and worked with James Stewart), Mann began directing films in 1942. He broke out of formulary quickies in 1947 with the extraordinary thriller *T-Men,* which contains a seminal Mann

"The anxious aspect of the look of the male": James Stewart in The Man *from Laramie.*

scene: an undercover agent must look on, impassively, while his close (male) friend and partner is being killed—a scene repeated in the bleakly cruel *Border Incident*. Mann's career overall falls into three phases: *films noirs* (plus a handful of negligible musical comedies) in the 40s, Westerns in the 50s, and epics in the 60s. Each time, the transition between phases/genres was marked by a single film, which also changed the visual register of his work. In 1950 there was the amazingly radical Western *Devil's Doorway*, shot in the manner of a *film noir*, demonstrating with merciless logic that the law is there to oppress people and that political power grows out of the barrel of a gun. In 1960, the transition from the Western to the epic was marked by *Cimarron*, the story of the settlement of Oklahoma right up to WWII.

The link between these archetypal yet exceptionally lucid and fascinating genre films appears to be something not easily grasped via content analyses: spectacle, in the sense of "offering a style without a theme," as Andrew Sarris put it in 1963. Mann's cinematic writing (with camera movements, light, colour, the inscription of figures into landscapes, multi-levelled deep-focus compositions, and so on) generates images that are echoed or re-doubled by the thematic structures of the plot.

In one sense, Mann's stories are mere excuses to replace one image by another, pretexts for the renewal of visual pleasure. The best example is the credit sequence of *Man of the West*. It opens with an image (in colour and scope) of an arid wasteland with one isolated figure, a man on horseback, quiet, doing nothing in particular, while the credits roll. The image and the figure in it are simply there to be looked at, to be enjoyed as pure pictoriality. While the following drama generates the rationale for changing the images, the image-track itself provides endless variations/elaborations of that initial picture. When it has run the entire gamut available in the genre, the film closes with a return to that first image, not to stop the flow, but to reactivate it as a loop. All Mann's amazing Westerns, with their justly celebrated "breathing" camera movements, play first and foremost on the "theme" of vision—not necessarily on a narrative level, but always in the presentation of the narrative.

And, as shown in *Man of the West*, this structure is pivoted on the look at the male figure: the male "in context," as it were. The viewer's experience is predicated on the pleasure of seeing the male "exist" (that is, walk, move, ride, fight) in or through cityscapes, landscapes or, more abstractly, history. And on the unquiet pleasure of seeing the male mutilated (often quite graphically in Mann) and restored through violent brutality. This fundamentally homosexual voyeurism (almost always repressed) is not without its problems: the look at the male produces just as much anxiety as the look at the female, especially when it's presented as directly as in the killing scenes in *T-Men* and *Border Incident*. This anxiety is marked in the images themselves: the shadowy world of the *film noir*, where Mann often relies exclusively on lateral, fragmented lighting and bizarre camera angles; then the contorted "neurotic" landscapes, shacks and ghost towns of the Westerns; in their turn replaced by the stylized opulence and giganticism of the imagery in the epics. The images always draw attention to themselves, never as fodder for the eye, but always "eye-catching," arresting the look. Spectacular in the true sense of the word.

It is the anxious aspect of the look at the male which is echoed in the thematic structures of the films—and which provoked the enthusiasm of the 60s auteurists, an all-male group obsessed with man's relation to nearly everything. This is most explicit in the Westerns, with the heroes ceaselessly trying to eradicate the memory of some real or imaginary "hurt" experienced, predictably enough, in the familial past. Moreover, given that the look is an integral part of the process of male identifications, the theme of the attainment of "true manhood" produces the hero as someone "searching for his identity," as the saying went a decade or two ago.

In Mann's films, this relation between spectacle and theme generates one consistently recurrent theme: the hero (or villain) pursued by a name. A father's name, or the name the hero wants to make for himself, or merely the name that makes you a target (as in the list of names in Robespierre's black book in *Reign of Terror*). The theme of the persecutory or triumphant family name traverses all the Westerns (ironically titled as anonymously as possible: *Man from Laramie, Man of the West)* and culminates in *El Cid*, whose honorific name wins the battle as he, a corpse tied into its saddle, rides out to meet the enemy. Mann's final film, *A Dandy in Aspic*, pushes this to its extreme: a double agent is ordered to kill his opposite number—who turns out to be himself.

It is now possible to see Mann's work as posing an eminently contemporary and urgent question: that of the operation of classic American cinema itself as a form of spectacle. In a way, Jean-Luc Godard already pointed to this in his rave review of *Man of the West* in 1959: "(Mann's style) reminds me of nothing whatsoever, for I have seen nothing so completely new since—why not?—Griffith....each shot shows that Mann is reinventing the Western. *Man of the West* is both course and discourse, beautiful landscapes and the explanation of this beauty, both the mystery of firearms and the secret of this mystery, both art and the theory of art; the result is that *Man of the West* is quite simply an admirable lesson in cinema—in modern cinema."

HE WENT THATAWAY:
The Form and Style of Leone's Italian Westerns

Marcia Landy (1992)

The western is a literary and cinematic form that has received a lot of commentary in American Studies and more recently in film studies. Like the treatment of much popular and mass culture, the attitudes toward history represented by writers on the western have been problematic. If there is a common denominator among the various discussions of the western, the commonality resides in the persistence of an adherence to seminal texts that treat the western as mythological discourse, valorizing, in one form or another, such works as Henry Nash Smith's *Virgin Land*, Frederick Jackson Turner's essays on the frontier, and lesser-cited but parallel works such as Leo Marx's *The Machine in the Garden* and R. W. B. Lewis's *The American Adam*.[1]

In the influential studies of the film western—such as Jim Kitses's *Horizons West* and Will Wright's *Six Guns and Society*—mythology has not disappeared but the western has been subjected to the rigors of structuralist analysis, which schematizes and codifies elements of the narrative according to the variant expressions of myth and to the concept of genre.[2] Nonetheless, the status of the discourse of history haunts discussions of the western, revealing, as with other forms of representation, the current crisis of historicizing. In George Fenin's and William Everson's study of the western, there is a bifurcation between the history of the settlement of the American frontier and the mythology to which it gave rise. Fenin and Everson complain that "reconstruction of historical events was and still is changed to suit the script," and they refer to the lack of "realistic pictures" and "authentic traditions."[3]

213

Kitses argues that westward expansionism is inscribed in the larger ideological project of nation formation and that "the western is American history," though the idea of the West is "an ambiguous mercurial concept."[4]

In his study of Clint Eastwood, Paul Smith addresses the ways in which the concept of the "real" has now shifted from the earlier binary conflict between two notions of history, one real and the other fantasmatic, to a conception of a "cultural and social imaginary" that subsumes the division between the real and the fictional, allowing for a more flexible and less monolithic conception of genre.[5] While there is little doubt about the variability of the forms adopted by the western (which can allow for Italian, German, Japanese, and Indian production), there lingers the sense that these forms are a North American property. The notion of a social imaginary comes closer to redressing complaints about lack of historical accuracy in the popular cinema and in the western in particular, opening the way for rethinking notions of myth and ideology that are all-encompassing, abstract, dismissive of countermemory, and useless for entertaining the historicity and heterogeneity of popular culture. Writings on the western, whether the authors' positions are overt or not, draw on some theory of the nature and role of history, and their models will inevitably reiterate positions concerning the status of knowledge and its relation to the dynamics of change.

In discussing the Italian western, it has become customary to make parallels between that form and the Hollywood western by comparing them to such films as *Stagecoach* (1939) or *My Darling Clementine* (1946) and to later films such as *Shane, Vera Cruz*, and *The Man Who Shot Liberty Valance* (1962). Discussions of the North American western stress abiding elements of structure, theme, and style. One of the most prominent motifs discussed by Thomas Schatz is the foundational narrative, or the struggle to create a civilization in the wilderness, as in *Stagecoach*. This narrative entails, along with the drama of forging a community, a struggle between the individual and the collectivity, the motif of "moral regeneration," and the archetypal binary conflict "between nature and civilization."[6] John Cawelti cites further the inappropriateness of European/Eastern values to the frontier, but the "basic premise of the classic western was a recognition of the inevitable passing of the old order of things, reflected in the myth of the 'old West,' together with an attempt to affirm that the new society would somehow be based on the older values."[7] According to Cawelti this formula was not suited to the exigencies of the post-World War II world and even less to the "more polarized social and political atmosphere of the 1960s."[8]

Much stress has been laid on the importance of community in relation to a savior figure who, for reasons of altruism, revenge, romance, or profit, becomes embroiled in the society for a period of time and who either stays or moves on after his goals are accomplished. The protagonist may enter the community as an agent of transformation, though he may ultimately choose not to be assimilated into it (as in *My Darling Clementine*). Or conversely, the community can assimilate the hero, as in *The Virginian* (1946) or *Stagecoach*. The male couple—the protagonist and his sidekick—who work in tandem for or against the community is also a familiar convention. It is customary in the critical literature to associate, as Cawelti has done, the earlier forms of the western with more idealistic notions of nation and to see a rupture in representation concomitant with the postwar era and with the Cold War.

Genre lines begin to blur, even to the extent of grafting the crime genre and film noir onto the western. Psychosocial and sexual treatments become increasingly evident.[9] A transformation in the ethical values can be detected, particularly in the more sympathetic treatment of the outlaw. The professional protagonist often replaces the idealist, "in the right place at the right time," as exemplified by *The Wild Bunch* (1969) and *Butch Cassidy and the Sundance Kid* (1969). This "job happens to be fighting whether for the law or against it."[10] Representatives of the law are also presented in more ambiguous terms.

Such general descriptions, however, can apply to any Hollywood genre, allowing for variations in the use of landscape, in the typology of the characters, in the use of stars, and in representations of the other. In a similar sense, the narrative schema can be read as characteristic of national narratives generally, allowing for the specificity of language and local customs. The problem is the inert nature of genre classification and the static nature of myth and archetype. The problem is also that foundational narratives rely on notions of linearity and progress, but instead of movement from disorder to order, the narrative trajectory often moves from order to disorder. A commitment to narratives of progression or regression occludes the possibility of seeing contradiction, of identifying the "excesses" of history. The insertion of a modernist perspective, the notion of increasing self-consciousness, Hegelian style, serves to impose a new narrative of progress, replacing action with self-awareness on the part of the auteur and his handling of genre.

To read Sergio Leone's films as remakes, as mere deconstruction of the Hollywood western, or as modernist in the vein of Antonioni and Fellini—though all such elements may be imbricated in the text—is to address cinema history and history in cinema schematically and reductively rather than analytically and interrogatively, univalently rather than heterogeneously. To read and judge the films from the unique position of auteurism is also problematic. For example, Sergio Leone has been regarded as an "opportunist" who has "simply yoked samurai gestures to western iconography."[11] His films deserve better; they deserve to be understood as repositories of social and cultural knowledge. They have gone a different route than most critical judgments of his use of the western genre assume, broadly engaging the moral concerns of neorealism in their dramatization of protagonists who struggle to survive in societies that are hostile to change and to collective practices. The films interrogate masculinity and its discontents, its complicity with violence and power, and they pose, though they do not resolve, ethical dilemmas about the forms of power similar in many ways to the historical investments of the Tavianis' films—especially *Padre Padrone* (1977)—which orchestrate the problematics of language, patriarchy, subalternity, masculinity, the family, social power, and the clash between rural and urban life and between tradition and modernity.

The Leone films rely on a certain dry and dusty desert landscape that comes to signify "the West" but that provides an arena of open space for action. This landscape is rarely associated with domestic space. Occasionally we see a contrast between open, contested public space and closed domestic space in *For a Few Dollars More* (1965) and *Once upon a Time in the West* (a film that particularly capitalizes on this disjunction). The images of towns such as Tucumcari, Agua Caliente, Sweetwater, and

"A certain dry and dusty landscape": the final showdown in The Good, the Bad, and the Ugly.

El Paso convey the sense of dirt, grime, and poverty that could apply just as easily to the underdeveloped terrains of Latin America, Africa, Sicily, or Sardinia as to the North American West. The ubiquitous fly (the most notorious example is seen in the opening of *Once upon a Time in the West*) serves as a synecdoche, a specific marker of the annoyances and discomforts inherent in this life and also of the physicality of the characters and of the *mise en scène*. The protagonists—Clint Eastwood with his familiar poncho and facial stubble, Eli Wallach in his stained clothing, the contrast between the meticulous Lee Van Cleef and the casual Eastwood, between the coarse Rod Steiger and the suave James Coburn—bespeak an attention to the relation between characters and environment.

The minutiae of this world are a distinctive dimension of Leone's film: the choreography of movement; the stylized use of faces; and the aversive uses of sound, represented by the grating sounds of wheels, the extra-loud noise of oncoming or departing trains, the ubiquitous buzz of flies, the sounds of eating, belching, and farting. These sounds fuse with the music, so that it is often difficult to know which are "natural" and which are "manufactured." Chanting, orchestral music, whistling, guitar music, the sounds of a flute or piccolo, and choral and instrumental themes mingle to provide a complex narration that acts as more than mere support to the narrative, more than mere atmosphere or filler. All of the critical work on the Italian western has singled out the music of Ennio Morricone for analysis (and for praise).[12] The scores for Leone's films serve a number of functions: as affective commentary on a character's actions or state of mind; as mockery, cliché, leitmotiv, thematic continuity; and hence as a comment on repetition, variation, or ironic reversal in the narrative. The music is a major carrier of the historical excess that creates the sense of openness and heterogeneity of narration. It enhances the melodrama and directs its affective strategies toward antimelodrama. As in opera, there is a union between verbal and gestural language and the music. The dialogue is often sparse, with the exception of *Duck, You Sucker*, which seems most committed to the use of words. Where there is dialogue, it is often restricted to one-liners, something Clint Eastwood will employ to advantage in both his western and nonwestern films (e.g., the infamous "Make my day"). There is a sense too that the dialogue, composed as it is of clichés, truisms, proverbs, one-liners, and commonsensical wisdom, works with the music and sound to punctuate, mock, comment on, or correct the banality of language. In many instances, the sparsity of dialogue is a sign that this world is more one of action than of thought.

In their dependence on physical action, Leone's films draw on traditions from Italian theatrical comedy and film comedy. The importance of farce, slapstick, and satiric allegory are evident in such films as *Once upon a Time in the West* and *Duck, You Sucker*. Moreover, the residual elements of the commedia dell' arte are evident in character typification and in the uses of gags, stylized gestures, *lazzi* (physical and verbal tricks), and repartee. Frayling has noted the relations between the Italian art of puppetry and the staging of the action in the Italian western. In the musical scores of Ennio Morricone in particular and in the choreography of body movement generally the films also evoke the characteristics of comic opera. Commenting on the persistence of the operatic in Italian culture, Gramsci linked the stylization of the operatic to a penchant for oratory, especially funeral oratory, and to the spectacle of district magistrate's courts, in which "the hall is always full of . . . people who memorize the turns of phrase and the solemn words, feed on them and remember them."[13] The turns of phrase and the instances of mock solemnity in Italian comedy have this mnemonic and oratorical attribute that is also evident in spaghetti westerns.

The fairy tale, "once upon a time" quality in Sergio Leone films[14] is related to Gramsci's conception of folklore. The films' dependence on the past, on "the West," is more than schematic and supra-historical myth: As folklore, it is "tied to the culture of the dominant class and, in its own way, has drawn from it the motifs which have then become inserted into combination with the previous traditions. Besides, there is nothing more contradictory and fragmentary than folklore."[15] Folklore, in the guise of fairy tale narration, in Leone's films calls attention to the commonsensical positions of the characters as a form of popular wisdom that is often revealed to be contradictory.

The strongly affective nature of Leone's treatment of the western has been described as emotional, "perhaps too emotional, for the audiences of Britain and America." While such comments may be more applicable to British than North American audiences, their invocation of the melodramatic and the operatic invites a comparison between Italian westerns and "Weepies, women's films."[16] Many of the spaghetti westerns are male melodramas, involving conflicts over identity and homosocial bonding. The films validate the connection between folklore, melodrama, and the operatic that I claim is central to popular representations of history. The nonverbal and affective strategies of melodrama and opera are conveyed in the iconography, in bodily movement (especially in the choreography), and in the use of intense close-up, particularly of the face. Bodies in motion are a hallmark of the films. Instead of the ballets of grand opera, there is the choreography of the shoot-out, of men riding through the landscape, of processionals; there is the choreography of ritual scenes, such as that in *Once upon a Time in the West* in which Jill and the other mourners observe the bodies of the dead McBains, and of the various ritual forms of violence itself interspersed throughout the film. The camera movement—pans, tilts, the use of handheld equipment—conveys the sense of a world of energy and motion, a world of bodies that collide. The music also serves to render the affective intensity of the bodily interactions. The choreography and the music call attention to the body politics of the films—more to the sexuality of the masculine body than to that of the feminine, since femininity seems confined to the few instances in which women are fantasized or dreamed about, or in which the homosocial relations suggest traces of tenderness in the brutal and violent environment.

Heterosexual romance is not a central motif and is subordinated to the motif of homosocial bonding. The relations between men—Mr. Mortimer and Monco in *For a Few Dollars More*, Cheyenne and Harmonica in *Once upon a Time in the West*, Tuco and Blondie in *The Good, the Bad, and the Ugly* (1966), and especially Juan and Sean in *Duck, You Sucker*—are central and complex, involving a form of coupling that is ambivalent. The relations are based on economic competition but also on something else that entails grudging admiration and respect, even if not affection and tenderness. Sex between men and women is circumscribed in this environment, and when present it is likely to be coercive and brutal. When women are present, they are usually carriers of economic value as kept women, prostitutes, or heirs to property, like Jill in *Once upon a Time in the West*, or figures of nostalgia, as in *Duck, You Sucker*. Maternal figures are either conspicuously placed in the background or entirely absent, or they violate conventional notions of service. Eroticism is conveyed primarily through scenes of eating, sparring, or killing.

The faces in close-up, so much identified with Italian westerns, contribute in many ways to an understanding of the world in the films. They serve a triple function: to intensify the affect, to interrogate the character and the situation, and to render them ambiguous. The close-ups are not reserved for the protagonists alone but are dispersed, associated with antagonists and with silent observers of the action.[17] Close-ups also contribute to the tragicomic nature of the situation, since characters are identified by their unshaven faces: dirt, moles, and in some cases spittle that is clearly visible. In the early part of *Duck, You Sucker*, the agonizing close-ups focus on fragments, on facial parts; especially the leering eyes and the masticating mouths filled with crushed and oozing food. The alternation between full-body shots and close-ups serves to underscore a conflict between the head and the body—a primary tension in Leone's films that centers on the relation between intelligence and force, creating questions about the dominance of one over the other.

The body mechanics are reminiscent of physical movement in Vsevolod Pudovkin and Sergei Eisenstein. They recall too the comic choreography of Chaplin—an icon of Americanism for many Europeans. Body movement in the films can be fruitfully identified with the Italian tradition of the commedia dell'arte. In contrast to opera,

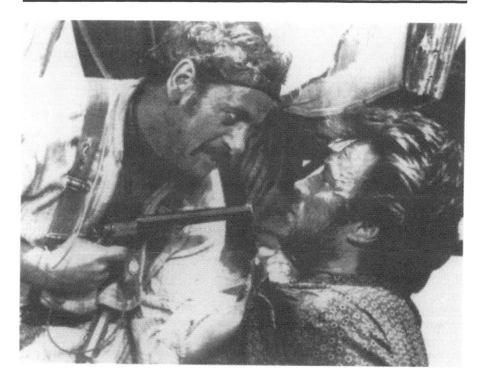

Homosocial bonding: Tuco (Eli Wallach) and Blondie (Clint Eastwood) in The Good, the Bad, and the Ugly.

the body in the commedia seems more in tune with a bustling street life caught unawares, even when performed indoors. The body in the commedia also expresses a paradox. While it refers to the slow-moving, deep structures of daily life, it is in constant motion. The body in the commedia, with its agility of a dancer and its careful choreography, nonetheless produces an effect of spontaneity. By virtue of movement, the body in the commedia resembles more a living document than a still monument.[18]

Leone's films mix the melodramatic and the comic, the monumental and the everyday. The foregrounding of the body communicates the constraints on the conforming body via an eruption of unruly antagonisms that signify the impossibility of total submission. The physical action in the Leone films, their emphasis on trickery and on violence, recalls the *lazzi* of the commedia as the characters engage in a range of physical actions and verbal wit to antagonize and outsmart their opponents.[19] The *lazzi* refer to "comic routines that were planned or unplanned," and they "allude to any discrete or independent, comic and repeatable activity that guaranteed laughs for its participants."[20] The *lazzi* were associated with "athleticism and clowning . . . tumbling, stilt walking, diving, and tightrope balancing."[21]

This masculine form of clowning is not only slapstick but also serves as a means of aggressiveness in attacking another or protecting oneself against attack. An instance of a *lazzi* is a scene in *The Good, the Bad, and the Ugly:* Clint Eastwood is cleaning his gun as Eli Wallach's hired assassins attempt to sneak up on him; with great agility and sangfroid he manages to dispatch them all. In the same film, the repeated gag of Tuco and Blondie taking turns hanging each other and then shooting through the rope, causing the victim to fall, recapitulates in humorous fashion the double-crossing tricks that Eastwood and Wallach play on each other. *Once upon a Time in the West* and *Duck, You Sucker* are filled with repetitive gags and reversals based on fast movement and legerdemain. A more bizarre episode of this trickery occurs in *A Fistful of Dollars:* The Man with No Name inserts himself between the Rojo and the Baxter families, propping up two dead bodies to lure the warring groups into fighting with each other. The play with repetition of physical objects as vehicles of recognition, revenge, and trickery can be seen in the use of the armor in this film or in the use of the locket in *For a Few Dollars More*. The repetition of routines works, along with the music, to highlight ironic reversals as well as narrative transformations.

The typology of the characters in the Italian western also resembles commedia types. For example, vestigial remnants of the braggart captain can be seen in such figures as Tuco in *The Good, the Bad, and the Ugly* and as Cheyenne in *Once upon a Time in the West* and in the rivalry between the two bounty hunters—Mr. Mortimer and Monco—in *For a Few Dollars More*. The pairing of figures, their competitiveness, and their exchange of serious and comic qualities are also reminiscent of the relations between *zanni*, the various clowning figures. According to Allardyce Nicoll, the *zanni* of the commedia (sometimes referred to as John) "appears as a stupid booby, but more commonly he mingles with his folly an element of wit, an element of liveliness, of good fun, of grotesquerie."[22] Also evident in the Leone films are the interchangeable figures of the *Dottore* and Pantalone: the older professional men who should be wise but who are pedants, traitors, or sunk in folly, such as Doctor Villega in *Duck, You Sucker*.

The comedy relies on common sense as a guide for action only to reveal the inadequacy of common sense in contexts that require innovation and wit. If common sense as folklore involves a stylized and naturalized commitment to past actions and behavior, the melodramatic and comic treatment of character and situation in the films serves to foreground historical excess. The dependence on physical action, on the body, and on the face sets up a tension between historical stasis and dynamic movement, between mechanization and spontaneity, and between the containing and the release of energy. Common sense is not a matter merely of words but of gesture and behavior, intimately related to the politics of the body and, therefore, to the body politic. While the Russian formalists objected to the mechanization of modern Fordist industrialism, Gramsci saw its possibilities for freeing the mind from the repetitive routines of production. Physical action in a Leone film can signify static repetition and routine mechanization, but it can also signify mental alertness.

The world created in the Italian westerns is not one of simple heroes and villains, though there are many Machiavellian characters. This is not the familiar Manichaean world of melodrama, though at times it appears to be binary. There is abundant affect and melodrama, but this melodrama coexists with the comedy; and the comedy tempers the melodrama but does not overwhelm it. Common sense is not defeated; it is shown in its contradictory dimensions: as a form of wisdom in the short run and as more questionable knowledge that requires interrogation in the long run. Clint Eastwood's comment in *A Fistful of Dollars* that "[e]very town has a boss. When there are two around I'd say there's one too many" is conducive to an understanding of the wisdom necessary for survival, but it also raises more questions than it answers: Why can there not be two? How does one know who is the boss? The statements may adequately characterize the competitiveness and violence that results from two bosses—the Rojos and the Baxters—but the resolution, getting rid of both, although it solves one problem, introduces more fundamental problems about power. There is no doubt that the pragmatic assessment of power works in immediate terms to both describe and diagnose problems that are integral to survival. The uses of history, the road taken by the films, does not lead to a future that is mapped but to one that is open, like the roads that the protagonists take as they ride out of town, alone as when they arrived.

NOTES

1. See John G. Cawelti, *Adventure, Mystery, and Romance: Formula Studies as Art and Popular Culture* (Chicago: University of Chicago Press, 1976), pp. 192-260; John H. Lenihan, *Showdown: Confronting Modern America in the Western Film* (Urbana: University of Illinois Press, 1980); Jack Nachbar, "Introduction," in *Focus on the Western* (Englewood Cliffs, N.J.: Prentice-Hall, 1974), pp. 1-9; Jennie Calder, *There Must Be a Lone Ranger* (London: Hamish Hamilton, 1974); Rita Parks, *The Western Hero in Film and Television: Mass Media Mythology* (Ann Arbor, Mich.: UMI Press, 1982); George N. Fenin and William K. Everson, *The Western: From Silents to Cinema* (New York: Bonanza Books, 1962); Jim Hitt, *The American Western from Fiction (1823-1976) into Film (1909-1986)* (Jefferson, N.C.: McFarland and Company, 1990).

2. Jim Kitses, *Horizons West: Anthony Mann, Budd Boetticher, Sam Peckinpah. Studies of Authorship within the Western* (Bloomington: Indiana University Press, 1969); Will Wright, *Six Guns and Society: A Structural Study of the Western* (Berkeley and Los Angeles: University of California Press, 1975); Thomas Schatz, *Hollywood Genres, Formulas, Filmmaking, and the Studio System* (New York: Random House, 1981); Lane Roth, *Film, Semiotics, Metz, and Leone's Trilogy* (New York: Garland Publishing, 1983); see also Bazin, *What Is Cinema?* vol. 2.

3. Fenin and Everson, *The Western*, pp. 10–12.

4. Kitses, *Horizons West*, p. 8.

5. Paul Smith, *Clint Eastwood: A Cultural Production* (Minneapolis: University of Minnesota Press, 1993), pp. 19-26.

6. Schatz, *Hollywood Genres*, pp. 45-80; Cawelti, *Adventure, Mystery, and Romance*, pp. 221, 225.

7.   Cawelti, *Adventure, Mystery, and Romance*, p. 251.

8.   Ibid.

9.   For a discussion of gender in the western, see Virginia Wright Wexman, *Creating the Couple: Love, Marriage, and Hollywood Performance* (Princeton, N.J.: Princeton University Press, 1993).

10.   Wright, *Six Guns and Society*, pp. 97-99.

11.   David Thomson, *A Biographical Dictionary of Film* (New York: Morrow Press, 1981), p. 344.

12.   Mark Kermode, "Endnotes," *Sight and Sound* (October 1994): 63.

13.   Antonio Gramsci, *Selections from the Cultural Writings*, ed. David Forgacs (Cambridge, Mass.: Harvard University Press, 1985), p. 380.

14.   Robert C. Cumbow, *Once upon a Time in the Films of Sergio Leone* (Metuchen, N.J.: Scarecrow Press, 1987), p. 129.

15.   Gramsci, *Selections from the Cultural Writings*, p. 194.

16.   Laurence Staig and Tony Williams, *Italian Western: The Opera of Violence* (London: Lorrimer Publishers, 1975), pp. 27-28.

17.   For a discussion of the affective nature of "faciality," see Gilles Deleuze, *Cinema 1* (Minneapolis: University of Minnesota Press, 1986), pp. 87-102.

18.   Angela Dalle Vacche, *The Body in the Mirror: Shapes of History in Italian Cinema* (Princeton, N.J.: Princeton University Press, 1992), p. 6.

19.   For a detailed discussion of the history of the commedia, see Allardyce Nicoll, *Masks, Mimes, and Miracles: Studies in the Popular Theatre* (New York: Cooper Square Publishers, 1963); for a discussion of the adaptations of the commedia to various cultural forms of representation from Shakespeare to modernity, see David George and Christopher J. Gossip, eds., *Studies in the Commedia dell'arte* (Cardiff: University of Wales Press, 1993); and for a specific discussion of the kinds of *lazzi*, see Mel Gordon, *Lazzi: The Comic Routines of the Commedia dell'arte* (New York: Performing Arts Journal, 1983). See also Flaminio Scola, *Scenarios of the Commedia dell'arte: Flaminio Scala's Il teatro delle favole rappresentative*, trans. Henry F. Salerno (New York: New York University Press, 1967); and Martin Green and John Swan, *The Triumph of Pierrot: The Commedia dell'arte and the Modern Imagination* (New York: Macmillan Publishing Company, 1986).

20.   Gordon, *Lazzi*, p. 5.

21.   Ibid., p. 9.

22.   Nicoll, *Masks, Mimes, and Miracles*, p. 276.

PECKINPAH RE-VISITED:
Pat Garrett and Billy the Kid

Jim Kitses (1998)

"**I** believe you know of *me* . . . ." Jack Elam's Alamosa Bill—walleyed, blackbearded, a "character"—introduces himself to Lincoln County Marshal Pat Garrett, then proudly listens as his fame is recounted, how he had "killed old G.B. Denning last year at Silver City for calling you a cheat at monte." "That'd be me . . . ", replies a pleased Alamosa, taken aback seconds later on being drafted for the hunt for Billy the Kid. Played stylishly by a dapper James Coburn, Garrett is here being barbered and has just asked an oddly-derbied Bob Dylan, sitting and drinking at a nearby table, who *he* is, only to receive the puzzling reply, "That's a good question." Earlier still, we had heard Garrett instruct an errand boy to alert his wife that he would be home for dinner . . .

If this conjunction of badge, barber, and bride would seem to point to a comfortable fit for Garrett with the settled life, the film everywhere complicates such notions. Although the film pauses with Pat at his house's picket fence, a return home seems less the occasion for his critical inspection before the barber's mirror ("Do me up good this time, Guiseppe") than his meeting with the Governor, an elegant turn by Jason Robards, who greets him with slick musings about the "fabulous melancholy" of rainy New Mexico evenings that hopefully bring one closer to "some greater design." However, the only design that the film bleakly maps is that of the increasingly destructive impact on the West of a squalid capitalism—incarnate in the Governor's mealy-mouthed guests—whose goals are achieved through Garrett, arm-in-arm with the Governor, and his grudging service to Chisum, giant rancher and creature of the state's money and political intrests that are closing down the frontier. This is the pow-

223

er structure the film defines as authorizing the manhunt and murder of William Bonney, a charming bad-boy Christ who kills people, a tarnished icon of independence and freedom, as constructed by Kris Kristopherson's soft performance and Peckinpah's direction. A film suffused with its own fabulous melancholy, *Pat Garrett and Billy the Kid* is a languorous dirge, a drifting death-poem, a post-modern lament for an earlier America, an Edenic time pre-dating our worthies' situation when life meant more than image and reputation ("That'd be me"). Peckinpah's vision of the closing frontier peoples it abundantly with outsize characters of renown such as Pat, the Kid and Alamosa—originals, eccentrics, ones-of-a-kind—but the authentic life, the autonomous self, are no longer possible. Style has replaced substance, the frontier a stage with a cast of drifters, unhinged, heroes without a referent. A rich tapestry of the West's final days, *Pat Garrett* is Peckinpah's ultimate statement, the tragic moment frozen, his final Western, his farewell to the Western.

In this ultimate elaboration of their historical plight, Peckinpah's characters find themselves in a world defined by compromise and betrayal, where the genre's mantle of heroic identity is a lie. "How good is he?" is a question often asked in the genre, ethics and expertise combined. Here we see the reality, the practice of social contracts such as the ten-step duel the film puts forward as the standard format for regulating violent conflict. Ironically, cheating itself has become a given. Alamosa Bill whirls to shoot on the count of eight; Billy has turned on three. At the end Billy will get similarly unsparing treatment from Garrett. The West is a combat zone where neither law nor honor exist, life a

Kris Kristofferson's "soft performance" as Billy the Kid.

cockfight. Billy shoots people in the back. There is no gold to be saved, no Elsa or Angel to rescue, no bad guys—only the range war with Chisum, but that's lost.

For all the echoes of Christ, Billy is as compromised as Garrett, as trapped in a righteous narcissism, a saviour without a cause. The film's prologue/epilogue structure, which records Pat's murder 27 years after the film's main events, has led some critics to see the action as if from his point of view, and to install him as its tragic hero.[1] But as the title, to-and-fro of the narrative, and evenhanded depiction of its epic characters suggest, the film is balanced equally on the shoulders of both men, ambiguous and ambivalent characters caught in a no-win deal, an historical Catch-22.

For men of charismatic authority and individual style, a life with honor and meaning is no longer possible, neither within the community nor on the shrinking open range. Trying to cross over, as befits his grey hairs, Garrett has become alienated, reminded by everyone of his compromised identity in serving Chisum. How dark this character becomes for us—an undertaker doling out death left and right—is quietly captured toward the end of his quest, in a gentle tableau that barely survived the studio's scissors. Resting in his manhunt by a river, Garrett's attention is drawn by gunshots from a barge floating downstream, a family aboard, a bearded patriarch firing at a floating target from the bow, womenfolk cooking behind. It is an image of the fragility and instability of the frontier community, a family at once both settled and transient, who appear to be living out Sheriff Baker's dream, "to drift out of this damn territory," its vulnerability thrown into stark relief when Garrett has a shot at the target, and the man aboard fires back. Garrett then takes aim, and the world of these strangers, drifting by on life's current, hangs in the balance. But the deadly Garrett refrains, the barge drifts on, and we are thankful that Pat's presence does not inflict a gratuitous violence on this family—as Billy's had the trading post's homesteaders who provide a mute audience for his murder of Alamosa in their front yard, after the meal they all share.

Pat's icy isolation is balanced by Billy's barely civilized life with cronies and whores, true to a meaningless bunkhouse existence, cynical, indolent, ever liquored-up, rustling Chisum cattle to recover back pay, all that's left. This narrow concern with personal cowboy justice bespeaks a self-absorption equal to the marshal's. Children are often in evidence around the Kid and his bunch, an ambiguous motif interwoven to suggest a kindred youth and hope, but indicating a lack of maturity as well. Neither man has a larger vision, something "to back off to," in the words of *The Wild Bunch*'s Dutch. Peckinpah takes the Western's stock melodrama of heartless corporations circumscribing free men of action to its ultimate, both men allowed a limited space for maneuver, a stage that makes for gestures rather than authentic action.

Peckinpah is no populist. Where John Ford foregrounds the foot soldier, the common man, the family in tension with the razzle dazzle of a *Liberty Valance*, ordinary people in Peckinpah's West are the anonymous underlings who have to live with snotty bosses, as in *The Wild Bunch*—"It's not what you *did* I don't like"—who survive by "standing in my own good hole," as the scurrilous sad sack whom Garrett turns over to Sheriff Cullen Baker puts it. However, if the director's heroes generally belong to an elite, *Pat Garrett* goes further, exploiting the genre's incipient dandyism to suggest "characters" in the late-frontier's shrinking outlaw society that carry the self-conscious, knowing air of celebrity and fame. These men occupy a charged space, a hyper-reality within which they play out their roles in a drama of historic proportions. As Alamosa lies dying he consoles himself—his name will be in reports on Billy's doings. Similarly, a bewigged Richard Jaeckel—another familiar face—on being pressed into action by Pat: "I hope they spell my name right." In contrast, we have Slim Pickens, the emotional epi-center of the film as Sheriff Baker, lumbering down to die by the river, supported at a respectful distance by Katy Jurado, the genre's Latin firebrand here recycled to mourn the passing of the West's last honest man, who shares the wisdom she first expressed about civilization's discontents long ago in *High Noon:* "This town is not worth it." Employing a favorite strategy for contrast, Peckinpah cross-cuts from the fading sheriff at the river's edge to Garrett maneuvering for a shot at a talky Black Harris, on the roof above, who is trying to distract the marshal with a running chat recalling their arrival in the county: "How long ago was that, Pat?" Meanwhile, as he dies, Pickens and Jurado exchange soulful looks, but are silent.

If that silence registers as protest, it is perhaps because the main business of language in the late-frontier appears to be its endless narrativizing of the "colorful" and violent events of a largely shiftless cadre, collectively constructing "history." There is no author of dime novels in *Pat Garrett*, no foregrounding of the myth-mak-ing process as in Arthur Penn's earlier treatment of the legend, *The Left-Handed Gun* (1958). Centered on Billy, as its title suggests, Penn's impressive debut was a Western of uncommon psychological complexity—"Oedipus in the West," as its director put it. Peckinpah's characters do not achieve analogous psychological depth, but then they are poseurs, inauthentics, in a world where even the ambiguous honor of revenge is not possible, as it had been for Paul Newman's tortured Billy.

Rather than document the formal construction of the myth in print, as both Penn's film and Clint Eastwood's *Unforgiven* do, what the film provides instead is a vivid grass-roots experience of the process, a preoccupation with events and their audiences ("Rode in from Seven Rivers to see you get hanged"), a pervasive telling of stories, anec-dotes, histories, incidents, jokes, and gossip, constantly flowing around the action and creating a kind of instant nostalgia, a nostalgia for the present, as it were. "That's a good story, Bell," Billy tells Matt Clark's runty deputy, the first of a large cast of supporting players behind Garrett. Bell has been describing a 40-mile trek he once made after his horse "locoed" on him, but primed with a six-gun discovered in the outhouse, Billy is ready for darker tales, and asks if J.W. knows how his friend Carlyle died. Although Bell has already heard about it, Billy wants to tell it his way, how he "shot him three times in the back—blew his goddamn head off," and having brutally set the stage, does the same to Bell, in a typically show-off, self-reflexive turn.

We hear innumerable frontier stories of death and dying—of Eben who drowned trying to escape a posse, of U.S. Christmas, the old man who expires in a ten-step with John Jones, who had stepped on his new boots, of a horse-thieving Jace Sommers dead by an artfully placed rattle-snake. . . . We see how events are kept alive in the memory, how stories are formed and circulate, how an oral tradition oper-ates, reputations are made and a heroic world, a mythology, grows up, a mythology which the film itself is both mourning and critiquing. Like *The Man Who Shot Liberty Valance, Pat Garrett* suggests that there is a gap between the shiny legends and the facts, between fame and greatness. The word cannot be trusted because signifier and signified have separated, image and action, aesthetic and ideology, are disjunct. And it is this haunting, incipient schizophrenia that gives the film its *angst*.

There is a preoccupation with image, style, and reputation in *Pat Garrett*. As the capitalists at the Governor's table make clear, a developing territory cannot be seen to accommodate the likes of a Billy the Kid. A danger less for what he does than what he represents, Billy is a signifier of an individual freedom and social anarchy of the past that threatens the new order. A writer interested in modernist re-workings of American myths, as in his screenplay for Monte Hellman's *Two-Lane Blacktop*, Rudolph Wurlitzer had produced a script for *Pat Garrett* that posited heroes who knew they inhabited a myth.[2] This attitude is visible in the film in the bearing of the characters. As opposed to the upright stature and moral drive of Joel McCrea's Steven Judd in *Ride the High Country*, Peckinpah gives us a languid stardom in *Pat Garrett*, characters who exhibit a kind of glamour. They look, they pose, they make speeches, they are legend. Inhabiting a cozy old-world global village, these privileged members of a frontier pantheon are introduced by Peckinpah in freeze frame cameos over the film's credits that immortalize this bunch, all insider looks, jokes, one-liners and tall tales ("So Pat said . . . "). Were ever images and characters so deliberate in the genre, actions so mannered? Toward the end of the film, when Billy has returned to Fort Sumner after aborting his escape to Mexico, he greets Beaver with a languid left hand, a Hollywood handshake on the frontier. Self-consciousness is everywhere.

This self-consciousness was evident in Peckinpah's intended design for the opening of the film, an associative montage worthy of the Russians which erects a future-time (1908) frame in which Garrett is being murdered by the capitalists he has served in his own murder of Billy. Intercut at the outset with the present-time (1881) action of the chicken-shooting show Billy is putting on, the action returns at the end as a fatal comeuppence for Pat after he has killed Billy. This complex structure establishes the treacherous modern world in bleak sepia, then bleeds in the rich colors of the film's present, underlining the dialectics of the actions being paralleled across the years by match cuts of the shootings, which suggest Billy and Pat are tied in a strange kind of double-murder/suicide. A flashy conceit that encapsulates the film's action— the death of the individual spirit at the hands of a corrupt corporate law—the frame is the kind of Brechtian brainstorm that was forever pitting the director against his producers, to act out battles that often seemed self-consciously to mirror the struggles and defeats of the characters in the films.

Three years earlier, the relatively modest, quirky *The Ballad of Cable Hogue* had suffered an indifferent release by Warners, its studio confused at the absurdist antics of a Mutt and Jeff in the desert. Like *Major Dundee* and *The Wild Bunch*, however, *Pat Garrett and Billy the Kid* was another ambitious Peckinpah epic doomed to traumatic final cuts against the wishes of its director, caught up once again in a power struggle with estranged MGM executives and producers. Along with the framing device, scenes of Garrett and boss Chisum, and Garrett and his wife, also vanished, together with numerous other bits, on the order of some sixteen minutes in all. The result was a disastrous reduction of the film. In cutting away the frame, a flash-back structure was lost which enunciates the basic theme of looking back, and the first hint of the key motifs of doubled characters—mirror-images—and of suicide. Equally damaging was the loss of the dandyish affectation inscribed within the freeze-frame credits which introduce some of the "players" striking poses and theatrically over-enunciating, as well as countless twists, tweaks and trims throughout, the total effect to produce an infinitely less stylized, more conventional film, diminishing the languorous, mournful, dreamlike tone.

After its disappointing reception, this release version was eventually followed by another cut, bowdlerized for broadcast television, of 103 minutes. An unstable text, *Pat Garrett*'s afterlife is complicated, the experience of the film modified depending on whether one is watching film or video, 16mm or 35mm, mainstream TV or cable.[3] Thankfully, a version closer to the director's design at 122 minutes is available on home video, although still absent two small scenes of Garrett's—with a bitter and unhappy wife, and with a hooker he abuses to locate Billy (which is in the release version). Mourn these cuts we must, but in my view their absence is not crucial. The male-oriented world of the Western in any case allowed Peckinpah to marginalize women (often having them provide vivid cameos, as with Jurado), and his work, espe-

Jason Robards, Jr. and David Warner in The Ballad of Cable Hogue: *"Mutt and Jeff in the West."*

cially if we take into account their representation and treatment in his other movies, clearly is bound up with a cult of masculinity.

Borden Chase, author of so many key Anthony Mann-directed scripts as well as Hawks' *Red River*, once defined the relationship between two men as "the greatest love story."[4] For Peckinpah, that love is always threatened. A dominant theme, loyalty provides the master code of value, loyalty to oneself, loyalty man to man, loyalty to codes, contracts and commitments. Loyalty to women is not an issue. But loyalty is an impossible ideal, the films tracing the contradictions and fallibility of the characters. Indeed, the action of many of the director's films begins under the sign of betrayal, original sin in Peckinpah. Jean Renoir once said the auteur makes the same film repeatedly. It is possible to discern in Peckinpah a master-text, all his work interconnected through and radiating out of the central binary of loyalty and betrayal, and the motifs of giving one's word, signing contracts, honoring friendships, bonds, commitments, and breaking faith, compromising, double-crossing, selling out, whoring. At its highest pitch, as in *Pat Garrett*, the drama of such ties and their transgression within the masculine sphere can express the depth, complexity and intensity of a love relationship. Asked why he doesn't kill Garrett early on, Billy ponders, then replies: "He's my friend." The sense of a private bond being violated is so intense it has led some critics to speculate there is a radical gay text struggling to surface in Peckinpah.[5]

Such speculative subtexts are understandable given the fraught air surrounding Peckinpah's antagonists. Pat Garrett, in particular, with its self-conscious theatrics and insistent mirror-image motif, lends itself to a quasi-autobiographical reading—Billy and Pat as co-stars in a glum saga directed by Garrett against his wishes for Chisum's producer (Barry Sullivan moving over from his role as director in Minnelli's *The Bad and The Beautiful*). Garrett as auteur of the show within the show—an ominous, exemplary text for the enlightenment of the territory—is a resonant notion, given his calling of the shots throughout. Within this perspective, Pat's meeting with Billy at the outset is perhaps less a warning than a provocative invitation to join the production, play the game of art, narrativize together. The master of *mise en scène*, Pat will shortly thereafter direct the action at the cabin's siege from on high—like a Ford or DeMille—but also show a flair for up-close, intimate scene-shaping, such as the later semi-comic humiliation of Billy's cohorts at a poker table, culminating in the killing of Holly. As befits the mind that holds the whole scenario, however, Garrett also displays a more deliberate, introspective side, increasingly hesitant, slowing the pace, contemplating, resisting the final action. In contrast, either with story or song, target practice or duel, Billy is always "on," the exhibitionist, perfect for star billing. Actors rarely look beyond their role, however, and at the end Billy—the naked, jilted lover—appears not to have realized how the action would play out, that he had been cast by his friend in a snuff film.

The aloof, imperious *auteur* and the madcap drinking buddy, the whore and the stand-up guy, the two halves of a perennially schizoid filmmaker are objectified here. This ultimate post-modern conceit centers on Peckinpah casting his own shadow in Garrett, egging his surrogate on at the end in his cameo as the coffin maker, and contemplating the treachery and murder that lie ahead at the hands of an ungrateful "business" in the frame's final dumb show and curtain, the director accurately foreseeing his own future marginalization and failures.

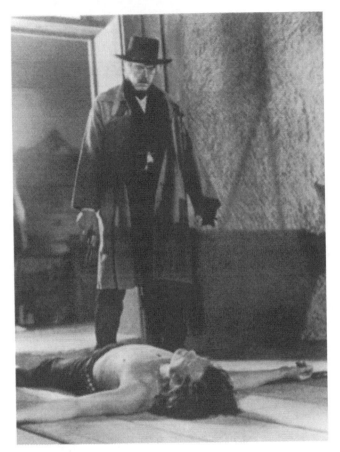

Key motifs: mirror-images, doubled characters, suicide. James Coburn as Pat Garrett.

To entertain such a reading is, of course, not necessarily to give credence to its image of the *auteur* as tragically compromised victim. It is tempting to speak sympathetically, as Paul Seydor has, of Peckinpah's films suffering "mutilation" at the hands of "money men," of *Pat Garrett* coming in, for all the vicissitudes of its production, "*only* twenty days behind schedule and $1.5 million over the original $3 million budget" (my emphasis).[6] But the truth is that the director was frequently unable to sustain the collaborative relationships essential to the quasi-industrial system of mainstream feature filmmaking. Peckinpah's early break-through successes coincided with the broad diffusion within the film community of *auteur* theory, as it was mistakenly called, and insofar as the premise of the director as author was seen as a theory of production rather than a critical method, its impact may well have been unfortunate within Hollywood.[7] Certainly Peckinpah's films and career stand for nothing if not a belief in the absolute primacy and authority of the gifted individual. That Peckinpah was aware that this was a doomed model, as the dramatic action of his films suggest, appears not to have deterred their director from aggressively attempting to live it out. In this he differed sharply from his early mentor, Don Siegel, who lived by compromising wherever necessary to make the best film that he could, a policy (shared by another Siegel protégé, Clint Eastwood) that acknowledges Hitchcock's famous maxim—"Ingrid, it's only a *mooovie.*" In contrast, Peckinpah conceived of his work as original and personal creation, "A Sam Peckinpah Film," signed on occasion with a witty self-reflexivity that literally, portentously, inscribes the director within the manly world of the film, as with *The Wild Bunch*'s frame freezing on his name and the line, "If they move, kill them!"

In *Pat Garrett* the credit is actually withheld until some three minutes after the producer's, until Garrett lays the gauntlet before Billy—he is asking the Kid to leave the territory, but if necessary will make him go—at which point Peckinpah freezes the image and imprints his name as author, branding the charged masculine space that his characters inhabit. It is hard to believe that Rudy Wurlitzer's script had the two never meeting until the very end. Peckinpah insisted on the opening scene where the two friends come together at Fort Sumner in the bloody, outrageously callous target practice—how jaded these worthies! Immediately introducing the dueling *dramatis personae* of the legend that provides the film's structure, the scene also reinforces the circular form of the framing device in the action, since Garrett will return to the fort for the showdown. The opening is also impressive for its nuances, balancing good feelings stemming from a shared past ("We did have some times") and underlying hostility at now-diverging paths, the beheading of the chickens immediately establishing aimless (for all the marksmanship) and spectacular brutality as a norm. The threat implied by Pat's gunfire interrupting Billy's is soon made good by the marshal's message: "The electorate wants you gone." Moving to the door of the saloon, Garrett stops and glances back, a pregnant, theatrical moment as the two trade threats and loaded looks, members of the bunch standing about, watching and listening to the *mano-a-mano.*

"How does it feel, Pat?" This question, put to Garrett by Billy, resonates throughout Peckinpah, and points to the ambiguous nature of the law, to how someone still "half-outlaw himself" can overnight become righteous, the system behind him. Looking at Garrett posed against the sky above Billy's cabin in his immaculate black business suit, the spectre of death and capitalism, a cigar jutting from his smiling face, a rifle balanced on his hip pointing to the sky, one would have to say it must feel pretty good. If Pat is in "poor company," as an equally posturing Billy will tell him, arms half-raised in a crucifixion shot borrowed from Penn's film, Garrett's pose up on high amongst the cactus communicates nothing so much as a personality convinced of his absolute right to rule over the landscape he inhabits.

Everyone strikes poses in this world. When Pat's ambush mortally wounds the half-pint Bowdrie, and he, Billy and O'Folliard hunker down in the besieged cabin, Peckinpah provides a measure of how self-conscious their larger-than-life act is by having them deal out a hand of poker while the bullets fly around them. A recurring notion in Peckinpah has it that life is just a game, albeit a deadly serious one. This scene paints the frontier's players as eccentrics reveling in such romantic whimsy, and suggests that when it was time to fold, they could go out in style, material for narrative. Played straight, a ploy that exaggerates the macho heroism, the scene presents the poker as a nihilistic affectation, the players themselves the only audience (apart from us) for their "cool" performance, and especially that of the scrappy Bowdrie, whose vision is blurring so he can't see his cards, and who consequently makes himself available as a decoy to draw fire.

As Robert Warshow pointed out, poker is a basic convention of the genre, a signifier of the inner serenity of the Western hero, of his grace under pressure. But in the degraded and decadent world of the late-frontier, such ideals can hardly survive intact and are here mocked in their excess, rendered even more absurd in a later scene where Garrett's search for Billy brings him to an encounter with Holly, Beaver, and Alias in a bar presided over by a thoroughly obscene Chill Wills. An invitation to poker there gets everyone to the table, but Garrett then draws his gun and indulges a showy, contemptuous power-play, forcing Alias to club Beaver unconscious, pull Wills' hat down over his eyes, and then stand by a shelf bizarrely reciting the contents of cans ("Plums . . . beans . . . succotash"), while Holly is compelled to drink himself drunk and into a fatal lunge for his knife. Ironically, the earlier poker game begun with Bowdrie and O'Folliard continues with Billy's incarceration, stressing the paradox of it all (like Billy dining with Alamosa before he kills him), the friendships continuing across the roles dictated by the law. Here the hands are played with Garrett and J. W. Bell under the vengeful eye of R.G. Armstrong, recycling his zealot's act from *Ride the High Country* as the hammy, demented Deputy Bob Ollinger. Here too, the poker is subverted, Bell folding a strong hand out of pity, as Billy's gallows outside provides a swing for a bevy of typical Peckinpah kids, innocence and death hand-in-hand. Once Garrett has left, however, it is Bell, shot in the back as he tries to run from Billy, and Ollinger, dead by his own shotgun and the sixteen thin dimes it holds, who are executed, not Billy, who continues his witty performance ("Keep the change, Bob") for a fascinated community of groundlings with his improvised song from up in the window, as he frees himself of his manacles. A far cry from the traditional, unifying melodies of the genre—memorably, everywhere in Ford, of course, and in Hawks' *Rio Bravo*—this solo ballad typically celebrates Billy himself and the towns he has seen, none of them "lowdown" as Lincoln.

Where did the weapon Billy finds secreted in the toilet come from? Theories include Pat himself, not such a radical notion if we bear in mind his ambivalence, the desultory pursuit, the possibility that he is following his own script. Or perhaps it is "the people?" In keeping with the legend, Billy is seen as a populist figure, dropping in on homesteaders for dinner, friend to the Mexican sheepherder, Paco, whose death at the hands of Chisum's henchmen will fatefully turn him away from the border and safety. Here, as Billy starts his ride out of Lincoln, he discovers the horse he has been supplied by the old Mexican peasant he has pressed into service is wild enough to unseat him. Cavalierly confiscating a superior mount, and tipping its stunned owner the bloody $1.60 in Bob's body, Billy again begins to ride out, but then stops, turns, and rides back to the same peasant, who is still holding Billy's poncho. A strange little encore—all smug smiles and deep glances by Billy—the retrieving of the poncho has the Kid grandstanding as a friend of old Mexico, a true democrat for all his charisma and the contempt expressed for Lincoln and its gawking, more "civilized" citizenry assembled in all their finery for a different show—his hanging. Finally, he does ride out, the whole town watching, and the Dylan score soars on cue to accompany a cosmic shot of Billy heading out to open range, an extended exit that eulogizes this out-law hero, rather like the serenade that italicizes the ride out by the Bunch from Angel's village, marking it as legendary.

Thereafter, the film neatly contrasts the journeys of its principals. Pat gets his hair cut, and then Peckinpah's design has him heading for his wife, the governor, and Chisum—to all of whom he is accountable now that he is, in Billy's jeer, "a working-man." In contrast, Billy heads out into open country and returns to his bunch, reclaiming his bed and whore from a resigned, lesser mortal, Harry Dean Stanton's Luke. Refreshed, a perky Billy arises bright and early to kill three bounty hunters over breakfast, during which he tells a story about another duel, that rambling narrative's similarity to the film's own drift and violence underscored by the rhyme of the two showdowns, the "let's get to it" of Billy's yarn extending a parallel invitation to the three silent visitors in his audience. Always the ham, here again Billy is self-reflexively staging and performing deadly action, his narrative a frame and punctuation for the duel, during which Billy also makes the acquaintance of Alias.

In casting Bob Dylan in an unscripted role and using his score (although he was finally unhappy with the music's pervasiveness), Peckinpah was boldly challenging his audience to make connections. Music was of course the dominant artistic voice of the period's counter-culture, and Dylan its soul. By employing Dylan alongside Kristofferson and Rita Coolidge (barely recognizable as Billy's girl after cuts), both of whom also evoked anti-establishment culture, Peckinpah erected a dialectical montage between his film's characters and events and those of the period. America's youthful protesters were like the West's last heroes, at the mercy of corrupt law and ruthless institutions, and the fate of Billy the Kid and his boyish bunch provided a mythic parallel for the victimization of an idealistic counter-culture in its struggle against the government and its Vietnam policy.

Jarring the illusion, kicking the audience out momentarily, Dylan's presence here has the distancing effect Peckinpah often aimed for in his work. Much comment-ed on, Dylan's iconographic potency combined with his lack of function opens an oddly disproportionate, privileged space in the film. He is "Alias," an enigma ("That's a good question"), vacant, a cipher, Mr. In-between. To understand Alias, it is helpful to see him in the film's overall design as positioned in opposition to its other privi-leged figure, Sheriff Baker. Always committed to casting for character, Peckinpah had turned to another veteran Western performer, a minor star of the genre in Slim Pickins, for Sheriff Cullen Baker, and had again, as with Alias, riffed on the script to enlarge his scene, in one fell swoop communicating a way of life unto death.

If Baker is to help Garrett go after Black Harris, he tells the Marshal, he wants payment—but when it comes to it, he puts on his badge and flips the coin back. Baker is thus constructed as a figure loyal to himself and a lifetime of service and integrity. A good soldier (as his costume suggests), Baker is defined by the past, the bearer of an identity now threatened by his duties to a law that serves the corporate powers creating the new West. Heart-sick, yearning for surcease and escape, for the possibility of drifting with life's currents, Baker is destined never to use the boat he has been building. Mortally wounded, he heads for the river, sits on its bank, dies, Dylan's mournful music cueing a whole world's passing. An ultimate signifier of loyal-

Bob Dylan as Alias, "a mirror of 'the Kid,'" in a production still.

ty, Baker's meaning is doubled in his partner, a wife who is also a deputy, a deputy who is also a wife, Jurado canonized for her own faithful service, the tears streaking her face as she watches her man expire, respecting him and the moment with her distance, but riding shotgun to the end.

All tics and twitches, a quirky Chaplinesque immigrant to the wild West, Alias has no past and no ties, walking off his printer's job in Lincoln after witnessing Billy's flashy performance and sizing up Garrett and his answering moves. No spouse for Alias; indeed he strikes us as pre-sexual, adolescent, epicene. He is thus a good fit with Billy and his bunch, sharing in the romance and adventure, the childishness and humor. Indeed, the film insists on its construction of Alias as Billy's double—the two swapping lines ritualistically—as an image of the pure child in Billy, a mirror of "the Kid," Billy's soul, balancing the parallel reflection that Pat provides of a more worldly, "grown-up" manhood, aging, housebroken, funereal, a shadow of who he was.

Where Baker unwillingly backs up Garrett, Alias volunteers his services, knifing one of the bounty hunters, a sidekick for Billy in their turkey-hunt hijinx. However, if Dylan's presence is a means of underscoring the anti-establishment spirit of the film, his fate within the diegesis as a signifier of uncertain identity, drift, the future, is both bleak and blank, Garrett making a stock boy of the character and using him to deliver messages ("Boy!"), like Lincoln's errand boy (played by the director's son, Matthew). Another icon becoming capitalist tool, a yuppie witness to "history," Alias is prominent in privileged close-ups as a spectator, grimly looking on to the end.

That history, *Pat Garrett* insists, is the suborning of the best spirits and skills of the West in order to destroy it. If Baker's service and death are the axis of the film, it is because of the characters that cluster together in a supporting system around him—their coercion by Garrett making up *Pat Garrett*'s spine—a gallery of venerable icons richly evocative of the genre, testifying to Peckinpah's determination to construct the West here as a paradise lost, a sad landscape peopled by die-hards and has-beens, the oppressed survivors of the genre's wars. Pickens and Jurado, Elam and Jaeckel, are joined by other classic personalities—Chill Wills' grumpy Lemuel and Emilio Fernandez, *The Wild Bunch*'s Mapache, as Paco, as well as other aging players such as Elisha Cook, Jr., fall guy in *Shane*, and *The Wild Bunch*'s Dub Taylor, both cruelly beaten by Poe, the capitalists' lackey, to give up Billy's whereabouts. As befits a cattle baron and the corporate overlord above this old-world power structure of reluctant retainers and vassals called on to end Billy's threat to the modern era, Barry Sullivan as Chisum aptly presents a face less coded (although still familiar from Sam Fuller's *Forty Guns*). Similarly, as his main agent, James Coburn's ambivalent Pat Garrett can be seen as neatly poised iconographically between the heroic past and a self-serving future, *Major Dundee* and *In Like Flint*.

Katy Jurado, "a wife who is also a deputy, a deputy who is also a wife."

Katy Jurado, (left)"riding shotgun to the end." Slim Pickens (right) as Sheriff Cullen Baker, "the last honest man."

In contrast to this icongraphic classicism drawn on to incarnate the old West and its executioners, the modernist strategy of "making strange" suggested by casting relative newcomer Kristofferson, in his first Western role, and Dylan and Coolidge as the rebellious younger generation, is further supported by a cameo from scriptwriter Wurlitzer as Tom O'Folliard, as well as the presence of little bespectacled Charles Martin Smith as Bowdrie, both of whom die at the cabin siege. L.Q. Jones and Harry Dean Stanton apart, Billy's bunch also includes a number of other less familiar performers, newer faces such as Kristofferson band member Donnie Fritts as Beaver, Richard Bright as Holly, and Luke Askew as Eno. The blankest slate of all is John Beck's Poe, a character without character, who has been forced on Garrett in an ironic comment on the genre convention of the sidekick, cruel payback for tracking Billy, and whom Peckinpah ironically provides with a white horse.

The death of the West is thus played out in a systematic elimination of the youth and frontier spirit of a community at the hands of its older generation, who are thus destroying themselves. The extent of this suicide is vividly apparent in a civil war that has Bowdrie and O'Folliard killed by Garrett's posse, Sheriff Baker killed by Black Harris, Black Harris and Holly killed by Pat, Billy killing Bell, Ollinger and Alamosa, Pat killing Billy, Poe killing Pat. This self-destructive logic is everywhere in the film, in its frame and narrative structure, in Billy's half-hearted attempts to escape, and in Garrett's typically self-dramatizing act, blasting the mirror after he has killed Billy, the image of who he used to be.

The stress on a declining, decaying and decadent world continues through its vignettes of grizzled old geezers, all reluctant accomplices, as the film drifts toward its end. After Baker and Lemuel, and the two greybeards Poe bullies, there is also Rupert, the sleazy bordello owner who reclines on his bar and supplies Garrett with four whores, Peckinpah's absurdist fantasies of sexual excess flaunting a typical invitation to his critics to construct him both as sexist and racist in the "scandalous" composition of a five-way sexual sandwich, a cheerful, sanitized orgy in which two white hookers are accorded the honor of an armpit, while two dark-skinned women are assigned a Garrett leg, and twirl each other's nipples.

Shortly thereafter there is Jaeckel's Sheriff McKinney, sourly chewing his whiskey, but for whose survival we will be grateful. The action will culminate at old Pete Maxwell's, with doddering old Pete doing what the very old do—re-living his glory, repeating old stories, talking to himself—as Pat and Billy describe a final dance, Pat going in, Billy coming out, Billy's love-making ("Jesus!") his final act before the marshal kills him. And of course we must not forget Will the coffin-maker, whom Garrett encounters as he finally approaches Pete's, Death walking in the blowing mist brushing up against a ghost, another icon for the insiders, another Brechtian joke, Peckinpah himself working on a small coffin—for the classical Western, surely—and like Godard's winking appearance in *Breathless* where the director points the cops to Belmondo, Peckinpah here directing Garrett on his way, "Go on—get it over with," and thus acknowledging his own complicity, his crucial role in the murder of the myth.

*   *   *

Writing about Peckinpah in 1969, I argued that on the evidence of his first four films, all Westerns—*The Deadly Companions* and *Ride the High Country* (1962), *Major Dundee* (1964) and *The Wild Bunch* (1969)—the genre was crucial to the director, that it made possible a "distinctive allegorical quality, the present igniting the past, the promise and pain of America brought alive on the screen."[8] Now weighing Peckinpah's overall career, taking into account all his work outside the genre, I find no basis on which to alter that early claim; indeed, if anything, the case for Peckinpah's special relationship with—and reliance on—the Western is immeasurably stronger, arguably self-evident.

If Peckinpah's films can be read as post-modern texts, it is in part because they look back with romantic longing at characters who in turn are perpetually looking back ("We had us some times, didn't we?"), characters forever in "the day after," barbed wire everywhere, El Dorado lost, the movies nostalgia films twice over, the director, characters, and audience, all implicated in a Narcissus-like play of gazes and reflecting surfaces. However, Peckinpah's Westerns are anything but escapes to a hermetic past. The director's basic narrative strategy was always the insistence on the closing frontier, "the times are changing" a line that runs through *Pat Garrett* like a mantra, as it does much of Peckinpah's work. This fin-de-siècle clash of old and modern worlds provided conflict that could stand in for contemporary wars, allowing Peckinpah to celebrate a mythic ideal of America set in the past, and to construct and critique a brutally violent modern world, authorizing the director to throw his bombs. It was because Peckinpah occupied his own frontier, torn between the romantic traditions of the classical form and the sensibility and instincts of a modernist, that he was able to turn the form on its axis, inflecting the genre with great originality and force to reflect the turmoil and divisions of a new era.

Peckinpah died in 1984, fifty-nine years old. There were only fourteen features, the product of some twenty-three years, six Westerns, *Pat Garrett* the grand finale, another broken monument. The director could not have known these would be his only efforts within the genre, nor how badly he would miss it. Peckinpah's allegiance to the form would be apparent in the re-working of its characters, themes and settings in much of his other work. There is of course the rodeo film, *Junior Bonner* (1971), the modern banditry of *The Getaway* (1972), the revenge-driven, Mexico-based *Bring Me the Head of Alfredo Garcia* (1974), and his penultimate film, *Convoy* (1978), the white-trash trucker movie set in the southwest with its motorized cowboys. And of course there are the recurrent elements—the theme of threatened identity, the masculine codes of behaviour, the preoccupation with savagery and violence—that are re-worked in the early, spectacularly controversial *Straw Dogs* (1971), as well as the war film, *Cross of Iron* (1977), and the political thrillers, *Killer Elite* (1975) and *The Osterman Weekend* (1983), Peckinpah's last hurrah.

It comes as no surprise that the two strongest works outside the genre proper rework the Western in contemporary forms, expressing the contrasting sides of Peckinpah's bipolar artistic personality. A charming film, *Junior Bonner*'s piquant tone depends in part on our shaky respect for its anachronistic, arguably arrested, aging rodeo heroes, father and son, whose family is constructed as the site of a divided America. And then there is *Bring Me the Head of Alfredo Garcia*, his most aggressively experimental, surrealist and personal work, a pastiche of *The Searchers* in which Warren Oates incarnates Peckinpah himself as desperate, demented hero holding aloft the symbol of a triumphant bestiality—or, alternatively, the head of John Ford, whose tomb he has burglarized—a film so challenging in its grotesquerie that for many it accomplishes what at times seemed the director's ultimate goal, total audience alienation.

Although much of his other work outside the genre was distinctive, to survey those productions, and the later films in particular, measuring the disparity between the enormous effort and the modest achievement, is to appreciate how much the Western mattered. Divorced from the romance and epic sweep of the form, Peckinpah's characters often seem to undergo a *reductio ad absurdum*, the gestures that would carry dramatic weight in ritualistic and mythic contexts appearing affectations in modern dress. Absent the historical frame of the frontier and its "tragic hero" motif that was Peckinpah's personal narrative paradigm, the problem the director faced was that the absurdist dilemma of his characters—trying to live out a heroic code in an unheroic, indeed post-modern world—always threatened to engulf the whole work in absurdity and inauthenticity, the theme overwhelming the material.

For a time, however, Peckinpah's great good fortune was to find his home as an action director within the greatest of action genres, the Western, within the most sophisticated and dominant of action cinemas, the American. The result was original and ground-breaking work that touched the very pinnacle of cinema. A consummate creature of the film medium, the director's great strengths were his inspired mastery of visual signs and forms, his gift for iconic representation on the one hand, and his impeccable dialectical instincts for challenging, often Brechtian, montage on the oth-er. In my view it was this command of the cinema's codes and modalities that allowed Peckinpah to inflect the Western genre with the force of an oppositional artist in his critique of American myths and ideologies. Ironically, in a final exchange of myth and reality, the effect of Peckinpah's critical re-invention of the genre, pushing the envelope to address a new era and audience, was to spearhead a revisionist exca-vation of the Western that contributed in no small measure to its virtual disappearance in the 80s, the director finally, irrevocably, living out the tragic myth of his gun-fighter-heroes whose acts help to close the door on their own freedom.

Paul Seydor would have us believe that the genre was incidental to Peckinpah's success, that the films are closer to psychological novels, the director a creative genius, his brethren Shakespeare, Melville and Mailer. We are to understand that Peckinpah is not a genre director, and his films are not Westerns "in the generic sense than in the sense of their being set in the West and in the Western past and of their being concerned with the subjects traditionally associated with the West . . . ." Apart from presumably validating Peckinpah as the totally original creative artist, this circumloquacious sophistry sets up the claim that the movies could be also classified and studied in other ways—"say, between his so-called 'violent' and 'gentle' films."[9] However, in a conveniently half-baked auteurism, Seydor wisely sticks to the Westerns, and fails to confront the decline in Peckinpah's work after *Pat Garrett.*

In my view it is foolhardy to deny Peckinpah the sustaining, creative tradition of the Western, the symbolic and allegorical dimensions of which were so valuable to the director. Clearly, a dialectical relationship obtained, the director taking as much as he gave. Peckinpah produced landmark works, an immense contribution, the collective impact of his work, and especially *The Wild Bunch,* bringing the form to a paroxysm, decisively mapping the genre's future. At the same time, it seems to me undeniable that the language of the Western in its turn brought Peckinpah alive, supplied his canvas, shielded him somewhat from his own toxic elements, and provided him with focus and direction.

*   *   *

For me, one image from *Pat Garrett* sums up Peckinpah's qualities and achievement. It comes after Billy has broken out of Lincoln's jail and ridden out into open country. As twilight falls, in a shot wholly black-and-white but for a thin orange streak where the sun has just set, Billy makes his way along the horizon, a dark reflection of the rider materializing in the water below as he descends by a small pond and a stand of trees dark against the skyline, pausing there to doff his poncho. Oddly accented in the film, nearly forgotten in Lincoln, then donned by Billy against the heat on the trail, the poncho is a minor icon that inevitably recalls Clint Eastwood's Man With No Name. In Leone's *A Fistful of Dollars,* however, the cloak had been a source of mystery and invulnerability (a protective shield underneath), suggesting a hero who, unlike our Kid, still retained traces of a messianic function. Given that lineage, it is appropriate that this snapshot frames Bonney's removal of the garment.

At first glance this striking image—dark rider and landscape reflected in the water—may seem simply a stock genre vista, a pretty example of Peckinpah's self-consciously painterly style. There is no dramatic weight, no brackets around it signifying "Tragic Hero," as with the shot of Pike riding across the dunes in pain and shame after falling from his horse in *The Wild Bunch.* There is, however, a haunting quality here that grows as the traveling shot pauses, the Kid stilling his horse to remove the poncho—the pause seeming to invite our own pause and reflection, nudging us to contemplate this reflected Billy, the "real" Billy above completely hidden in shadows and visible only in the reflected image, the shadow rider and the dark leafless trees heavy in the water beyond him—the pause encouraging us perhaps to understand

Above, John Ford's Rio Grande. *Below, Billy's pause creates "an inverted Ford icon . . . a post-modern emblem for the genre."*

that this is our reflection, too, America in the dark and dead in the water, asking us to turn the cowboy over in our mind, and to discover that, as always, Peckinpah is exposing the negative of the myth and its classical iconography. Employing his masterful compositional effects, Peckinpah here creates a magisterial visual design that both evokes and subverts, constructs and critiques, the image that is the very bedrock of the grand tradition of the Western, the silhouette of the lone cowboy against the sky but *reversed* here, Billy revealed to us as an inverted Ford icon, a shadow reflected upside down in the water, the cowboy a dark figure in the dark, visible only as a double or dead ringer.

Both the spontaneity and the calculation of the Peckinpah style, the invitation to contemplate the past as a mirror to our own era, the complexity of the relationships with both heroes and genre, the love for what the Western was and the necessity of seeing it anew, of turning it all upside down, the classicism and the modernity, the loyalty and the betrayal—everything is there, crystallized in a post-modern emblem for the genre. Peckinpah holds the shot well after Billy has left, brooding on the dark landscape of the West reflected in the still water, the mirror image of America's golden dream in its twilight.

Apart from the spaghetti Western, Peckinpah explicitly refers to two other classics of the form in *Pat Garrett—High Noon*, with Jurado and her judgment on the unworthiness of the new order, and *Shane*, the boy casting the stones at Garrett as he rides away from Bonney's corpse at the end. However, Peckinpah's indebtedness to the collective tradition of the Western is everywhere apparent, and I like to think it is partly re-paid here, in this supreme image that defines his core as an artist, this self-referential sign so evocative of the Western myth and of Ford, the earlier master of Western horizons whom he had succeeded.

NOTES

1. Paul Seydor, *Peckinpah: The Western Films* (Chicago: University of Illinois, 1980). An expanded second edition, *Peckinpah: The Western Films—A Reconsideration*, was published in 1997. Seydor's voluminous scholarship positions him as a leading Peckinpah scholar. However, Seydor's roots are in literary and *belles-lettres* traditions, and his project is to appropriate Peckinpah for a privileged pantheon of American writers (although Shakespeare is prominent, too) from Emerson and Twain to Hemingway and Mailer, who represent a tradition, innocent of ideology, centered on "the masculine principle."

   Seydor constructs the films as a kind of dense visual literature, and treats their heroes as complex psychological characters rather than signs or types, who learn (and thus can teach us) how to "face reality and its imperatives unflinchingly" (1980, p. 226). Empathic with the heroic artist, the critic is authorized to become a creative partner in the "writing" of Peckinpah's text. Thus Seydor's account of the film as Pat Garrett's tragedy rests in large measure on seeing the main body of the work as subjective, a record of events from Pat's point of view, despite his being off-stage during half the film's action and the absence of any cues in the text that invite or endorse such an interpretation.

But, of course, Garrett hasn't figured it out, and it won't be over
for the better part of three decades. Even then, after years of turning it
over and around and upside down, he still can't figure it out, still can't
make it come any clearer or better or straighter. And when it passes
before him for one last time as the bullets tear through his body, the
most that he achieves is a dim, tragic recollection that he was a link in
the chain of causality which has brought his life to this dying fall.
(1980, p.209)

More than any other American filmmaker in the post-war period, Peckinpah has
generated big books, large claims, voluminous research, exhaustive analyses, a Boswell-
like devotion, aptly epic undertakings. Apart from Seydor (whose *Reconsideration* runs
nearly 400 pages), there are Garner Simmons's *Peckinpah: A Portrait in Montage* (Austin:
University of Texas Press, 260 pages), and David Weddle's *"If They Move . . . Kill 'Em"*
(New York: Grove Press, 1994, 586 pages), among others. Although one is grateful for
the detailed research into the various versions of the films (Seydor), the extensive production histories (Simmons), and the blow by blow account of the director's bouts with
studios, wives and addictions (Weddle), reading these studies, it is difficult to escape the
impression of a collective idolatry. Peckinpah's career and films often suggest that he
had heavily invested his persona in the cults of personality, masculinity and the artist. It
was perhaps inevitable that he would find collaborators in his romantic myth of the
"indomitable," tortured genius, critics and journalists who heroically rescue the films
from a non-existent neglect and promote them as amongst the supreme achievements
of the 20th century.

2. Quoted by Jan Aghed, "Pat Garrett and Billy the Kid," *Sight and Sound* (Spring, 1973), pp.
65-9. Peckinpah's interest in the legend was long-standing, his first feature script in 1957
having been based on Charles Neider's *The Authentic Death of Hendry Jones*, which in turn
had been based on Garrett's memoir, *The Authentic Life of Billy the Kid*, and which became
Marlon Brando's *One-Eyed Jacks* (1960), although largely transformed and long after
Peckinpah and numerous others, including director Stanley Kubrick, had moved on.

3. Paul Seydor, *Peckinpah: The Western Films A Reconsideration.* The second edition usefully
includes a detailed record of the different versions of *Pat Garrett* (p. 298).

4. Jim Kitses, "The Rise and Fall of the American West," *Film Comment,* (Winter 1970/71),
p. 17.

5. Brad Stevens, *"Pat Garrett and Billy the Kid,"* Ian Cameron and Douglas Pye, eds. *The Book
of Westerns,* (New York: Continuum, 1996).

6. Seydor (1980), p. 196.

7. Of course ambitious producers who were in charge of the bucks could also seize on the
concept. As Charles B. FitzSimons put it apropos producing *The Deadly Companions:* "Sam
shot an ending for the picture that I couldn't use . . . that was the Peckinpah version . . .
But you have to understand . . . I am a great believer in the auteur theory as it applies to a

producer." Quoted in Garner Simmons, *Peckinpah: A Portrait in Montage* (Austin: University of Texas Press, 1982), pp. 38-9.

8. Jim Kitses, *Horizons West* (London: Thames & Hudson/British Film Institute, 1969), p. 169.

9. Seydor, *Peckinpah: The Western Films*, pp. xvi, xvii. In his *Reconsideration*, Seydor drops the quoted equivocations about the genre, and concedes of the non-Westerns that "it is doubtful they can be grouped together as cogently or coherently as the Westerns" (p. xxiv).

Clint Eastwood in Joe Kidd *(1972) and with Will Sampson in* The Outlaw Josey Wales *(1976).*

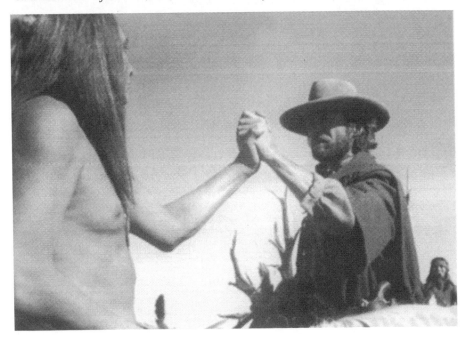

A FISTFUL OF MEMORIES:
Interview with Clint Eastwood

Kenneth Turan (1992)

While other people complain about the absence of Westerns, Clint Eastwood continues to make them. *Unforgiven*, the tale of a reformed killer tempted to fall back on his old ways, is his 10th, the latest in a steady skein that dates from Sergio Leone's *A Fistful of Dollars* in 1964. Eastwood's associations with the genre go back further still, to his 1959 debut as hard-bitten Rowdy Yates on TV's *Rawhide*.

Eastwood's Westerns, usually employing a variant of the emotionless Man With No Name persona he created for his three films with Leone, reached a kind of apocalyptic crescendo with a trio he directed himself *High Plains Drifter*, *The Outlaw Josey Wales* and *Pale Rider*. Yet he has also done quasi- musical Westerns (*Paint Your Wagon*), modern-day comic Westerns (*Bronco Billy*) and even police dramas that were really Westerns in disguise (*Coogan's Bluff*). Given all this, it seemed an appropriate time to explore Eastwood's thoughts on the Western and the actor-director, looking fit and relaxed in his quiet bungalow on the Warner Bros. lot in Burbank, was willing to oblige.

Question: Why did you want to do another Western?

Answer: I never want to do any particular genre or any particular film for the sake of the genre: it's always the individual story. One of the things I do like is that it goes back to my roots as an actor coming of age in Western films.

245

Q: How did you come across David Peoples' script?

A: This is a project that was written years ago, in the late 70s. It was optioned to Francis Coppola, but he was going through some hard times and couldn't get it together. It was called to my attention in the early 1980s, when I was looking for a writer to do some stuff for me. I thought, "Gee, I really like this, it's too bad it's all tied up." But when I called the writer's agent he said, "Francis gave up the option two days ago; the script is available." So I bought it and sort of sat on it for years. I always thought it was a little gem, but I figured I had to age into it.

Q: What did you like about it?

A: I don't know whether it's revisionist or whatever people want to call it, but it's different, it's unusual, and it's hard to find stuff in the Western vein that's unusual. You can't quite predict it; from the very beginning you don't know quite where it is going. You don't quite know who's going to be the hero of the piece, and the protagonist is inept at certain things.

Q: The first glimpse of you, in fact, is very non-heroic, as a farmer falling down in the mud chasing some pigs.

A: I've never pictured myself as the guy on the white horse or wearing the white hat on the mighty steed, though I've ridden some good horses periodically. I've always liked heroes that've had some sort of weakness or problems to overcome besides the problem of the immediate script. That always keeps it much more interesting than doing it the conventional way.

John Wayne once wrote me a letter telling me he didn't like *High Plains Drifter*. He said it wasn't about the people who really pioneered the West. I realized that there's two different generations, and he wouldn't understand what I was doing. *High Plains Drifter* was meant to be a fable; it wasn't meant to show the hours of pioneering drudgery. It wasn't supposed to be anything about settling the West.

Q: Have you always been a fan of Westerns?

A: When I was a kid there was no television, but you had Westerns on the second half of the bill in theaters a lot. I grew up watching all the John Ford and Anthony Mann Westerns that came out in the 1940s and 50s, John Wayne in all those cavalry kinds of Westerns and Jimmy Stewart. The B-Westerns too, the ones with Randolph Scott. Some of them were good, some were not so good, but we enjoyed them just for the adventure of it all. I grew up through a whole era of them.

One of my favorite films when I was growing up was *The Ox-Bow Incident*, which analyzed mob violence and the power of the mob getting out of control. I saw it again recently and it holds up really well. I don't know how the public feels about those kinds of films, but I just felt it was time to do one again.

Clint Eastwood as The Man With No Name.

Q: *Unforgiven* **also seems to emphasize the cost of violence.**

A: I've done as much as the next person as far as creating mayhem in Westerns, but what I like about *Unforgiven* is that every killing in it has a repercussion. It really tears people up when they are violent, and I felt it was time for that kind of thing in the world. And it became more contemporary during the last year with law enforcement events here in Los Angeles. An incident will trigger decisions, maybe the wrong decisions or the wrong reactions by people, and then there's really no way to stop things. But the public may say "Yeah, I get the morality of it, but I like it better when you're just blowing people away."

Q: **Did you think you'd be doing Westerns for so long?**

A: When I first went and did *A Fistful of Dollars*, there were a lot of predictions in the trade papers that Westerns were through. And I said, "Swell, now that I'm doing one they're through," but that film turned out to have its place in the world.

Eastwood as William Munny in Unforgiven: *"Maybe the last film of that type for me."*

The funny thing was that a few years before I'd gone down to a theater on Western Avenue in L.A. that ran Japanese films. A buddy of mine, a big aficionado of samurai films, had taken me to see this film called *Yojimbo*. I remember sitting there and saying, "Boy, this would be a great Western if only someone had nerve enough to do it, but they'd never have enough nerve." So it was ironic when, a few years later, someone handed me a script for what became *A Fistful of Dollars*, and about five or 10 pages in I recognized it as an obvious rip-off of *Yojimbo*.

Q: *Unforgiven* is dedicated to the memory of Sergio Leone and Don Siegel, both of whom directed you in Westerns. Is there anything about the film that makes that especially apropos?

A: It is a favorite script of mine. Sergio and I hadn't seen each other for many years until *Bird* opened in Italy and we hung out for a few days. It was almost like he was just saying goodby because he died right after that. Don and I were really good buddies; I loved his cantankerous, rebellious ways. We had some good times together and made some good films that were important in my life. It seemed a logical film to dedicate to them because either one of them would have liked to have made this type of story. Don, especially, would have loved this script.

Q: *Unforgiven* brings to mind other elegiac Westerns—for instance, Sam Peckinpah's *The Wild Bunch*. What did you think of that?

A: It was a good movie, but I've never been one for the slow-motion technique, the ballet of violence. It was very effective, and the predecessor to a lot of people trying to do the same thing, but I never liked it. I've always thought that drama is really the anticipation before the action happens, the buildup to it, and the action itself is like shuffling a deck of cards, so fast it's kind of unreal.

Q: And what do you think about *The Searchers*?

A: Well, it's got some wonderful things in it. I don't think it holds up in the sense that there's some sub-characters that wouldn't play today. I think that whole thing with the ingenue and Jeffrey Hunter would be considered pretty edgy by today's standards. But I think Wayne gave one of the best performances he ever did.

Q: Having made so many Westerns, how does it feel to get the gear on one more time?

A: It's like a little nostalgia twinge, all of a sudden you go, "Here I am again, 35 years later." I wear the gear around for a while, I live in the shirts and pants. Hats especially you've got to wear around a little bit.

A lot of modern Westerns have disturbed me because the hairdos make them look like they took place in 1965. If you look back at old photos, people always had their hair short. If they were going to pay for a haircut, they were going to get their money's worth. For *Unforgiven*, I just took sheep shears and cut.

I thought *Dances With Wolves* was an admirable project, and the visuals were quite stunning. But it was kind of a contemporary guy out West who was interested in ecology and women's rights and Indian rights. If you did it like it was, people probably could've given a crap less about that in those days, but maybe that's what is needed to get a newer generation of moviegoers interested.

Q: What is it about the Western that makes it so resilient?

A: I guess because of the simplicity of the times. Now everything's so complicated, so mired down in bureaucracy that people can't fathom a way of sorting it out. In the West, even though you could get killed, it seems more manageable, like a lone individual might be able to work things out some way. In our society today, the idea of one person making a difference one way or the other is remote.

Q: Would you want to do another Western after this one?

A: If I was ever going to do a last Western, this would be it because it kind of sums up what I feel. Maybe that's why I didn't do it right away. I was kind of savoring it as the last of that genre, maybe the last film of that type for me.

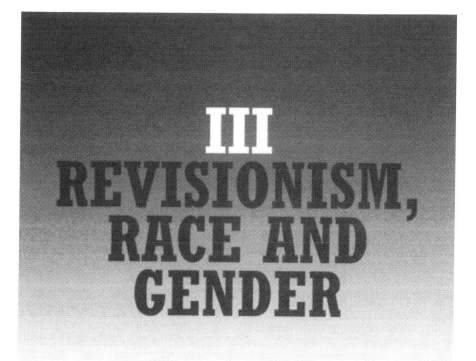

III
REVISIONISM, RACE AND GENDER

MY HEROES HAVE NEVER BEEN COWBOYS & RESERVATION DRIVE-IN

Sherman Alexie (1993)

MY HEROES HAVE NEVER BEEN COWBOYS

1. In the reservation textbooks, we learned Indians were invented in 1492 by a crazy mixed-blood named Columbus. Immediately after class dismissal, the Indian children traded in those American stories and songs for a pair of tribal shoes. *These boots are made for walking, babe, and that's just what they'll do. One of these days these boots are gonna walk all over you.*

2. Did you know that in 1492 every Indian instantly became an extra in the Great American Western? But wait, I never wondered what happened to Randolph Scott or Tom Mix. The Lone Ranger was never in my vocabulary. On the reservation, when we played Indians and cowboys, all of us little Skins fought on the same side against the cowboys in our minds. We never lost.

3. Indians never lost their West, so how come I walk into the supermarket and find a dozen cowboy books telling me How The West Was Won? Curious, I travel to the world's largest shopping mall, find the Lost and Found Department. "Excuse me," I say. "I seem to have lost the West. Has anybody turned it in?" The clerk tells me I can find it in the Sears Home Entertainment Department, blasting away on fifty televisions.

4. On Saturday morning television, the cowboy has fifty bullets in his six-shooter; he never needs to reload. It's just one more miracle for this country's heroes.

5. My heroes have never been cowboys; my heroes carry guns in their minds.

6. *Win their hearts and minds and we win the war.* Can you hear that song echo across history? If you give the Indian a cup of coffee with six cubes of sugar, he'll be your servant. If you give the Indian a cigarette and a book of matches, he'll be your friend. If you give the Indian a can of commodities, he'll be your lover. He'll hold you tight in his arms, cowboy, and two-step you out-side.

7. Outside it's cold and a confused snow falls in May. I'm watching some western on TBS, colorized, but the story remains the same. Three cowboys string telegraph wire across the plains until they are confronted by the entire Sioux nation. The cowboys, 19th century geniuses, talk the Indians into touching the wire, holding it in their hands and mouths. After a dozen or so have hold of the wire, the cowboys crank the portable generator and electrocute some of the Indians with a European flame and chase the rest of them away, bareback and burned. All these years later, the message tapped across my skin remains the same.

8. It's the same old story whispered on the television in every HUD house on the reservation. It's 500 years of that same screaming song, translated from the American.

9. Lester FallsApart found the American dream in a game of Russian Roulette: one bullet and five empty chambers. "It's Manifest Destiny," Lester said just before he pulled the trigger five times quick. "I missed," Lester said just before he reloaded the pistol: one empty chamber and five bullets. "Maybe we should call this Reservation Roulette," Lester said just before he pulled the trigger once at his temple and five more times as he pointed the pistol toward the sky.

10. Looking up into the night sky, I asked my brother what he thought God looked like and he said "God probably looked like John Wayne."

11. We've all killed John Wayne more than once. When we burned the ant pile in our backyard, my brother and I imagined those ants were some cavalry or another. When Brian, that insane Indian boy from across the street, suffocated neighborhood dogs and stuffed their bodies into the reservation high school basement, he must have imagined those dogs were cowboys, come back to break another treaty.

12. Every frame of the black and white western is a treaty; every scene in this elaborate serial is a promise. But what about the reservation home movies? What about the reservation heroes? I remember this: Down near Bull's Pasture, Eugene stood on the pavement with a gallon of tequila under his arm. I watched in the rearview mirror as he raised his arm to wave goodbye and dropped the bottle, glass and dreams of the weekend shattered. After all these years, that moment is still the saddest of my whole life.

13. Your whole life can be changed by the smallest pain.

14. *Pain is never added to pain. It multiplies.* Arthur, here we are again, you and I, fancydancing through the geometric progression of our dreams. Twenty years ago, we never believed we'd lose. Twenty years ago, television was our way of finding heroes and spirit animals. Twenty years ago, we never knew we'd spend the rest of our lives in the reservation of our minds, never knew we'd stand outside the gates of the Spokane Indian Reservation without a key to let ourselves back inside. From a distance, that familiar song. Is it country and western? Is it the sound of hearts breaking? Every song remains the same here in America, this country of the Big Sky and Manifest Destiny, this country of John Wayne and bro-

"God probably looked just like John Wayne."

ken treaties. Arthur, I have no words which can save our lives, no words approaching forgiveness, no words flashed across the screen at the reservation drive-in, no words promising either of us top billing. Extras, Arthur, we're all extras.

RESERVATION DRIVE-IN

The French Connection

"Drive, damn it, drive," Seymour yells as we fishtail through the reservation drive-in at noon, weave between speaker stands, over speed bumps, circle the snack bar where pioneers cower and refuse to let go of their popcorn. Once again, we chase the tail of some Crazy Horse dream, chase the theft of our lives. What matter if there's a case of beer bottles in the back seat? What matter if Seymour is farsighted in one eye and nearsighted in the other? What matter if the drive-in manager calls the Tribal Police? What matter if the change in the ashtray is only enough gas money to get us

"We're all extras": Apache, Winchester '73.

halfway? What matter if we break into the projection booth and run the movie in broad daylight? What matter if Gene Hackman drives us quickly into the unsteady future?

Rocky

Do you remember those Yakima Indian boys played the theme song from *Rocky* ninety times straight one summer day in 1978, played it on secondhand trumpets, played it in their garage, door open wide, the first and last reservation amphitheater? They were always barefoot, their toes so Yakima we all knew they didn't belong on the Spokane Indian Reservation, but there they were: the barefoot, bareback, Yakima Indian boys' secondhand trumpet duet. Do you remember the name of that goddamn song? Was it *Gonna Fly Now*, and did they fly after their station wagon, packed full of reservation souvenirs, left all of us Spokane Indians behind? Didn't Arnold find one of those trumpets years later in the trash and blow it hard, blow air loud until he couldn't breathe, his heart punching against his rib cage?

Enter the Dragon

Suddenly, the Indian boy is Bruce Lee. Maybe he's only the Bruce Lee of the reservation playground, kicking every other child aside on his climb to the top of the slide. *But tell me, Mr. Lee, what's the use?* There is no soundtrack for the rest of that Indian boy's life, no sudden change in music to warn him of impending dangers. Mr. Lee, in your last movie, in your climactic battle with Han in his hall of mirrors, it was beautiful when you smashed those mirrors and won the war with yourself, that interior battle. But you died soon after that movie, Mr. Lee, and never finished the next. Now, there is a photograph of the Indian boy kneeling beside your Seattle gravestone. He looks straight into the camera; he does not know what comes next.

Star Wars

Dick from Somerville calls in the middle of the night. "The next astronaut to set foot on the moon is to be an Indian," he tells me. I walk out into the reservation starry night where the moon hangs low on the horizon, another bright and shining promise, another measure of the distance between touching and becoming. Sometimes it is too much to ask for: survival. There are too many dangers, a fresh set of villains waiting for us in the next half-hour, and then in the next, and the next. They murder us, too, these heroes we find in the reservation drive-in. The boy, Luke Skywalker, rises up against his dark father and the Indian boys cheer, rise up and fall out of car windows, honk horns, flash headlights, all half-anger until the movie ends and leaves us with the white noise of an empty screen. Over and over, we make these movies our own promises, imagine our fathers never lose, pretend our mothers slice their skin a hundred times in testament. Soon, we will sit around old drums and sing songs: "You promised us the earth and all we got was the moon."

The Bicycle Thief

Charlie Chaplin was a Spokane Indian. He was drunk in the Breakaway Bar when someone stole his bicycle. For weeks, he waddled around the reservation on foot, his Levi's hung low on his hips, nothing surprising—until another bicycle was stolen from between the phone booths outside Irene's Grocery, and then a bike was missing from the community center, then two from the Longhouse. The Tribal Police Chief had no comment, the Tribal Council called a general meeting but not one Skin arrived. Every Indian was on foot. They walked and walked, raised arms in greeting, but never said a word. The bicycles were all gone but not one Indian said a word. Charlie Chaplin was braiding his hair when he cleared his throat and said, "Now." Surprised by the sound, he said it again, louder, shouted it as he ran across the reservation. "Now," he said. He said, "This is not a silent movie. Our voices will save our lives."

LOOKING AT LOOK'S MISSING REVERSE SHOT:
Psychoanalysis and Style in John Ford's The Searchers

Peter Lehman (1981)

During the opening credit sequence of *The Searchers*, we hear an all-male singing group asking:

What makes a man to wander?
What makes a man to roam?
What makes a man to leave bed and home?

What, we may also very well wonder, must a woman do? The answer comes in the first shot of the film: wait for the man to get done searching. The opening shot of the film is curious since it begins in mid-action. Nothing has been established (it is so dark, the entire screen is black); a door opens and we see a woman frozen in the doorway looking out. It is as if her function were to wait and open the door at the right moment. We see her open the door, we do not see her involved in any activity from which she is distracted. She seems to exist waiting, immobile, looking out. Thus, the credit sequence with the all-male group singing about masculine concerns excludes any place for the woman, and the first shot of the film gives her the only place possible: if men must search their whole lives through, women must wait at home for them to return.

An ideological analysis of *The Searchers* reveals a serious problem concerning the place of women in general within the film. In this article, however, I wish to examine an even more specific ideological problem concerning the place of one woman—the Indian squaw whom Marty inadvertently marries. It is important that this character's name not be thought of as "Luke." Her name, in fact, is "Look" and the distinction is significant. It is easy to understand how some might think of Luke as her name. We hear Marty say, "Aw, look," and "Hey, look" to her. Once, desperately trying to communicate with her, he repeats, "Aw, look." She responds in her native language and Ethan Edwards, overhearing the exchange, translates for Marty, "She says her name is Wild Goose Flying in the Night Sky, but she'll answer to 'Luke' if that pleases you." Ethan pronounces the name as that commonly spelled L-u-k-e in the English language. But it is his pronunciation; it is not what Marty calls her. In a film which deals extensively with epistemological questions relating to language and perception, this is of obvious importance.

I have written extensively elsewhere about the centrality in *The Searchers* of situations involving how characters gain and communicate knowledge.[1] Direct visual perception is contrasted with mediated accounts; what the eye sees is contrasted with what one hears or reads about. Even the phonetic alphabet is contrasted with other kinds of signs such as an arrow shape constructed on the ground out of rocks. Part of the complexity of this epistemological theme in *The Searchers* involves the cross-cultural situation of whites and Indians. Briefly, Marty, because of ignorance of Indian culture, marries a woman without knowing it. He thinks he has traded for a blanket, not a woman. When he learns otherwise, he tries to explain the situation with an

Marty, because of ignorance of Indian culture, marries a woman without knowing it. "Aw, look."

"Aw, look." In a film so concerned with the act of looking and language encoding, the implications of the name are clear.

But what interests me here is something more than this thematization of Look's place in the film. Ford uses carefully structured off-screen space as a major formal strategy in *The Searchers* to develop the epistemological theme. There is much in the film which we don't see and which the characters don't see. All of this, however, a good formal analysis can account for with reference to the notion of style. Part of the style of *The Searchers*, in other words, involves absences, things which we don't see. What I want to investigate in this paper is a single shot where we don't see Look—a shot which may be an absence of a different kind than that which could be included under the rubric of style.

The moment in question comes in the scene where Look acquires her name. Ethan sits by the campfire, drinking a cup of coffee. Marty, despairingly, goes off to sleep. He lies on top of a hill and Look goes up and lies down next to him. In a two shot, we see Marty sit up and kick her down the hill. She rolls out of the frame and Ford cuts to a shot of Ethan laughing heartily at the spectacle. Suddenly, Marty runs up to Ethan and exchanges words with him. Each time that I have seen the film with an audience, there is wild laughter when Marty kicks Look down the hill. In fact, the laughter is always so uproarious that it drowns out the ensuing dialogue between Marty and Ethan.

This part of the scene has always disturbed me. In fact, I was recently surprised when someone proposed to me that Ford intended the moment as comic. I always wrote the audience laughter off to their insensitivity. This moment in the scene may have struck me as bad or brutal, but certainly not comic. Being forced to think about it, I'm not certain now that the moment isn't indeed comic. Look is, after all, treated as a comic character. The part is cast with a woman (Beulah Archuletta) whose body type and face are meant to suggest an undesirable, silly chubbiness. Look has her own musical theme on the soundtrack and it is lighthearted and comic. I don't have the slightest idea whether Ford intended Look's being kicked down the hill to be funny. Nor do I care. And I say this not just because of the obvious way that the question leads one into the intentional fallacy. Whether the moment was meant to be funny or serious, whether the audience is "right" or "wrong" in laughing, the moment is equally profoundly disturbing. Why?

My own personal reaction to the moment has undergone something of the following process of change. First I dismissed the whole thing as an irrelevant embarrassment in the midst of a brilliant film. Upon reflection, however, it became clear to me that Marty's kicking Look down the hill was anything but irrelevant. The scene and the moment have a formal complexity within the film. Briefly, it is a variation on the central narrative situation. The obsessive search is motivated by the profoundly irrational fear of sex taking place between a white woman and an Indian man. Ethan is maniacally driven by fear of this type of miscegenation. Yet, when faced with the sexual reversal of a white man with an Indian woman, he merely finds the whole thing funny. He obviously doesn't make any conscious connection and sees no contradiction. He laughs when he first realizes that Marty has married Look and thus the apparent motivation of the cut to him after Marty kicks Look down the hill; the whole thing is nothing but joke to Ethan. Then there is the larger formal context which contrasts courtship rituals between cultures: while Laurie reads about the event, we see the ludicrous spectacle of Charlie McCorry's courtship of her. Suddenly, the Indian custom whereby Marty ended up with Look doesn't seem so strange.

Approached in this light, I changed my original opinion of the scene. Far from being an irrelevant embarrassment, it now seemed to me a highly sophisticated scene with many references and reverberations throughout the film. Which it is. But it is, unfortunately, at the same time, something more or perhaps less.

It is not at the level of narrative or thematic formal relationships that the disturbing problem in the scene lies; rather it is in the way Ford spatially and temporally structures it. He manages to shoot and edit the scene in such a way that we never see the consequences of Look being kicked down the hill.[2] This need not to look at what he has done to Look drives Ford to place a slight spatial and temporal discontinuity at the heart of the moment.

The obvious Hollywood convention used to structure the scene would be to follow the action. Thus, for example, there could be a reverse shot showing Look roll down the hill, or, at the very least, a pan shot which would follow her movement. But Ford chooses another Hollywood convention—the cut to a reaction shot. However, he never returns to the action involving Look. The shot sequence is as follows:

1. LS—frontal view, Marty kicks Look down the hill; she rolls out of the frame.
2. MS—frontal view of Ethan laughing.
3. LS—as before, Marty gets up and rushes out of the frame.
4. Cut just as Marty exits the frame to a LS side view of Ethan as Marty enters frame right.

Thus, once Look rolls out of the frame in shot 1 of this shot sequence, we don't see her again until after the action of the fall is completed. But the need to not look at Look falling raises a problem for Ford—how to get Marty over to Ethan's space in such a way that we don't even get a glimpse of Look in the rear of the frame. The problem is that she lies between the two men. Ford does this with shots 3 and 4. He waits until Marty exits the frame in shot 3 and chooses a setup in shot 4 where Marty can enter frame right almost as the cut takes place. But something is wrong—a moment in space and time is missing and it is not just the innocent Hollywood elision of boring insignificant moments. Marty reaches Ethan too quickly considering the space to be crossed. The cut which takes place on his exit in shot 3 and entry in shot 4 suggests a continuity which is not there. The reason that Marty seems to arrive too quickly is that there is a bit of space which he doesn't cross-precisely that space where Look lies. Not only doesn't Ford follow Look's action in the fall, he can't even allow a glimpse of it in the rear of the frame.

After Marty and Ethan talk, Ethan gets concerned that Look has overheard them and walks out frame right, followed by Marty. Ford cuts to an empty frame (only a bit of the top of Look's head is barely visible in the lower right hand corner of the frame) which Ethan and Marty then enter. They reach down and pull Look up into the frame. Even this shot is odd. It contains another spatial problem. We last saw Look rolling out of a long shot at a high velocity. Given the establishing shot of the scene, we have some idea of where she would be, but she is nowhere near there. In fact, she may be closer to the place from which she was kicked than when we last saw her roll out of shot 1.[3] And why the empty space for a moment at the beginning of this shot? Ford doesn't even want us to see the spectacle of Look lying on the ground. So she suddenly reappears and the narrative continues.

To complete an analysis of this scene, we have to pay careful attention to another scene in the film. Marty and Ethan discover the ruins of an Indian village after the cavalry has attacked. Ethan enters a teepee and looks intensely at something offscreen. He calls for Marty and then Ford cuts to a shot of Look lying dead on the ground. We see Ethan approach her body, kneel down, and with gentleness and reverence, cover her with a blanket. Here, in a profound sense, is the missing reverse shot, displaced into another scene. There is no question of the brutality and seriousness of this moment, and Ford has no trouble looking or letting us look. If he (and Ethan) were horsing around earlier, this is for real.

How may we account for what has happened to Look in this film? *The Searchers* deals with a number of highly charged sexual and racial themes such as incest and miscegenation. In the 1956 social context, the real American racial tensions (which were, of course, highly sexualized—i.e., the "well-hung" black stud) lay between whites and blacks. The conventions of the Western allow Ford to displace those tensions

Opposite, and following pages: The Searchers *(frame blow-ups).*

into the past and onto another race.[4] The American Indian was no longer actively contemplated, yet alone feared by the average white American in 1956. But the subject of interracial sexuality (particularly between black men and white women) was very much alive. And I think no case needs to be made about the intense sensitivity of the subject of incest and its threat to the family. Ford handles these topics with surprising maturity and formal complexity throughout *The Searchers* with what is perhaps the sole exception of the treatment of Look. And it is within this context that we can best understand what has happened.

Ford has let "too much" into the film—that is, there is too much dangerous, repressed, sensitive material being dealt with. Ford confronts and controls throughout 99% of *The Searchers* such things as Ethan's destructive, incestuous love of Martha and Ethan's maniacal and racist fear of Scar. Indeed, the film is a turning point in Ford's increasingly critical analysis of white culture in general and the cavalry in particular. It is as if for one moment the "great artist" has to behave like a high school kid. The almost unbearable tensions raised by *The Searchers* need an outlet. Ford's momentarily vicious and brutal treatment of Look is that outlet. He, more than Marty, needs to kick Look down the hill; he, more than Ethan, needs to laugh at it. Then, by not looking, he does not acknowledge what he has done.

This kind of psychoanalytic reading of *The Searchers* raises serious questions in relationship to what we usually call style. Specifically, we can pose the question as follows: how do we know that the absence of following Look's fall is an absence of a different kind than those carefully structured, controlled absences which define so much of the film? As described here, the absence is wildly out of control; it is a symptom—a tear or fissure.

But the question is even more complex than this. On the one hand, if we are going to posit out of control moments, are they all of the same kind? Obviously not, as the very scene with Look will demonstrate. The scene ends with a dissolve to a shot of rocks in the shape of an arrow on the ground. Ethan Edwards enters frame left but we only see his legs and feet. Ford then cuts to a shot of Ethan kneeling down by the rocks; we see the full body including his feet. There is a drastic mismatch between the boots worn by the figure in the first shot and those worn by John Wayne in the second shot. Clearly, this moment could be said to be out of control, but it is not out of control in the same way that the moment with Look is. In fact, it is a totally uninteresting and trivial observation to make unless one wants to demonstrate that Ford is frequently careless with certain Hollywood continuities, a point which is easily proven.

Thus, we have to distinguish between out of control moments; some are profoundly and symptomatically out of control and others are insignificantly out of control. But the situation is even more complex than this simple distinction. What about the moments that appear under con-

trol? Certainly they are not exempt from a psychoanalytic reading. Could Ford have shown us Ethan's discovery of Lucy's body? Probably not, but on one level that elision functions in a complex way within the film. Still, the fact remains that the structured absences reveal an important part of the ideology of a film; the out of control or unstructured absences reveal yet another aspect of ideology.

Indeed, at certain levels, Hollywood style encodes such absences. Consider for the moment the multitude of scenes in Hollywood films where someone has to shoot a horse in the head to put it out of its misery. We frequently see the gun put to the horse's head (e.g., Blake Edwards' *Wild Rovers)*, but we *always* cut to a reaction shot when the trigger is pulled. Always the cut; always the absence of the moment of the shooting. It is fairly easy to see how ideology works here, and the example is of little more interest than that of the mismatched boots.

If we are going to apply psychoanalysis as a cultural tool to the study of films, we have to be very careful in discriminating between levels of application. In the past, for example, film criticism in general has not paid nearly enough attention to the way in which a director like John Ford will formally structure absences or violate so-called Hollywood sacrosanct rules of continuity. It would be a serious mistake to treat all absences in *The Searchers* as somehow equal—as if they reveal an ideology of things that John Ford "cannot" look at. Thus, the importance of the project showing how structured absences work centrally in the film. In fact, it is only by acknowledging those that we can approach and fully understand the bizarre absence of the moment with Look. At the very least then, we are faced with discriminating between three levels: absences which are structured and thus partially controlled, wildly out of control absences which are profoundly ideologically symptomatic, and trivial absences which point to little more than carelessness. This demand for sensitivity on the part of the film analyst has its obvious parallel with the institution of psychoanalysis and the role of the psychoanalyst.

If film texts are to be perceived as heterogeneous and symptomatic, how does this relate to the question of aesthetics? Indeed, one film scholar has argued with me that *The Searchers* is a lesser film than *The Man Who Shot Liberty Valance* precisely because the out of control treatment of Look mars this otherwise brilliant film. She simultaneously asserted that *Liberty Valance* was free from any such moments. Both points seem to me profoundly erroneous. An examination of the history of Hollywood films reveals that it is the greatest films that contain some of the most disturbing, out of control moments. The reason for this, I think, can be seen from *The Searchers* example. Important artists frequently let more into their films than they can handle. They are less restrictive and censoring (no doubt, largely on an unconscious level) than more mediocre artists. Their films are thus more likely to glaringly reveal the tears and fissures—the symptoms that cannot be controlled.

This brings me to the second point. The assertion that *Liberty Valance* is free from blemishes is naïve. If we are going to be consistent in applying psychoanalysis to film and if we are to view the text as heterogeneous, then that must be true for all films. We must do away with the myth of, say, Blake Edwards, totally in control of his films—every shot worked out ahead of time for precisely the right reason, every shot under control. If psychoanalytic and ideological criticism have taught us anything, it is

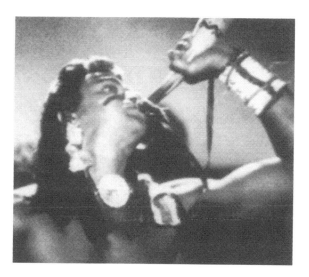

Henry Brandon as Chief Scar, The Searchers.

that no filmmaker (or artist of any kind) is ever totally, consciously in control of his/her style. Edwards may have had a reason for cutting from the pistol being fired by the horse's head in *Wild Rovers*, but I know another reason.

Much as the clinical institution of psychoanalysis turns largely on the sensitivity of the analysts, the same will be true for psychoanalytic film criticism. We need to be sensitive to different kinds of problems, to recognize what is comparatively in control and what out of control, and then to recognize the profoundly out of control from the trivially out of control. And finally, I think we have to be very careful with the harshness of judgments. If such judgments are to be made at all we certainly should not hold disturbing, symptomatic moments as an aesthetic weapon against the film. We all know human beings whose behavior is manifestly symptomatic of some psychoanalytic problem. But that does not mean that those people are less interesting or valuable as human beings in comparison to their so-called "normal," apparently under control neighbors. Indeed, the opposite is frequently the case and we would do well in the rush to apply psychoanalysis to film to not simplistically condemn *The Searchers* as a film or John Ford as a man because of the disturbing treatment of Look. Lesser artists than John Ford would never have had the nerve or the intelligence to work themselves into that horrible position in the first place.

NOTES

1. Peter Lehman, "An Absence Which Becomes a Legendary Presence: John Ford's Structured Use of Off-Screen Space," *Wide Angle*, 2, No. 4 (1978), 36-42. See also my chapter on *The Searchers* in William Luhr and Peter Lehman, *Authorship and Narrative in the Cinema* (New York: G. P. Putnam, 1977), pp. 85-135.

2. I am indebted to David Bordwell who formulated the problem in the scene in this way during a discussion of a draft of my doctoral dissertation. This paper grew out of that discussion. Thanks also to David Prince for his help in analyzing the various continuity problems in the scene. Although the analysis was carried out on a 16mm print, I have since seen a projected 35mm print. All of the fundamental points concerning space and composition made in this argument remain accurate.

3. Indeed, this entire scene is riddled with continuity problems. The log that we see in the first establishing shot is not even close in shape to the one that we see Ethan sitting against throughout the rest of the scene. But not only the log has changed, it is also now at a different angle. Thus when, prior to the part of the scene I have analyzed in detail here, John Wayne glances off to the left of the frame as he talks to Marty and Look before they go up to their sleeping place, the eyeline makes no sense in relationship to the previous establishing shot. Furthermore, when he then glances off frame right during the shots I have described there is a jarring confusion. It is very difficult for the viewer to grasp the spatial continuity of this entire scene. One can only speculate about the unusual number of continuity "errors" in this short scene. They may be unrelated to my main point or they may be symptomatic of the bizarre nature of the scene in general.

4. Interestingly, in *Sergeant Rutledge*, another cavalry western, Ford overtly confronts similar racial tensions in relationship to a black man and a white woman.

ANGELS GAMBOL WHERE THEY WILL:
John Ford's Indians

Tag Gallagher (1993)

John Ford's last film, *7 Women* (1965), is about Christian missionaries in China, and to some Chinese it is an offensive film. The white characters show contempt for the Chinese and use racist terms; the story's details contradict historical fact; its Chinese speak the wrong languages: and its Mongolian bandits are played by a Ukrainian (Mike Mazurki) and a black (Woody Strode).

What can be said in Ford's defense?

Primarily, that Ford did not intend an authentic China. His China is fantasy, like Kipling's India, a background for the whites' story. Its authenticity is token and suggestive, not a moral imperative. As is the case with most art.

Authenticity as a moral imperative is a recent obsession. It was accorded relatively little importance during most of the last hundred thousand years, even (and especially) by historians. Authenticity was thought unachievable. And for good reason. The past, after all, does not exist, except in our individual imaginations, and no two of us can imagine even yesterday in the same way. Thus what we call "history" is what we ourselves create, our story. History is not written by the hand of God, nor by Nature (and dialectical materialism has no hand). The past's only relevance is what it means to us today. This is why Renaissance paintings of the Crucifixion or Nativity set Biblical events in contemporary contexts, with medieval villages in the background, and angels gamboling where they will.

History—in prose, verse, picture, or object—once had no illusion that it was anything but myth. Nor did it aspire to be. Only recently has it been primping itself as a science; always before, myth was its highest aspiration.

To the Chinese offended by *7 Women*, however, such arguments are confirmation of Ford's racism, his cultural centrism. Ford is therefore not the myth we want today. And do we not have every right to choose our myths? By such choice human reality is created.

Yes. Yet the question now comes: Is not racism or centrism inherent in any profoundly human utterance? Who of us can claim to be pure? Is it not impossible, no matter how hard we try to speak for the whole human race, to shed our family, tribe, language, religion, and cultural tastes? If what we speak will have any truth at all, do we not first of all have to speak the truth we know most intimately: the truth of our self?

Isn't great art always conscious of the limits of understanding? If art is so often—one might even argue, always—religious, is it not because it stares at what it cannot see?

There is a moment in *7 Women* when a white missionary preaches to Chinese children. We see their faces staring back with total incomprehension. The movie's theme is people—white and yellow, white and white, yellow and yellow—staring at each other uncomprehendingly. In rare instants, an *I-thou* moment breaks through.

We can trace a similar theme through the highpoints of most of Ford's hundred-and-more films: characters staring into space, after people who have gone, or are leaving, or are right in front of them. These are beautiful images, compelling. Always there is alternation of community and privacy, and the intolerance, the racism, the nonrecognition of our neighbor.

In this sense, Ford's treatment of Indians is profoundly racist. And it is Ford's Indians that I am coming to, via Ford's China. His storyworld is still the white man's. He is not telling the Indians' story, he is looking at them from the sensibility of his whiteness, they are his symbols. Perhaps Ford could not have done otherwise; apparently he chose not to try. For that matter, it is difficult to think of any white person's film that has not made the same choice.[1]

Probably (although I cannot judge) Ford's depictions are superficially accurate: he read a great deal, spoke some Navajo, and, partly because he provided good jobs, had been adopted into a tribe with a Navajo name, Natani Nez, "Tall Soldier." But if the depictions are accurate, so what? We have seen letter-perfect depictions on television for decades of Palestinians, Japanese, and Reaganites, of pro-choicers and pro-lifers, and all these decades of accuracy have not contributed much to understanding, have not therefore really given us faithful renderings, have not permitted us to see what these people would regard as the essential aspects of themselves. Perhaps, sometimes, we know them better from depictions that are blatantly racist; for the point of view is less synthetic, less unconscious. Mechanical honesty—the camera's honesty—is insufficient.

I am thinking, for example, of a startling photo I saw of President Reagan in a European paper in the mid 1980s—startling because Reagan's expression was so untypical, so horrific, so menacing: here certainly was a man more beast than man. "It's not accurate," I objected; "he's *never* shown this way in the United States."

Sal Mineo in Cheyenne Autumn. *"Art and history have preferred myth and fantasy."*

"This shows the *real* Reagan!" my host retorted.

But of course every photo of Reagan showed "the real Reagan." The choice of photo was a choice of which reality to emphasize, of which story to tell.

"Nasty Reagan," I wanted to argue, was misleading historically, even if Reagan were Hitler, because Americans never saw this Reagan. As Louis XIV observed, one rules by appearances, not by the true nature of things. So we have to understand the appearances, or the true nature of things will be murkier than ever. If today we understand why there was enthusiasm for Stalin, but do not grasp why there was enthusiasm for Hitler, it is partly because we still know Stalin through the images contemporary Russians saw of him, whereas we experience Hitler through images that bear little relation to what German Nazis saw, which were images of a patriarch of peace and righteousness. By "correcting" Hitler's image, we may have served valid goals, but we may also have doomed ourselves to finding Hitler inexplicable, and to repeating "history."

Thus art and history have preferred myth and fantasy. Ford sacrificed accuracy willingly. His Apaches smoke pipes, not cigars, and his Comanche don feather bonnets to ride into battle. Were I to learn that his Comanche chief's makeup and costume correspond to no actual Comanche's, I should not be surprised. Even when Ford made *The*

Quiet Man (1952), about Ireland, which he knew intimately and by blood, he preferred myth. And some Irish were indignant: "I cannot for the life of me see that Ford's Ireland has any relation to the Ireland I or anyone else can have seen or known," one critic (Hilton Edwards) complained. So naturally Ford's Indians are equally mythic, inspired less by the reality of the Indians he knew or the scholarly books he read, than by the reality of Winslow Homer, Frederic Remington, and Charles Russell, of the dime novel and hundreds and hundreds of movies, and before them of the Puritans, Rousseau, Chateaubriand, and Cooper, and the thousands of imitators they spawned.

It is awesome to contemplate the sheer quantity of European and American images of the Indians, to consider the constant fascination and inspiration these images have held for five hundred years, and to recognize how terrifyingly irrelevant this overwhelming hoard of images has been to what individual Indians actually were, and therefore how relevant these fantasies became to forming white attitudes toward those individuals, to forming the prisms, the icons, through which we perceive Indians; and how responsible these fantasies are for what was done to those individuals. This is what Ford is about.

Ford's most extensive essay in this vein, on Indians, is *The Searchers* (1956). The Indians are mythic apparitions, appearing repeatedly and always suddenly out of nowhere, icons of savage violent beauty dread, and so entirely projections of white fantasy that Ford himself termed *The Searchers* "a psychological epic." For the white Ethan Edwards (John Wayne), the Comanche Scar is the "Other" that he can stare at but cannot see. Worse, he is Ethan's doppelganger, everything in himself that he despises. Specifically, Scar has raped Ethan's brother's wife, for whom Ethan himself nursed desire so obsessive that, before the picture begins, he has been wandering for seven years in order to escape her allure. Thus Ethan must kill Scar in order to destroy the complex of violence within himself, and will spend the picture's story-time—a second seven years—searching to do so. "A man will search his heart and soul, go searching way out there," goes the movie's title song, alerting us that Ethan's physical search is only a search for himself, to come to terms with his own solitude. And the search will resolve not with the death of Scar (whom Ethan finds dead and thus cannot kill), but with a transmutation of Ethan's violence, solitude, and racism into love, community, and (the antonym of racism?) fraternity.

For this drama the Indians are basically props, so much so that the fact that Scar is played by a white actor (Henry Brandon), rather than a red actor, seems entirely appropriate. Ford's "psychological epic" makes no claims to realism. Quite the contrary: in an opening title card, it identifies the myth-evoking landscapes of Arizona's Monument Valley in 1955 as "Texas 1868," and follows this with a series of Charles Russell imitations and painterly compositions bathed in expressionist light. This movie is a myth based on other myths based themselves on still other myths, without beginning. It is an attempt to write "history" to serve to clarify the subjectivity of the historian, the mythmaker—who, from colonial times, has sown the ideologies that have prescribed how Indians would, in actuality, be treated by American authorities.

It is because of Ford's evident consciousness of this fact that his treatment of the Indians is "profoundly racist"—that is to say, not racist at all, but confessional: a confrontation with the limits of understanding, the sin of solitude, the intolerable violence wreaked by our callous adhesion to ideology (myth: *ideas* of what other people are, rather than *I-thou* contact). Evil in Ford is always good intention gone astray; and tradition, which sustains us, is always the humus where evil has its roots. Thus to the whites, in *The Searchers*, the violence done by Indians is too terrifying even to be imagined, but also it has the allure of archetypal fire, of the raw reality that ideology expels from our consciousness. In contrast, violence perpetrated by whites is a Biblical romp: "For that which we are about to receive, O Lord, we thank Thee" prays Ford's Shakespearean fool (Hank Worden as Mose Harper), as he aims his rifle to start slaughtering Indians. And although the violence and ideological myopia in Ethan are transmuted eventually, they are not *recognized* by Ethan, still less so by his white community, who would exterminate an ant colony with the same degree of moral inhibition and much less jubilation.

Myths sustain societies in Ford, but poison them as well. They define the limits of understandings, but are seldom perceived. They rule and regulate our lives.

The tragedy of the American Indians for Ford is not only that they themselves were virtually exterminated: it is also that their story is lost, or rather, that their story stays with them. Their story has not become part of our story. It is a story that, as the images of *She Wore a Yellow Ribbon* (1949) capture so movingly, passes momentarily across the horizon, like yesterday's herds of buffalo and virgin forests. Hence it is nature that destroys the Custer-like cavalry regiment in *Fort Apache* (1948) rather than merely the Indians, who are at one with land, rocks, and dust. In both pictures, the *dramatis personae* are white, never red, and Ford's interest is, as in *The Searchers*, with the traditions and community values that render otherwise decent individuals into willing agents of imperialism and genocide.

An Indian story in the middle of *The Searchers* depicts the limits of understanding. It is about an Indian named "Look" whom none of the whites can see, whose story is smothered by white stories. It begins beside the fireplace of a white home, when a girl gets a letter from her fiancé, whom she has not heard from in two years. There is much play between her agony, the opportunism of a rival courter, her father's insensitivity, her mother's distress. The boyfriend writes he has gotten a squaw, and then in flashback we see that John Wayne and the boyfriend inadvertently purchased Look, a plain, chubby girl, when they thought they were just buying a blanket. Wayne makes fun of her and the boyfriend kicks her out of his bed. Both the flashback and the letter-reading are played as comedies, dependent on indifference to the suffering of the two girls. Audiences, identifying with Wayne's humor, identify also with his racism. Then Look is found dead, a victim in a cavalry massacre, and we are jerked into consciousness of Wayne's morality—and our own morality. Look's story, scarcely perceived by the six whites from whose perspective it is told, has been only a joke for them, a foil in the drama of their insensitivity toward each other. No one sees Look.

Since the Indian story cannot be told, no individual Indian can emerge as a rounded character. Ford's strongest, most communicative images of Indians are iconic, which is why they stir us: they are images constructed by the myths that we, the whites, have constructed.[2]

Dolores Del Rio and Carroll Baker in Cheyenne Autumn, *where the Cheyenne are "a Greek chorus to highlight a white drama."*

I know of no white film that has tried to assume an Indian's point of view. Perhaps the effort has always looked doomed to failure—and indecent. As Ford observes in *Cheyenne Autumn* (1964), it is white words, white language, that have been our most potent weapon against Indians. Are we, the descendants of their destroyers, now to presume to tell their stories in the language that destroyed them? Is it time, yet, to acknowledge the responsibility to make their stories part of our common heritage?

NOTES

1.   One common device is to have an empathetic white character take up a semi-Indian style of life, by marrying into a tribe; for example—*Broken Arrow* (Delmer Daves, 1950), *Run of the Arrow* (Samuel Fuller, 1957), *Dances with Wolves* (Kevin Costner, 1990), *Little Big Man* (Arthur Penn, 1970). But such films do not tell an Indian story: quite the contrary, they specifically look at Indians from the white characters' point of view and interpret Indian life in terms of European concepts. In such films, the Indian characters are foils for a

white drama and do not themselves emerge from stereotypes as rounded human beings: the roles played by Chief Dan George in *Little Big Man* and *The Outlaw Josey Wales* (Clint Eastwood, 1976) are excellent examples, all the more so as George's role in the former is probably the richest part any actual Indian has played in a white film, and yet is nonetheless purely iconic. Indian roles are more usually played by Caucasians or Orientals, particularly if the parts are substantial: e.g.., Burt Lancaster in *Apache* (Robert Aldrich, 1954), Rock Hudson in *Taza, Son of Cochise* (Douglas Sirk, 1954), Anthony Quinn in *The Savage Innocents* (Nicholas Ray, 1959). I would argue that here again it is a white point of view that is being presented. *The Savage Innocents* possibly comes closest to a nonwhite point of view of any film by an important filmmaker: it goes out of its way to render the strange and bizarre as normal, and succeeds so well in inducting us into the alien sensibilities of its Eskimos that, by the time a white man shows up, we feel him as the abnormal one.

A true Indian film would be one made entirely by Indians in their language and, in the sense intended here, by Indians whose sensibilities are substantially formed by precontact heritage. Such a film would also require a genuine artist whose style was not derived from American, European, or Asian models. Unfortunately I have not had an opportunity to see any films made by Indians.

2. Such too is the case with Ford's *Cheyenne Autumn* (1964), which rather than foregrounding Indians as individuals, as in Mari Sandoz's source novel, turns them into a Greek chorus to highlight a white drama of encroaching awareness. How the film would have been different, had Ford been in better health, is impossible to say. Ford, prematurely aged at 70, depressed, and much under the influence of "the creature," accepted a bad script, did not submit it to his customary rewrite, and, by failing on many days to emerge from his bedroom, reportedly spent $2 million more than his $4 million budget.

Renaming: Lord Morgan becomes A Man Called Horse, Lieutenant John Dunbar becomes Dances With Wolves.

GOING INDIAN:
Discovery, Adoption and Renaming Toward A "True American," From Deerslayer to Dances With Wolves

Robert Baird (1996)

While lying there listening to the Indians, I amused myself with trying to guess at their subject by their gestures, or some proper name introduced . . . It was a purely wild and primitive American sound, as much as the barking of a chickaree, and I could not understand a syllable of it.... I felt that I stood, or rather lay, as near to the primitive man of America, that night, as any of its discoverers ever did.

—Henry David Thoreau[1]

As soon as possible after my arrival, I design to build myself a wigwham, after the same manner and size with the rest.... and will endeavour that my wife, my children, and myself may be adopted soon after our arrival. Thus becoming truly inhabitants of their village, we shall immediately occupy that rank within the pale of their society, which will afford us all the amends we can possibly expect for the loss we have met with by the convulsions of our own. According to their customs we shall likewise receive names from them, by which we shall always be known. My youngest children shall learn to swim, and to shoot with the bow, that they may acquire such talents as will necessarily raise them into some degree of esteem among the Indian lads of their own age; the rest of us must hunt with the hunters.

—J. Hector St. John Crevecoeur[2]

With thanks to the Blackfoot tribe who adopted me.

—Leslie A. Fiedler[3]

277

Taken together, the three epigraphs above are good examples of a very old, and still ongoing, process of the American imagination: the White discovery of, and the renaming and adoption into, the tribal society of the American Indian. "Going Indian" describes an imaginative mythopoeic process, recurring often enough in American history, letters, and media to merit more attention, especially after the apparent resurrection and further development of this gesture in Kevin Costner's tremendously popular *Dances with Wolves*. This film was released too long after any other great epic Western to be anything but a boondoggle—or so we thought, until "Costner's folly" was seen by millions and had won seven Academy Awards.

A traditional ideological goal in American literature and film has been the search for Americanness. Crevecoeur's third letter as an American farmer was titled "What Is an American," and his famous melting-pot response was lengthy and detailed, testifying to the seriousness with which the question was met. Tautologically, the defining American characteristic has been the attempt to define the American character. It is the question itself—indeed, that the question has been open for so long—that marks this nation as unique. One answer to the question of national identity proposes that the original inhabitants of North America represent "True Americans," whose character deserves emulation. *Dances with Wolves* accepted this not-new proposal and sought to convince modern motion picture audiences that only by going backward into history, back into tribalism, could the American hero hope to go forward.

D. H. Lawrence argued that Europeans "came to America for two reasons:

1. To slough the old European consciousness completely.
2. To grow a new skin underneath, a new form. This second is a hidden process."[4]

Leslie Fiedler praised Lawrence's insight, suggesting that

> He knew something . . . which we are born not knowing we know, being born on this soil . . . that the essential myth of the West and, therefore, of ourselves . . . is the myth of Natty Bumppo and Chingachgook. Here is, for us—for better or for worse, and apparently forever—the heart of the matter: the confrontation in the wilderness of the White European refugee from civilization and the "stern, imperturbable warrior."[5]

This meeting, Fiedler noted, occasioned two possible outcomes: "a metamorphosis of the WASP into something neither White nor Red" or "the annihilation of the Indian."[6] Although the latter option was the most frequently chosen path of story makers for the "penny dreadfuls" and nickelodeons, the metamorphosis of White into Red developed rapidly in the 1950s with the "sympathetic Western," and it is in *Dances with Wolves* that the myth reached its culmination and logical end.

Three famous theories help explain how a motion picture of the 1990s would, first, attempt a big-budget dramatization of the going-Indian myth and, second, reach an appreciative audience in the process. The first theory is Claude Levi-Strauss' notion that myths and narratives reconcile cultural contradictions and bring opposing forces and values together. With the going-Indian myth, the contradiction is between nature and industry; hunting and agrarianism; innocence and decadence; manifest destiny and the sacred homeland. Thus, *Dances with Wolves* is a cinematic myth that addresses still-unresolved traumas and contradictions of American history, as well as current contradictions between industrialism and environmentalism, tribal society and industrial society, the melting-pot theory and ethnic pride movements.

The second theory was propounded by R.W.B. Lewis in *The American Adam*, wherein the author described the historical development of the idea of a new American hero who would be "emancipated from history, happily bereft of ancestry, untouched and undefiled by the usual inheritances of family and race."[7] That the American continent triggered images of the Garden of Eden among European immigrants has been ably documented by many scholars. But the Garden of Eden was not empty, and for those uncomfortable with the demonization of native inhabitants of this continent, the American Indian provided a ready-made Adamic figure. The American Adam and Garden of Eden myths were easily transposed into American Westerns and musicals, including the mythic and cinematic forerunner of *Dances with Wolves*, Delmer Daves' *Broken Arrow* (1950), considered the first of the sympathetic Westerns of the 1950s. This film traces the transformation of an Indian fighter (played by Jimmy Stewart) into a man who befriends Cochise, marries an Apache maiden, and fights to establish some truce between the land-hungry settlers and the Apache. The American Adam undercurrent is manifested in *Broken Arrow* during a pastoral honeymoon scene that takes place on the banks of a wild pond. Stewart and the Apache maiden Morning Star have just been married. Stewart is reclining beside the still waters as the camera follows Morning Star, who walks majestically toward her lover, then lies in his arms:

Tom Jeffords (James Stewart) and Morning Star (Debra Paget) in Broken Arrow. *"The dream of Pocahontas cannot last too long."*

Morning Star: "You are asleep?"

Stewart: "No . . . I'm quiet because I'm so happy. I'm afraid if I open my mouth my happiness will rush out in a funny noise like, Ya-hoo!"

Morning Star: "What does that mean? It is an American word?"

Stewart: "Uh huh. I think it was a word made by Adam when he opened his eyes and saw Eve."

The dream of Pocahontas cannot last too long, however, and even in this first sympathetic western, Morning Star dies before the last reel. In contrast to the deluge of conventional Westerns, *Broken Arrow* was, for its time, the most pointed liberal critique of manifest destiny and the sad history of relations between Indians and Whites.

The third theory comes from Sigmund Freud's limited work with the "family romance," in which he attempted to account for certain fantasies of young children who denied their literal parentage in favor of more noble, imaginary mothers and fathers.[8] Freud claimed, in *Der Familienroman der Neurotiker*, that all young people must break with their parents at some point—that each generation must break with the previous one. A family romance might be created in response to various motivations, for example, to compensate for loss of parental love, or because of fear of breaking the incest taboo or with realization of parental fallibility.

This theory suggests a psychological mechanism that can account for the success of those narratives wherein the white protagonist goes Indian. Working on the personal and collective psychological levels, the romance of Native American parentage would satisfy the wish for a return to the Garden of Eden, where strong and noble parents live in an environment of abundance and harmony, free of the decay, pollution, and anxiety of industrial society. Crevecoeur's epigraph was written during the troubled context of the American Revolution, when the author found himself pulled between British allegiance and colonial rebellion. His romance of living with the Indians was never enacted in reality, but it was exactly the tale of the noble savage that Europeans would find appealing.[9]

Elizabeth Stone provides evidence that modern, adult Americans have engaged in family romances of Indian ancestry. In a study of the psychological dynamics of family stories, Stone interviewed Black and White Americans who claimed Indian ancestry even against rather conclusive evidence to the contrary. In spite of the truth of a family's history and the Indian's oppression and negative stereotyping in our culture, Stone found a number of Americans who claimed Indian blood in the manner that others would pridefully recall European royalty or illustrious Puritan ancestry. It is "the idea of the Indian," "a powerful symbol, especially since World War II," that Stone found in American literature from Ernest Hemingway to Ken Kesey, an idea "suggestive of our mourning for our lost pre-industrial Eden."[10]

These three theories offer a rudimentary dynamic in which *Dances with Wolves* can be seen to function as mythical *narrative* (Levi-Strauss) among the *collective conscious* (Freud) and in the context of American *history* (Lewis). As such, this dynamic helps contextualize historical and fictional prototypes of the going-Indian myth in *Dances with Wolves*.

Thoreau and Russell Dance with Wolves

Thoreau was, Leslie Fiedler believed, "at his mythological core an Indian himself, at home in the unexplored regions where women flinch," and Fiedler added that Thoreau himself claimed that "all poets are Indians."[11] Thoreau's Walden adventure strikes me as a case study on the limits on how far a Harvard man can go Indian, and although Thoreau never entertains the notion of becoming a "squawman," the "idea of the Indian" infuses every page of *Walden*. At one point in his masterpiece, Thoreau mused: "My days were not days of the week, bearing the stamp of any heathen deity, nor were they minced into hours and fretted by the ticking of the clock; for I lived like the Puri Indians, of whom it is said that 'for yesterday, to-day, and to-morrow they have only one word, and they express the variety of meaning by pointing backward for yesterday, forward for to-morrow, and overhead for the passing day.'"[12] Besides the explicit reference to living "like the Puri Indians," I also like the notion here of near timelessness, so central to any mythological state, as well as the privileging of the Indian lifestyle in contrast with the rush to keep European time. Although Thoreau drew no special attention to it when he mentioned it, the story of the naming of Walden Pond, the naming of Walden in *Walden*, offers evidence, both literary and historic, of the claim "the Indian" holds not only on the American landscape, but on Thoreau's and our imaginations: "My townspeople have all heard it in their youth, that anciently the Indians were holding a pow-wow upon a hill here . . . and while they were thus engaged the hill shook and suddenly sank, and only one old squaw, named Walden, escaped, and from her the pond was named."[13] Thoreau best shows where he has been and where he would like to go in *The Maine Woods*, where he admitted, "One revelation has been made to the Indian, another to the white man. I have much to learn of the Indian, nothing of the missionary. I am not sure but all that would tempt me to teach the Indian my religion would be *his* promise to teach me his."[14]

Thoreau never wrote the great work on the Indian he had been planning. His notebooks, though, were full of carefully collected details of native dress and behavior. Most important, his greatest book may have captured more of the "idea of the Indian" than any scientific work he could have written.

Although he called himself an illustrator,[15] Charles M. Russell is, along with Frederic Remington, the most famous of the Western artists. Russell, who began life as the son of a wealthy St. Louis family, eventually lit out for the territory of Montana.[16] As a painter, sculptor, and writer, Russell focused his attention on the lifestyles of cowboys, trappers, desperadoes, and Indians, all of which he captured in his seemingly simple, rough-hewn style. In a 1922 painting of a squaw man titled, "When White Men Turn Red," Russell depicted a leather-clad, mounted White man descending into a river valley with his two Indian wives, three horses, and four dogs. Russell has poured a luminous golden sunlight over the distant mountain range and lower sky of this painting, and this golden sidelight outlines his figures, the effect being boldly romantic and serene. In commentary accompanying this painting in his *Remington and Russell*, Brian W. Dippie noted that "Russell himself had felt the lure of Indian life and knew that he, like several of his cowboy friends, would have been

Dances with Wolves: *The buffalo hunt. Dunbar (Kevin Costner) wins over Wind-in-His-Hair (Rodney Grant).*

quick to take an Indian wife had the right woman come along."[17] Dippie mentioned a short story from Russell's *Trails Plowed Under*, titled "How Lindsay Turned Indian." In this tale, Russell related how, as a young boy, Lindsay ran off from a mean stepfather (a fictional "literalization" of Freud's family romance?) to eventually find himself following a tribe of Piegan Indians, as he had nowhere else to turn. After meeting the rearguard of the traveling Piegans, the young Lindsay uses his magnifying glass to light the pipe of the Piegan chief. Of course, for a people who worship the sun, this is no small feat, and the chief intones, "The grass has grown twice since my two sons were killed by the Sioux . . . my heart is on the ground; I am lonesome, but since the sun has sent you, it is good. I will adopt you as my boy . . . Child of the Sun, it is good."[18] Much like Lieutenant John J. Dunbar, in *Dances with Wolves*, Lindsay's important transition comes with his first buffalo hunt. In both cases the adopted Whites get their first kill, eat the fresh liver of their killed animal, and consider that moment as the important point of no return in their going Indian: "My boy . . . that's been sixty-five years ago as near as I can figure. I run buffalo till the whites cleaned 'em out, but that's the day I turned Injun, an' I ain't cut my hair since."[19]

The hunt has long been an initiation ritual for many different groups, and the buffalo-hunt scene and subsequent feast in *Dances with Wolves* mark Dunbar's almost complete assimilation into the tribe, shown by his trading of pieces of his cavalry blues for Indian gear; his winning over of Wind-in-His-Hair (who was earlier a strong doubter of Dunbar's intentions toward the tribe); and his participation in the culturally important role of storyteller, when Dunbar recounts his own hunting feat over and over to the tribe's great enjoyment. In short, the buffalo hunt's central position in Plains tribe culture would have made it the perfect path, both fictionally and historically, for any non-Indian to follow if he sought access to the flesh-and-bone existence of a tribe.

Getting Past the Massacre

Ever since Mary Rowlandson's Captivity Narrative (first published in 1682), any White seeking to go Indian has had to confront "the massacre." The historical and mythic power of the massacre is so pervasive that it seems all Westerns that deal with the confrontation of White and Red must address this issue in some manner.

An interesting negotiation of the massacre occurs in *Broken Arrow*, in which Jimmy Stewart's character saves his own life by having aided a wounded Cheyenne boy. When Stewart and the young boy are eventually surrounded by a group of warriors, the grateful young Cheyenne successfully pleads for Stewart's life with the menacing warriors. But when a group of unsuspecting Whites interrupt the Cheyenne just as they are about to release Stewart, he is bound and gagged and forced to watch the resulting massacre. He must witness as well the torture of three White survivors of the battle—two are "crucified" and one is buried up to his neck, smeared with cactus pulp, and eaten by ants. Later in the film Stewart must pass through the civilized, industrial equivalent of the Indian massacre nightmare—the lynching—when his own society tries to string him up for his defense of the Indian; he is only saved at the last minute, with the rope already around his neck. Stewart's near-lynching by the townspeople, like Dunbar's beating at the hands of his fellow Cavalrymen in *Dances*, signifies the one side of the cultural dialectic that the hero must pass through in order to prove his commitment to the synthesis of cultural contradiction. The binding and gagging of Stewart is evocative of the deep psychological chasm that the modern liberal conscience must negotiate between the archetypal Massacre and the Noble Indian; that is, atrocities of history cannot be erased but must be witnessed, then passed through. Although sometimes suppressed, historical atrocities will, when they eventually force their way into cultural narratives, be dichotomized into the poles of evil aggressors and innocent victims; sometimes this dichotomy is inverted, as when the good (morally or historically justified) Indians attack the U.S. Cavalry in *Dances With Wolves* and in the made-for-television *Son of the Morning Star*.

Arthur Penn's "progressive" Western *Little Big Man* begins with (what else?) a massacre of the family of the young Jack Crabb. However, the film, and Thomas Berger's book upon which it is based, cannot exhaust the psychic energy and mythic trauma of the massacre with this single bloodletting. Therefore, following the general reversal of the Western tale we find throughout *Little Big Man*, Penn gives us another slaughter by inverting the conventions of the massacre, presenting Custer's infamous "battle" with the Cheyenne beside the Washita River. This time the cavalry does the massacring.

Almost twenty years after the sympathetic Western *Little Big Man*, the even more sympathetic *Dances with Wolves* cannot circumvent the massacre, and in fact, includes three massacres, one of which is told as a flashback of Stands-with-a-Fist (a White adopted by the Lakota Sioux, who becomes Dunbar's wife). The Stands-with-a-Fist flashback is as distilled and powerful an embodiment of the massacre trauma as has ever been presented by Hollywood. Shot in soft focus and at sunset, the scene begins, slow-motion, as an idyllic view of a rustic farm and cabin; two frontier families are eating outdoors on a large table when ominous looking Pawnee warriors ride slowly in on

Traumas and contradiction: Jack Crabb (Dustin Hoffman) in Little Big Man; *Dunbar and the Sioux in* Dances with Wolves.

horseback, their faces painted in bilious blues and bloody reds. At first it seems a peace-ful meeting of the two cultures, but then a tomahawk flies through the air, and the scene takes on added poignancy as the edit returns us to the horrified gaze of the young wit-ness and, by a film dissolve, to the still-haunted Stands-with-a-Fist.[20]

The third massacre in *Dances* transforms the horror associated with that depic-tion into the Hollywood-sanctioned celebration of dispatching the badmen—the U.S. Cavalry. Dunbar has been captured by the cavalry as a renegade and is being taken by wagon in shackles to a frontier prison. When the Lakota attack and kill Dunbar's tormentors, one realizes that—even with ninety years of Hollywood history turned on its head—we have here the same cheer for the good guys; the skillful and precise application of violence in order to right the world; the promise of "regeneration through violence," which Richard Slotkin has so eloquently elaborated upon.

Another strategy for resolving the historical trauma and contradiction of the massacre is, through sleight of hand, to present viewers with a tribe of Noble Savages (the Sioux in *Dances* and the Cheyenne in *Little Big Man*), and then with a tribe of just plain old-fashioned savages (the Pawnee in both films). This strategy has the function of addressing White historical fear and guilt within the same narrative, providing a way in which a *fiction* can remain simultaneously *true* to contradictory emotional responses to history.

Renaming

In *A Man Called Horse*, Lord Morgan (Richard Harris) is captured by a band of Sioux in 1825. Yellow Hand decides to save this strange White man for a slave of some sort and, after tying a rope around his neck, proceeds to ride Morgan like a horse before the other laughing warriors of the raiding party. Taken back to the Sioux camp, Morgan is mistreated until he eventually earns the Sioux's respect through his endurance, his slaying of attacking Shoshone braves, and his successful completion of the Sun Dance ritual. Although never explicitly mentioned in the film, Morgan's Indian name itself is transformed from the beast-of-burden connotations of that word to the more noble connotations for *horse* one would expect from a horse culture. *Little Big Man*'s young Jack Crabb (Dustin Hoffman) gets his name from old Chief Lodgeskins (Chief Dan George), who gives Jack his name—Little Big Man—by way of a story the old chief tells the rather short young man to inspire his confidence. Later, Jack kills a Pawnee during a war party and further strengthens his bond to the tribe, eventually becoming a squaw man in more ways than one.

In *Dances with Wolves*, Lieutenant John J. Dunbar is named, at first without his knowledge, by his Sioux brothers who have seen him "dancing" with his "pet" wolf, Two Socks. Dunbar had been trying to get Two Socks to return to his fort as he rode out to the Indian camp, but the wolf would playfully snap at his heels when Dunbar tried to chase him back. The Indians watched in the foreground of the shot, incredu-lous that a White man could have such a relationship with a wild animal. This scene in the film is presented with no fanfare, narration, or dialogue that signifies its tremendous importance to the film's mythopoeic task. Thus viewers take Dunbar's frolic with Two Socks as just another day-in-the-life event for John Dunbar, that is, as natural and spontaneous. Because viewers do not hear the Lakota warriors name Dunbar and because they already know the title of the film, the scene achieves two brilliant effects. First, the renaming scene is one of the most calculated moments of the film, yet it comes off as an utterly natural occurrence (accentuated by being filmed in long shot and soft focus, with a PBS nature-documentary style). Second, Costner, in effect, lets every viewer rename Dunbar with his Lakota name, since the scene plays sans dialogue or even gesture from the Lakota. This has the effect of making filmgoers active participants in the sacred ritual of renaming a man into nature and the tribe.

Although this renaming fits nicely with the standard Hollywood story convention of depicting an *evolving* character, this infrequent, but telling, tendency says more about American romantic concepts of the Indian and the natural than it does about Hollywood storytelling. This renaming of a White man with a natural name and his shedding of his European name is the quintessential American myth—the self-made man rediscovering both America and, most important, his own true self in the process. Freed from the oppressive yoke of European tradition, self-made even to his name (founder of his self—the task of Walt Whitman's *Leaves of Grass*), this character of literature and film has, after two hundred years, become only more solidified in our consciousness. From a string of names with no "direct relation to the universe"— Natty Bumppo, Lewis Henry Morgan, Lord Morgan, Jack Crabb, and John Dunbar— emerge Indian names, true names: Leather Stocking/Deerslayer/Hawkeye; Tayadaowuhkuh; Horse; Little Big Man; Dances-with-Wolves. European interest in Indian names did not develop solely from fictional romances of the noble savage; the real contrast between Indian naming and European naming sparked the imaginations of many explorers, trappers, and immigrants who sought to communicate and understand that first task of language, naming.

The naming process in Indian cultures was an apparently less rigid and legalized endeavor than modern-day Americans are accustomed to. A Cheyenne boy might, after returning from his first successful war party, be named after his "most outstanding predecessor."[21] In the Sioux tribe, a young man could be given a new name upon initiation into one of the important warrior or police societies of the tribe, and a "town crier" (a poor old man hired by the boy's father) might be asked to announce to the village the boy's new name.[22] Birth as well as death were occasions for naming in Sioux society, and the dead would be given, after the proper rituals were observed, a "spirit name," by which they would be called from that moment on.[23] After the birth of one Sioux girl who was given twenty-two hand-crafted cradles from friends and family, she was named in such a way as to memorialize this impressive gift-giving: They-Love-Her. Children could be named after an important grandparent, a father's military exploits, or "in reference to a dream he had experienced."[24] If those sources were not enough, a Sioux child might even gain a name from a *winkte*. A Sioux young man who could not or did not want to join in the hunt or war party adopted the female role of *winkte*, or transvestite; the *winkte* was both respected for his supernatural powers and feared for his transgression of the sexual taboos. Blue Whirlwind discusses the *winkte*'s naming function within the tribe: "There is a belief that if a winkte is asked to name a child, the child will grow up without sickness. My grandson was given the name Iron Horse when he was three days old by a winkte, and I gave him a horse. Fathers will go to the winkte and flirt with him. Whatever the winkte says will become the secret name and this he will name the child. Winkte names are often unmentionable and therefore are not often used. Girls never had winkte names."[25] Since an Indian might begin life with a pet name, take a formal name at the age of six, and be renamed for every important achievement or event of later life, the federal government sought to stabilize things with the imposition of a single Christian name at census times: From elaboration to consistency, from poetry to legalese.

Indian names gain in appeal through their correspondence between the bearer and experience. Indian names develop out of the life of the tribe or the individual. Modern names are, at best, in honor of some favored relative, at worst a name one's parents felt "sounded nice." Few refer "directly to the universe" in any Emersonian way. Like Adam's naming of the animals, the taking of an Indian name is the earning of a moniker that has grown spontaneously out of one's life and character in the archetypical Garden. Indian names seem something the poet-Indian can respect as living language, not fossilized nomenclature. Indeed, how many of us can say that we have earned our names? Or say what it is they mean?

Dances and the Developing Myth

As I heard my Sioux name being called over and over, I knew for the first time who I really was.
—from the diary of John J. Dunbar

Dances with Wolves seems to me to be the latest, most important development in this mythopoeic founding of the "only real American."[26] It is a different myth than the one Fiedler called the "anti-feminist" myth, in which the runaway male flees from the White woman to his native, dark-skinned companion. Lieutenant John J. Dunbar marries Stands-with-a-Fist, a White survivor of the massacre, who has nearly forgotten her first family and language. *Dances with Wolves* accomplishes, I think for the first time in our American imagination, the transmigration of the White family unit into the mythical hunting ground of the Indian. By the end of the film, Dances-with-Wolves and Stands-with-a-Fist have already transfigured into buckskins, the Sioux language, the Sioux way. Edward D. Castillo, a Native American academic, has written an excellent review of *Dances with Wolves* that explores many of the same issues analyzed here. Castillo has asserted that *Dances* is "really about the transformation of the white soldier Lt. John Dunbar into the Lakota warrior Dances with Wolves."[27] Recalling Dunbar's hope to "see the frontier . . . before it's gone," Castillo noted: "That simple childlike desire touches an unspoken yearning in many Americans, young and old."[28] His words "childlike desire" recall Freud's family romance as well as the wish-fulfillment aspect of *Dances*. Even more interesting is this passage in Castillo's essay: "While exchanging parting gifts, Dances with Wolves tells Kicking

Bird, 'You were the first man I ever wanted to be like. I will not forget you.' Indians know that no white man or woman can become Indian, but many of us hope those who have learned of our cultures and appreciate their unique humanity will be our friends and allies in protecting the earth and all of her children."[29]

Since *Dances with Wolves* starts with Lieutenant John J. Dunbar near death on a Civil War operating table and never once flashes back to any fictional family or past, Dunbar's line to Kicking Bird—"You were the first man I ever wanted to be like"— becomes illustrative of a close adherence to the imaginative logic of the family romance. Through a brief examination of only some of the material, this chapter has shown how the generic logic of the family romance was embossed in *Dances with Wolves* with the American Adam myth and the historical legacy of Native American cultures. In retrospect, one should be surprised neither at *Dances with Wolves*' enthusiastic reception nor at the many modern Americans who found going Indian a still viable trail to follow through the American imagination.

Postscript: (The Return of) *Dances with Wolves*

During the November "ratings sweeps" of 1993, ABC broadcast a new, expanded version of *Dances with Wolves*. At fifty minutes longer than the original, the new *Dances* exploited the television Western miniseries formula that worked so well with *Lonesome Dove*. The new *Dances* was originally composed by Costner and producer Jim Wilson for foreign distribution and simply reintegrated footage originally trimmed for the American theatrical release. As can be expected, much of the footage simply expanded on plot, characters, and themes in the original American version. A few additions bridge minor gaps in the narrative and flesh out issues that might have puzzled some original viewers. The crazy Major Fambrough, who sends Dunbar on his "knight's errand" is shown, through added footage, to be certifiably insane. The environmental destruction theme is pushed even further in a number of additions and in one wholly new scene. One addition has the slothful mule driver Timmons littering as he crosses the prairie, tossing a tin can to the ground as Dunbar registers the appropriately modern reaction of indignation. The horror of Fort Sedgewick's polluted pond grows through the addition of animal carcasses and by witnessing Dunbar having to swim into the pond, bandanna over nose, to struggle with the wet dead weight of the animals before he burns them. The wholly new scene of environmental devastation occurs when Kicking Bird and Dunbar journey alone to the sacred Sioux mountains (Kicking Bird: "The animals were born here.") but find instead an ominous silence and the remnants of a hunting camp strewn with animal corpses and empty whisky bottles. The mystery surrounding the prior inhabitants of Fort Sedgewick is also settled. Before Dunbar reaches the deserted fort, the last of the fort's troops are shown cowering in their caves until their officer assembles them, commends them for staying after the others deserted, and suggests they mount an orderly mass desertion with, "The army can go to Hell!" The new version also fleshes out a few of the minor characters. Two Socks, Dunbar's friendly wolf, gets much more on-screen time, and the trio of young Sioux boys that includes Smiles-a-Lot turn up in a number of scenes of "teenage" drama and hijinks: last-minute jitters before the unsanctioned raid on Dunbar's horse, a vigorous but denied attempt to join the men during the buffalo hunt, and a foiled prank to close the smoke flap on the tepee of the honeymooning Dances-with-Wolves and Stands-with-a-Fist. The inversions of cultural prejudice occasionally seen in the original film are seconded with one more quite pointed gibe that takes place during the massacre of Timmons. A Pawnee brave starts to take Timmons' quilt for a trophy until he sniffs it suspiciously, throws it on the ground in disgust, and cleans his hands with dirt. On a more romantic note, the new film elaborates on the courtship between Dances-with-Wolves and Stands-with-a-Fist, including Dances' need to rely on tribal gifts of horses and clothing in order to purchase his new bride, in the traditional Sioux way, from her father-guardian, Kicking Bird.

But the most substantial difference between the new and original versions of *Dances* involves the night scene just before the buffalo hunt. In the original film, this scene is one long take that lasts for only twenty-eight seconds. The Sioux camp appears in the background, ponies in the middle ground, and Dunbar, resting on his bedroll, is stretched out in the foreground, his voice-over narration intoning: "As they celebrated into the night, the coming hunt, it was hard to know where to be. I don't know if they understood, but I could not sleep among them. There had been no looks, and there was no blame. There was only the confusion of a people not able to predict the future." One assumes simply that Dunbar is finding some time alone before the next day's big hunt. In the expanded version, however, the scene contains two minutes of footage and twenty-five shots that change not only the meaning of this single scene but imbue the entire film with a greater moral complexity. The scene begins with Dunbar riding into camp with a small band of warriors. A large fire is burning in the center of camp as the Sioux dance around it. Dunbar holds back and sizes up the situation. He notices a wagon, filled with buffalo hides. His voice-over narration explains things:

> It was suddenly clear now what had happened, and my heart sank as I tried to convince myself that the white men who had been killed were bad people and deserved to die, but it was no use. I tried to believe that Wind-in-His-Hair and Kicking Bird and all the other people who shared in the killing were not so happy for having done it, but they were. As I looked at the familiar faces I realized that the gap between us was greater than I could ever have imagined.

The narration accompanies a building intimacy of shot scales, growing closer to the dancing Sioux as well as including Dunbar's reaction shots. Two crucial insert shots provide gory emphasis: a severed white man's hand tied in rope and hanging over the flames of the campfire; a long blonde scalp at the end of a pole, reflecting the reddish glow. This unexpurgated scene then ends with the same thirty-second shot and voice-over found in the original; but now Dunbar's comment about not being able "to sleep among them" takes on a pointed meaning. The scene in the original *Dances*, then, is literally a repression of the novel and the shooting script, a repression of the massacre.[30]

Whereas the other material in the film merely expands and explains themes already extant in the first release, this reincorporated material marks a radical addition, I should say a *return*, to the film. While trimming *Dances* to a tight (!) 181 minutes kept the film distributable and positioned for Oscar contention, Costner might have deflected a great deal of subsequent criticism that his Sioux were too wholesome by keeping just this one moment of unbridgeable cultural difference in the original film. (He might also have included, as the new film does, another moral complication of the Sioux: A brief scene early in the narrative makes it clear that Stands-with-a-Fist's husband died, not while defending the tribe from the marauding Pawnee, but during a raid *on* the Utes, explicitly undercutting the assumption the first film may have given that *these* Sioux practice only defensive tribal warfare.) This is not to deny *Dances'* radical inversion of the Western. Whereas *The Searchers* turns on a White man's obsessive attempts to find and retrieve a White woman from her tribal life, *Dances*, at midpoint, gives us a White cavalry officer who returns a White woman to her tribal life as a simple matter of course. But what I find so interesting is how the latest model in the progressive Western cannot live by genre inversion alone, but rather ends up negotiating, deflecting, and ultimately retrieving the massacre. Neither version of *Dances*, I think, is the definitive, authoritative edition—the "director's cut." Multiple versions of narratives, sometimes, betray tensions not so easily written off as just more of the same. Thus, I think we have two films now: *Dances with Wolves*, and *(The Return of) Dances with Wolves*.

NOTES

An earlier version of this essay was published as "Going Indian: In and Around *Dances with Wolves*," in *Michigan Academician* 25 (1993), pp. 133-146. Reprinted with permission.

1. Henry David Thoreau, *The Maine Woods* (New York: Harry N. Abrams, 1989), pp. 184-185.

2. J. Hector St. John Crevecoeur, *Letters from an American Farmer* (Gloucester, Mass: Peter Smith, 1968), p. 225.

3. Leslie A. Fiedler, *The Return of the Vanishing American* (New York Stein and Day, 1968), epigraph preceding the title page of this book.

4. D. H. Lawrence, *Studies in Classic American Literature* (New York: Viking Press, 1923). p. 53.

5. Fiedler, *Return of the Vanishing American*, p. 167.

6. Ibid., p. 24.

7. R.W.B. Lewis, *The American Adam: Innocence, Tragedy, and Tradition in the Nineteenth Century* (Chicago: University of Chicago Press, 1955), p. 5.

8. Sigmund Freud, *The Standard Edition of the Complete Psychological Works of Sigmund Freud* (London: Hogarth Press, 1959), vol. 9, pp. 236-241.

9. Richard Slotkin, *Regeneration Through Violence: The Mythology of the American Frontier,*

1600–1860 (Middletown, Conn.: Wesleyan University Press, 1973), p. 263. Slotkin's book is an exhaustive examination of American myth, with brilliant work on the "Indianization" theme.

10. Elizabeth Stone, *Black Sheep and Kissing Cousins: How Our Family Stories Shape Us* (New York Penguin Books, 1988), p. 131.

11. Fiedler, *Return of the Vanishing American*, p. 106.

12. Henry David Thoreau, *The Illustrated Walden: With Photographs from the Gleason Collection* (Princeton: Princeton University Press, 1973), p. 112.

13. Ibid., p. 182.

14. Ibid., p. 248.

15. Charles M. Russell, *Trails Plowed Under* (New York: Doubleday, 1935), p. xx.

16. Harold McCracken, *The Charles M. Russell Book: The Life and Work of the Cowboy Artist* (Garden City, N.Y.: Doubleday, 1957), pp. 13-36.

17. Brian W. Dippie, *Remington and Russell* (Austin: University of Texas Press, 1982), p. 156.

18. Russell, *Trails*, p. 139.

19. Russell, *Trails*, p. 144.

20. Men are not the only ones to gain an Indian name. The historical figure Virginia Dare, who was the first European child born in the new world and disappeared in 1587 with the rest of Sir Walter Raleigh's colony, has presented a puzzling mystery to historians ever since her disappearance. In a children's book titled *Virginia Dare: Mystery Girl* (New York: Bobbs-Merrill Co., 1958), part of a series called Childhood of Famous Americans, Augusta Stevenson created a fictionalized conclusion to Virginia's story. Given the problems of presenting a children's story that must deal with the massacre, Stevenson seems to have followed the mythical tradition, giving Virginia an adoptive tribe and an Indian name: White Flower.

21. E. Adamson Hoebel, *The Cheyennes: Indians of the Great Plains* (New York Holt, Rinehart and Winston, 1960), p. 94.

22. Royal B. Hassrick, *The Sioux. Life and Customs of a Warrior Society* (Norman: University of Oklahoma Press, 1964), pp. 18–19.

23. Ibid., p. 303.

24. Ibid., p. 313.

25. Ibid., pp. 134-135.

26. Charles M. Russell left a number of comments concerning his vote for the true American. In a 1914 letter to Judge Pray, Russell used pen, ink, and watercolor to depict a rather forlorn, mounted Indian. Handwritten beside the brave, Russell inked, "This is the onley [sic] real American. He fought and died for his country. Today he has no vote, no country, and is not a citizen, but history will not forget him"; from Janice K. Broderick, *Charles M.*

Russell. American Artist (St. Louis: Jefferson National Expansion Historical Association, 1982), p. 84. Russell expressed much the same sentiment in another letter to Joe Scheurle, possibly around 1916: "The Red man was the true American. They have almost gon [sic]. But will never be forgotten. The history of how they fought for their country is written in blood, a stain that time cannot grind out"; from *Good Medicine: The Illustrated Letters of Charles M. Russell* (New York: Doubleday, 1929), p. 127.

27.   Edward D. Castillo, review of *Dances with Wolves, Film Quarterly* 44 (Summer 1991), p. 16.

28.   Ibid., p. 19.

29.   Ibid., p. 20.

30.   Michael Blake's novel (*Dances with Wolves* [New York: Fawcett Gold Medal Book, 1988]) makes Dunbar's cultural anxiety even more apparent than the expanded film does. Some relevant passages: "Suddenly it was clear as a cloudless day. The skins belonged to the murdered buffalo and the scalps belonged to the men who had killed them, men who had been alive that very afternoon. White men. The lieutenant was numb with confusion. He couldn't participate in this, not even as a watcher. He had to leave." (p. 167). The scene concludes with Dunbar racked with existential anxiety over his indeterminate place in the world: "More than anything he wanted to believe that he was not in this position. He wanted to believe he was floating toward the stars. But he wasn't. He heard Cisco lie down in the grass with a heavy sigh. It was quiet then and Dunbar's thought turned inward, toward himself.Or rather his lack of self. He did not belong to the Indians. He did not belong to the Whites. And it was not time for him to belong to the stars. He belonged right where he was now. He belonged nowhere. A sob rose in his throat. He had to gag to stifle it. But the sobs kept coming up and it was not long before he ceased to see the sense in trying to keep them down" (pp. 167-168).

WOMEN AND THE WESTERN

Pam Cook (1988)

R ecently, the American West has once again become disputed territory.
Historians have turned their attention to women's participation in the westward trek and have discovered, to no great surprise, that their real contribution was far
more extensive and diverse than traditional histories and literature have led us to
believe.[1] When it comes to movies, the picture is much the same: the impoverished
range of female stereotypes on offer (mother, schoolteacher, prostitute, saloon girl,
rancher, Indian squaw, bandit) never matches up to reality. In the epic battle between
heroes to tame the wilderness, the heroines who fought to change the course of history
(the suffragettes, farmers, professional women) fare badly—even the maligned
American Indian has been afforded the dubious luxury of liberal reassessment.

It's tempting to put this down, as many critics have,[2] to the male oedipal bias
of the Western, a narrative based on a masculine quest for sexual and national identity which marginalizes women. Fruitful though this approach may be, it has not really
come to terms with the dual, contradictory role of women. On the one hand she is
peripheral (Budd Boetticher: "What counts is what the heroine provokes, or rather
what she represents. She is the one ... who makes him act the way he does. In herself
the woman has not the slightest importance."). On the other hand she is central
(Anthony Mann: "In fact, a woman is always added to the story because without a
woman the Western wouldn't work."). By the same token, the demand for more realistic images of women does not account for the fact that what lingers in the memory,
refusing to be dismissed, is a series of extraordinary heroines, from Mae West's

Feminine ideal and adventurer: Phoebe Titus (Jean Arthur) in Arizona.

Klondike Annie and Doris Day's Calamity Jane, to Joan Crawford's Vienna and Barbara Stanwyck's Jessica Drummond. The search for realism is perhaps rather self-defeating in a genre which is more concerned with myth than historical accuracy. It might be more illuminating to shuffle the deck (bearing in mind that female card-sharps in the Western are few and far between) and see what permutations emerge.

Following Henry Nash Smith, the frontier has often been seen in symbolic terms as a boundary or barrier between opposing ideas: the Garden/Wilderness dichotomy translating into Culture/Nature, and so on. This formulation has both a relationship to actual events (the breaking down of the barrier between East and West under pressure from eastern expansion), and also a link with psychic and social reality (the loss of boundaries of sexual difference, as eastern "feminine" values came into contact with the "masculine" Wild West). Not surprisingly, then, many Westerns work away at the problem of re-establishing sexual boundaries: it's unusual for the woman who starts out wearing pants, carrying a gun and riding a horse to be still doing so at the end of the movie. Suitably re-clad in dress or skirt, she prepares to take her place in the family, leaving adventure to the men.

Of course, the hero's destiny is also circumscribed: rather than remain a nomad, he has to become civilized and participate in building a new society inside rather than outside the law. In both cases, the rehabilitation can be ambivalent, but the results are different. Over and over again, the woman relinquishes her desire to be active and independent, ceding power to the hero and accepting secondary status as mother figure, educator and social mediator. If she is allowed to be active, it is in the hero's cause rather than her own; in *High Noon* (1952), the young Quaker wife puts aside her pacifist principles to support her husband's heroic stand.

This pattern is remarkably consistent, but the most interesting Westerns explore its inherent tensions. *Stagecoach* (1939), directed by John Ford, whose reverence for motherhood and family is legendary, produced some significant reverberations: the East/West conflict is centred on two women, the respectable Lucy Mallory and the prostitute Dallas, and is played out at the point of life and death as the stagecoach and its motley group of passengers come under attack from savage Apaches. The hope for future civilization (revolving around who is a "good mother": Mrs. Mallory, who gives birth during the journey, or Dallas) lies not with the effete, class-conscious visitors from the East, but with the westerners, who in spite of their "illegality" have an instinctive compassion and sense of right and wrong. Dallas herself, reviled by the snobbish easterners, is presented as a more "natural" mother than Lucy Mallory: shots of her cradling Lucy's baby while the stage is under attack are quite transgressive, since prostitutes are outside the family and the law. It's true that the resolution is entirely conventional: Dallas is the civilizing force that brings the outlaw Ringo back into society. Nevertheless, she remains an ambiguous figure, half prostitute, half wife, partly because of the positive value attached by Ford to renegades and social outcasts.

Similar tensions are worked through in *My Darling Clementine* (1946), where East meets West in the confrontation between schoolteacher Clementine and westerner Wyatt Earp. Clementine is a civilizing influence on Earp, but he makes the passage from Nature to Culture unwillingly, as though resisting the colonizing impetus of the East; and while the wild saloon girl Chihuahua is banished from the scene, her memory lurks in the shadows as a reminder of what civilization represses.

Male ambivalence towards home and family is also at the center of *The Lusty Men* (1952), but here Louise Merritt's resistance to the virile, itinerant world of the rodeo to which her husband Wes becomes attached is given a positive critical force. Jeff, Wes' friend, wants to quit that world, and is attracted to Louise; tragically, he is unable to escape either the rodeo's competitive ethos or the male alliances on which it is based. The film's focus on its heroes' crisis of identity paradoxically allows space in the masculine Western scenario for Louise's own problems with her wife/mother role.

A mother who resists her secondary status is Ma Callum in *Pursued* (1947), a film noirish Western which approaches its subject in an unusually introspective way. The hero, Jeb, is prevented from achieving proper manhood by Ma Callum's refusal to give him essential knowledge about his past. Only when she tells him the truth, in effect relinquishing the control she has guarded so jealously, can he pass into adult masculinity. Simultaneously powerful and powerless, mothers in the Western do indeed reflect the two sides of the Mann/Boetticher coin.

If the good mother represents the feminine ideal in the Western, what then of the "bad girls," the law-breakers against which the ideal is measured? These shady ladies threaten to upset the applecart by challenging men on their own ground; adventurers all, they demand equal status and refuse to take second place, at first, anyway; they wear pants and brandish guns, own land, property and business, demand sexual independence. It's true that this is usually only temporary—if the tomboy has not abandoned her transvestite garb for the arms of the hero by the end of the movie, then she comes to a sticky end. (In *Arizona* [1940], Phoebe Titus' independence is revealed as masquerade and she cedes the struggle to laconic westerner Peter Hunsey.) Nevertheless, the passage to femininity is not always smooth; the bad girl's vacillation between tomboy and wife, with its attendant cross-dressing games, offers some interesting possibilities.

Calamity Jane (1953), contains some extraordinary gender confusions which its somewhat arbitrary double wedding finale does not entirely iron out. Calamity's feminization is not quite complete—at the end of the movie she is back in buckskins as gun-toting guard of the Deadwood Stage, while her marriage to hero Wild Bill Hickok is haunted by the spectre of the scene in which, for the slightest of narrative excuses, he dresses as an Indian squaw. The combination of a comedy-of-errors with the utopian structure of the musical and Western conventions enables an egalitarian fantasy (one which the traditional Western mobilizes in order to undermine) to prevail.[3] In a different way, Marlon Brando's dressing up as a pioneer woman in *The Missouri Breaks* (1976) also brings to the surface some of the unspoken contradictions in the Western's privileging of masculine desires.

Both these films exploit and expose a potential perversity at the heart of the genre, its regressive drive to elude the law of the father, to play forbidden games. The tomboy offers a different sort of erotic pleasure from the mother, one focused on her bottom, and which provokes the desire of the hero to spank her. This sexual tussle, usually played for laughs, is a kind of parody of the father/daughter, father/mother power relations which will eventually put the tomboy in her place. In *Dodge City* (1939), Errol Flynn offers to spank Olivia De Havilland when she has the temerity to want to work on the town newspaper and contribute actively to the town's political development. Their rough and tumble is a playful prelude to a more serious confrontation, apparently a reversal of roles, in which De Havilland lays out for Flynn the moral necessity of his defending the burgeoning community against the villain. De Havilland's passage to mother figure is played out against two other feminine stereotypes, seen as less than ideal: the saloon girl, who sides with the villain, and the comically ineffectual, repressive temperance league women. The heroine's successful putting aside of her tomboy identity brings the errant hero back into society, and so ushers in progress.

There are women whose status as good or bad Western heroines is less easily defined, sisters to the *femmes fatales* of film noir. These duplicitous creatures often inhabit revenge Westerns, which focus on the hero's obsessive drive to seek out and kill his *alter ego* for a crime committed against his family. The woman takes on a sphinx-like quality: she both represents, and holds the key to, the enigma he must resolve. In *Winchester '73* (1950), the neurotic hero, Lin McAdam, is matched by an ambivalent heroine, Lola Manners, who may or may not be a prostitute, may or may not be complicit with villain Waco Johnnie Dean, but is indirectly responsible for the latter's death at the hands of McAdam. Her ambivalent status is maintained until the end: as she and McAdam embrace, his long-time buddy High Spade looks on with a quizzical expression as if to question his friend's judgment.

Occasionally, the duplicitous heroine takes on a more sympathetic, tragic hue. In Fritz Lang's extraordinary Brechtian Western, *Rancho Notorious* (1952), the hero Vern's obsession with avenging the death of his wife turns him into a ruthless, inhuman monster whose sadistic attitude towards the woman, Altar Keane, whom he believes holds the secret to his wife's murder, turns out to be an error of judgment with dire consequences. Believing Altar to be complicit with the murderer, Vern realizes his mistake too late, after Altar dies saving his buddy Frenchy's life. Partly because of distancing techniques used in image, sound and narrative, this is one of a few Westerns in which the overriding male perspective is brought into question: Altar is explicitly seen as a victim of Vern's need to project on to an external image his own violent, destructive urges. In *Rancho Notorious,* women are finally evacuated from the scene completely, as Vern and Frenchy ride off together.

Hannie Caulder (1971) puts its heroine in the vengeful hero's place. Hannie sets out to avenge her own rape and her husband's murder, acquiring sharp-shooter skills and much-abbreviated masculine garb (a hat, boots and man-with-no-name-style poncho, but no pants). In spite of an obvious intention to titillate, *Hannie Caulder* also manages to produce some interesting reflections on male heroism. Hannie learns from her mentor (who later dies—no easy romantic transition here) the practical and emotional skills required to be a westerner. No room for compassion or love—Hannie must stand alone in the wilderness. She succeeds in killing the villains, satisfying justice, and at the end she is not returned immediately to home and family. But in an elegiac conclusion, she comes face to face with a mysterious man in black who has haunted her progress, and whose presence is a reminder of a final boundary Hannie can never cross. For women can never really be heroes in the Western: that would mean the end of the genre.

The Western is haunted by the fear of miscegenation, the myth of the rapacious Indian bent on capturing and breeding with white women. When white women mate with Indians, the results are generally catastrophic: the woman is seen to be contaminated by the primitive (polygamous) laws of the wilderness and henceforth unfit for monogamous family life. It's different when a civilized white man mates with an Indian woman. Surprisingly, perhaps, Indian women are often quite positively portrayed as noble, brave, intelligent and self-sacrificing. But this is merely a variation on the mother figure, whose function is to smooth the way for the male transition to maturity. In *The Big Sky* (1952), Teal Eye enables the relationship between Jim and Boone to move beyond the latently homosexual to a mature friendship, also allowing the younger Boone to overcome his hatred of Indians, while in *Run of the Arrow* (1957) Yellow Moccasin supports O'Meara through his crisis of national identity, even to the extent of giving up her Sioux nationhood to return with him to the States when the crisis is over.

Sometimes, however, the race/sex/nation conflict is less easily resolved. Ethan Edwards, the hero of *The Searchers* (1956), is a classic westerner. Solitary, asexual and taciturn, he is driven to seek out and destroy his *alter ego,* the Comanche chief Scar, epitome of the primitive sexuality Ethan's culture represses. Ethan and his quest are imbued with epic overtones: nevertheless, his rescue of his niece Debbie from Scar's clutches is seen as a highly ambiguous act on a par with Scar's original act of abduction, since Debbie makes it clear she wants to remain with the Indians. Debbie's refusal to see herself as a victim, or to accept a position as object of exchange between the two cultures, doesn't affect her final destiny; but it does allow a criticism of Ethan's racist puritan code to surface, a criticism not entirely erased by the elegiac overtones of the hero's final act of walking out alone into the desert. Five years later, in *Two Rode Together* (1961), Ford's criticism becomes more explicit. Marshal McCabe (James Stewart) rejects the racist attitudes of cavalry and white settlers by leaving for California with Elena, a kidnapped white girl turned Indian squaw.

King Vidor's magnificently melodramatic *Duel in the Sun* (1946) unusually focuses on a woman's crisis of identity. Its racially ambiguous heroine, Pearl Chavez (daughter of a white father and Mexican Indian mother) vacillates between two lovers (the "good" brother Jesse, epitome of civilized eastern values, and the "bad" brother Lewt, barbaric and brutal), who represent the struggle within herself between good and evil, wife and tomboy. Pearl is unable to accept her feminine role as Jesse's wife and pursues her transgressive desire for Lewt. On one level, the struggle is between the "primitive" Indian and "civilized" white in Pearl—her inability to control her sexual desire is partly responsible for her death. But melodrama's characteristic focus on female desire turns the normal moral order on its head: the forces of civilization become forces of repression which lead precisely to the excess which brings about Pearl and Lewt's deaths. Pearl Chavez's tragedy is that of all the Western's tomboys, writ large.

One reason for the Western's decline could be its resistance to the impact of social change. One attempt to capitalize on an emerging women's movement was *The Ballad of Josie* (1967), a comedy Western starring Doris Day as Josie Minick, the wife of a violent alcoholic in nineteenth century Wyoming territory, forced to become an independent woman after his death. After a succession of menial jobs, she uses her savings to set up a sheep farm in what has traditionally been cattle country, provoking a range war. The film attempts a blending of contemporary feminist issues (wife-battering, child custody, job discrimination) with historical material like prostitution and women's suffrage, set against the characteristic trajectory of the Western heroine from tomboy to wife; but the feminist influence sits uneasily with the Western narrative.

Perhaps the nearest Hollywood has come to a feminist Western, *Johnny Guitar* (1954), predates the modern women's movement by more than a decade and does not deal directly with social issues at all. Set in a timeless desert wasteland with only the most perfunctory signs of civilization in evidence, *Johnny Guitar* is overtly presented as myth. Vienna, the film's extraordinary heroine and one of the most compelling female images the Western has produced, has often been seen as a feminist ideal, a woman who survives on equal terms with men (though reservations have been expressed about the misogynist representation of Vienna's opponent, Emma Small, and the disappointing shoot-out between the two women).[4] Vienna is certainly unusual: a powerful combination of several Western heroines in one (a gunslinger, a musician and a successful entrepreneur who outwits everyone by buying up land to capitalize on the coming of the railroad, she is sexually independent but also mother to the disillusioned Johnny and the Dancin' Kid's gang). Feminine in her white dress, masculine in black shooting gear, she moves between tomboy and mother figure with

The Ballad of Josie *(right)*, Hannie Caulder *(below)*, Duel in the Sun *(bot. right)*: *"Women can never really be heroes in the Western: that would mean the end of the genre."*

ease, demonstrating and maintaining a level of control allowed to very few women. But the film's feminism goes deeper than this, extending to a criticism of the Western's male values. Destructive masculine drives have gone out of control, creating a world dominated by death, betrayal and revenge. Emma Small is complicit in this process, while Vienna keeps a distance, speaking out against moral disintegration, expressing perhaps director Nicholas Ray's own disillusionment with the U.S. in the grip of McCarthyism. It is in this light, rather than as a failure of her positive qualities, that Vienna's half-hearted shoot-out with Emma Small can be seen. Vienna has had enough of death and revenge; she and Johnny leave the ranchers, bankers and outlaws to their own devices. At the end of *Johnny Guitar*, still in pants, still more than equal to any man, having successfully resisted all attempts to bring her down, Vienna bids farewell to the Western.

NOTES

1. Sandra L. Myres, *Westering Women and the Frontier Experience 1800-1915* (Albuquerque: University of New Mexico Press, 1982). Julie Roy Jeffrey, *Frontier Women: The Trans-Mississippi West* (New York: Hill and Wang, 1979).

2. For example John Cawelti, *The Six-Gun Mystique* (Bowling Green: Bowling Green Popular Press, 1971).

3. Mandy Merck, "Travesty on the Old Frontier" in *Move Over Misconceptions: Doris Day Reappraised* (London: British Film Institute, 1980).

4. Jacqueline Levitin, "The Western: any good roles for feminists?," *Film Reader* no. 5, 1982.

SALOON GIRLS AND RANCHERS' DAUGHTERS:
The Woman in the Western

Blake Lucas (1998)

O f all the misconceptions which have come to attach themselves to the Western, none is more saddening or wrong-headed than the notion that women are unimportant in it. When they are conceded a place in accounts of the genre, it is customarily a marginal one or at best a significant but strictly symbolic role. The myth that the traditional heroine of a Western is a passive and pallid figure has inevitably led to the belief that her role must be subverted, and it can be interesting for a woman to literally shoot her way into the center of the action. But scorn of the more familiar types of Western women presents to us the depressing possibility that the classical Western—a genre without equal in its 1946-1964 golden age—may come to be undervalued and rejected as a model, and that along with this many Western heroines who have never been truly appreciated and celebrated will be forgotten. It's time to see the Western in a different light—not as a masculine genre but as one supremely balanced in its male/female aspect and one of the finest places for women characters in all of cinema.

Some kind of alchemy blesses artistic forms which are especially rich—think of the sonnet or the string quartet—and of narrative forms, the Western movie is one of the most satisfying, its combination of landscape and dramatic motifs endlessly stimulating. Here and in the older forms cited, expressiveness and invention go hand in hand with a respect for the specific limitations of the form. So the best Westerns tend to cleave closely to familiar outlines, the same basic characters and situations steadily recurring but revitalized by individual artists and at times given the force of revela-

"A genre supremely balanced in its male/female aspect": Jeb Rand (Robert Mitchum) and Thorley Callum (Teresa Wright) in Pursued.

tion. This ritual quality is an overriding one which suggests that something very universal is at work; and without doubt, the genre is not just about specific American history, or even the interplay of history and myth, but a *form* which gives a supple choreography and voice to everlasting archetypes and to archetypal human experience. We will be more rewarded if we think of characters in Westerns in these terms rather than taking the facile approach of labeling them as stereotypes. Let's keep this in mind as we look at the saloon girls and ranchers' daughters and the many variants of these types of women who have populated Westerns.

The rancher's daughter/saloon girl duality reaches far back into all forms of narrative and cultural consciousness—she is in essence the madonna or whore, settling down here on the American frontier with a specific yet still eternal resonance. The insightful artist sees something of each archetype inside all women, but also understands that respect for archetypal models encouraged the genre to evolve. Discerning practitioners have always handled both types of women with empathy and creative attentiveness, and it's hard to think of a good Western from any period in which the wholesome heroine is pure and simple or the "bad girl" fallen forever.

In the single film which did most to revitalize the Western in the sound period, *Stagecoach* (1939), director John Ford cannily realized he could cover the most ground by assertively bringing together all the archetypes he could crowd into and onto a single stagecoach, doing especially well with good outlaw the Ringo Kid (John Wayne), disillusioned gentleman gambler Hatfield (John Carradine), and the two women. So Louise Platt's Lucy Mallory, an army wife, is of one type, and Claire Trevor's Dallas, a prostitute, is of the other, and they are wonderfully signalled in direction, acting, writing (the estimable Dudley Nichols), and character-defining costumes by Walter Plunkett. Like many directors, Ford shows more empathy for the prostitute, but he does not lack a measure of sympathetic feeling for Lucy, too. Both characters remain as vivid as ever and resonate in harmony with Hatfield and Ringo, often in unspoken ways, as in that nocturnal walk through Lordsburg of the main couple.

It's intriguing—and one of the sources of tension and richness in relationships between men and women within the genre—that hero and heroine are not usually so linked in perfect harmony of purpose as Ringo and Dallas. Though it's a wonderful and never-stale motif to intimate the settling down of the couple on a little ranch after the fadeout, the essential natures of male and female are defined as different in the Western: the man is the restless wanderer and figure of action, while the woman is physically more passive and can embody the values of civilization while standing in the doorway of her homestead. Resolution for the couple can as often mean separation as union, though some Westerns neatly evoke the feelings of both endings, as in *My Darling Clementine* (1946, directed by John Ford), *The Man From Laramie* (1955, directed by Anthony Mann) and *Seven Men From Now* (1956, directed by Budd Boetticher).

In many Westerns, the hero simply rides off, seemingly never to settle down. Not so in the neglected *Saddle Tramp* (1950), in which Joel McCrea's persona turns this loner into the gentle Chuck, but here, ironically, the happy ending provides a deeper sense of how hard ambivalence is to tame. In Harold Shumate's deceptively easygoing screenplay, realized with characteristic grace and precision by Hugo Fregonese, the protagonist rides into the landscape of the opening scene musing in an inner monologue about wild geese and how free they are, concluding "That's me." But involvement with orphaned children and pretty heroine Della (Wanda Hendrix) inevitably changes this, and so, in the movie's piercing last scene, Chuck sends the boys off to school telling them how good it is to settle down, then stands in the yard of his ranch with Della and looks up to see those geese passing once again. I cannot evoke the look on his face and sound of his voice as he watches them, momentarily possessed of an almost inexpressible yearning, but what makes this one of the great moments of the genre is that Fregonese keeps the couple in two-shot as Della picks up and concludes his thoughts while both look at the sky in one accord, tenderly observed from overhead. Chuck has picked the right girl—the one who understands the part of him that still wants freedom. But are people's natures settled so easily? And doesn't Della's empathy for Chuck's wanderlust suggest that, just maybe, women too have a part of their souls that wants only to be wild and free?

At the least, the *Saddle Tramp* epiphany suggests that the heroine is more interesting than most accounts of the Western suggest. Still, the Fregonese film is about the male journey and not woman's destiny. Yet that destiny has always been just as viable a subject, as readily proven by one obvious but still magical example— *Westward The Women* (1951). This female journey is made by a multiplicity of variations on the two basic archetypes, all capable, physical and sexual—rounded figures of heroic will (and brought to life with a wonderful vitality by Denise Darcel, Lenore Lonergan, Marilyn Erskine, Hope Emerson, Julie Bishop, Renata Vanni, Beverly Dennis, et al., none of whom ever had another opportunity this good). Director William Wellman and cinematographer William Mellor fill the work with eloquent black-and-white images of women in command of their own fate—pulling a wagon up a mountain with ropes or pushing one across the arid flats after it has lost a wheel or leading the men they've chosen into a graceful dance at journey's end.

Even if heroines don't usually step out into the center so forcefully, in the classical period they are commonly treated with the same stimulating flexibility, as is evident in the works of acknowledged masters of the genre. John Ford, for example, had known how to bend archetypes since his earliest films. This is well-demonstrated in *Hell Bent* (1918) in which Cheyenne Harry (Harry Carey) meets the decent heroine Bess (Neva Gerber) when she goes to work in a dance hall—a subtle, sophisticated relationship forms between them, and her presence in his life determines the flow of the narrative. In the Western's mature years, archetypes continue to recur in Ford—notably in *My Darling Clementine* with its reconceived saloon entertainer (Linda Darnell) and girl from the East (Cathy Downs), both sympathetic and engaging—but the earlier films had proven how perfectly he understood them and they are now only a starting point. So, he is free to go on to things that interest him more—ideas, moods, spiritual states.

Types of women in Ford are as diverse as there are characters. He's matchless in his appreciation of mature women, as shown in his marvelous portraits of cavalry wives—Mrs. Collingwood (Anna Lee) and Mrs. O'Rourke (Irene Rich) in *Fort Apache* (1948) and Abby Allshard (Mildred Natwick) in *She Wore A Yellow Ribbon* (1949); and he can still etch pleasing contrasts between different types, as with aristocratic captive Elena (Linda Cristal) and wholesome if troubled rancher's daughter Marty (Shirley Jones) in *Two Rode Together* (1961). Continuity within life is the constant of the Ford woman—he sees the dreams and sexual yearning of youth, mature love and marriage which can host a range of complex feelings and be troubled in some ways yet fulfilling in others, motherhood with its joys and heartbreak, and the spiritual example a woman can become who really knows life. Ford is interested in families and communities, so he tends to favor women whose journey has brought them to a place where they are likely to be a part of those families and communities. But he never suggests that their journey has been naive and that they are not whole women. A shining example is Carroll Baker's Deborah Wright in *Cheyenne Autumn* (1964)—a Quaker, she is this film's spiritual center, balancing her priorities, both intimate and communal, with beautiful poise, and its single character who tries to look beyond the troubled present to a better tomorrow.

If the Ford heroine is characteristically the enlightened good girl who seeks a place in the wider community, the Raoul Walsh heroine is most strongly felt as an individual whose worldly experience is considerable and needs no apology. Warm and honest, she is comfortable within her body and at ease with her feelings. As surely as his male heroes, she is an adventurer who will ultimately wind up side by side as an equal partner with a sympathetic man who prizes her independent nature and has no wish to steal any part of it. Walsh's is the cinema of the couple to an extent that no other director can claim. All of his Westerns bear this out; they even tend to rise and fall in interest and stature according to how compelling the couple is and how well their story is told.

Walsh tends to take the characters as the scripts come to him, so there are plenty of examples of both female archetypes in his films. He can do well with the lady, but the more worldly the woman the more likely she will be the heroine (almost invariably true in his work when both archetypes are present). Rosie (Julia Adams—Julie after 1954) in *The Lawless Breed* (1953) is introduced in a saloon, in the same scene in which trouble begins for John Wesley Hardin (Rock Hudson); we feel immediately her capability for traveling the hard road with him as a soulmate in a way his homespun fiancee (Mary Castle) never could. She is also like Colorado (Virginia Mayo) in *Colorado Territory* (1949) in having a story of her own which runs parallel to that of the hero. For Rosie, it's the progression from woman on her own in a rough world of saloons, to outlaw's lover enjoying the good life his gambling provides, to a wife who discovers settling down is what she really wants, to a mother raising on her own a son obsessed with his father's reputation, her wholeness and centeredness making possible a family reunion that is finally joyous rather than tragic. For half-breed Colorado, it's the return to sources—the land she grew up in; here, she "lives over" the life that had led her low with a new result—true and eternal love with Wes (Joel McCrea)—in much the same way he "lives over" his outlaw life to finally transcend it as time and space reunite them in death.

So it is with the purest Walsh Western, *The Tall Men* (1955). Again, the parallel stories of hero Clay (Clark Gable) and heroine Nella (Jane Russell) are given equal weight, so that a richly satisfying third story, of their evolution as a couple, is traced as an intimate journey against the narrative's more expansive one. The heroine is especially interesting—a synthesis of the two archetypes, though closer in spirit to the saloon girl, she is sexually experienced and anxious to find a rich and powerful partner but finally elects to hang her hat at Prairie Dog Creek with Clay, who dreams small but is the right guy if there ever was one. She also gets to be a kind of one-woman Greek chorus singing about her own story ("I want a tall man, don't want a small man..."), and it's this delightful running commentary, with the content of the lyrics changing depending on how she's feeling about men at any given moment, which gives the film its special charm. *The Tall Men* is a pleasing example of how the production code couldn't keep a good relationship down—the couple clearly sleeps together early on while sharing a little cabin along the trail, and Walsh amusingly seals the breach which follows as they each move to their own corners of the vast CinemaScope frame to retire separately. The film celebrates the mutual sexual enjoyment in their lusty, humor-inflected relationship, especially when her change of heart reunites them at the end. For Walsh, the moment when strong men and strong women find each other is the moment of highest emotion.

Then there's Anthony Mann. Even his name evokes for many the masculine conflicts which seem almost invariably to animate his world. Yet this is one director who actually said: "Without a woman, the Western wouldn't work." And sure enough, the heroine figures strongly in every Mann Western and tends to have a decisive influence on how the narratives play out. Mann's heroes, especially as played by James Stewart, readily compel attention—they're driven, obsessive, divided men of clear dramatic dimension—and the same goes for his villains, so often charismatic and engagingly amoral when they are not powerfully evil or driven by their own demons. By contrast, the Mann heroine often plays in a quieter or "lighter" register, as is com-

"Mutual sexual enjoyment": The Tall Men.

monly true within the genre, but this should not be treated dismissively. The reflective and gentle side of a Western is as valuable and important as the most violent and cathartic action. In fact, the counterpoint of the two tones, and how well it is handled by a director, may be more essential to the Western than anything else.

With that thought in mind, let's consider that for all his acknowledged brilliance with space and landscape, revenge motifs, and climactic gunfights, Mann would not deserve his place as a key figure and defining force in the genre's classical maturity if his women were as weakly drawn as some have alleged. The limitation, though, is in those who take that view, for it's hard to think of a director who has given us a more fetching and varied group of women (all played by different actresses) within one decade's worth of Westerns—from Paula Raymond to Julie London by way of Barbara Stanwyck, Shelley Winters, Julia Adams, Janet Leigh, Ruth Roman, Corinne Calvet, Cathy O'Donnell, Aline MacMahon, Anne Bancroft, and Betsy Palmer, they are all effective. In Mann's first Western, *Devil's Doorway* (1950), Paula Raymond sets the tone with her pensive, handsome portrait of frontier lawyer Orrie Masters, a woman of intelligence, insight and courage as well as ladylike composure and adult passion. Betsy Palmer's Nora Mayfield in *The Tin Star* (1957) has an essential place in the story—widow of an Indian, mother to a half-breed boy (Michel Ray), sympathetic and warming confidante to another outcast, bitter bounty hunter Morg Hickman (Henry Fonda)—if very few scenes in which the actress can flesh her out; Palmer gets the job done, though, as her director allows her those few vital extra moments within the scenes for a feeling to be lyricized, a look or gesture or word to reveal substance, unforced allure, and a complex nature. Then there's Corinne Calvet's disarming and humorous Renée Vallon in *The Far Country* (1955), wandering the Alaskan goldfields with nerve and verve, a touch of naiveté, and wonderfully uncultured charm; here is arguably Mann's freshest and most endearing heroine, as subtly sexy as she is obviously the movie's moral voice.

As the Mann villain doubles the hero's darker, more violent side, the heroine mirrors the life-affirming energy of his nature—she is the one who calls with the voice of finer, more decent impulses and of romantic yearning and so reawakens feelings in the male hero which rebalance him. There's surely no question that the most powerful example is Janet Leigh's Lina Patch in *The Naked Spur* (1953)—a woman alone among four men in a rugged and perilous wilderness, she is the one of five characters who is truly the strongest, able to make this story change course so that Howard Kemp (James Stewart) will not be consumed by his bitter past. The movie peaks not in its stunning climactic sequence of rocks, river, and death, but in the aftermath. It's an achingly beautiful moment when Howard turns to face Lina, his eyes full of tears, and sees in her face the light of unconditional love and a new beginning, and if it's mainly Stewart's moment—one of his greatest ever—it wouldn't be nearly as moving without the softer yet no less vibrant intensity of Leigh. Again and again, the woman in Mann registers in this way. Try to pull her out of the film and all that would be left is men giving in to their basest impulses—a spectacle of slaughter awash with pessimism instead of these finely wrought moral dramas in which men and women alike seek a wholeness of existence within the emerging communities of the frontier.

From the beginning of the great post-war years, this interaction of men and

Canyon Passage, *"a film equally about women and men."* Susan Hayward and Dana Andrews.

women in emerging communities is an essential element of the Western. *Canyon Passage* stands with *My Darling Clementine* as a seminal 1946 work and has some remarkable resemblances to that film. In each, there are two male friends—one a natural leader working out private concerns as well as communal ones (here Dana Andrews' Logan) and the other self-destructive, or in this case, simply weak (Brian Donlevy's George, who loses his moral sense), while the heroine (Susan Hayward's Lucy in this instance) moves from the second man to the first. *Canyon Passage* places its central triangle within an even more elaborate weave, for Logan is engaged to a farm girl, Caroline (Patricia Roc), loved by still another man, Vane (Victor Cutler), while George is attracted to gambler's wife Marta (Rose Hobart) and seems ambivalent about Lucy—in an especially amusing moment, Logan shows George how she should really be kissed. It is surely no accident that this wonderful portrait of an Oregon settlement just finding its way—a film equally about women and men, with some lives in renewal and others in decay—would attract the brilliant Jacques Tourneur to the genre at this point in his career. The source material was by Ernest

Haycox, who originated *Stagecoach*, and the producer, Walter Wanger, is the same as on that film; it plainly aspired to the same level of nuance and maturity and needed a director of Tourneur's subtlety and sensitivity, one not so interested in who is hero or villain but in how each one plays his part, gracefully observed with the director's special synthesis of quiet sympathy and calm dispassion in a way that mirrors the wry yet lovely commentary within the film of Hy the balladeer (Hoagy Carmichael).

The two 1946 films underline what many other examples confirm: romantic triangles in Westerns, if marginally less plentiful than climactic showdowns, are just as vital to the character of the genre. Women in these triangles are sometimes perceived as overly reticent, but a film like *Shane* (1953, directed by George Stevens) shows that notion is at best a half-truth while presenting a vision of the triangle which often has a special depth and poignancy within the genre—all three characters are decent and sympathetic and the woman loves both men in different ways. A woman in this situation must balance the intensity of the unexpected attraction against deeply held ideas about her life. She can let herself feel romantic feelings for the outsider, as Marian (Jean Arthur) does for Shane (Alan Ladd), without being able to hide them from her husband (Van Heflin), yet act so unassailably within a personally felt code of conduct that she cannot be reproached. Marian has to reconcile all of this within herself, and it's clearly a painful process. She has to let her yearning side hang out a bit in order to come to rest, then makes a believable choice. What Westerns which dramatize this kind of triangle can show so expressively is the heartrending intimate spectacle of complex feelings absorbed into the flow of history and the nurturing of a land which could one day become a paradise if faith is kept.

If this kind of willed repression of desire is one motif of the genre, eroticism and passion are also familiar faces, and the Western has boasted memorable physical love scenes as well as quietly tender communions. An example of the former is the moody nocturne of *Yellow Sky* (1948, directed by William Wellman), with its eloquently erotic images of the sudden expressiveness with which miner's daughter Mike (Anne Baxter) responds to outlaw leader Stretch (Gregory Peck). Another magical, if much quieter, discovery of love occurs in an ineffable moment midway through *The Outriders* (1950, directed by Roy Rowland), when Jen (Arlene Dahl), who has offered to break her ladylike reclusiveness and dance with all the men on a wagon train after an especially hard day, finally gets her chance with Will (Joel McCrea); she changes her shoes and the music changes to a gentle waltz, and as she and Will dance away from the others, a romantic spell lifts this obscure movie, sealed as Will speaks softly: "You never showed yourself like this before." Scenes like these often don't get the attention they deserve because the Western never lingers on anything too long. There's a train to catch or meet, cattle to be taken to journey's end, an outlaw double to be vanquished—but a good filmmaker can always poetically charge the moment where intimate feeling is revealed or expressed.

Love—sexual, romantic or spiritual—is only one face of the male/female communion so essential to the genre. But the impulse to love, which typically feels so natural to the characters in a Western, always prompts that communion into being. The hero will talk to the heroine as he has never talked to anyone, haltingly perhaps but very eloquently. Wonderful examples of this occur in the cycle of Randolph Scott movies directed by Budd Boetticher, notably in scripts by Burt Kennedy. In the revelatory journey of *Comanche Station* (1960), Cody (Scott) tells Nancy Lowe (Nancy Gates) that in the long years he has been searching for his lost wife captured by Comanches, the first ease he has felt has been in the time spent traveling with her. This is a film which treats with great sophistication the theme of masculinity—gentle natured Dobie (Richard Rust) becomes a man when he turns his back on doing wrong, costing him his life at the hands of Ben Lane (Claude Akins), while the husband who did not try to rescue his own wife from the Comanches turns out to be blind. In this context, the quiet registration of Cody's flash of tender feeling—a side of this stoical hero that longs for a woman's gentle gaze and loving touch rather than an endless quest in hard, forbidding country—is both affecting and crucial to the expressiveness of the whole. A more elaborate instance of a man showing a deep, hidden part of himself to a woman occurs in *Jubal* (1956), in a scene especially well-realized by director/co-writer Delmer Daves. This occurs when the eponymous hero (Glenn Ford), who now wants to solve his problems, tells Naomi (Felicia Farr), the rawhider heroine, how his father's death by drowning provoked his mother to express her wish that it had been Jubal, then a boy, instead. The revelation explains a lot about this trouble-prone character, but it's the scene's visual mood which seals its effectiveness—Jubal stands beside a softly flowing river as he tells his story while Naomi stands away from him listening sympathetically and attentively. As in *Comanche Station*, the contrast between the rugged action of the narrative and the unaccustomed voice of the hero's introversion suggests that the women have drawn these men into an unusually impressive and powerful intimacy.

Make no mistake about these "listening" scenes: the ability to listen to a man does not make a woman a passive vessel. It is only in naïve perspectives on the American cinema that women are respected in relation to how much they are imitative of men as figures of action. It is this view that has dismantled a formerly fine tradition of women's roles in American movies, with the Western in particular now pretty much bereft of the kinds of heroines I have been describing. World cinema as a whole has always understood the nature of a heroine. While men have commonly driven the action of a film in an external way, women have often driven it from within themselves (in films by Renoir, Rossellini, Ophuls, Mizoguchi, Naruse, et al.). *L'Histoire d'Adèle H.* (1975) does not have the content of a Western but it has the dramatic momentum of one, with director François Truffaut's heroine (Isabelle Adjani) moving toward a climactic moment as cathartic as a well-staged gunfight. And what about *L'Avventura* (1960)? Of its two adventurers, it is clear that director Michelangelo Antonioni conceives of the woman (Monica Vitti) as the stronger and that she is the one who both centers and leads the narrative. One film that has deep affinities with a Western is *Les Rendez-vous d'Anna* (1978)—here, there is a listening woman (Aurore Clement) who is also a figure on a journey. Just as Randolph Scott or James Stewart might sit by the campfire at night drinking coffee and engaging in unaffected philosophical conversations with the villains and other traveling companions, director Chantal Akerman's heroine lends herself to transient social interaction without straying from an essentially solitary path—a perfect alternative title would be *Anna Rides Alone*.

So the woman in the Western can act on its narrative with a subtle but real forcefulness, helping the hero to his destiny while also finding her own. And in the process, archetypes often intriguingly merge. Army wife Ellen Colton (Julie London) in *The Wonderful Country* (1959), a magnificent achievement by director Robert Parrish, is promiscuous and might be seen as a bad woman looking like a lady, except that the truth is more complex—a man to her is someone who can lay down his guns, something Martin Brady (Robert Mitchum) finally does. The marvelously moody opening scene of *Joe Dakota* (1957, directed by the talented Richard Bartlett) finds a stranger (Jock Mahoney) riding into an almost-deserted town in which the sole inhabitant, young Jody (Luana Patten), looks like she might be the town trollop as she leans provocatively against a wall—but she's really a good girl (though branded by a mysterious event which lies at the film's heart), whose unusual ideas about life make her a good soulmate for the hero, with whom she quickly bonds. Then there's Mariette Hartley's Elsa in *Ride The High Country* (1962, directed by Sam Peckinpah), memorably at the center of one of the Western's finest sequences—her wedding in a brothel, with its nightmare atmosphere, subjective shots, comic yet perceptive speech about marriage by drunken judge Edgar Buchanan, and above all, the spectacle of a wholesome and innately sensible girl, who has remained in touch with herself despite

Elsa (Mariette Hartley) and the wedding in the brothel in Ride the High Country. *"Romantic dreams broken against frontier realities."*

her father's attempts to totally repress her nature, seeing her romantic dreams broken against frontier realities.

As the experience of many of these movies suggests, the heroine does not easily move to the center of a Western, and is usually a little off to the side of the hero, but good filmmakers have traditionally compensated by becoming palpably sensitive to her, so that she registers far more affectingly than her place in the narrative might suggest. Naturally, not every outstanding Western is a model. Sometimes a character is good enough but the actress is weak—*The Bravados* (1958, directed by Henry King) has a viable heroine, an old flame of the revenge-obsessed hero (Gregory Peck) with whom he shares the film's more reflective moments, but Joan Collins fails to animate her (imagine Ava Gardner in this role). On the other hand, women may be decently realized yet still pale in interest beside the male characters, as in *Vera Cruz* (1954); here the two women (Denise Darcel and Sarita Montiel) contrast with each other and serve the story well, but there's no question that it's the interaction of affably wary comrades-in-arms Joe Erin (Burt Lancaster) and Ben Trane (Gary Cooper) that makes this one of the most enduring works of director Robert Aldrich. Still, it is the rule rather than the exception that the strongest Westerns tend to be those in which women are most well-realized and vital to the whole.

That's confirmed, often in a negative way, in post-classical films, especially those of the so-called "revisionist" phase. Forcefully executed but at heart simple and sentimental, a film like *The Wild Bunch* (1969, directed by Sam Peckinpah) is more full of sound and fury than substance and reflection, and it's surely significant that in all of Peckinpah, women are at their most peripheral and one-dimensional here. I find it depressing that this film—so representative of the "Men without Women" sub-genre that has pervaded these later years—is so often taken as one of the genre's touchstone works, but at least Peckinpah has real feeling for the West. A director like Arthur Penn seems not to belong in the genre at all, and the caricatures of *Little Big Man* (1970) are only one indication of his failure to imbue women in his Westerns with the dimension they often have in other of his films; far more serious is the hip, smirking attitude of *The Missouri Breaks* (1976), which dooms any chance of giving the rancher's daughter archetype a new vitality despite the presence of an actress, Kathleen Lloyd, who might have thrived in a good Western. Somewhere between Penn and Peckinpah is Robert Altman whose *McCabe And Mrs. Miller* (1971) shows a genuine understanding of the contours of the genre but is undone by the director's characteristically cynical and contemptuous attitude toward the characters, their feelings and dreams, and, by extension, the frontier world of which they are a part (compare the treatment of an emerging community, as well as the male-female relationships, in a classical work like *Canyon Passage*!). With Constance Miller (Julie Christie), Altman rings a fresh if finally opaque variation on the saloon girl archetype—replacing any vestige of warmheartedness with cold-blooded pragmatism and emotional vacancy. We are a long way from the great couples of the Western at this film's denouement, with McCabe (Warren Beatty) dying in the snow while Constance lies in an opium den, oblivious.

In the better films of these later years, archetypes and motifs evolve, but the filmmakers treat both genre and characters with the sensitivity and respect of their predecessors, and like Peckinpah, they are best when the female presence is strongest. So, in *Will Penny* (1968), director-writer Tom Gries recalls a classical model like *Saddle Tramp* in his character study of a wandering cowboy (Charlton Heston) and the woman who would settle him (Joan Hackett), but the love story has a rueful resolution which conveys painful emotional limitations as an aspect of the hero's rootlessness. *Unforgiven* (1992, directed by Clint Eastwood) takes up the related theme of restless, wild hero coupled with stable, moral heroine through the powerfully evoked relationship between Will Munny (Eastwood) and his dead wife Claudia—the movie's central one—but the film is darker than the models because remorseless outlaw Will's redemption through love of Claudia may finally have been only one episode in a never resolved odyssey of unsettled identity. These movies are exceptions to the general tendency of recent Westerns, which derives in part from a symbiosis between filmmakers and criticism rooted in ideology and psychoanalytic theory. It is not politically correct to embrace any concept of the traditional woman, and feminist naiveté will only tolerate "empowered" women who can masquerade as men or shoot it out with the boys. Never mind that in classical Westerns, we often admired male heroes for the power they gave up, like turning away from gunplay; for the ideologically conditioned Western heroines of recent years, power is a grail—the key to female identity. It is these years—and most of the Westerns produced within them—which have, in most people's minds, marginalized women within a genre in which they once thrived.

There is a female iconography in the Western as much as a male one, at least in the classic era, which includes actresses like Susan Hayward, Virginia Mayo, Julie Adams, Julie London, and a range of others—among them Olive Carey, Debra Paget (in her Indian roles), and Katy Jurado. Heroines can be as young as Kim Darby's Mattie in the still underrated *True Grit* (1969, directed by Henry Hathaway), a prim but game girl, mercurially naïve and mature by turns, and so well-realized that she stands as one of the genre's freshest figures. With archetypes as a starting point, Howard Hawks brought his kind of woman to three great Westerns—*Red River* (1948), *The Big Sky* (1952), and *Rio Bravo* (1959)—with *Rio Bravo*'s Feathers (Angie Dickinson) the apotheosis of the director's type. There have also been some memorably malevolent women pushing the action of certain Westerns, like Veronica Lake's Connie in *Ramrod* (1947, directed by Andre de Toth) and Millie Perkins's mysterious lady in *The Shooting* (1966, directed by Monte Hellman), though the standout in this group is an easy choice: Mercedes McCambridge's Emma in *Johnny Guitar* (1954); within Nicholas Ray's inspired *mise en scène*, McCambridge has created a mesmerizing antagonist who fills the drama with warped passion and a strong if twisted will worthy of any of the great male villains. In general, though, it is the traditional heroine who has been served best by the Western—without moving too far from the archetypes, she has shown how well the natures and experiences of women have been served by a genre that really cares about them. Here, in ascending order, is a personal choice for the best of all.

10. Lolly (Colleen Miller) in *Four Guns To The Border* (1954). Lolly, a girl poised between late adolescence and womanhood, is traveling home with her tough, protective father Simon (Walter Brennan). The two encounter a group of four outlaws, including Cully (Rory Calhoun). Later, all six wind up at a desert way station, where Cully catches Lolly in a disturbing kiss. What happens at the 26 minute mark is extraordinary. In a nocturnal storm, Lolly, unable to sleep and dressed in a white cotton slip, moves through the store in a choreographic manner, pausing by a line of rain leaking from the roof and touching her face with the water, then goes out to the shed to comfort the horses. Cully follows her. Aroused but uncertain, she retreats shyly, then kisses him happily, then withdraws fearfully as he becomes more ardent, then, regretful after she throws a pitchfork at him, comes into his arms with abandon in a riveting rainswept embrace. Cut to Simon and a tense resolution, followed by a coda which finds Lolly back at the window looking out as she was when the sequence began. In just over six minutes and 37 shots, this lyrical love scene in an obscure programmer from Universal-International describes the moment of sexual awakening in a young woman with matchless intensity and insight, a fine cinematic suppleness, and a rare command of mood. The brilliant direction is by actor Richard Carlson, who realized only a few movies but here created one of cinema's most erotic sequences. As for Colleen Miller, who plays Lolly with such affecting naturalness and vibrancy, at least one viewer who saw *Four Guns To The Border* on first release is still enamored of her.

Lolly (Colleen Miller) and Cully (Rory Calhoun) in Four Guns to the Border.

9. Catherine (Jenny Agutter) in *China 9, Liberty 37* (1978). In her yearning spirit, she might be an older sister to Lolly, but Catherine is married, and the story describes an interlude in her life—after Clayton Drum (Fabio Testi), a gunfighter hired by the railroad, chooses not to kill her husband Matthew (Warren Oates), she stabs Matthew in the back and runs away with Clayton. Director Monte Hellman's portraits of women can be harsh, but *China 9, Liberty 37* reveals what's really in his heart. The warmth and sympathy with which he realizes Catherine—glowingly interpreted by Jenny Agutter—is everywhere evident: in her captivating "Red River Valley" duet with sister-in-law Barbara (Isabel Mestres) at a family picnic, in her little girl happiness watching a circus rehearsal, in the laughter she shares later with the husband she thought she had killed, and in sad, intimate exchanges with Clayton during the most beautiful stretch of the film, the lovers' last night together. The romanticism of *China 9, Liberty 37* was antithetical to the cynicism of the 70's Western; sadly, it went virtually unreleased in America.

8. Kathleen (Maureen O'Hara) in *Rio Grande* (1950). The last film in John Ford's beloved cavalry trilogy registers the same finely shaded complexity of feeling about the processes of history as its predecessors while narrowing to an intimate focus on three members of a family broken apart. The estranged wife of a devoted-to-duty but affectingly vulnerable Lt. Col. Kirby Yorke (John Wayne) and protective mother of a still soft but very determined trooper, Jeff (Claude Jarman, Jr.), Kathleen is like them a character of mingled qualities and attitudes. Too proud of her Southern past but rightfully demanding her deep feelings for it be acknowledged and still in love with her husband but also profoundly let down by his failures within their marriage, this is a woman seen whole. It's hard to convey the singular way she inclines her head toward Kirby, in a quiet rush of feeling unobserved by him, when the regimental singers serenade the two with "I'll Take You Home Again, Kathleen," or her sly look as she twirls her parasol during the concluding "Dixie." The entire presentation of Kathleen is studded with this kind of behavioral beauty. Ford here paired O'Hara with Wayne for the first time, and the palpable chemistry between them not only makes for a stirring love story but enhances both of their characters even when they are not together on screen.

7. Thorley (Teresa Wright) in *Pursued* (1947). Screenwriter Niven Busch gave his stories a basis in modern psychology and linked them to the great dramas of antiquity, and like director Raoul Walsh, he was one of the first to thrive when the post-war Western turned to specifically adult subjects. Here, because of a forgotten traumatic event in his childhood, Jeb Rand (Robert Mitchum) is so reticent and passive that he ends up taking actions he would not choose. By contrast, his adoptive sister Thorley moves decisively through the narrative at every turn, even if wrongly at times—her feelings are always open and projected with an admirable intensity. The differing but complementary registers in which Wright and Mitchum play contribute much to a sense of these characters and their unusual relationship, and they are alike in radiating sincerity. *Pursued* is deepened even more by the genre's most imposing, complex mother—Judith Anderson played Medea around this time and one feels Euripides himself would have liked her Ma Callum. Women in Westerns are often figures of light, but here Ma shadows the action in an unhappy way; her climactic action finally links her in a positive way to her daughter, giving extra dimension to a final image which finds a Walsh couple riding away, not into the sunset, but out of the darkness.

6. Callie (Lee Remick) in *These Thousand Hills* (1959). Made when the genre had reached a peak of refinement and emotional suppleness, *These Thousand Hills* is representative of how the Western at its most mature could still do everything it needed to do with the basic archetypes. Here, a warm and open dance hall girl and a ladylike banker's niece are both present in the melancholy character study of a flawed hero, Lat (Don Murray), cowhand turned powerful rancher. Callie is the dance hall girl and sometime prostitute who falls in love, and the sequence in which she takes Lat home is beautifully observed; though he wants her, he's too reluctant about it to stay, and her realization that she is the more sophisticated of the two and has found a different kind of man than she's used to is perceptively played by Lee Remick, who uses the moment to artfully signal her character's dimensionality. Once the affair does begin, Callie finances his start, but the sexually troubled Lat marries Joyce (Patricia Owens), who appears to be as repressed as he is, and in his puritanism pulls away from his best friend Tom (Stuart Whitman) as well as from Callie. Finally, he does defend Callie by fighting Jehu (Richard Egan), her jealous and brutal tormentor, but this ends with Callie shooting Jehu in the back to save Lat's life. That moment is the film's true emotional climax—as Callie looks at Lat, her face shows the sad knowledge that she has given away all she is out of love for a man who could never really respond in kind, but that her own nature made no other choice possible. *These Thousand Hills* does not play as downbeat despite its subject, a tribute partly to Alfred Hayes' fine adaptation of A. B. Guthrie, Jr.'s novel but even more to the direction of Richard Fleischer, who finds just the right tone to unite action and landscape with a reflective treatment of relationships.

5. Denver (Joanne Dru) in *Wagon Master* (1950). Worldliness and unapologetic sexuality may go hand in hand with the saloon girl archetype, which traveling show-girl Denver fits at least visually, but John Ford neatly dissolves the difference between archetypes with this character, who, however different in style and experience, is as much a down-to-earth girl looking for love with one of the two heroes, Travis (Ben Johnson) and Sandy (Harry Carey, Jr.), as her Mormon counterpart Prudence (Kathleen O'Malley). Joanne Dru is wonderfully alluring in the role, fleshing out the character with an uncommon subtlety—she surely has no more than twenty lines of dialogue in the whole movie. With a knowing look or in confident but oddly awkward movement, Denver displays a natural eroticism as well as an appealing blend of vulnerability and resilience, never more than in the magical scene in which Travis proposes to her: she reacts with an inarticulateness equal to his, stumbles as she moves away from him, and then is seen in close-up riding away on the back of a wagon, her eyes reflecting her thoughts as she smokes a cigarette in provocative reverie.

4. Emmy (Felicia Farr) in *3:10 To Yuma* (1957). In the little town of Bisby on a near-still, sun-baked afternoon, within a saloon given a special ambiance by Charles Lawton, Jr.'s moody black-and-white images and George Duning's haunting music, one of those erotic encounters which always have a special charge of feeling in the Western takes place, and this one—between Emmy, sad but sweet young barmaid with brown eyes, and Ben Wade (Glenn Ford), a ruthless outlaw who is tender with women—stands by itself in lyricizing the quiet yearnings of the day and evoking how much the experience of an hour can play into the essence of one's self and one's whole life. The last of three appearances by Felicia Farr in the Westerns of Delmer Daves is the shortest but most memorable—a singular portrait of a romantic sensibility seeking expression on a lonely frontier. Emmy is the character who shows most affectingly how well the two archetypes can merge in one appealing young woman—in looks, dress, and manner she seems in every way the wholesome good girl, yet in conversation with Ben, she happily acknowledges that she once sang at the Blind Irishman in Dodge City; the saloon girl has come to a dryer climate for her health. But there's no one to sing for in Bisby, just a chance for a moment of love and a memory. For all its brevity, the sequence is so suggestive that one almost feels one has seen the character's own journey retraced. Daves seems acutely aware of this, punctuating its end with a loving flourish: he cranes up as the stagecoach carrying the captured Ben leaves town, cuts to a reverse angle—craning down and facing a solitary Emmy who stands in the middle of the street watching, then cuts back to the first shot—from overhead and behind Emmy as the coach disappears amidst dust swirls in the distance.

3. Alice (Leora Dana) in *3:10 To Yuma*. With two great heroines to its credit, *3:10 To Yuma* takes pride of place here. Made in the genre's best decade, it's as close to perfection as any Western, with a screenplay by Halsted Welles at once concise and allusive, and masterly direction by Daves. Its subject is the natural order of things and how it both challenges and nurtures relationships between men and women, especially in marriage. As drought is the central visual metaphor, marriage is the motif—it's in the central relationship between ranching couple Alice and Dan Evans (Van Heflin), in the honeymoon suite in Contention City where Dan and his prisoner Ben wait for the train, and even in the amusing exchange in which a hotel clerk (Guy Wilkerson) and outlaw Charlie Prince (Richard Jaeckel) wonder why wives run off. It's also the relationship Ben and Emmy will never have; and the connection between the two couples, stable but dispirited husband and wife with two sons, and free-spirited but drifting outlaw and barmaid—nicely underlined in a scene where, for a few moments, the captive Ben charms Alice too—is vital to the whole. The two women resemble each other, giving continuity to the suffusion of female energy which is felt throughout, but the film can invest more in Alice, whose sorting out of priorities is so eloquently felt in Dana's superb performance, because for all that she and Dan are a couple in crisis, she travels with him spiritually throughout these tense hours. The action builds to a natural miracle, and the powerful images of both drought and rain—from opening crane shot which begins on parched earth and moves up into a pale sky to final shot of the train rushing through the pouring rain on its way to Yuma—show in the purest way why a subject like this one can achieve fullest expression in a Western. The metaphor is so unstrained, so naturally poetic, and so perfectly attuned

"Two great heroines": Emmy (Felicia Farr) with Ben Wade (Glenn Ford), and Alice Evans (Leora Dana) and her husband Dan (Van Heflin) in 3:10 to Yuma.

to the relationship. Daves' ultimate crane shot—moving up from an overhead view of Alice as she gazes rapturously up at Dan passing on the train, the rain pouring down on her face—not only provides the unifying stylistic moment but instills in the film a profound eroticism which traverses the space between temporarily separated husband and wife and imbues their sustained love with uncommon emotion.

2. Jill (Claudia Cardinale) in *Once Upon A Time In The West* (1968). An awesome heroine, Jill, rather than three strongly realized male characters, is the expressive central presence of this operatic Western. In her unusual relationships with each of the men and in the way her personal odyssey intersects the playing out of the greater myth of the frontier, this prostitute who has married and come West to share in a vision of the future and who must then begin again is arguably the single character to show most effectively how a woman can be placed in the genre in a transfiguring way. Compare this film to director Sergio Leone's three previous "male" Westerns; texture and tone—and even Ennio Morricone's music—are completely different, as a sardonic attitude transforms into a gentle humor, violence becomes less pervasive and more purposeful, and irony gives way to an expansive romanticism.

1. Hallie (Vera Miles) in *The Man Who Shot Liberty Valance* (1962). The Western's best heroine may seem prosaic. In the flashback of her younger days which makes up most of this film, she works in a restaurant, must learn to read and write, and wears only a few costumes (albeit designed by Edith Head). Yet this is the kind of character many artists dream of creating, unaffected but evocative of a whole world. Without bravura but with quiet daring, John Ford here deals out his best cards from the top of the deck—the communion on a buckboard of an older Hallie and ex-town marshal Link Appleyard (Andy Devine) as they ride out to a burnt-out house and look at the cactus roses takes place within the first ten minutes, yet it has the emotion of the whole film behind it. As exquisite as anything in cinema, the sequence benefits from its simplicity, grave pacing, concise dialogue, the sublime acting of Vera Miles and Andy Devine, and the wistful Ann Rutledge theme of Alfred Newman, but most of all from a cut to a different, slightly lower angle of the same two-shot that occurs

"The Western's best heroine": Vera Miles as Hallie in The Man Who Shot Liberty Valance, *returning with her husband Rance (James Stewart) to Shinbone, greeted there by Link Appleyard (Andy Devine).*

between Link's line "There's his house down there...what's left of it...blossoms all around it" and Hallie's "He never did finish that room he started to build on, did he?" The cut is almost invisible, yet in a moment quiet, intimate, personal feelings become elevated, heroic, transcendent—it's a stroke of genius comparable to what one would expect of a Bach or a Rembrandt in their late works. *The Man Who Shot Liberty Valance* is about many things, all consciously drawn from the motifs of the genre, but most of all it is about a woman between two men, of how her feelings for each man answers a deep part of herself and so can never be dispelled, and how the tragic irresolution has pervaded her life and theirs as well. What is so admirable about Hallie is not her sadness but that she bears the choice she made with such grace and dignity. In this, she is profoundly suggestive of the heroine (Nina Pens Rode) of a work far from the Western, *Gertrud* (1964, directed by Carl Dreyer)—which *The Man Who Shot Liberty Valance* anticipates by two years—and the affinities of the two films are indeed great, in specifics like the even, incantatory line readings and old age makeup of the respective framing scenes and epilogue, and beyond into the bold stylization and uncommon soulfulness of each. Finally, though, Hallie is firmly of her world, the prairie flower blossoming through all the seasons. "It used to be a wilderness . . . now it's a garden." The line evokes the course of her life, but it goes far beyond this, resonating with an empathy for the West rare in any character—for what it was in the past, for what it has become, and for what it may still be someday.

THE COMPETING TUNES OF
JOHNNY GUITAR:
Liberalism, Sexuality, Masquerade

Jennifer Peterson (1996)

N icholas Ray's eclectic 1954 western *Johnny Guitar* has supported dramatically divergent readings by its critics over the years. American journalists at the time of its release were disappointed by *Johnny Guitar's* nontraditional use of generic conventions. "It has not only male, but female gunfighters," a writer for the *New Yorker* sneered, declaring: "It was probably inevitable that sooner or later somebody would try to change the pattern of Westerns, but I can state authoritatively that this twist is doomed." *Time* proclaimed it "a crossbreed of the Western with a psychoanalytic case history," while *Commonweal* criticized it for self-parody, "refus[ing] to take the script or . . . actors seriously," and *Variety* accused it of having too much "pretentious attempt at analysis."[1] In fact these critics were correct in apprehending the film's revisionism, for Ray indeed set out to challenge convention by making his hero female (and by casting Joan Crawford to play this hero[ine]) and by turning the paradigmatic western conflict between individual and community into an anti-McCarthyist allegory. What is less perceptive and more symptomatic about the above criticisms is their disapproval of this generic revisionism.[2] These critics, in fact, represent just the attitudes about convention that I will argue *Johnny Guitar* wants to challenge. Contemporaneous with and in direct contrast to the film's American critical rejection, French New Wave critics applauded it, celebrating Nicholas Ray as an *auteur*, a "poet of nightfall." François Truffaut praised the film as "a Western that is dream-like, magical, unreal to a degree, delirious."[3] This positive appraisal demonstrates a concern with poetics and pathos rather than aesthetic conventionalism and seems inspired by the film's overinscribed stylistic elements (high-

321

ly saturated Trucolor film stock, quirky sets, flamboyant acting); in fact, it is precisely the film's unconventionality that attracts Truffaut. By presenting itself as an exploration of conventionality and unconventionality, *Johnny Guitar* has produced several decades of criticism along the same lines, criticism that fails to move beyond the terms the film sets up for itself.

Johnny Guitar is hard to pin down. To a greater degree than many films it supports multiple and contradictory discourses, and analysis of it has usually focused on one or another discursive level at the exclusion of others. A responsible reading of the film must recognize these oppositions, for this very polyvalency is its key. Its plot is simpler than it appears: female saloonkeeper Vienna is accused of harboring a gang of criminals, and the townspeople—led by the vindictive Emma Small, whose brother was allegedly killed by this gang—try to drive her out of town. Johnny Guitar arrives just as this conflict between Vienna and the townspeople is beginning to brew; he tries to rekindle his past relationship with Vienna, competing with gang member the Dancing Kid for her affections. Vienna's saloon is torched and many characters are killed over the course of the narrative, but finally Vienna is vindicated: she shoots and kills Emma and pairs off with Johnny as the film ends. Such a conflict between a righteous individual wrongly scapegoated and an angry community is particularly significant to the film's early 1950s context as an implicit (and explicitly stated) critique of McCarthyite anti-Communist fervor. However, the film's representations of gender complicate any ostensibly simple political polemic. What concerns me here is the deployment of *Johnny Guitar*'s "liberal'" anti-McCarthy agenda and the dependence of this political deployment on a misogynous caricature: the hysterical, undersexed Emma Small (played by the ever-pathological Mercedes McCambridge). In this apparent critique of repressive and conservative postwar American society, Ray actually reveals new anxieties about sexuality and gender. His "liberal" critique of conformity and repression projects culpability onto the woman who is the community leader, thereby gendering persecution mania and anti-Communist fervor female. However, even a recognition of this first ideological U-turn does not fully illuminate the film, for while it presents its "liberal"/misogyny theme, the film also provides a figure of female power in the enigmatic character of Joan Crawford's Vienna. Finally, the film filters all these issues through a thick veil of campy self-consciousness, which qualifies its stances on politics and gender by making it virtually impossible to take them seriously.

Johnny Guitar engages the familiar western icon of the lone hero in a new way: she is a woman; and the part of the villain, though represented in a general way by the frenzied community, is also personified primarily by another woman. This has led critics to see the film as either a protofeminist narrative of affirmation or as an ominously masculinist narrative of female containment because of the film's not-quite-serious treatment of these female characters. Thus we have the rather starry-eyed 1970s proclamation that "director Nicholas Ray, in very overstated terms, showed how women's liberation could and did come to the West long before contemporary society took up the hue and cry."[4] Conversely, we find the equally wholehearted conclusion that "*Johnny Guitar*'s hidden thesis is that the possibility of women gaining power through money makes both the encroaching civilization from the East and even the old western community dangerous."[5]

In a 1990 *Cinema Journal* article, Leo Charney makes a similar argument that the film is an antifeminist narrative; he does not concede any female triumph to Vienna, claiming instead that the film is ultimately and principally concerned with Johnny. The film begins and ends with Johnny, it is titled with his name, and "Vienna's struggle results not primarily in her victory over Emma or in her business success but in her reunion with Johnny. The film's containment strives to keep both women and excess in their place."[6] Thus the criticisms have come full circle, from dismissing the film for even having female lead characters to attacking it for its "'contained" female characters. These criticisms all move back and forth on a linear axis; either the film is unsuccessful or it is successful, either it is feminist or it is conservative and antifeminist. In contrast, I argue that the film represents competing discourses about gender; on the one hand, Vienna is granted a somewhat qualified female strength, while on the other, Emma is made a completely pathological woman. A linear model is inadequate for an explanation of *Johnny Guitar*. The film defies the symmetry (both formal and thematic) of the classical Hollywood cinema;[7] it embodies all the above politicized elements to some extent simultaneously but ultimately represents something entirely other, enigmatic. It is this inscrutability that provides room for the programming of whatever reading a critic finds useful to his or her purpose.

In particular, I want to address Charney's criticism, the most recent and rigorous of those outlined above yet still bounded by its insistence on only one discourse. Charney uses *Johnny Guitar* as a vehicle for discussing Roland Barthes's notion of "excess," which is expanded to incorporate the relationship of a film's narrative to the social context of its production, in this case embodied in the acknowledged anti-McCarthy parable mounted by the film. Charney argues that the film's structure requires it to "acknowledge excess, [it] must bring it forward in the attempt to contain it."[8] In this configuration, anti-Communist hysteria is evoked by the film to be discredited, contained. Charney goes on to argue that the film's containment doesn't stop at the level of the McCarthyist plot but continues on to subsume the Vienna/Emma plot underneath that of Johnny, thereby containing the female characters for the reinstatement of male subjectivity. "The film's opening clearly establishes Johnny as its center of perception," and the film's closure "tips the balance of the film's gender tensions, structurally subordinating the female plot to the reaffirmed masculinity of Johnny Guitar."[9] I take issue with this argument because it fails to account for the varied and opposing discourses of the film. What about the film's theme song, sung by a female voice at the film's close intoning "My Johnny"? What about the film's self-parody? Charney forces his own argument into a balanced formality of double-containment when the film itself is in no way so neatly structured.

Liberalism

Nicholas Ray made a point of emphasizing the allegory of McCarthyist hysteria he intended in *Johnny Guitar*. Once a member of the Communist party himself, Ray was surprisingly not blacklisted, though he was sympathetic to the plight of those who were. Casting was a significant factor in the creation of this allegory. Sterling Hayden, who played Johnny, had been an informer before the House Un-American Activities Committee and was looking for a way to expiate the guilt he felt over his infamous act. "Vienna [Joan Crawford] also mirrored reality. Under fire from McCarthy, she refused to inform," Ray explained.[10] *Johnny Guitar*'s screenwriter, Philip Yordan, said in an interview: "we played a good trick on Ward Bond, who was, as you know, one of the members of the fascist party in Hollywood. We had him play the role of the head of the posse, an extreme fascist causing a reign of terror. And he thought the character was a hero, a good sympathetic guy. He didn't understand anything."[11] Ray and Yordan thus identified with Vienna's ostracized situation and attempted to coerce the audience into doing so as well in a sort of Hollywood version of a morality play. Following their own binary politics, they styled themselves as "liberal" revisionists of western conventions, typified by films such as *My Darling Clementine* (John Ford, 1946), for example, in which civilization triumphs over lawlessness and in which individualistic values are integrated into the community. In Ray and Yordan's reconfiguration, the civilized community is made into a vindictively conservative mass that threatens the freedom of the individual. *Johnny Guitar*'s persecuted individuals are forced into the role of outlaws by mob violence; thus the community violates its own traditional values (responsibility, family, lawfulness) and becomes a grotesque profaner of American individualism (and by extension the concomitant individualistic values of freedom, self-reliance, and personal integrity). Yordan said in the same interview: "There were other things in *Johnny Guitar:* a violent attack against puritanism in the character of the old crazy girl, played by Mercedes McCambridge."[12] The wording here is significant; it belies a smugly "liberal" and reactionary transfer of blame from one site to another, from blaming the "'Communist" for societal ills to blaming the "puritan[ical] . . . *old crazy girl."* The film's gender constructions are the key to breaking it down, for while ostensibly granting women heroic status, the film actually displaces most of its disgust for McCarthyist hysteria onto the female figure of Emma Small.

The anti-McCarthyist parable certainly works on an implicit level and can be extensively drawn out. While much of the film's character symbolism may be apparent, I quote one account of it at length partly for its conciseness but also to indicate the limitations of an uncritical reliance on allegory, as if film were some sort of crossword puzzle. The parenthetical comments are in the original text:

> The "'outlaws" become symbolic communists (besides living and working communally over their mine shaft, they are also the town's "whipping boys," constantly blamed for real and imagined transgressions). Johnny, the ex-gunman is the ex-Communists (now mere entertainers) called before HUAC. (At the time, Sterling Hayden was still famous for renouncing his past Party membership under government pressure.) Vienna—consort of the outlaws, and also the town progressive—is a "'fellow traveler." Emma Small, driven by hysteria and jealousy, suggests those vindictive witnesses and politicians who used the investigations to destroy the careers of hated rivals. McIvers is big business, going along to protect threatened interests and bending the law to his will. ("I thought it was kind of a nice inside joke to cast Ward Bond that way," Ray has said.

Director Nicholas Ray and Joan Crawford on the set.

Bond, of course, was an anti-Communist zealot in the early fifties.) The fair but power-less marshal is the good men in government, caving in under McCarthy's bluster. And the townspeople are the American middle class—the film's audience.[13]

Though drawing out the film's McCarthyist subtext may be an entertaining exercise, there are problems with leaning too heavily on such a direct analogy, partic-ularly when the filmmakers stated that such analogy was intended. This sort of analy-sis lays so much stress on a simplistic, one-for-one parallel that it merely reproduces the film's own self-stated codes, thereby masking any more rigorous criticism of the work—the McCarthyist parable is useful, but it does not tell the whole story. In fact, the anti-McCarthy allegory betrays itself by merely scapegoating another marginalized figure: Emma. *Johnny Guitar*'s negative forces are not defused but relocated. Although I would not argue that the film is simply misogynistic, for Emma's evil hysteria is bal-anced by Vienna's composure, its inability to deal with the force it is trying to deni-grate leaves the film with hardly the liberating significance it ostensibly intended.

Sexuality

Johnny Guitar's anti-McCarthyist allegory combines with its gender portrayals to create a telling conflation of the sexual and the political. Emma's villainousness is uniquely pathological, implicitly stemming from her sexuality (or lack thereof). This transfer of blame along a linear axis—from "Left" back to "Right"—catches up women along the way, using them as politicized pawns. Ray represents the Right as repressed, paranoid, and misguided—by a woman. The Left is comprised of innocent individualists such as Vienna, who is merely trying to do her business and play by the rules but whose alien presence ("You're nothing but a railroad tramp, you're not fit to live among decent people,'" Emma says to her) is inherently repugnant to the isolationist Right. It is perhaps fruitless to speculate why Ray used women to personify this binary; but the effect is quite illuminating, and certainly the space of a western is a good location in which to fight it out. Despite its pridefully antitraditional crusade, however, the film's "liberal" assertion of the individual's right to live free from persecution is actually quite conventional, mirroring the exploration of individualism found in earlier westerns such as *Stagecoach* (John Ford, 1939) and *Shane* (George Stevens, 1953), for example. Ray seems to be attempting a social critique that would provide an argument for tolerance and progressive ideals in an era he viewed as repressive and intolerant. Yet as has been demonstrated by Michel Foucault, reading modern society as repressive, particularly regarding sexuality, is actually a misreading. For Foucault the 'repressive hypothesis'" of power relations is a false configuration that is "in fact part of the same historical network as the thing it denounces (and doubtless misrepresents) by calling it 'repression.'"[14] Using Emma as a sexually caricatured figure who must shoulder the blame for all society's ills merely reproduces the power structure Ray thinks he is critiquing. In a similar manner, D. W. Griffith "liberally" condemned those who tried to censor his *Birth of a Nation* for its racism by representing them as prissy female spinsters in *Intolerance*.[15] Once again, repression is gendered female, and a political debate is deflected onto gender. Foucault speculates that "'there must be another reason that makes it so gratifying for us to define the relationship between sex and power in terms of repression: something that might be called the speaker's benefit. If sex is repressed, that is, condemned to prohibition, nonexistence, and silence, then the mere fact that one is speaking about it has the appearance of a deliberate transgression."[16] Ray is all too eager to place himself in the role of the deliberate transgressor out to foil repression; his extreme revisionism in *Johnny Guitar*—making fun of the idea of the western itself, as if it were below him—demonstrates this. Certainly in 1954 one could be misogynistic and still think himself a liberal, but viewed today the film's portrayal of Emma seems quite reactionary. The surprise is perhaps that there exists an alternate discourse to that of female hysteria: Vienna's undemonized manipulation of female power.

Mercedes McCambridge's performance as Emma enforces this conflation of politics and gender through a mixed use of pop-psychology metaphors. (The 1954 *Time* review called her a "sexological square knot who fondles pistols suggestively and gets unladylike satisfaction from watching a house burn down."[17]) Emma is clearly the origin of the (significantly all-male) community's persecution mania, and she is the character the film works to discredit. It is she who whips the men into a frenzy, thus underscoring the men's own failed masculinity; she spurs them on at every turn to chase after the Dancing Kid and his gang, to banish Vienna from town, and to hang Turkey. Though it may be the community that carries out these deeds, Emma is always to blame for goading the community to follow its worst inclinations. Emma is a half-crazed, pathological caricature. Her facial expressions are excessively dramatized: thick eyebrows persistently raised, nostrils flared, mouth agape, always half-breathless with an airy, high-pitched voice. She is a truly hysterical subject, mono-maniacal in her mission to oust Vienna from town. As a female character, Emma is a vehicle well suited to be the carrier of hysteria, a condition historically associated with women. Steven Heath, quoting Freud, has said that "the hysteric will not play the game, misses her identity as a woman: 'Speaking as a whole,' writes Freud, 'hysterical attacks, like hysteria in general, revive a piece of sexual activity in women which existed during their childhood and at that time revealed an essentially masculine character.'"[18] Emma infects the townspeople (all men) with this hysterical quality as though it were a virus, and the only way these men can restore order is by disassociating themselves from her, as they do just before her death. At the end of the film, when Emma and Vienna are about to duel, one of the townspeople says, "Mac, me and the boys have had enough of this killin'." McIvers replies, "'So have I. It's their fight, has been all along. Run and tell the others there'll be no more shootin'." In this way the infected, hysterical agent (woman) is jettisoned from the all-male community.

Emma is often referred to by the term "'puritanical"; screenwriter Yordan labeled her a " puritan," and many reviewers, including Charney, point to this as a central quality of Emma's subjectivity, claiming that her "neurotic vengeance vividly embodies a breakdown of Puritan self-restraint."[19] This term in its common usage implies that Emma is ultraconservative and prim, anxious to deny all sexuality; using the pejorative "puritan" enacts the repressive hypothesis of power and sexuality. However, I would suggest that Emma is not exactly an asexual character but rather a classic depiction of the pathological lesbian. Indeed, the virus metaphor for Emma's pathology fits with the characterization of homosexuality in the fifties; as John D'Emilio and Estelle Freedman write in their history of American sexuality, homosexuality during the Cold War "took on the form of a contagious disease imperiling the health of anyone who came near it."[20] Thus when the men eject Emma from their society they are ridding themselves not only of a woman but of a homosexual—Communist scapegoating has turned into the scapegoating of yet another generic Other. Though Emma makes isolationist speeches saying that Vienna represents the future of a town "squeezed between barbed wires and fenceposts" to justify her senti-ments, the film implies that her motivation for obsessively persecuting Vienna springs from a twisted, thwarted jealousy of Vienna's sexual relationship with the Dancing Kid, whom she loves but perversely won't admit to loving. Vienna explains that the Kid "makes her [Emma] feel like a woman, and that frightens her." Emma is a hodge-podge of sexually aberrant signifiers; her "masculine" qualities—aggressiveness, shortly cropped hair, thick eyebrows, plain, makeupless face—are all stereotypical indicators of lesbianism, along with her pathological attitudes about sexuality, simulta-neously decrying sex and yet seeming to need more of it. Her mourning dress also bears an uncanny resemblance to a nun's habit, another clichéd reference to sexual repressiveness. As one of only two women in the film, Emma is in a sense punished for taking part in the action and not having a male love interest, for not rewarding the viewer with a pleasurable female spectacle for the male gaze. Ray and Yordan meant to indict sexual repressiveness with Emma and thus draw a parallel with societal repressiveness in general, but because this sexual denial is inscribed on the figure of a woman, and because none of the many male characters are punished for their lack of sexuality, the film ultimately replays a patriarchal emphasis on woman as sexual object. Emma's punishment is thus two-pronged: she is punished for her audacious female leadership, and she is punished for her misdirected "lesbian" sexuality. By

The 1954 Time *called Mercedes McCambridge's Emma a "sexological square knot who fondled pistols suggestively."*

infusing Emma's behavior with a bit of pop-Freudian motivation and by claiming an allegory of anti-McCarthyism, the film tries to claim a liberating agenda for itself, but Emma's characterization is merely another example of the classical cinema's masculinist articulation.

Although it is important to acknowledge *Johnny Guitar* as a lesbian camp classic, it is admittedly somewhat reading against the grain to see Emma as a closet lesbian, since her flaw is primarily a lack of identity mobility. Her two-dimensionality is an easy target for the film to discredit, thus deflecting criticism from the film's own two-dimensional political spectrum. Emma's pathology does revolve around an aberrant sexuality, however, and granting that it is acceptable and even necessary to read texts against the grain, her gender problem can thus be analyzed as lesbianism. With this outlook in mind, it is indeed telling that Ray would use a homosexual caricature to deflate the power of McCarthyism, for homosexuals, like Communists, were another target of the purges of the McCarthy era. D'Emilio and Freedman write that "'homosexuals suddenly found themselves labeled a threat to national security and the target of widespread witch-hunts . . . [in] 1950, the same [year] that Senator Joseph McCarthy initially charged that the Department of State was riddled with Communists . . . the Senate authorized a formal inquiry into the employment of 'homosexuals and other moral perverts' in government.... The Cold War against Communism made the problem of homosexuality especially menacing."[21] Ray and Yordan, then, engage in the same homophobic practice as the dreaded McCarthy in their use of Emma as society's evil incarnate. The film's "liberal" stance is highly problematic in its simplistic reversal of the power equation: it blindly reproduces the same social prejudice as the "conservative" McCarthyites, albeit under the guise of an alternative ideology. "Male and female homosexuality played to a variety of sexual fears just at a time when an ethic of sexual liberalism had sunk roots into the middle class," D'Emilio and Freedman write.[22] Ray and Yordan are a part of this sexual "liberalism" that is in fact not free from its own form of intolerance. Ray falls decisively short of his self-applauding noble purposes by using contemporary homophobic strategies to discredit Emma. However, Vienna's character significantly complicates a simple reading of the film as misogynous.

Masquerade

While Emma's problem is her rigidly pathological identity, Vienna's strength is in her gender mobility. Vienna goes unpunished in the plot as a strong, sexual woman; she is a leader in her own way: quiet, solitary, self-possessed, gaining allies through respect rather than intimidation. Contrary to Leo Charney, I argue that Vienna is the undeniable heroine and focus of the film. The narrative is motivated and propelled by her conflict with Emma, and Vienna maintains the power to choose her own course of action throughout. Vienna and Johnny both are allowed the power to repeatedly mask and change their identities; Vienna changes from pants to dresses, Johnny switches from guitar wearing to gun wielding, Johnny has changed his name, Vienna has changed her profession. Vienna's identity in particular resists pigeonholing; it fluctuates throughout the film and allows her a greater power than Emma, stuck in a hysterical bell jar. To further complicate the film's identities, there is also a theme of false identification surrounding other characters. The Dancing Kid and his gang are accused of a holdup they didn't commit, Vienna is repeatedly accused by the townspeople of masterminding crimes she had nothing to do with, and Turkey, trying to escape hanging, lies that Vienna was a part of the bank robbery he committed. Identity is thus continually in question in *Johnny Guitar*; in effect, the film deconstructs identity and assigns a power to gender fluidity that is unavailable to characters stuck in narrower categories. Vienna's inscrutability forms a buffer space around her, protecting her individuality from the prying eyes of the conformist crowd. She is able to masquerade as either male or female, as the costume suits her fancy.

Joan Riviere's notion of the masquerade is therefore useful in analyzing Vienna's empowered position in the film. "Womanliness'" in Riviere's configuration is put on as a mask to disguise a female's "masculine" possession of phallic power. "Womanliness therefore [can] be assumed and worn as a mask, both to hide the possession of masculinity and to avert the reprisals expected if she [is] found to possess it."[23] Vienna is in possession of such phallic power: she is financially independent, runs her own saloon, and is the boss of several male employees. She is also in control of her sexual relationships, able to choose for herself which man she wants (the Dancing Kid or Johnny), rather than being chosen by them. She performs the female masquerade, particularly at crucial moments in the plot, to save herself when this visible power becomes construed as a threat by the male community. Most notably, when she puts on a white dress to meet Emma and her angry mob of townspeople Vienna plays at female innocence and decorum. This white dress is not merely white, it glows with luminous spotlessness. Made of layers of sheer, fragile-looking material, its voluminous skirt billows out from her trim waist, exuding placid feminine righteousness. She has chosen to use this dress as a sign of her innocence, along with her solitude and moody piano playing; the excessiveness of this dress clearly indicates Vienna's self-conscious choice (via the film's costume designer, Sheila O'Brien) to wear it as a costume, unleashing the significant cultural import of the white dress as a sign of purity. Later, when running from the mob with Johnny the dress no longer serves its purpose and in fact catches on fire, hindering her progress and emphasizing that the charade of the white dress is no longer needed. At this point Vienna changes into pants. Her pants wearing and her dress wearing are both a drag performance of sorts, but the costumes also have some "truth" value for Vienna since she does embody both "masculine" and "feminine" qualities—she is at home in either outfit. Vienna is willing to "play the game'" of female masquerade, unlike Emma, who possesses some power, albeit pathologically inspired, but who is not so careful (or able) to disguise it. "'Hysteria is what? *failed* masquerade," Steven Heath proposes, describing a situation akin to Emma's.[24] And as Mary Anne Doane puts it in a description applicable to Vienna, "masquerade is anti-hysterical"[25] because it creates a space between the self and one's perception by others, thereby masking desires that others would find aberrant and threatening in a woman. In a sense, then, the masquerade is a necessary defense mechanism for women, a means of maneuvering some power out of a prescribed position of disempowerment.

Judith Butler points out that the masquerade (in Lacan's analysis, but still applicable here) can be construed as either "performative production of a sexual ontology'" or as a "denial of a feminine desire that presupposes some prior ontological femininity regularly unrepresented by the phallic economy."[26] I would argue that in the case of Vienna, we have the former example of "performative" femininity. Vienna is clearly performing, and she is in control of her desires—particularly for men. Butler's continuing description of the first understanding of masquerade as "performative'" is particularly applicable to Vienna. "The former [understanding] would engage a critical reflection on gender ontology as parodic (de)construction and, perhaps, pursue the mobile possibilities of the slippery distinction between 'appearing' and 'being,' a radicalization of the 'comedic' dimension of sexual ontology only partially pursued by Lacan."[27] In Vienna's case, repression and denial are not at the core of her masquerade. Her costumes—pants, boots, and a gun when she is "masculine," dresses, particularly the white one, when she is "feminine"—are so extremely at odds with each other that they do indeed engage a parodic deconstruction of gender. She has another notable costume: the red negligee-like gown she wears when she and Johnny reaffirm their romantic relationship. This is Vienna's sexy outfit (red, clingy, just as obvious as the white dress), though she remains a fully sexual woman while not wearing the dress as well. Though she is most helpless when in a dress (unable to stop the bank robbery, unable to prevent Turkey's lynching) and she is most powerful when in pants (the initial confrontation in her saloon, the shootout with Emma), there is a crossover between outfits; for example: she cooks breakfast for Johnny while wearing pants. Each of these costumes enhances qualities Vienna already embodies; they serve as icons in themselves, oversaturated with significance to highlight whatever quality is most opportune at the moment. Vienna is not made to deny her desires; rather, she plays with power relations, always retaining control of her outwardly perceived identity.

Vienna's masquerade is not only of "'womanliness" but of "manliness" as well—though Riviere's and other discussions of the masquerade do not speak of women masquerading as men since this changes the equation from one of disguising desire out of fear into an appropriation of power for similarly manipulative purposes of disguise. Vienna's masculine attire at times seems to mask a certain sadness that lies beneath her veneer of phallic power; this sadness shows forth in her reunion with Johnny, when she admits to a deep loneliness, and in her wistful maternal tenderness for Turkey, both while wearing pants and dresses. She is "femininely" vulnerable, yet at the same time Vienna seems to possess a certain fighting spirit and self-control that looks awkward in a dress, indicating that perhaps she is truly at home in neither costume. In Heath's words, "The pertinent question remains: what is behind the mask of womanliness?"[28] Butler implies that it is masculinity, but this seems inadequate. Vienna demonstrates the pose that is gender identity, but is there an essential identity beneath this mask? Returning to Riviere, we find an answer: "The reader may now ask how I define womanliness or where I draw the line between genuine womanliness and the masquerade. My suggestion is not, however, that there is any such difference; whether radical or superficial, they are the same thing."[29] I suggest that Vienna embodies a certain enigma that is incorrectly represented by either gender mask. It can be argued that Vienna acts out a radical critique of the binary gender construction itself, demonstrating that a full character is inadequately pigeonholed by rigid identities. These identities are the only framework available, however; thus the method of subverting them is to demonstrate their constructedness.

Vienna is validated by *Johnny Guitar* as a figure of female power in the traditionally male-dominated West; in fact, she is almost superhuman. She has it all, both breasts and a gun, and remains intact even after her saloon has burned down; she is a rugged, tough individual with a solid presence that the film respects—or does it? Such vehement validation of a female character in fact verges on grotesque parody, particularly since this character is played by Joan Crawford. The film's camp can be read as either containing or liberating, depending on one's attitude toward gender play and strategic misreadings. It is possible to read Vienna's powerful position as undermined by the film's camp. Pamela Robertson, however, makes a compelling argument that the film's camp elements work in precisely the opposite direction not to bring about containment but to work in favor of a feminist reading. While it is true that Vienna could be seen as merely inappropriate rather than critically transgressive (the camp-as-containment argument), in Robertson's critique, camp is the primary force through which "certain marks of excess undermine the film's narrative strategies of containment."[30] Vienna may resemble a campy castrating woman (who, like Emma, could even be pigeonholed as a lesbian because of her possession of phallic power and certain visual clues such as her short hair and her pants wearing), yet it is this very camp excess that undermines the film's misogynous elements. Camp thus enters into the picture as yet another contradictory force, potentially discrediting Vienna's position as the film's heroine yet also allowing space for Vienna's fluid gender-bending performance of the masquerade. Despite the film's camp (or, rather, because of it), the film can be seen as mounting a critique of stability and containment on the level of gender, as it tries to do with politics. *Johnny Guitar* lacks stable gender roles, except in the character of Emma, who is made freakish by the very rigidity of her sexual identity. Vienna's ostensibly threatening gender play is shown to be a red herring as Emma is discovered to be the real threat; Emma's real threat of social conformity-gone-hysterical is defused upon her death, leaving Vienna to emerge triumphant, still wearing pants and in possession of *her* Johnny. *Johnny Guitar*, then, does allow Vienna to retain heroic status in a straight reading *despite* its campy treatment of a conflict between two women, in a camp reading *because* its camp allows for such transgressive gendering in the first place. The film encodes at least three different attitudes about female gender: Emma is misogynistically portrayed as hysterical, Vienna is celebrated for her female power, and Vienna's masquerade, the flip-side of the film's camp, provides the means to this power through the deconstruction of gender identity. I agree with Robertson's claim that *Johnny Guitar* is a "fundamentally incoherent text,"[31] for in my argument, this incoherence is what allows for the programming of so many diverse readings.

Johnny, too, is endowed with the ability to change his identity. He embodies the myth of the ex-gunfighter, a western convention, but with a twist: he has changed his name from Johnny Logan to the ridiculous and flamboyant Johnny Guitar, an example of the film's intentional self-parody. His guitar is a feminizing prop (though

Sterling Hayden and Joan Crawford: "Johnny's feminization, along with Vienna's masculinization, is part of the film's revisionist stance."

he still carries his guns in his saddle bag), and when he first emerges to confront Emma and the angry townspeople in Vienna's saloon he carries a tiny blue-flowered china teacup in his hand. For a male lead in a western, he is notably inactive throughout the film, mostly standing on the sidelines looking on while Vienna interacts with others. This inaction, along with his guitar, renders Johnny "feminine," particularly when compared with other male western leads such as the paradigmatic John Wayne. Johnny's feminization, along with Vienna's masculinization, is part of the film's revisionist stance toward the genre, though here again the film retains a conventional western trope with Johnny's strident individualism. He rides into town on a horse like a typical western hero, big, strong, and silent, yet he rides with a guitar slung over his shoulder instead of packing a gun.

Vienna berates Johnny for being "gun-crazy," a code word for violent loss of self-control (like Emma's) that also implies a too-great fascination with phallic power, or perhaps with the gun/phallus itself. This can be read as Vienna's desire that her man not be too violent and that he need not be overly masculine. But without stretching the text too much, the term "gun-crazy" could be read as a sign of latent homosexual desire. Christopher Castiglia traces such male homosexual desire in Ray's subsequent film *Rebel Without a Cause* (1955). In this film there is an apparent tension surrounding male sexuality located in the adolescent crisis of Jim (James Dean). Jim's evolving sexual identity is influenced by his two friends, who compete for his attention: the nymphlike Plato (Sal Mineo) and the attractive teenage Judy (Natalie Wood). Homoerotics are thus dramatized in triangular romantic competitions, ultimately resolved through the traditional heterosexual coupling.[32] Although the homosocial/sexual elements of *Rebel* are clearly indicated in that film and are not as implied in *Johnny Guitar*, a strategic misreading of *Johnny Guitar* as filled with homosexual tensions is helpful in understanding its gender constructions, even if the idea must be highly qualified.

Gender fluctuation is central to Vienna's character, as we have seen, and Emma's converse position of gender fixity figures strongly as part of her discrediting as a maniacal dyke figure. Johnny's own inaction might be understood as misplaced phallic potency: he's put his gun away and must get it back again by the end. Johnny's physical appearance is as important as Vienna's: he is large and oafish-looking, very fair-skinned, always looking like a little boy with messy hair. Johnny's guitar playing is a comedic parody; he rarely picks up his instrument, and when he does it is only briefly to play a weepy sad song and then some absurdly dramatic "Spanish" chords. These examples indicate Johnny's participation in a male masquerade. Gaylyn Studlar states that "the tantalizing pleasures of the masquerade depend on the mobility of desire and the pleasurable exchange of identity. Males as well as females participate in masquerade that delays consummation through the changing spectacle of mobile desire."[33] Johnny's participation in the game of identity mobility parallels Vienna's and is equally centered on gender bending. These constructions allow the film to explore gender slippage while still upholding the traditional heteronormative understanding of sexual relationships, an understanding also at play in *Rebel*. However, Johnny is not completely feminized, nor is Vienna characterized as unhealthy for her androgyny; they are clearly sexually involved, and there is no ambivalence on Johnny's part about his attraction to Vienna. He demonstrates his possession of Vienna with his bantering with the Kid and with his body movements, as when he fastens Vienna's belt for her in front of the Kid. Reading the film as a latent homosexual text is therefore only partially accurate, though in its explorations of gender it is perhaps a foretaste of things to come in *Rebel*.

Despite her gender—or more accurately because her gender is not static but floating, both "'feminine" and "'masculine"—Vienna is allowed to stand as a self-sufficient individualistic western hero. Vienna is certainly not a depiction of the female as lack, nor is she entirely a castrating woman. She has phallic presence and is unable to be possessed unless she allows it. At the same time, however, this presence is a spectacle. Her male saloon employees make a point of commenting on this unusual gender behavior. Sam says, in a nearly direct address to the camera and the viewer: "Never seen a woman who was more a man. She thinks like one, acts like one, and sometimes makes me feel like I'm not." Tom speaks similarly of Vienna: "I never believed I'd end my years workin' for a woman . . . and likin' it!" The female image, it seems, can never escape its function as spectacle; here it is Vienna's very power that makes her visually fascinating. Despite the many point-of-view shots the film grants her, Vienna's female heroism could be interpreted as mere spectacle, a function of the film's campiness and overt revisionism. Indeed, the duel staged at the end of the film between women instead of men lacks the dramatic veracity of a typical western—this stand-off mimics a catfight more than it does a shootout. The duel takes place at the Kid's hideout, which itself resembles a 1950s ranch home more than it does an outlaw's lair, perched atop a mountainous rock and silhouetted against the blue sky. The women fight it out on the porch of this domestic, homelike space. While Emma creeps up the hill to Vienna on the porch, McIvers and the townspeople watch, along with Johnny and the Kid, as the nondiegetic dramatic string music builds. When Emma reaches the porch there is a pause; the music stops momentarily and Vienna and Emma each get a quick medium camera shot. The women face each other on the porch, above the men watching them from below as if they were on a stage. Then there are three brief shots of the men watching, first McIvers, next Johnny, then the Kid, each accompanied by a rising horn note on the soundtrack as a counterpoint to their shot. Emma shoots Vienna in the arm, and Vienna falls down limply backward onto the planks of the porch. Emma, crazy with rage, begins shooting at everybody, landing a bullet in the Kid's forehead. Vienna finally shoots her from where she lies wounded on the floor and Emma falls dramatically off the porch, her black, witchlike skirt swishing around her, rolling down the hill face down into a stream. This spectacle of two women fighting can be compared with the male-oriented lesbian sex scenes of much straight pornography, particularly in the extent to which it is staged for the men watching from within the diegesis. The scene's violence is the consummation of the conflict between Emma and Vienna, which has hinged on sexuality all along. Pamela Robertson writes: "Emma is a woman possessed. But what desire possesses her? Presumably, her repressed desire for the Dancing Kid. But she directs all her manic energy and enmity toward a former dancing lady, Crawford's Vienna."[34] Clearly, Emma's intense desire is in a twisted way directed mostly at Vienna. This shootout is a classic moment of the female spectacle and can certainly be interpreted as undermining any straight-faced female heroism. However, I maintain that Vienna does emerge triumphantly affirmed by the narrative, and her performance of spectacle (as demonstrated by the masquerade) has all along been her means to maintain power. Though the shootout is a different kind of performance, it does not necessarily undermine the affirmation of Vienna's discourse.

Vienna may be a heroic female figure, but the question remains whether the film actually articulates any female subjectivity. As Emma's characterization demonstrates, *Johnny Guitar* does not have an overtly feminist agenda, and the staging of the female shootout only underscores this point. However, because Vienna is the hero of the film, the spectator identifies with her as the protagonist, despite the film's title. Peggy Lee's song at the film's close reasserts Vienna's presence over Johnny's: "There was never a man like my Johnny, like the one they call Johnny Guitar." These words, sung by a female voice, assert Vienna's point of view, as if the entire film has just been narrated by her. Johnny is positioned as the object of the song; he is Vienna's

"Vienna does emerge triumphantly affirmed by the narrative."

possession, "*my* Johnny,'" hers to marvel at. The song, like the rest of the film, is also ironic: pop music vocals enter the film's western environment as if by mistake from a teen flick or melodrama. *Johnny Guitar* is intentionally misnamed—the male lead is not the active focus of the film and even disappears altogether for a time after Vienna pays him off. This title is yet another facet of the film's revisionism, a revisionism so thorough and yet so contradictory that the film nearly falls apart at times—yet it is all the more intriguing for that incoherence.

Though I maintain that *Johnny Guitar* has the ability to support any critic's most expedient reading, this of course should not deter us from drawing our own conclusions. I argue that gender mobility, then, is the key to understanding *Johnny Guitar*.

The film engages in a critique of identity through its use of the masquerade to powerfully illuminate the workings of the gendered power imbalance. To reiterate Riviere once again, there is no distinction between "genuine womanliness and the masquerade . . . whether radical or superficial, they are the same thing."[35] It is *Johnny Guitar's* strength and innovation that it recognizes the constructedness of gender in similar de-essentializing terms and rewards the characters that utilize this knowledge to their own benefit. *Johnny Guitar* points straight to the constructed spectacle of masquerade as a mechanism of power and fantasy. The masquerade is at once a role-playing game that masks and heightens desire and a means to maintaining phallic power otherwise unavailable to marginalized figures such as women and "outlaws."

NOTES

Many thanks to Miriam Hansen, Pamela Robertson, and Brian Calvin for their valuable comments and suggestions on this essay.

1. *New Yorker*, June 5, 1954, p. 65; *Time*, June 14, 1954, p. 109; *Commonweal*, June 18, 1954, p. 270; *Variety*, May 5 1954, p. 6; this is just a small sample of the remarkably unisonous (and today, often-quoted) first reviews of the film.

2. Though genre is still a complex and vexing issue, most film scholars can at least agree that it works on just such revisionist terms, operating in cycles of repetition and similarity but always with a difference in order to remain compelling and apparently new. What remains intriguing about genre is the degree of difference within each individual film, and how this degree of difference within repetition reflects a political subconscious. See Christine Gledhill's chapters on "Genre" and "The Western" in Pam Cook, ed. *The Cinema Book* (New York: Pantheon Books, 1985), pp. 58–72, for a useful overview and bibliography of genre criticism. Also see Barry Keith Grant, ed. *Film Genre Reader*, (Austin: University of Texas Press, 1986), especially Rick Altman's "A Semantic/Syntactic Approach to Film Genre," which provides one model for complicating certain simplistic oppositions genre revisionism might tempt us to make.

3. François Truffaut, "A Wonderful Certainty,'" in Jim Hillier, ed. *Cahiers du Cinema, the 1950s* (Cambridge: Harvard University Press, 1985), pp. 101–8.

4. James Robert Parish and Michael R. Pitts, *The Great Western Pictures* (New Jersey: Scarecrow Press, 1976), p. 166.

5. Jacqueline Levitin, "The Western: Any Good Roles for Feminists?" *Film Reader* 5 (1982), p. 100.

6. Leo Charney, "Historical Excess: *Johnny Guitar's* Containment," *Cinema Journal* 29 (Summer 1990), p. 31.

7. See David Bordwell, Janet Staiger, and Kristin Thompson, *The Classical Hollywood Cinema: Film Style and Mode of Production to 1960* (New York: Columbia University Press, 1985).

8. Charney, "Historical Excess," p. 28.

9. Ibid., p. 31.

10. Speech by Nicholas Ray at the Orson Welles Cinema, October 23, 1973; quoted in John Francis Kreidl, *Nicholas Ray* (Boston: Twayne Publishers, 1977), p. 49.

11. Bertrand Tavernier, "Interview with Phillip Yordan," *Cahiers du Cinéma* 128 (February 1962), p. 18; quoted in Kreidl, *Nicholas Ray*, pp. 48–49.

12. Ibid., p. 50.

13. Michael Wilmington "Nicholas Ray's *Johnny Guitar*," *Velvet Light Trap* 12 (Spring 1974), p. 23; parenthetical comments in text.

14. Michel Foucault, *The History of Sexuality*, trans. Robert Hurley (New York: Vintage, 1990), 1:10.

15. For one account of this, see Miriam Hansen, *Babel and Babylon: Spectatorship in American Silent Film* (Cambridge: Harvard University Press, 1991), esp. chaps. 5 and 6.

16. Foucault, *The History of Sexuality*, p. 6.

17. *Time*, June 14, 1954, p. 109.

18. Steven Heath, "'Joan Riviere and the Masquerade" in Victor Burgin, James Donald, and Cora Kaplan, eds. *Formations of Fantasy* (London: Routledge, 1986), p. 51.

19. Charney, "Historical Excess,'" p. 9.

20. John D'Emilio and Estelle B. Freedman, *Intimate Matters* (New York: Perennial, 1989), p. 293.

21. Ibid., pp. 292–93.

22. Ibid., p. 294.

23. Joan Riviere, "Womanliness as a Masquerade" (1929), in Burgin, Donald, and Kaplan, eds., *Formations of Fantasy*, p. 38.

24. Heath, "Joan Riviere," p. 51.

25. Mary Anne Doane, "Film and the Masquerade: Theorising the Female Spectator,'" *Screen* 23 (September-October 1982), p. 82.

26. Judith Butler, *Gender Trouble: Feminism and the Subversion of Identity* (New York: Routledge, 1990), p. 47.

27. Ibid.

28. Heath, "Joan Riviere," p. 55.

29. Riviere, "Womanliness," p. 38.

30. Pamela Robertson, "Camping under Western Stars: Joan Crawford in *Johnny Guitar*," in *Guilty Pleasures: Feminist Camp from Mae West to Madonna* (Durham and London: Duke University Press, 1996), p. 104.

31. Ibid. , p. 105.

32. Christopher Castiglia, "Rebel Without a Closet," in Joseph A. Boone and Michael Cadden, *Engendering Men* (New York: Routledge, 1990), pp. 207–12.

33. Gaylyn Studlar, *In the Realm of Pleasure: Von Sternberg, Dietrich, and the Masochistic Aesthetic* (Chicago, University of Illinois Press, 1988), p. 166.

34. Robertson, "Camping Under Western Stars," p. 109.

35. Riviere, "Womanliness," p. 38.

Unforgiven: *"paradigms of masculinity."*
Gene Hackman, Clint Eastwood, Morgan
Freeman.

"MAYBE HE'S TOUGH BUT HE SURE AIN'T NO CARPENTER:"
Masculinity and In/competence in Unforgiven

Janet Thumim (1993)

The shortcomings of Sheriff Little Bill Dagget/Gene Hackman's carpentry, noted and condoned by his deputies, are measured against his competence in being a man: it is his acknowledged "toughness" which earns him the fear and respect of his fellows. As the narrative unfolds, however, this very toughness is continually put under the spotlight of audience attention—it is observed, recorded, analyzed, questioned. This exploration, this measurement of masculinity is couched in terms both of being tough—equated with fearlessness, brutality, single-minded-ness—and of competence since the paradigm for masculinity in the western is the gunfighter who must, by definition, be competent—else he's dead. What is so interesting about this western—Clint Eastwood's "return" to the classic western—is the way in which competence is privileged, being examined not only in the context of gun-fighting and toughness, but also in relation to other and diverse activities—carpentry, farming, story-telling. The idea of competence, as foregrounded in this film, invites a meditation on history—the stuff of the western—calling into question both the morality and the veracity of propositions about America's past as delivered in western myths. That this is not a new project is clear in the near ubiquitous reference, in reviews of the film, to the western before 1964 (which Eastwood, with Sergio Leone, "colluded in undermining"[1]) and particularly to the John Ford/John Wayne films, and often specifically to The Searchers (John Ford, 1956). The conflict-

341

ing generic demands of melodrama and realism produced fractures in the episodic narrative of *The Searchers*, most striking in Ethan/John Wayne's *volte-face* when he catches up with Debbie/Natalie Wood near the end of the film and, against all expectations, rescues her despite what he regards as the defilement of her life as Scar's squaw. In *Unforgiven*, however, the two modes are woven together so intricately that each becomes a part of the other: the truthfulness of the melodramatic axis is measured against its consequences in a realist discourse, and the adequacy of a realist account is constantly checked in terms of its moral implications. The marker of the interchange, the place where the two axes intersect, is in the idea of competence, hence this film suggests competence is central to masculinity. *Unforgiven* is not only a classic western, it is also *about* the western and thus, necessarily, it is also *about* masculinity in both its personal and its public, or social, manifestations. The complex moral and epistemological questions it poses reach far beyond the confines of the genre or of the historical moment, 1880, in which it is set—it is not simply (if it were simple) a matter of making a western as powerful and compelling as *The Searchers* or *Shane* (George Stevens, 1953), or *Rio Bravo* (Howard Hawks, 1959), but of insisting on our attention to the meanings underlying the myths of the west—for America, for men, for all of us.

An on-screen title informs us that the film is set in Big Whiskey, Wyoming, in 1880. A cowboy, visiting the town brothel euphemistically named Greely's Billiard Hall, is mocked by a whore and is so enraged that he responds by slashing her face. The Sheriff, Little Bill Daggett, dispenses summary justice by ordering the cowboys to compensate the Saloon and Billiard Hall owner, Skinny/Anthony James, for his loss of the whore's earnings. Outraged by what they see as an *unjust* refusal to consider compensating the woman herself, Delilah/Anna Thomson, the whores put up a bounty for anyone who will avenge her by killing the cowboy. This sets the narrative in train, and a succession of bounty hunters is expected in town. Amongst them is Will Munny/Eastwood and his erstwhile partner Ned Logan/Morgan Freeman, brought out of their farming retirement by the young Schofield Kid/Jaimz Woolvert who wants to prove himself against what he imagines to be the "truth" of the legendary western heroes of whom he has heard (as we have) so many stories. English Bob/Richard Harris is also attracted by the bounty and, accompanied by his "biographer," the writer Mr. Beauchamp/Saul Rubinek, arrives in town first, only to be beaten and humiliated by the Sheriff who is determined not to allow a re-run of the mythic western free-for-all in his town. Eventually Will, Ned and the Kid track down and kill the cowboy and his partner, and Ned is caught and beaten to death in reprisal. This event triggers Will's anger—not the professional bounty hunter now, but the moral outrage of an avenging partner—and in a final and spectacular set-piece he shoots the Sheriff and deputies before returning to his two children, his run-down pig farm and his wife's grave. An end title informs us that he subsequently disappeared and was said to have "prospered in dry goods" in San Francisco.

Carpentry and Competence

I don't deserve this, to die like this
I was building a house.

Even as the butt of Will Munny/Eastwood's rifle hovers above Little Bill/Hackman's chin in the final scene, Little Bill laments his unfinished house. The gun fighting, violent sheriff, survivor of the legendary tough towns whose names he invokes like a litany punctuating set piece displays of his sadistic violence—"Kansas, Missouri, Cheyenne . . ."—was looking forward to a peaceful old age. He thought he would sit on his porch, the violence and competencies of his life now behind him, smoking a pipe as he watched the sun set over the lake. The film's imbrication of melodrama and realism is invoked in the Sheriff's last words: his mode of death is undeserved—the moral axis because he was engaged in a practical and forward look- ing enterprise, he was building a house—he was participating in the functional here- and-now of realism.

In this film the men keep talking. But what do they talk about? They talk of desire, fear, power and death; of the past, of remembering and forgetting and know- ing. These concerns weave in and out of talk about competence and incompetence, about gun fighting and, above all, about stories of the old west in which these two terms, competence and gun fighting, are synthesized. When the Schofield Kid rides up to Will Munny's pig farm in search of "the worst, meaning the best" gun fighter to be his partner and is witness to a grey-haired and muddy display of half-heartedness and incompetence in pig handling, he is disappointed. He finds, he thinks, "nothing but a broken down old pig farmer." When Will Munny, recognizing his limits as a pig farmer in an eloquent sigh as he leans on the pigs' corral, decides after all to join the Kid in his bounty hunt, he can't even mount his horse. His struggle to gain control of the animal is a recurrent motif—part tragic, part comic—of the narrative. Is he also engaged in a struggle to control his own "animal" self, formerly responsible for the acts of violence, brutality and drunkenness of which his recently deceased, God-fear- ing, law-abiding wife Claudia had "cured" him? Was it through her agency that he was able to control himself? The interesting question of what it was about him that elicited her support—something her mother, as a title tells us, could never understand—isn't answered. The film is not about its women. The tragedy in the motif of Will's struggle with his horse is the consequence of the man of action's loss of prowess, its comedy is based in the unlikely spectacle of his *in*ability even to reach first base—to get on his horse. As in the classic clown's device, laughs are in response to the clever perfor- mance of incompetence: here is a simultaneous recognition and undercutting of skill. The audience's laughter both applauds the clever performance and delights in the cathartic ridicule of "prowess." Will Munny's problems with his horse are excessive and, as if to underline the point, the narrative also delivers this spectacle to excess. When Will and his partner Ned catch up with the Kid they discover that, despite his extravagant claims the Kid's eyesight is so poor he can only hope to hit close range targets—he is practically blind: a blind gun fighter, too, is a comic absurdity. But these are not only comic moments for the audience but also serious and disabling deficien-

Clint Eastwood as "'the worst, meaning the best' gunfighter," William Munny, and Jaimz Woolvett as the Schofield Kid.

cies in the skills on which each character depends for his livelihood. All the central male characters are shown to be deficient in a skill that they themselves value and need. Their inadequacies are not just shown in passing, revealed at a tangent to some more pressing concern of the narrative, they are emphatic—leitmotifs, almost: Will's falling off his horse, the Kid's near blindness, the Sheriff's diabolical carpentry

The event that sparks off the narrative concerns a man's inadequacy: when Delilah, who "didn't know no better"—who was too inexperienced to have learned never to laugh *at* a man—giggled at the sight of her cowboy client's "teensy little pecker," his enraged, almost anguished response was to slash her to bits. In its attention to the question of in/competence, the film proposes a distinction between the moral axis, good:bad, and the functional one, competent:incompetent. Social order requires a balance of the moral and the functional, which the Law attempts to negotiate. Woven through the fabric of the film is Will's refrain, sometimes assertive, sometimes questioning, sometimes plaintive that "I ain't like that no more." He has changed: he has *been* changed by dear departed Claudia since, for Claudia, to be a skillful gunfighter is to be a bad man. So Will claims that he is no longer a Bad Man, a gunman. It isn't his competence that is at issue but his motivation, which he understands as pertaining to the realm of the moral. Hence one of the serious questions posed in the film is the relation between these two axes. Competence (gun-fighting, love-making, carpentry) is *necessary* to a convincing demonstration of masculinity, but moral rectitude (right action, responsible concern for the self and others, the knowing use of hindsight and foresight) marks maturity. Does this produce a paradox? How can competent masculinity be marked as mature? Is it, perhaps, a question not so much of knowing how to act, but of knowing when? "I ain't like that no more" doesn't mean Will *can't* operate competently as a gun fighter, but that he *can* distinguish judiciously as to when such skill is appropriate. Will's lesson is eventually learned by the Kid who, initially full of bravado, is so chastened by the actual experience of violent bloodshed that he is ready to accept his inadequacy, to relinquish both his share of the bounty and his gun: "I'd rather be blind and ragged than dead."

Gene Hackman as Little Bill, "rough and ready, one might say, like his carpentry."

But Little Bill's is a more complex and fractured character, living with crude, pragmatic and often flawed judgments—rough and ready, one might say, like his carpentry. It is in this character that the film's dialectic of melodrama and realism is most finely balanced. His inadequate justice, his barely controlled sadism, not to mention his complete oblivion to the shortcomings of his woodworking skills, exist in an utterly convincing tension with his avuncular bonhomie and the engaging pleasure he takes in building his house. Like John Wayne's Ethan Edwards in *The Searchers*, Little Bill is at once appealing in his verisimilitude and anachronistic in his values. Ethan knows how to track and, eventually, to find Debbie, he knows what to expect from the various renegades from the old west encountered during the long search—but he doesn't know how to fit into the settled, social Texas of post-civil war, post-frontier America. Little Bill knows how to deploy terror in his exercise of control, but he can't acknowledge the justice of the whores' complaint. How does the narrative resolve the conflict it proposes? The future, it would seem, is to belong to the survivors, the repressed Will, "prospering in dry goods in San Francisco" and the near-blind, ragged Kid. Little Bill's "mature" masculinity is inadequate now, it's a fiction. As Sheriff, in his negotiation of the moral and functional imperatives, he has failed. He has been incompetent in his delivery of the Law, and he's been out-gunned by a bounty hunter.

Gun Fighting

But the Duck was faster and hot lead blazed from his smoking six guns.

While questions of skill, competence and adequacy might loom large in men's private assessment of themselves and their peers, the issue of gun fighting is also about competition, dominance and power—overtly about the relations *between* men. No matter the size of the pecker—the gun can be depended on to spurt hot lead on demand. One of the attractions of Little Bill's complex character is his apparent recognition of this, and the consideration of motive and consequence evident in his discussions with—or rather his monologues addressed to—the writer/observer Mr. Beauchamp. Little Bill, Sheriff of Big Whiskey, Wyoming, in 1880, and Gene Hackman, accomplished veteran of Hollywood, seem to be laughing in unison over the extract from Mr. Beauchamp's dime novel, *The Duke of Death*. We're invited to smile, too, at Little Bill's mispronunciation; but from his position of power he dismisses Mr. Beauchamp's correction—command of language (and storytelling, and history, and myth-making) is secondary, for Little Bill, to command of the situation at hand. But as the narrative unfolds Little Bill's rough and ready approach, his crude pragmatics, is found wanting. His summary and fatally mistaken dispensing of justice, avoiding the "fuss" of a trial and compensating Skinny for his "investment" rather than Delilah for her cut-up face, turns out to have been as incompetent as his carpentry. Though his opponent, Will, reminds him that "deserve's got nothing to do with it" before delivering the final shot, still the elegant narrative composition balancing, as it does, classic western oppositions, attributes and motives in a harmony fit to delight any structuralist,[2] invites an explanation for his death.

What kind of man do Eastwood as director and Hackman as actor construct, in their production of Little Bill ? His easy-going pleasantness is succeeded by a chillingly passionate violence perceived by observers both on screen and in the films' audiences as bordering on the pathologically sadistic. Philip French, reviewing the film in the *Observer*, wrote:

> The middle-aged Daggett disarms Bob and with a sadistic glee destroys him physically and mentally as an example to others.[3]

and, in a similar vein, Sue Heal's *Today* piece described the character as

> the terrifying Hackman who will brook no vigilantes in his town and treats all-comers with an unbridled physical force that turns law-keeping into abuse.[4]

In three set-piece scenes, each more savage and distressing, Little Bill's beatings of the would-be bounty hunters English Bob, Will Munny and Ned Logan are the object of meticulous, lavish—some would say excessive—filmic attention. There are other depictions of violence from the initial slashing in the brothel to the shoot-outs at the Bar T and the final showdown at Greely's Saloon, but the camera, in these other scenes, doesn't dwell on victim or aggressor in such lascivious detail but rather delivers an atmospheric interpretation of western motifs. Little Bill is distinguished amongst the film's male characters by his engagement with physical brutality—and it is indeed a physical engagement as he whips, kicks and punches his victims. The only time we see him using a gun it is as a club.

As most reviewers have noted, however, the film also goes out of its way to deglamorise the violence typical of the genre.[5] Not only is Little Bill's physical brutality clearly coded as excessive, but also the gunfights which the film delivers are notable for the attention paid to the fear, suffering, anxiety and, again, the incompetence which, it would seem, were their real and inevitable accompaniments. The excessively long drawn out shooting of the first cowboy, Davey, during which Ned cannot shoot and the Kid cannot see, is an example. The dying cowboy calls piteously for water and Will, apparently exasperated by the western's demands for clean and callous dispatchings, breaks all the rules when he calls to the cowboy's comrades to bring him water, promising not to shoot while they do. Not for this film the gunfights sanitized in long-shot which contributed to the cultural status of early western heroes. The competitive strategy of the gunfighter is to inspire fear in his opponent, and fear is evidence of weakness, if not of submission. The film is relentless in its delineation of fear, noting it in heroes, villains and bystanders alike, and, in so doing, problematising those categories. It is no longer clear, by the end of the film, who *were* the heroes, villains or bystanders, nor even, perhaps, what a hero is. From reminiscences about "the west" of history and legend, the narrative proceeds to "replay" a paradigmatic western event, emphasizing all the discomfort, anxiety and pain conventionally omitted in the interests either of glamour or of a lascivious dwelling on spectacular brutality and bloodshed such as in Peckinpah's *The Wild Bunch* (1969).

The careful cataloguing of the signs of fear is worth recalling partly because the implicit acknowledgment of the protagonists' frailty is productive in the interests of a realist re-assessment of the western legends, and partly because they account for the survivors' rejection of the "meaner than hell cold-blooded goddamn killer" role. Will, once the most cold-blooded killer in the west, will prosper in dry goods, and the Kid, avid consumer of western stories and would-be dandy and gun-fighter, vows never to touch his Schofield model Smith and Wesson again. The sweating and shaking deputy, standing in the Sheriff's office, a framed picture of a stag visible on the wall behind him, argues that anyone can be scared. The almost palpable presence of fear is brilliantly suggested in the following scene when, as Mr. Beauchamp reaches into his shoulder bag for the book which will substantiate his claim to being a writer, the tense silence is broken first by the sound of the nervous deputies' clicking rifles, and then by the trickle of liquid forming a pool on the ground by his feet as his bladder gives way. But it isn't only novice deputies and visiting writers who experience fear in the face of western (or should I say masculine?) violence and lawlessness. English Bob, bloody, beaten and imprisoned, knows enough to be frightened by Little Bill's cat and mouse game as he instructs Mr. Beauchamp in the subtler intricacies of gun fighting. Will, in his delirious fever, sees grotesque and terrifying visions from beyond the grave and tells Ned "I'm scared of dying," his admission followed closely by an acknowledgment that this fear is somehow shameful (emasculating?): "don't tell anyone the things I said, don't tell my kids." And then there is the Kid, whose quest for the reality behind the western myth fuels the narrative, and whose own admission of fear is in many ways a more cathartic moment than the final shoot out, or than Will's operatic departure from Big Whiskey. It is the Kid's acknowledgment of his fear which allows his (and the audience's) recognition of the tawdry and brutal reality underlying the western fiction. The narrative's project, to re-educate the Kid, raised as he has been on stories of the west (stories of the masculine) is in a sense completed here in the scene between the man and the youth under the lone pine. What follows—Will's resumption of his discarded persona as the most cold-blooded killer in the West—can be seen as the last repeat of the western melodrama's tragic chorus. Suddenly carpentry, pig farming or even dealing in dry goods, even though they may not enjoy such spectacular sound, lighting and effects, seem preferable alternatives.

The film's articulation of fear is amplified by its recognition of the multiple and intricate connections, in the masculine psyche, between sexuality and violence. It is this, the powerful opening scene suggests, that makes for such a heady concoction when a private inadequacy is played out in a public contest—particularly when the terms are guns and whiskey. The links, for masculinity, between sexuality and power (the latter *always* coded as violence in the western) are acknowledged in several references to the penis. It is the "teensy little pecker" that is the initial cause of all the trouble; Two Gun Corcoran is so called, Little Bill tells Mr. Beauchamp, not because he carried two guns but because "he had a dick that was so big, it was longer than the barrel on that Walker Colt," and Ned refers to the Kid's penis as his "pistol," when they make their precipitous escape from Greely's billiard hall. But whereas reference to the analogic relation between the penis and the gun is no doubt intended to amuse, to be a lighter moment in the textual construction—albeit (as Delilah discovered) a comedy fraught with danger—there is, I think, a more profound and more troubling relation between male sexuality and the exercise of violent power lurking beneath the surface of the film, half acknowledged, half concealed. Here I return to the film's excessive concentration on the details of Little Bill's grotesque and barely-controlled physical attacks.

After the first of these, when he has finished kicking English Bob around the main street of Big Whiskey he is suddenly "spent," his power and energy wasted. Limp and alone, his opponent vanquished, he returns the gaze of the shocked onlookers as if seeing them for the first time and, irritated by their intrusive presence at his "post-coital" depletion, sends them away:

> What are you all looking at?
> Go on, get out of here, scoot.
> Go on, mind your own business.

When he whips Ned, stripped to the waist and gripping the cell bars, the camera lingers perhaps just a little too long on the extreme close up of Ned's face, Little Bill's face just behind, whispering threats. Is it Ned's shallow breathing, his glistening skin, or is it Little Bill's intensity, his whispering, that lends this scene such a sexual charge? Little Bill's violence is not expressed through the stand off, the shoot out, the exercise of skill and cunning in hunting, tracking, aiming and so on, but in the sweaty intimacy of (almost) hand to hand combat—except there's no combat here, just beating, which is what makes the scenes so hard to watch. Once again I'm reminded of Ethan Edwards in *The Searchers*, and the grim retribution he exacted from his opponent, Scar. What is less clear is how far the film is condoning or even legitimating the dubious pleasures of spectacularly sexualized violence, how far the propitiatory jokes about guns and penises are offered as a mask, a cover for a more disturbing model of male sexuality, one which requires a powerless partner (should I say victim, opponent?)

Story-Telling

> Hell, I even thought I was dead but I found out it was just that I was in Nebraska.

Whereas the classic western characteristically glamorizes violence and romanticizes the arduous frontier life, this film works to deconstruct, even to undermine those myths. The emphasis on competence as the measure of moral adequacy in the melodramatic mode and of functional adequacy in the realist mode requires the film's protagonists to evaluate each other's past and present actions—to deliver the measurement. Thus the very processes of storytelling, of men's talk, are at the center of the film, embodied in the characters of the writer/observer Mr. Beauchamp, author of *The Duke of Death* and in the would-be gun fighter—we might say the consumer of western fictions—the self-styled Schofield Kid. Both these characters propose "histories" which are corrected by the central pair of protagonists, Little Bill Dagget and William Munny. Through this device of doubled pairs of storyteller and listener the film draws attention to the gap between the event and its recounting, and hence to the formation of the story—and of history. Various sources purveying western myths are emphasized in our glimpses of the newspapers, the *Cheyenne Gazette*, the book, *The Duke of Death,* in the traces of the Kid's Uncle Pete and his reminiscences, in Little Bill's eyewitness corrections to English Bob's falsified accounts and, finally, in Mr. Beauchamp's faltering attempt to begin a history of the massacre he (and we) have just witnessed.

Mr. B:	You killed five men. You're single-handed.
Will:	Yeah.
Mr. B:	That's, ah, that's a Spencer rifle, right?
Will:	That's right.
Mr. B:	Who, er, who did you kill first?
	When confronted by superior numbers an experienced gunfighter will always fire on the best shot first.
Will:	Is that so?
Mr. B:	Yeah. Little Bill told me that.
	Then you probably killed him first, didn't you.
Will:	I was lucky in the order.
	But I've always been lucky when it comes to killing folks.
Mr. B:	Is that so?
	Who was next?
	It was Clyde, right?
	It must have been Clyde. Well it could have been Deputy Andy.
Will:	All I can tell you is who's going to be last.

In this way the audience itself is implicated in the recording, preservation and recycling of stories and their transformation into myths—both the myths of the western *and* the myths of the masculine. It is impossible to ignore the film's demands that its audiences consider the politics of storytelling as well as its consequences for culture and history—for social formation. At the same time it is a story and it is *about* stories.

Storytelling assumes this crucial importance once hindsight allows the recognition, frequently reiterated by both Will Munny and Little Bill in their re-tellings, that the protagonists of the legendary events were too drunk to shoot straight half the time, let alone to remember who shot who, and why. Thus the film works to reveal, as we have seen, not only the complex and unsettling links between male sexuality and violence, and their centrality to the western genre, but also the uncertain and provisional understandings of reality embodied in both contemporary and historical accounts of western history. As Philip French put it in the *Observer* review "it is a meditation on history and the American experience, and an allegorical commentary on the state of the union."[6] So men's fictions are laid bare. Could this be the offense implied in the film's resonant title?

There is a clear distinction, in *Unforgiven*, between "men" and "boys," between those (men) who remember the real west because they were there, they have earned their status as "men" by virtue of their survival which has required their competence as gunfighters, and those (boys) who know *of* the west, but do not *know it*. The older characters—Little Bill, William Munny, English Bob, legends in their own time—must educate, discipline and protect the younger ones—the group of deputies, the "hard-working" cowboys, the Kid and, through the figure of the writer, the readers of the future—the audience for the stories. It is here that the implied synonymity between "the west" and "the men" is instrumental in defining masculinity. Herein too lies the film's fascination for the female audience, because in deconstructing the myths of the west the film is also obliged to deconstruct the myths of the masculine. Just as the "teensy little pecker" summarizes, retrospectively, the in/adequacy: sexuality: violence matrix at the center of patriarchy's construction of the masculine, so the resonances of the initial event, the cowboy cutting Delilah's face, constitute a paradigm for western storytelling. The pivotal scene in the melodrama/ realism dialectic ordering the narrative is the meeting between Will and Delilah, when he first sees her for himself. He is recovering from a fever contracted after his ride to Big Whiskey in torrential rain and his brutal beating at the hands of Little Bill in Greely's Saloon. For three days he's been hovering, delirious, near death. His old, stubbled, bruised face half buried in unwholesome blankets is seen in medium shot, in the shadows of a dilapidated shed. Delilah, her scars healed but still visible, is tending him. She seems a little hesitant, awkward, frightened perhaps, an ordinary woman in her dull coloured dress and enveloping cloak, from the homestead or wagon train of any western. But to him she is, as he says, a "beautiful woman with scars"—his summary, in itself redolent of melodrama's central paradigm, invites the audience to take a second look at the scene. Now the characters' latent meanings to each other, and to us, come to the fore. She is beautiful because she has suffered; he is frightening because he is unknown. The symbolic possibilities of melodrama transform the characters, the landscape, they shift the focus of our attention. But as our attention is shifted, realist and melodramatic codes are simultaneously in play, and realism's damaged man/scarred woman are balanced by melodrama's threatening male/suffering female, the equation offered as exemplary of patriarchy's masculinity and its feminine Other.

The film opens with a low lit medium close-up of a cowboy "riding," in the whores' own parlance, a semi-clothed woman. The rhythmic creaking of the bed-springs is interrupted by the sounds of cries and commotion from the adjacent room which the couple (and the camera) run to investigate. All is chaos: the medium and close-up shots of the dimly lit and crowded interior make it impossible to distinguish people and actions; a claustrophobic urgency pervades the scene. Silence and order are achieved by a threatening gun to the head of the enraged cowboy whose "pecker" had so amused the sadly ignorant Delilah. Thus, in the very construction of this scene the film suggests the impossibility of answering the question "what happened" in any but the most partial manner. The contingency of truth is subsequently demonstrated through the various (and varying) accounts both of the incident and of Delilah's face, which punctuate the film. Alice/Frances Fisher, in her fury at Little Bill's misogynist prioritizing of Skinny's property rights over Delilah's own rights, refuses Davey's conciliatory offering: "She's got no face and you bring her a goddamn mangy pony?" The Kid, in his efforts to enlist Will as his partner, claims that Delilah's eyes, ears and "teats" were slashed, as well as her face and, as in a game of Chinese whispers, this version is repeated, with elaboration, to Ned. Delilah's narrative function here recalls

Anna Thomson as "a beautiful woman with scars."

that of Debbie in *The Searchers*, whose seizure by Scar and his band motivated the long search chronicled in that film. Both Will and Ned, seasoned gunfighters though they are, are shocked by the story they hear:

Ned: All right, so what did these fellas do?
       Cheat at cards?
       Steal some strays? Spit on a rich fellow? What?
Will: No, they cut up a woman.
Ned: What?
Will: Yeah.
       Cut up her face, cut her eyes out, cut her fingers off,
       Cut her tits.
       Everything but her cunny I suppose.
Ned: Well I'll be darned. Well—I guess they got it coming.

The retribution required by moral order leads, just as it did in *The Searchers*, to the quest, the contest—but though it is *activated* by the woman it really concerns the *exchange* between men, self-appointed as executors of the Law. When, somewhat later, we get to see Delilah's scarred face for ourselves we are invited to compare our view with others' descriptions. Alice says she's got "no face"; Skinny says she's so ugly no-one would pay for sex with her; Will when he finally meets her takes her, in his delirium, for an angel. Later, as the film shifts effortlessly from realism to melodrama, he calls her a beautiful woman with scars—the version with which the audience is invited to concur. Both Delilah herself in the flesh, as it were, and references to her in the accounts of other characters appear repeatedly throughout the film, insisting by their presence on the relativity of truth in that continuous relay and replay of record and interpretation which constitutes the social world. This paradigmatic tale, Delilah's "story," allows fragments of other stories—"I was in the Bluebottle Saloon in Wichita the night English Bob shot Corky Corcoran. . . ."; or "You remember the night I shot that drover in the mouth and his teeth came out through his head . . . ," or "You were *there*, at . . . ?"—to reverberate around the cavernous space the film creates with its sweeping landscapes, its cyclic time marked by the passing of seasons, its echoing fictions counterpointed with rolls of thunder.

Whether Little Bill is in Death, Nebraska, or Big Whiskey is, in the Wagnerian climax, immaterial. Despite some reviewers recognition of a "feminist streak" patriarchal order is, on the evidence of this film, secure enough to risk if not a little giggle at its pecker, at least some navel-gazing. The fact that to today's audiences—or at any rate to this audience member—the whores' outrage, if not its consequences, is utterly convincing and justifiable is a credit to Eastwood's recognition of a feminist agenda. It's certainly a development from the narrative pretext of *The Searchers* which was to prevent an unthinkable miscegenation. But the misapprehension of those men sympathetic to a feminist agenda who thought that Eastwood could produce a "feminist western" is amply demonstrated in the film's ultimate inability to sustain a female character central to both the moral and the functional axes of the film. With the possible exceptions of William Wellman's *Westward the Women*, (1951) and the flawed but alluring *Ballad of Little Jo* (Maggie Greenwald, 1993), the western and feminism seem to be contradictory terms. Women, though certainly not absent from the film, are freely acknowledged in their classic role, marking the boundaries of the masculine. Delilah's mishap motivates the contest, and she and her "sisters," the whores at Greely's saloon and billiard hall, mark the progress of their revenge, standing silently together in the windblown garden or on the raised wooden sidewalk, watching, waiting, subject to the outcome. Claudia's gravestone frames the narrative and the whores' revenge gets it moving. In between it's men's talk.

NOTES

My thanks to Gill Branston, Pat Kirkham and Lee Thomas for helpful comments on earlier versions of this essay.

1. *Sunday Times*, 13 September 1992, pp. 22-23.

2. For example, Will Wright, *Sixguns and Society*, University of California Press, 1975.

3. *The Observer*, 20 September 1992, p. 53.

4. *Today*, 18 September 1992, p. 33.

5. See, for example, review articles on the film in *Cineaste*, December 1992; *Literature/Film Quarterly*, Volume 21, Number 1, 1993; *Films in Review*, December 1993; *Sight and Sound*, October 1992.

6. *The Observer*, 20 September 1992, p. 53.

7. For example, Amy Taubin in *Village Voice*, 18 August 1992, p. 52; Jonathan Romney in *New Statesman and Society*, 18 September 1992, pp. 31–32; Alexander Walker in *Evening Standard*, 17 April 1992.

OUR HEROES HAVE SOMETIMES BEEN COWGIRLS:
An Interview with Maggie Greenwald

Tania Modleski (1995)

W hen a woman film-maker stakes a claim to genres like the Western does she betray feminism by adopting male stories and male myths? When a woman makes a Western about a cross-dressing female hero, should we read it as an allegory of the female director in Hollywood? Does female success in the world of popular entertainment mean that a woman's gotta do what a man's gotta do?

In the early years of feminist film theory, writers such as Claire Johnston urged feminist film-makers not to abandon the formulas of the entertainment film which have given so much pleasure to women, but rather to work at transforming them. Many feminist critics began to study women's genres like Hollywood maternal melo-dramas and television soap operas in order to examine how women's fantasies have been shaped and how feminists might begin to reshape them. Although the fantasies of many women have surely been influenced by male genres too, we didn't really think much back then about how women might appropriate these genres. At the time, such an appropriation might have struck many of us as an affirmation of the very values and storytelling traditions we wanted to subvert.

In those days female "transvestism"—a term we used figuratively to designate an identification with the opposite sex—was often held to be a sorry condition; in fact it became a major metaphor for the tragic plight of the female spectator, who because she was forced to project herself onto a male hero was thought to be unable to "achieve a stable sexual identity,'" as Laura Mulvey put it in her analysis of *Duel in the*

Suzy Amis with writer-director Maggie Greenwald on the set.

Sun. Recently, however, transvestism has taken on a more positive meaning, and the idea that one should strive to achieve "a stable sexual identity" has increasingly come to be seen as retrograde and severely limiting. Marking this shift in attitude is Maggie Greenwald's 1993 Western, *The Ballad of Little Jo*, a landmark in the history of women's cinema and a major artistic achievement by almost any standard. Partly about the pleasure and freedom enjoyed by a woman who cross-dresses as a man, the film invites us to rethink the position of woman in and at the movies, as well as that of the woman behind the camera.

Greenwald is among the most talented of a new breed of women directors emerging today who refuse to remain confined to their traditional spheres in the realm of fantasy, but range freely across both male and female territory, transforming the land they roam.

The Ballad of Little Jo—the first Western written and directed by a woman since the silent era—stars Suzy Amis, who gives a stunningly subtle performance as a young Eastern society woman cast out by her family when she has a child out of wedlock. Initially frail and vulnerable, Josephine Monaghan comes out West, adopts male dress, and becomes Little Jo Monaghan, a self-sufficient sheep farmer who successfully fights off the brutal Western Cattle Company when it attempts to force the sheep farmers off their land.

The film retains what feminist critic Annette Kolodny has seen as the hallmark of female fantasies of the landscape: a sense of intimacy with the land and its creatures. At the same time, with its breathtaking cinematography, it assumes the tradi-

Suzy Amis as both Josephine and Jo.

tionally masculine prerogative of glorying in the sublimity and solitude of the West. *Ballad* is not Greenwald's first incursion into male worlds. *The Kill Off* (1989), Greenwald's second film (after *Home Remedy* in 1987, which the director describes as "a black-comedy about an anti-yuppie's crisis in a yuppie world"), is to my mind the most successful and interesting adaptation of the work of the *noir* novelist Jim Thompson. Greenwald is relentless in exploring the seediness of Thompson's settings and his characters' moral and psychological degradation. Yet "transvestism" in the case of the Greenwald-Thompson interaction works both ways: in adapting the book, Greenwald faithfully adhered to the male writer's vision, but at the same time, . . . she actually detected and elicited a "feminine" current in the work of a writer whom many would consider the ultimate hard-boiled novelist. . . . When it was released abroad in 1990, it created a great stir—at Cannes as well as other festivals (including the Torino Film Festival, where it won the Best Director Award).

The Ballad of Little Jo was highly praised in a variety of quarters, but it encountered some critical resistance as well. Because such resistance can tell us much about the stakes of feminist film-making, especially the kind which seems to encroach on male genres, I asked that we begin by trying to analyze this resistance.

Maggie Greenwald: Because there are so few, everybody wants films like Ballad to represent themselves, to say whatever it is they want to say. Someone like the lesbian critic Ruby Rich, who criticized the film for not being about lesbian desire, wants a different movie—one which should be made. I felt that she misunderstood that this wasn't a film about sexuality but about gender.

Rich's desire to have a film about lesbianism is understandable, but it's more dubious when a similar criticism comes from the mainstream press.

Tania Modleski: There was a review in the Los Angeles Times—by Peter Rainer. . . .

Some of these white men criticized this women's film, this feminist film, for not dealing more with the gay issue, in effect siding with gays against me as a woman (even though the gay press has been on the whole very positive about the film). "See, we didn't like her Western for our reasons. But we didn't like it for your sake too. She didn't represent gay people fairly. We of the mainstream press side with you marginalized folk. Let's join together against her."

Some of the reviews were fantastic and wonderful, but some accused me of negative portrayals of the men, saying that the male characters were generic, and also that the film should have some gay content. There was in the script a whole subplot involving one of the female characters coming on to Jo. Unfortunately it had to go because it disrupted the flow of the piece as a whole. What's left are subtle moments in which the woman flirts with Jo. We realize that what she, Jo, has triggered in this character is another dimension of the existence she has chosen.

What would you say to those critics of the mainstream press who criticized the "negative," "generic" portrayals of men?

One of the things I found very unfortunate in these attacks, which made me see how defensive and sexist many of these reviewers are, is that not one of the reviewers, not one, took their thinking a step further to say, "Gee, this is what it's like for a woman to go to the movies for her whole life and watch herself portrayed through the eyes of men." To me that was a profound disappointment. Instead, for example, one reviewer said, "The film made me want to go home and watch Bonanza." I feel the press is obligated—particularly at a time when point of view is such a controversial issue—to take that thinking to the next step. But by siding with minorities, the white male-dominated press sidestep this obligation and go on the offensive, saying, for instance, that Allison Anders shouldn't have made Mi Vida Loca [a film about Latinas in gangs in Los Angeles]. It's a divide-and-conquer tactic. Trying to turn Latina women against white women. If someone gave some money to a Latina film-maker we would have an opportunity to see her point of view. Allison's the first film-maker who could get financing who was even interested in Latina gang girls. It's infuriating—I could go on and on.

The criticism about negative portrayals of men in *Ballad* doesn't seem to me even to be accurate.

I think there was more complexity and depth to the male characters than in the average portrayal of women, even in films that are supposed to be about a woman. For that matter, the male characters are more fully drawn than most male characters in mainstream films by and about men. That was something I wanted to explore, to show how men and women relate to one another, how, for example, someone who is very decent and very kind is also capable of being very brutal and very cruel. . . .

How were you able to go on and get funding for *Ballad?*

Well, because *The Kill-Off* is so renowned among the independent film community's distributors and executives, Ira Deutchman, head of Fine Line Features, was interested in what I was doing. I went in and told him about two things I was working on. He raised an eyebrow when I gave him a one-line pitch about *Ballad*, and I thought, Well, he's really interested in that one, so I went home and wrote a rough draft in three weeks. Fred Berner, one of the producers, got involved at that time, and we took the project to Ira, who committed half the financing. It took a year and a half to raise the rest of the money. The other great hero of the financing story is Aline Perry, who green-lighted the film through Polygram Filmed Entertainment. Right now, perhaps, the idea of a cross-dressing Western sounds very trendy, but almost four years ago there was no *Crying Game* or *Orlando*. And *Unforgiven* didn't open until a year and a half after I'd written *Ballad*. So there was nothing to suggest that this would be a commercially viable project.

Why a Western ?

From a very young age, I felt what I consider a very primal connection to the landscape of the West; to the idea of surviving against nature, in nature; to images of someone riding across a plain on a horse. I refuse to accept that these are male images; I think they are human images. In films that were more buddy kind of movies, the idea of friendship and fighting for a good cause with friends appealed to me. The Western is just a majestic, fabulous genre. And the few stories that have women as main characters were not so interesting to me.

Such as . . . ?

The woman in *High Noon*—not very interesting, though I might be more interested now than when I was a kid in telling her story. Barbara Stanwyck as a land baron—not interesting. Or Doris Day in *Calamity Jane*.

I don't know if you've seen that film recently. It's a lot more interesting than you may remember. It's about cross-dressing too, and there's also a strong current of female homoeroticism that we might be more inclined to see today than people were in the 50s. What about *Johnny Guitar*?

I didn't see it until I was an adult. It's very outrageous and I love it as a film, but I didn't connect in the way I've described.

Enjoying *Johnny Guitar* depends to some extent on believing that it is outrageous for women to inhabit the West and the Western genre (other than in very restricted roles). Whereas what you're saying is . . .

. . . that we belong.

So are you simply putting women into a genre without changing the conventions or are you critiquing the genre by, as it were, changing the subject?

I think that critiquing comes by the way. It was not an intention, but the very act of making a film like *Ballad* is so subversive that it becomes a critique. I wanted to make a Western and I knew I wanted to make a Western that had a woman as the main character. When I stumbled upon information about the real Little Jo I saw that her story was a classic Western story about a rugged individualist who carves out a place for herself in the American West. American history is full of women who did exactly that. Women came from all over the world to make lives for themselves, the same as men did. But the story does change when a woman is put at the center. And I would be a liar if I said there was not a tremendous amount of me in it. As a film-maker I'm working on male terrain and my subject matter is also "male terrain."

You're cross-dressing too, in a way.

Right. Just as Little Jo learned about being a woman through cross-dressing, the process of making the film involved my accepting myself as a woman, saying, Yes, I can be a director and be a woman and don't have to accept anymore what has been shoved down women's throats in the last 20 years or so—that in order to succeed you have to be like a man.

Exactly what is known about the real Josephine Monaghan ?

Very little. The only thing that's known is what was published in the newspaper article when she died, which gave me the information for the beginning and the end of the story. She was a society girl who had a child out of wedlock. It's believed her sister cared for the child, or someone else may have adopted him. Her family threw her out, and somewhere between the time she left the Northeast and arrived in the West she assumed the identity of a man and lived her whole life that way. She worked as a ranch hand, and I believe she sent money to her sister for the rest of her life to support her child. Her existence was pretty meager and lonely; she—he—was considered a very strange little fellow. She spent a period as a bronco buster, and was very successful at it, but she quit, maybe because she was attracting too much attention. She did eventually own her own homestead, but was never self-sufficient; she always had to work for others to get by.

She was tiny, five feet tall, and very feminine looking. Long after I wrote *Ballad*, someone sent me a copy of Julie Wheelwright's book, *Amazons and Military Maids*, about women who have cross-dressed in the military throughout history. The book is loaded with photographs and portraits of women who today we wouldn't believe for two seconds were men. But we're so used to women wearing jeans and suits and such that we don't realize the extent to which your outer appearance dictated what you were accepted as being. So while I have no doubt that people were a little suspicious of Jo and considered her somewhat peculiar, there's no record of anyone digging deeper.

In the film that suspicion is there throughout, just under the surface and sometimes reflected in the way people look at Jo or speak to her.

It was quite a scandal in the territory when it was discovered that Jo was a woman.

You have been talking a lot about the actual West, so I assume you did research on it.

Most of the research I did was through photographs. I wrote the script surrounded by photographs. The reality was far more fascinating than anything you could make up. For instance, looking at the photographs it occurred to me to ask, What happens when you suddenly decide to build a town in the middle of a forest? You end up with tree stumps in the middle of the road and mud all over the place. The buildings are shelters in these photographs—well, what are they made of? And you suddenly notice that something's got a piece of paisley and that part of a roof or a window may be someone's scarf. It was a matter of using anything that was available to work with. I felt it was important to give the film that kind of texture. More than anything I wanted the land to be a character in the film, it's so vast and so imposing. For the people who went out there, the land was their main obstacle as well as the source of the life they built there. Jo's relation to the land is as central to what goes on in the story as her relationship with Tinman or Frank Badger.

It's interesting that you didn't use Cinemascope.

Yes, we talked about it, but we wanted an intimate story. The hugeness of the landscape comes through anyway, and we thought that with Cinemascope the images would be out of proportion with the story, it would destroy the intimacy.

Annette Kolodny wrote a book called *The Lay of the Land,* which is about male fantasies and the desire to conquer the "virgin" territory, and so on. How does Jo's relation compare?

Speaking for myself, when I got out there I looked at the land and couldn't begin to figure out how you would conquer it. When I sent her out to spend the winter alone with the sheep, I showed that Jo learns to use the land to survive; she learns to co-exist with it. I think she would have been destroyed if she tried to conquer it.

In another book, *The Land Before Her*, Kolodny talks of women's fantasies and argues that they were very different from men's (though the period of which she is writing is earlier than the period of *Ballad*). The women want to come and create little gardens and have clinging vines around their cottages. . . .

For an Eastern woman to come out West and make a garden might be the same mentality as the male fantasies, which are about the need to impose oneself on the land. To bring roses in and to force them to grow where they don't normally grow is like bringing the railroad in, isn't it?

Could we switch gears and talk a bit about the narrative, the part that was your construction, and some of the issues it gives rise to? You said that this was not a film about sexuality but about gender. Do you mean that it's not about homosexuality?

It's a question of asking how someone's perception of both the outside world and of herself changes when she stops wearing a skirt and puts on a pair of pants. When I first started writing the film I thought I was writing a film about a woman who becomes a man, but I realized very early on that I was writing a story of a woman who gets to become a true woman. By throwing off the trappings of socialized femininity which is connected to victimization, Jo is forced to find out who she really is. The first thing she does is learn how to survive and how to work, and she takes a job tending sheep out all by herself with no human company for months on end. She finds out what she likes, and they're all solitary things.

Which is amazing. What other films have dealt with the pleasures of solitude for a woman ?

I feel it's my human right to know how to take care of myself and survive. That's something that traditional socialization denies women. We're caretakers of others, but we're supposed to be taken care of. That same socialization also denies women their sexuality because it punishes them for it; women have throughout time been denied the right to sex outside of marriage. So after learning how to take care of herself, the next important thing for Jo was to reclaim her sexuality. And I think that's what you mean when you say the film is about sexuality. In creating the story of Jo I searched the landscape for a mate for her. I came across the Chinese railroad worker, whose health has been destroyed by years of labor and who becomes Jo's "houseboy" after she saves him from lynching.

I was interested in your choice of a Chinese man to play the leading man; of all the ethnic men inhabiting the West—Native Americans, Mexicans, even African

Americans—the Chinese man has been the most marginalized and in fact has usually been invisible.

Native American men are depicted as more "masculine" because it's a so-called "primitive" culture. To cast a Native American in the role wouldn't have pushed the gender issues in the same direction. In our history and our popular culture, the same thing has been done to Asian men that's been done to women. In Westerns, they're extras, they're in the background, or they're in the kitchen. They're asexual, and they're slaves who work their whole lives taking care of white men. I felt the two would connect with each other through a similar experience of life. And by the time they connect in the story it's not like she's the man and he's the woman; he is absolutely the man and she is absolutely the woman. They just happen to do jobs that are not conventional jobs.

You completely avoided sentimentality in your treatment of the relationship between Jo and Tinman, which is especially impressive considering the tendency is always—and certainly in the Western—to portray Western culture's "others" as subhuman or to idealize them. Ruby Rich called your depiction of this relationship subversive, though she spoke of it as stereotypical as well. A *Village Voice* reviewer also thought she detected a "drift toward stereotype" in your delineation of this character.

But I've used stereotypes throughout the whole film. The film is about stereotypes. I set out to make a conventional Western and to dig below the surface to find out what's underneath the conventions. All of the characters start out as types: the Frank Badger character, for instance. Percy . . .

Yes, we should talk about Percy because he has been a somewhat controversial character too.

Because Ian McKellen played him, Percy becomes more unusual than he would have if someone who is not an out gay actor had played him.

How so?

Because conventional Westerns are full of these marginalized men who are alone . . . and you don't know who they are and they never really connect, and they are someone's sidekick, or they're someone who is scary and bad and does one good deed. Who are they? And it's not just Westerns, but stories about seamen or pirates, anybody who has run away.

But the objection might be that the suggestion of repressed homosexuality in a character who violently attacks a prostitute links homosexuality to misogyny.

I don't get the connection. It's certainly not my thinking. We explored this character's lack of awareness about himself. Is he gay? Is he straight? It's possible that he is homosexual and that his repressed homosexuality does connect to his hatred of women; his sexual experiences with women could have been full of rage or shame. But if I had cast someone else—a straight actor or an actor who the world thinks is straight—the same inference might not have been made. Women are beaten up and brutalized all the time. But I'll take the accusation and accept that one is free to make it because Ian was cast in the role. I'll take it even further: Ian and I did talk about whether this character is a gay character who has fallen in love with a boy, or is a straight man who is attracted to Jo because she is a woman. And what I found really fascinating was the ambiguity. Who knows? I could say he's a straight character who thought it would be safe to have a boy around and is in fact attracted to Jo because Jo is really a woman. I like that complexity.

I was very interested in the moment in the film in which Jo decides to allow her son to believe she is dead and rather than going back East to be with him, she chooses to remain in the West.

I put myself inside the morality of Jo's day. As adulterer and as bastard, both mother and child were outcasts. I always knew Jo couldn't go back, though there would come a time when she might want to, might come to crisis and have the urge to flee back to the familiar. While it might be satisfying to a contemporary audience to have her go back and claim the child and say, "I am a woman, I will defy you all," it wouldn't have been believable for the time. And given the morality of the time, such an act wouldn't be doing anything for the child. By giving him up, though, she gave him legitimacy and removed the social stigma of his birth. But I do construct it as a choice. The moment of decision has to come.

Tell me about casting Suzy Amis as Jo.

I saw hundreds of women, both famous and unknown, in casting the part. I wanted to cast someone who was not well known. I thought it would be more difficult for the viewer if someone well known was in the part. Even if our budget had permitted us to have a Jodie Foster, for instance, Jodie's so famous you couldn't forget who she was for five minutes.

She did *Maverick* instead!

The experience of the movie involves completely forgetting whether you're watching a man or a woman. Especially for the men who liked the film, this was an important aspect of it. So it was crucial to find someone who had great range as an actress, someone who was "feminine" enough to be believable in the role of the Eastern debutante and at the same time was capable of taking on the physical challenges of the rest of the film. And Suzy was the only one. Because she was away during much of the time we were casting, we didn't see her until we were three months into the process. A lot of the women who came to read for me dressed up in cowgirl outfits for the reading. But when I walked out in the hall the day Suzy was there, she was wearing skin-tight black pedalpushers and a low-cut black shirt, and she had black mules on and a pink bow in her hair, and her hair was down to her waist. Well, no one had come to read for Jo dressed like that. When she read, her reading was beautiful and natural, and all of the girly stuff fell away; I saw this wonderful androgynous quality begin to emerge.

The reviews of her performance were extremely favorable. In fact, though we began by focusing on the negative reviews your film received, many praised it lavishly. You must have been pleased by those.

Yes, very. And for the sake of this discussion I fear we haven't acknowledged these reviewers (mostly white men and some women) properly. Which I do here, now. Yes! But remarks like "made me want to go home and watch *Bonanza*" prevented the important discussion from happening. I thought when I read that, You want to go back to . . .

. . . Hop Sing?

Yes . . . to the Western where there's no women around telling these three guys that they're not okay and where the Chinese man has no dick? That's where you want to go back to? Well, you can't. It's over.

Well, but is it really over? After all, many mainstream reviewers don't appear ready to get beyond their defensiveness, and they are the ones who control the information that gets out about films. For instance, they helped Clint Eastwood make pots of money on *Unforgiven* by praising its originality and revisionary impulse. How will you and others who are making radically revisionary work which expresses different points of view keep going ?

A lot of people are still seeing my work. The video of the film is doing extremely well, and I get almost as many calls now as I did a year ago. If the work gets made, it gradually creates a market for itself. Anything that's this new has no market for itself yet. Of course, there's a market for Quentin Tarantino; it's the 90s reworking of very traditional and conventional popular culture, told from the point of view of the usual subjects—white men. I'm actually very optimistic; it's a matter of making the work and getting it out there, and little by little it will build a following. In the marketplace there is already the knowledge that women between 14 and 40 constitute a huge untapped market. Two years ago, no one acknowledged that.

By the way, since it's come up, what do you think of *Unforgiven?*

I'm actually an Eastwood fan, but I don't like *Unforgiven*. I'm confused by people who consider it revisionist. To me it's the same old stuff. I like much of Clint's work a lot, though. I like the fact that he's a man explicitly making work out of his experience as a man and has been doing so since his first, fabulous film, *Play Misty for Me*. His characters are never idealized, they're very human. His women characters are always strong and interesting; he's consistently done positive things with them. I mean, the portrayals are not full. because he's not that interested. People may think I mind, but I don't. I'm just saying that a man making such films should acknowledge, as Clint does, that it's his point of view of the world, not the way the world is. It's his experience of life and the world and *his* fantasies. His myths. But they're not mine. And I get to have mine. I want to have mine.

And what are you working on now?

I'm adapting the classic Yiddish play *The Dybbuk*, which takes place in a shtetl in the 1870s and is full of Jewish mysticism, folklore, and magical images from the Cabala. It's about star-crossed lovers: the boy dies, and the girl becomes possessed by his wandering spirit.

Another variation on the theme of cross-dressing!

In the play the girl is very much a spiritual cypher. I've approached the adaptation from her point of view. I'm very interested in creating the kinds of female heroes that would have meaning in our culture. Little girls need heroes too.

AN EXEMPLARY POST-MODERN WESTERN:
The Ballad of Little Jo

Jim Kitses (1998)

*T*he Ballad of Little Jo* is the post-modern text *par excellence*.
In its ingenious deployment of the cross-dressed cowboy, its tale of the Eastern society woman who passed as a man out West and thus straddled her own "peculiar" frontier, the film elegantly exemplifies Charles Jenks' argument for double-coding as the semiotic structural base for post-modern art and culture.[1] Going West, Josephine Monaghan discovers America and achieves its dream, carving out independence and freedom, the wilderness allowing her to escape the prison of civilization. But in its hybrid and feminist style, *Little Jo* is also a maternal melodrama, Jo's destiny less manifest than covert, the sacrifice of her child and her own gender the price of her salvation, an earlier, homespun, camouflaged Stella Dallas.

Josephine Monaghan's first lesson in the West—one she takes to heart—is that appearances can be deceiving, the result of her trusting Rene Auberjonois' chummy peddler, who promptly sells her to two ex-Union soldiers. Slavery may be over, but neither emancipation nor the West's nomadic life-style extend to women "vagrants." To save herself, Josephine takes action, the privilege and duty of the truly autonomous self. Molly Greenwald was a picture and sound editor before directing, and the experience shows in the complex and economical montage that captures Josephine's metamorphosis into Jo, transitioning from a victim of melodrama, seduced and abandoned, to a Western actor (in both senses), a character of agency. Distilling her Victorian back story—we see the cad, the hard-hearted patriarch, the

A victim in a Victorian melodrama, Josephine becomes Jo, a Western actor (in both senses), a character of agency. Above, Suzy Amis and Sam Robards, below Amis and Ian McKellan as Percy.

"bastard" left behind with the sister—the images trace Josephine's tearful farewell to herself, the removal of skirts and corsets, the painful cutting away of her past, the emergence of her self-construction, the simulacrum cowboy.

Yet Jo will be the real thing, the masquerade allowing her to become a player in manly domains, a Jo-of-all-trades—prospector, stable boy, sheepherder, homesteader. Although there will be heroic moments, too, the film basically revises the mythic character's job description. This is a *working* cowboy, and the film, remarkably, provides image after image of actual labor—panning for gold, stable duties, sheepherding and shearing, carpentry and homesteading. As the "kid"—Jo's feisty, quietly charismatic masculine persona—she soon attracts mentors, a favor she will later return to another immigrant youth, the chain and skills of masculine experience passed on. This, too, is how the West was won, the film suggests, and little Jo was part of it.

At once both traditional and revisionist, *The Ballad of Little Jo* recycles the classic Western but also goes beyond it, an affectionate yet ironic vision that borders on parody in its emphatic de-centering of the white male, subverting what has been considered the most macho of genres, to champion an inclusive frontier. "They've got as much right to be here as you do, mister." Given her own exile, her odyssey of suffering, Jo's sensitivity and compassion are understandable, as when she rebukes rowdy Frank Badger and his mates for their inspection of the newcomer's socks, ironically, to ensure she is not effeminate, a dude. "Dudeness" is of course kin to gayness, which increases the irony given that the town regular who speaks up in defense of Jo—"Why don't you leave the boy alone, Frank Badger? He just wants to go his own way"—is Percy, whose own sexuality the film puts in question, in part through its casting of Ian McKellen, a gay actor.

Indeed, one of the unsettling, illuminating effects of Greenwald's premise, an attractive hero whom only we know to be both male and female, is that virtually all relationships in the film are ambiguously eroticized. Given that desire often works in mysterious ways, we are on uncertain ground, as indeed are all of Jo's "friends," in pinning down exactly what is going on. Precisely who is it that the flirtatious saloon gal, Mary, whose eyes follow Jo—or Percy, who mentors Jo in the tasks and rituals of manhood—or Badger, who forces a housekeeper on Jo, worrying about her because he "can't help it"—who is it that these characters respond to, and how can we define or characterize that response? Remarkably, it is the achievement of this fine film to raise these crucial questions in order to go beyond them, to suggest that in some measure they are unanswerable, and that desire and gender are more complex and elusive than binary oppositions allow for.

These ambiguities reach a sustained pitch after Jo is forced to take in David Chung's Tinman, the Chinese immigrant who becomes Jo's menial. Jo saves Tinman from a mock-lynching, from being badgered by Badger, a character more complex than suggested by the apt name or his arguably badger-like looks as portrayed by Bo Hopkins, a macho Peckinpah regular left over from "the old days," and amusingly recycled by Greenwald to invoke Peckinpah's spirit, all the better to interrogate it. Irony, one of the most prevalent of post-modern stylistic markers, reverberates throughout *Little Jo*, but reaches a peak in this little vignette, where Tinman is forced on Jo in part to preclude his taking a white man's job. That he might aspire to a white

Rene Auberjonois' chummy peddler and Josephine: "Appearances can be deceiving."
Below: Bo Hopkins, "a macho Peckinpah regular," as Frank Badger.

Little Jo and Tinman "forge their own family."

man's *woman* in the sexually deprived frontier that Greenwald etches is not even imaginable, of course, yet this will be the final outcome of Badger's act. To be fair to Badger, his boisterous joke also disguises a real desire to help his young, isolated friend. Given this complex of factors, we can perhaps understand his rage at the end when the dead Jo has been unmasked, a fury so outsize and destructive it may recall that of a colossus, Charles Foster Kane, rampaging through his wife's room, outraged at the independence and betrayal of the feminine.

Having saved Tinman from his distress, Jo and he play out their reversed social roles, Jo the herder, hunter and carpenter, Tinman the cook, housekeeper, assistant. For a while the masquerade continues, Tinman's own performance pitched to hide a sensitive intelligence behind the ancient stereotype of the comical Asian monkey—"Yes, Mister Jo!." But eventually the couple will give in to their own desire, and forge their own family, one so far beyond the unenlightened conventions of their time that they would be killed if found out, as Tinman puts it, "unquestionably, brutally." A de-masculinized male by the predatory, chauvinist norms the film describes, Tinman is man enough to share Jo's world as her silent partner, and provide support when she falters in fearful anticipation of the ultimate test of the heroic West—the violent confrontation with its repressive forces.

Of course the scarred and sickly Tinman knows of what he speaks, having labored on the railroad fifteen years to unite America, one of the thousands of anonymous Chinese depicted in John Ford's epic *The Iron Horse*, which allows its coolies a grin as the golden spike is driven, "the buckle in a girdle of a continent," but no speech. In a quiet moment in bed—one of a number, for this is a love story too—Tinman and Jo compare scars. The final touch when she had invented herself, Jo's gash is the mark of castration, although not the sign of phallic lack, but rather the gaping wound of the mutilated mother, the price of entry to the land of the free. Likewise, Tinman's multiple, various scars establish his body as a political site of the hidden side effects of a driven new nation's violence, racism and imperialism. That these two should come together in an unspeakable love is, of course, the logical outcome of their parallel marginalization, their lack of place as their own persons in the promised land.

In this dynamic, *Little Jo* recalls an earlier, very different film, Zhang Yimou's *Ju Dou* (1989), the sumptuously mounted, tragic melodrama that similarly inscribes a victimized couple and a forbidden love. There, on the Chinese frontier, it is the new wife, ridden like a horse and whipped for her failure to conceive a male heir, whose body becomes the site of patriarchal oppression. Trapped in a loveless, unbearable marriage, Ju Dou discovers that her tyrannical old husband's nephew is spying on her while she is at her morning ablutions. In one of the film's peaks of inspired creativity, Zhang has the tortured woman ingeniously appropriate the power of the male gaze by exposing herself to it, a weeping Ju Dou performing a humiliating strip, exploiting her nakedness and revealing the gross marks of her oppression, the closed system which imprisons the wife generating its own rebellion, the erotic and political fused, implicating the voyeur.

It may seem inappropriate to invoke a work which springs from such different production circumstances—a late-modern art film from China so epic and grand in its emotional range and visual design—an ill-advised strategy, given our modest $4 million Western. Such condescension should be avoided. *The Ballad of Little Jo* is a major achievement by any standards, and it too provides a supreme moment, a visual image of breathtaking intelligence and beauty that, as in *Ju Dou*, brilliantly sums up the complex forces at work in the film's diegesis.

The moment comes before the couple have revealed themselves, at that stage when Jo is becoming increasingly uncomfortable at sharing her close quarters, in masquerade, with a man. This image too, involves a character being spied on in their bath, an image coded for erotic, visual pleasure, involving the act of looking and, in Laura Mulvey's resonant phrase, a character connoting "to-be-looked-at-ness." And here again, as in *Ju Dou*, the power dynamic is reversed, the spy ensnared, the object of the gaze, here unwittingly, in the ascendant, although now it is the woman who is the voyeur behind her male disguise, and it is the man who is spied upon. As Jo leads her horse from the corral early one morning, she looks up and we see—the shot traveling in to a close-up—that she is taken aback to discover Tinman, nude to the waist, bending to splash water up to his face and arms, his long hair uncoiled and hanging free down to the sun-drenched river's surface in which he is reflected. Greenwald cuts to Jo turning slowly away to mount her horse but then looking back, the editing's precise, ironic parallelism balancing Jo as she climbs up into the seat of power with her servant, the "weaker" character down below, but erect now as he turns his head in a free and easy gesture, swinging the long, wet hair back over his shoulder. As Jo rides out, there is a third shot, Tinman for the first time looking up, feeling the weight of her gaze, as the "master," devastated, attempts to recuperate her power: "I've left you some mending."

Although years of labor have hardened Tinman, his body firmly muscled, there is a shapely, curvaceous quality to his upper torso which interacts dynamically with his long hair, his free and artless movements, his state of casual undress, a shirt tied loosely around his waist. It is an image of nonchalant sensuality, of ambiguous erotic force, italicized by virtue of being seen from our tightly wrapped hero/heroine's point of view. This graceful tableau of Tinman in dishabille exerts a mysterious energy, reminiscent of a statue from Greek antiquity whose serene nudity and epicene beauty can compromise the viewer, whatever the genders involved, the gaze rendered uni-sexual, multi-sexual. Looking on, we too feel the force and attraction of this visual pleasure, and can understand why Jo is so thoroughly unmanned, as the next shot, which has her communing with her sheep, eloquently suggests. In one transcendent image, Greenwald creates a post-modern pin-up, as natural, direct and free as Tinman's own gestures, which forces us to confront and experience, as Jo has, the limitations of our society and its reductive categories. It is a great moment.

Finding love and peace with Tinman, Jo becomes her own person, her own woman. But if Jo achieves a measure of autonomy, it is, paradoxically, at the cost of a fragmented identity, a denial of the feminine, a loss of self and a journey of self-dis-covery. However, because that journey is undercover, Jo a sexual double agent, her, masked point of view takes on a special intensity and displaces the genre's traditional gender dynamics, feminizing the West. The uniqueness of *Little Jo* is that it introduces a sustained female subjectivity into the Western, not through the spectacular excess of a Stanwyck or Crawford seizing phallic power, but out of a heightened perception of what it felt like to be—and not to be—a woman on the frontier.

The Ballad of Little Jo can be seen as a late entry in Hollywood's role-swapping cycle initiated in the 80s by the success of *Kramer vs. Kramer* (1979) and *Tootsie* (1982). These films cast the mold for an affirmative action cinema, a wholesale revisionist interrogation of the white male which clearly relates to the Western's fall from grace as a viable metaphor for the period. Through switches, masquerades and reincarnations, a generation of middle class white men learn to be better human beings by giving up power and privilege. Following a cross-cultural narrative, the films all involve trading places and learning about stereotypes, Dustin Hoffman's humbled single parent the prototype.[2]

In contrast, Jo appropriates power, but rather than "improve" she undergoes a profound suffering that finally gives her character a spiritual stature, a glow in the darkness of the frontier. If Jo is nearly torn apart by the film's action, it is because in ideological terms her double-coded identity puts her at the mercy of the genre's traditional binary conflicts—East versus West, individual versus community, nomadic versus settled—normally dramatized across a range of characters. However, for me, what makes *The Ballad of Little Jo* a unique and moving experience is the incorporation of Jo's painful journey in a thoughtful, intimate, near-Bressonian *mise en scène*. A tightly organized action, stately beat, and genuine thrift in the film's deployment of landscape, performance, camera, and music, create a rigorous and mysterious tone so

David Chung as Tinman: "A post-modern pinup."

much in evidence that any release guarantees a powerful affect. Jo's introduction after her metamorphosis also introduces the style. The shot begins in tight on the horse, the frame line cutting the rider off at the waist, then tracks with it through the trees, cutting to behind the rider as he proceeds down the muddy main drag of the primitive Ruby City, the suspense building further as the cowboy dismounts, head down, hitches his horse, and finally turns, head still down, to answer the two who have asked—"What's your name, kid?"—the hat finally coming up slowly toward us, the masquerade revealed: "Jo Monaghan, sir." But for an occasional bashful smile with Mary, or a happy moment with immigrant neighbors, the serious, almost forbidding look will stay persistently in place. As a result, Jo will seem positively to thaw, the Keatonesque stoneface cracking into a crinkly smile, when she and Tinman finally introduce themselves ("Is your name really...?"), the person materializing, the cowboy kid humanized at last.

The *mise en scène* evidences a spareness and an intensity of gaze throughout, as aware of the pussy willows in the foreground as the high country beyond, a circumspection which accords well with Jo's *modus operandi*, one of caution, restraint, repression. But in a final irony, given Greenwald's post-modernist yarn of a mock-male, this deliberate, evocative style also creates a tone and rhythm appropriate for a celebration of the feminine. Like panels on a polished, classic Greek vase, the stately images track a narrative that limns all the stages of the frontier female's existence, and the triumph of a womanhood intensely alive to the world, a spirit sensitive to processes and relationships, to the wholeness of being and sacredness of life. Transcending the trends of the day, *Little Jo* is far from the pyrotechnics of a *Dances With Wolves*, the "ecological Western" with its foregrounded reverence for nature. Avoiding the rhetoric of both the sublime and the picturesque, the film is quietly holistic, creating a re-enchanted West, attentive to the moon, the mornings, and the mountains. And we should not forget the river that saved Jo from rape, and that supplies a daily source of precious water, serves her homestead like a moat, and provides the luminous, magical setting for her seeing of Tinman anew.

It would be easy enough to hail Greenwald as an auteur, but the significance of the film is post-authorial and political, embodied in a feminist critique that goes beyond pastiche and self-referentiality. For all the nostalgia that the film as ballad

Little Jo rides out: "The spy ensnared."

evokes in its images and haunting score, *Little Jo* is a resistant text that recycles the past to advance difference and otherness and to interrogate myth, underlining our own era's culpability.[3] And the Western's myth here is crucial, allowing for a vision both critical and inspirational, and an empowering force impossible in contemporary formats such as neo-noir—the grim *Manhunter* a canonical text—with their obsessive focus on the paralyzing, pathological symptoms of a postmodern society.[4]

Evidencing a blue-collar conscience and feminist commitment, a populist soul cued by an evocative, ethnic-coded folk melody score, the film uses the nuances cast by Jo's presence to highlight ordinary "womanly" behaviors such as cooking, serving, washing, the family and domestic chores invisible in the background of thousands of Westerns, here thrown quietly into relief by virtue of our hero's freedom from them, as they go on about her.[5] Women's powers, their indispensable gifts to the frontier, in flesh and spirit, are celebrated in two sharp, contrasting cameos. Elvira, the mute prostitute, rides into the mining camp of Ruby City like a queen, a goddess in white on her snowy mount, but once darkness falls all hell breaks loose, the infernal lighting and demented dancing cueing a lust and license that finally culminate in a facial scar for Elvira too, from Percy's knife for refusing to "put it in her mouth," a male grievance if ever there was one. This abuse of frontier women, the rape of the goddess, is balanced by the neglect of Ruth Badger, quietly ennobled by Carrie Snodgrass (formerly of *Diary of A Mad Housewife*) for her wise woman's many nurturing contributions—loving care, a steady hand, and remedies to break Tinman's temperature and save his life. She is the healer, the mother, her mysterious art carefully detailed—spoonfuls of kerosene, onion-slice bandages, a piney solution. "Come on back, little feller... Come on back," she calls to Tinman, who's "got one foot on the other side."

As in this little vignette, *The Ballad of Little Jo*'s ultimate affirmation of life carries the conviction of a land whose pioneers paid their dues. The film's sacred signifier of America, the Russian family that Jo had brought to their "homestead ... homestead," are the martyred victims of the Western Land Company, the film's embodiment of the genre's stock capitalism. As in John Ford, the family is holy, America's immigrants, Jo's surrogate family, whom she leads to the promised land, accepting a teddy in payment from the little girl who alone may sense the truth and appreciate the joke. Jo breaks bread with them, mentors the son who takes over her herder's job for Badger, but has to watch as the helpless mother—in a horrific replay of Jo's own past—runs desperately, encumbered by her skirts, from the faceless horsemen who gun her down, and in time will come to Jo as well. Shot first from on high and then in close, Greenwald cross-cutting the struggle of the powerless woman dragging through tall grass with the mounted riders, unstoppable, behind, the chase insinuates a revisionist analysis of the "noble" horse in terms of the frontier's sexual politics, no ranchers' daughters in the saddle here. It is a crushing blow for Jo, whose frequent visits with the large family of many children we sense had helped assuage the profound loss, the pain so vivid in her correspondence with her sister. There is a bright moment, the family delighting in Jo's gift of an orange, that testifies to their closeness, high spirits, and sense of shared adventure. The camera describes two intimate circles, panning from face to face, culminating in Jo, the family stirred by the mysterious, fulfilling ritual, smelling the new fruit, then each taking and tasting a crescent, like a sacrament under the open sky, the open prairie all around them.

Was ever America's dream, the spiritual promise of the open frontier, so warmly, intimately, economically, evoked? Maggie Greenwald's film everywhere extends an invitation to enjoy the close observation of a frontier existence in its details, a strategy distant indeed from the epic and heroic excess to which we are all accustomed. *Little Jo* achieves its profound effects precisely because of its human scale, avoiding the god-like Peckinpah/Leone paradigm of both *Bad Girls* (1993) and *The Quick and the Dead* (1995). This should not suggest, however, that Jo does not face and pass the genre's obligatory tests, that she is unworthy, not a legitimate fantasy figure. Describing the classic trajectory of the tenderfoot who undergoes an education in the West, Jo becomes a sheepherder and mountain man, and teaches herself survival skills such as the gaining of gun lore, one of the genre's most satisfying rituals.

Indeed, little Jo ultimately reveals "himself" a stand-up guy, a post-modern cowboy hero who stands up for the dude, the whore, the "China-man," minorities all, and finally for herself, killing two of the combine's henchmen. No Sharon Stone, it takes four revolver shots to take one man down, but Jo scores the second as he recedes into the distance at full gallop with a breath-taking crack rifle shot—and then weeps, still herself beneath the mask for all the brutalizing hardships undergone. The mask belongs to Suzy Amis, whose taut performance is often all eyes and voice, and who sports a dapper cowboy wardrobe of sharp hats and dandyish suspenders that frame a lean and boyish body. She/he stands tall, or at least erect, in a careful, controlled body language not unlike the stiff, almost wooden moves of an earlier bearer of the law, Henry Fonda's and *My Darling Clementine*'s Wyatt Earp. However, the balancing act the latter performs—between personal justice and public order—is far more mundane than the queer equilibrium Jo's posture disguises.

Although there is an open-air marriage and celebration in a sunny spot surrounded by vaulting mountains beyond, not unlike in John Ford's film, it is of course not Jo who weds, but the tavern maid, Mary, who has had to put her crush on Jo aside to accept the older man who happened by, and is now spiriting the sweet young thing off to share his life in Texas. Nor is there an American flag fluttering above, Mormon extras dancing. Greenwald's style throughout provides a close study of the small data of a life, rather than the large propositions of a community.

Stylistic excess is one of the hallmarks of post-modern film texts—from the rhetoric and hyperbole of both Peckinpah and Leone, to dystopic tech-noir like *Blade Runner* and *The Terminator*, to grim serial killer-noir such as *Manhunter* and *Blue Steel*. Greenwald takes a different approach, trusting that all contemporary audiences are not jaded, one that avoids the flatness, the "waning of affect" that chill so many contemporary films. It is precisely because the film goes about its frontier melodrama in so restrained a manner—rather like the movements of its hero—that its tightly reined-in emotions eventually achieve such full-blooded expression.

In keeping with its genre fusion, *Little Jo* mounts two distinct climaxes. The duel with the combine's masked enforcers, Greenwald typically pausing over its aftermath rather than the violence, satisfies the masculinist demands of the form. However, there is an earlier test, a turning point that in fact precipitates the bloody shoot-out. True to her hybrid text, Greenwald has Jo face another moment of truth in a classic

"The woman at the window": Little Jo gazes at "a lost past."

scene from the family melodrama, the woman at the window, looking back with yearning at a lost past, a life she had to sacrifice. For Jo, however, the moment is not one of resignation or despair. Gazing out at who and what she might have been, an image provided by the fussy wife of her ranch's prospective buyer nagging her little boy to keep clean, Jo decides not to sell. In part she is prompted by Tinman's miraculous rise from the dead, his fever finally breaking, but equally there is the sense here that, as Jo stands by the window, the light falling on the scar of years ago, she finally ends her journey, another miracle, peace at last, accepting the cards that life had dealt her. Mysterious, evocative, passionate, *The Ballad of Little Jo* creates a West both mundane and sacred, an apt landscape within which to play out its affecting drama, the education and salvation of its cross-dressed cowboy hero.[6]

Writing back in 1957 in *Cahiers du Cinema*, Andre Bazin welcomed "an exemplary Western," Budd Boetticher's breakthrough success, *Seven Men From Now*, for its intelligence, for avoiding both philosophy and psychology, and for "constantly surprising us, despite its rigorously classical plot."[7] Five years later, interviewed by *Cahiers* about his own work, Jean-Luc Godard could be heard praising Sam Peckinpah's *Ride the High Country* and the Americans for having "a gift for the kind of simplicity which brings depth."[8] Greenwald's extraordinary achievement strikes me as having precisely the kind of integrity and substance that the French found so praiseworthy in those earlier, outstanding efforts. Indeed, *Little Jo* may be best considered a Bazinian Western, a transcendental Western, in its purity and immanent vision of America, affirming the spiritual despite the de-humanization of a society that prefers the image to the real.

Double-coded to the end, *Little Jo* leaves us with a final ironic and ambiguous image, another post-modern pin-up, the dead cowboy tied to his horse in a pose for posterity, the lady photographer, Greenwald's stand-in, asking that they "open his eyes." Sam, one of Jo's old mates, complies, and corrects his sidekick who has echoed the request: "*Her* eyes, Lyle." Appropriately, the image records the resurrection of a female cowboy savior, the ascension of an ordinary woman who had an extraordinary life, one Josephine Monaghan, to a special place in the history of pioneer America. It is a process which Greenwald's film—"inspired by a real life"—respectfully repeats, in tribute to a woman who insisted on standing up and being counted, on having a vote—in advance of her sex—in the forming of America.

It comes as no surprise, given her obvious respect for and command of the form, to find that our writer/director has wanted to make a Western since a child, that she has always felt a "primal connection to the landscape of the West."[7] With *The Ballad of Little Jo*, Maggie Greenwald has produced a distinguished contribution to that tradition, a Western deserving of attention from any student of the genre. It is an indispensable film.

NOTES

1. Jenks, "The Post-modern Agenda," *The Post-Modern Reader* (New York: St. Martin's, 1992). Jenks also addresses the hybridization of the sign with special emphasis on architecture in *What is Post-modernism?* (London: Academy Editions, 1996), pp. 29-35.

2. A man becoming better for becoming a woman is also featured in *Switch* (1991) and *Mrs. Doubtfire* (1993). Roles are swapped with a child in *Like Father, Like Son* (1987), *Big* and *Vice Versa*, both 1988; with an African-American in *Soul Man* (1986) and *Heart Condition* (1990), the homeless—*Life Stinks* (1991), the disadvantaged—*Regarding Henry* (1991), a medical patient—*The Doctor* (1991), and so on. The cycle culminates in the cross-cultural blockbuster, *Dances With Wolves*, Hollywood finally cashing in bigtime on multi-culturalism with Kevin Costner's version of the traditional Western's racial narrative, that Robert Baird characterizes as "going Indian" in his contribution to this volume.

3. The claim put forward here for *The Ballad of Little Jo* draws on a key distinction often advanced in post-modern critical literature, between the so-called conservative text, wherein re-cycled codes seal off the work from any critique of culture and society, an empty spectacle, as it were, and the resistant text that questions and comments on cultur-

al myths and contemporary concerns. Such a great divide, however, is easier to sustain in theory than in practice. The norm is perhaps closer to a film like *Posse* which embeds its African-Americanization of the frontier with a blatant misogyny, a blend of progressive and regressive elements.

4. Based on a Jim Thompson novel, Greenwald's distinguished second film, *The Kill-Off* (1989), was her own venture into the neo-noir darkness. A highly stylized work whose haunting images and mesmerizing score give it an expressionist quality, the film is absolutely uncompromising in its portrait of a whole community of low-life characters trapped in a cycle of violence and despair. In many ways, this Sartrean vision of existential hell, a post-modern nightmare, is the reverse of *The Ballad of Little Jo*.

5. Rarely does a score so sensitively express a film's spirit. That its director and composer should have fallen in love and married, as Molly Greenwald told me, only confirms the impression of a charmed production.

6. Although by no means in the radical manner of a Bresson or Ozu, the film would appear to achieve some of its spiritual quality through the approximation of a design Paul Schrader defined in his *Transcendental Style in Film: Ozu, Bresson, Dreyer* (Los Angeles: University of California Press, 1972). Schrader postulates that by employing "screens" to hold emotion in check, the filmmaker can create a repressive regime and achieve epiphanies on minimally relaxing the style's constraints. After moving on to writing and directing, Schrader experimented with the effect himself, as at the end of his *American Gigolo* (1980), an early and influential post-modern neo-noir in its commentary on a society of narcissistic surfaces.

7. Andre Bazin, "An Exemplary Western: *Seven Men From Now*," *Cahiers du Cinema* No. 74 (August/September, 1957).

8. "Interview with Jean-Luc Godard," *Godard on Godard* (New York: The Viking Press, 1972), p. 193.

9. The quoted passage comes from Tania Moldleski's interview in this volume. Greenwald discusses the Western and her film further in "Private View: Cowgirls," in *Sight and Sound* (Oct. 1994), p. 61. Modleski champions *Little Jo* in "A Woman's Gotta Do ... What A Man's Gotta Do? Cross-Dressing in the Western," in *Signs: Journal of Women in Culture and Society* (Spring, 1997), and provides an analysis of the film in relation to theories of fantasy in feminist scholarship. The journalistic reception of the film suffered in some camps from ideological determinations. Thus the film was attacked for failing to exploit its potential as a lesbian text (B. Ruby Rich, "At Home on the Range," *Sight and Sound* (November, 1993), and *Cineaste* (Karen Backstein, "*The Ballad of Little Jo*," 1993) critiqued the film's politics as insufficiently feminist in its acceptance of male codes for the measurement of little Jo's success. The film was even seen as an ersatz Western for not being violent enough, and for focusing on a sheepherder as hero; however, these bizarre notions were fortunately minor lapses in an otherwise sharp review by Claire Monk (*Sight and Sound*, April, 1994).

THE WESTERN UNDER ERASURE:
Dead Man

Gregg Rickman (1998)

> Every Night & every Morn
> Some to Misery are Born.
> Every Morn & every Night
> Some are Born to sweet delight
> Some are Born to sweet delight,
> Some are Born to Endless Night.
> —William Blake, "Auguries of Innocence"

The Two Blakes

Jim Jarmusch's western *Dead Man* drew generally baffled reactions upon its release in 1996, many commentators perplexed that the innovative filmmaker had abandoned the laid-back whimsy and diegetic game-playing of his earlier features (*Stranger Than Paradise, Down by Law*, et al.) in favor of a violent, albeit still somewhat comedic, exercise in a dead genre. Of the film's defenders Jonathan Rosenbaum was the most articulate, blaming negative commentary on reviewers and audiences unable to "sit still for movies that require even a modicum of adjustment."[1] That *Dead Man* offers an adjustment away from both contemporary Hollywood entertainment and the lineage of the classical western is certainly true; an adjustment *toward* what remains in question. One way to begin making sense of *Dead Man* would be to parse some of the film's many references to the British poet William Blake. The film's story is set in the Old West of the 1870s. A Native American named "Nobody" (Gary

381

Farmer) mistakes—or recognizes, if you will—wounded accountant Bill Blake (Johnny Depp) as the poet. Nobody takes it as his mission to guide Blake back to "the bridge made of waters," the ocean, where he will be "taken up to the next level of the world—the place where William Blake is from—where his spirit belongs." Blake, however, had been fatally wounded in a gunfight back at the Western town of Machine. His physical body dies just as his spiritual journey is supposed to begin. Our last glimpse of Blake is of the canoe bearing his body drifting off over the horizon.

The poetry of the historical William Blake is drawn from at key junctures in the film, most notably the verse from "Auguries of Innocence" used as this essay's epigraph. Blake (1757-1827) was in his day a foe of both the ancient regimes of Europe and of the oncoming Industrial Revolution, which he saw as based in the deplorable rationalism of the Enlightenment and thus destined to destroy the balance between humanity and nature. Blake remains something of an artistic hero to many today, of many different beliefs, perhaps particularly to those of Jarmusch's generation. (Born in 1953, the writer-director told interviewer Charlie Rose on PBS "When I first read Blake it kind of blew my mind to read this kind of thought from centuries ago.") Blake's revolutionary impact is suggested by one scene in *Dead Man*: as a child Nobody, captured by British soldiers and taken across the Atlantic as an exhibit, "mimicked them, imitating their ways," until the boy by chance discovers Blake's poetry. We see Nobody's story in cameo-like flashbacks accompanied by his narration. As he speaks we see a young Indian in English clothes of the period open one of Blake's books. Nobody says of that moment: "I discovered the words that you—William Blake—had written. They were powerful words, and they spoke to me." Nobody is so moved by Blake's words that he escapes his captors and eventually returns home.

Blake's writings comprise a lifelong investigation of the relationship between unmediated Innocence and hardened Experience. This opposition appeared early in his works, perhaps his most famous poetic sequence being his *Songs of Innocence and Experience* (1789-94), in which the child-centered view of one group of poems is matched by the sadder maturity of the other. The poem "Auguries of Innocence," from which both Nobody and Bill Blake quote in the film, is from a later period of Blake's career. It was written circa 1800-1803, never published in Blake's lifetime, and remained unknown until its discovery in the so-called Pickering MS, left to a B. M. Pickering in 1866. (Nobody would have to have been markedly well placed to have read "Auguries of Innocence" during his sojourn in England, datable to the 1850s, given that *Dead Man's* action is set in the 1870s.[2]) In his classic study of Blake's writings *Fearful Symmetry* (1947) Northrup Frye argues that the poems in the Pickering MS "were apparently intended to explore the relationship between innocence and experience instead of merely presenting their contrast," as in the Songs.[3]

The relationship between innocence and experience is explored throughout *Dead Man*. The more worldly Nobody recites the "Auguries of Innocence" verse cited above upon first hearing Bill Blake's name. Later a less innocent Blake, accepting his new identity and Nobody's dictate that his future poems be written in blood, asks two lawmen "Do you know my poetry?" before shooting them. He then recites the line "Some are born to endless night" while examining their bodies.

The key encounter between Innocence and Experience comes early in the film, when Bill Blake, the accountant who arrives in Machine in search of a position with Dickinson Metal Works, meets Thel (Mili Avital), who befriends Blake after the company refuses his application. He is Innocence incarnate, initially presented as a naive bumbler from the East of a type common to many westerns (the effeminate man mocked in Ford's *The Iron Horse*, the "dude" stripped of his plaid socks in Greenwald's *The Ballad of Little Jo*). Thel, on the other hand, bears the marks of much bitter Experience. By seducing the evidently virginal Blake Thel is introducing him to the sensual world, which the film associates with the mud of Machine's streets: Blake first sees Thel when she is pushed into that mud, and he finally leaves her room by falling into the mud himself, from out of her window. In both instances Thel's white paper flowers, which she makes and sells, are seen to be scattered about in the mud, a Griffithian image of soiled purity.

Moreover, unlike Blake and his long drawn-out death, Thel's finish is quick, brutal and violent. She is shot dead by her ex-lover Charlie Dickinson (Gabriel Byrne) after his discovery of her in bed with Blake. Charlie was aiming at him, not her, death coming as she tries to shield Blake from Charlie's bullet (the fate of many experienced women of the West, as with saloon entertainer Marlene Dietrich in *Destry Rides Again*, and entrepreneur Ruth Roman in *The Far Country*, who both die catching bul-

Innocence and Experience—Bill Blake and Thel. Note white paper roses, at rear left.

lets meant for James Stewart). Blake fires back and kills Charlie, but the bullet that kills Thel passes through her to lie close to Blake's heart, giving him, like so many other heroes of myth, a wound which will not heal. Experience has tried and failed to shield Innocence: Blake must experience the Fall (from her window), and spend the rest of his short life in flight.

The character of Thel appears to be Jarmusch's variation on the title character of Blake's poem *The Book of Thel* (1789). Thel is an unborn spirit dwelling in "the vales of Har," which to quote Harold Bloom in his reading of the poem is "a lower paradise and seed bed of potential life which undergoes its own cycles but never dies into the life of the human experience and so never becomes altogether real."[4] This young female spirit's name means "wish" or "will" in Greek, according to Bloom, and "Female Will" in a persuasive recent reading by Hilda Hollis.[5] Thel is afraid of what the harsh realities of Experience might bring her, and questions various denizens of Har in an attempt to understand what Experience is like. Ultimately she is invited by a Clod of Clay to enter into her house and prevision sensual existence. As Bloom notes, "The Clay is the red earth of which Adam was formed, and so 'the matron Clay' is inviting the virgin Thel to accept incarnation."[6]

Thel accepts the opportunity to preview sensual existence:

> Thel enter'd in & saw the secrets of the land unknown.
> She saw the couches of the dead, & where the fibrous roots
> Of every heart on earth infixes deep its restless twists:
> A land of sorrows & of tears where never smile was seen.

What Thel perceives, says Bloom, is the "terrible world" Blake had already shown in his *Songs of Experience*.[7] Finally coming "to her own grave plot," she hears her own posthumous voice, a "lament from out of the hollow pit of natural destruction," and flees with a shriek "unhinder'd" back into paradise. The conceptual theme of the poem, in Bloom's reading, "is the failure to move from Innocence to Experience." More recently feminist critics have offered alternate readings justifying Thel's reluctance.[8] Deborah McCollister's reading of Thel's cry is convincing: "With a loud shriek, his heroine, in effect, cries 'No!' to the experience of the earthly woman."[9]

Now compare Jarmusch's Thel: we first see her being pushed into the mud of Machine's filthy streets (clods of clay, perhaps even "the red earth of which Adam was formed"). Her victimizer is a drunk who says "We liked you better when you was a whore." This Thel, then, reversing the flight from Experience of her namesake, has entered "the house of Clay" and is experiencing the lot of earthly woman. She is fully sexualized, a point made further with her seduction of the film's Blake and also by her past as mistress of Dickinson's son. Her efforts to free herself from exploitation with her new career, making and selling white paper roses, is a suggestion perhaps of "the Lilly of the valley," Thel's first encounter in the poem.[10] Her death finally leads her to "her own grave plot . . . the hollow pit of natural destruction." The pattern of inversion suggested by the trajectory of the film's Thel compared with that of the poem's tallies with what will be a consistent pattern throughout *Dead Man*: what is promulgated in previous poetry, myth, or films in the western genre is upended and reversed—canceled out—by Jarmusch's screenplay and direction.

Urizen's West

Further comparisons between Blake's poetry and the events of *Dead Man* can no doubt be made. Nobody's association of Bill Blake with the poet, for example, is furthered by his occasional quotations from Blake's *Proverbs of Hell*, which as Rosenbaum notes "sound like Native American sayings to Blake and to us . . . conversely some of Nobody's pronouncements sound like the poetry of Blake."

Also interesting is a correlation that can be posited between the elder Dickinson (Robert Mitchum)—the metal works owner whose rage at the death of his son leads him to hire bounty hunters to pursue and kill Blake—and the recurring character of Urizen in Blake's poetry. Urizen, like Dickinson an angry, powerful near-deity, is associated with smoke, flame, and metal. As *The Book of Ahania* asks, "Shall we worship this demon of smoke"? Dickinson rules over Machine and his Metal Works the way Urizen rules over his despotic domain of the Earth in Blake's poetry, "the changes of Urizen" that he causes to be worked upon the world being *metal worked* on a "dark bellows . . . forging chains new & new" (*The Book of Urizen*).

Urizen, moreover, is associated with the world of reason, of mathematics and logic ("He form'd a line & a plummet / To divide the Abyss beneath; / He formed a dividing rule; / He formed scales to weigh"—*The Book of Urizen*). Bill Blake applies to work for Dickinson as an accountant, and is received by a roomful of Dickinson's accountants.

Robert Mitchum as Dickinson: "Shall we worship this demon of smoke"?

When Urizen's son revolts against him, as Charlie Dickinson evidently tried to do by courting Thel, Urizen defends himself with the "broad Disk" of his rationalism, "forg'd in mills" of logic.[11]

The name Urizen is in part drawn from the Greek word Horízein, to bound or limit, the root of our word "horizon."[12] Edward Larrissy has discussed the poet's interest in bounds, boundaries, frontiers and horizons in a catalogue of Blakean motifs that includes "'bound,'" "veil," "outline," "circumference," "garment" and of course Urizen's "horizon.'"[13] To this list we might add the western frontier, site of so many films, and note *Dead Man's* final images of a Blake floating off into the far horizon. Urizen is also a pun on "your reason," the Enlightenment which Blake rejected along with the smoking machines that were its works. Throughout his life Blake expressed horror at the Industrial Revolution that so transformed England in his lifetime. The glimpses we see of Dickinson's Metal Works conform with Blake's portrayal of "(t)he tyranny of Urizen, the rationalist" as symbolized by "slaves grinding at the mill."[14]

In his *Milton* Blake wrote of "dark Satanic mills." Machine, appropriately, is referred to as "hell" by the smoke-blackened train Fireman (Crispin Glover) who serves as Virgil to Blake's Dante in *Dead Man's* prologue. Blake arrives in Machine in a train that billows smoke, an image that tallies with the powerful images of menacing trains in Leone's *Once Upon a Time in the West* (1968), and inverts the positive symbolism associated with trains as instrument of civilization in classical westerns from *The Iron Horse* (1924) to *Union Pacific* (1939) to *How the West was Won* (1962).

One late classical western does, however, also invert this symbolism, a film comparable with *Dead Man* in several ways. That it's a film Jarmusch knows can be seen in his claim that *Dead Man* might be the first black-and-white western since *The Man Who Shot Liberty Valance* (1962), John Ford's elegy to the passing of the Old West.[15] In that film's opening scenes U.S. Senator Ransom Stoddard (James Stewart), the film's unwitting symbol of compromise and denial, arrives with his wife in the western town of Shinbone on a modern train, "the traditional symbol of progress and the pioneering spirit," that nonetheless is now "a polluting and corrupting force."[16] At film's end an express train speeds the pair back East, away from this site of their youth, an immediate canceling of Stoddard's claim that he wishes to return and retire there. Stoddard, despite his efforts in the film's intervening narrative to tell the truth about himself, is unable to escape his destiny any more than the film's other characters—or those of *Dead Man*.

The name Shinbone echoes with the bones we see piled high in Machine. Stoddard has built his reputation on his supposed killing there of the outlaw Liberty Valance, a name and character symbolic of licentious freedom.[17] Liberty's true killer is the late Tom Doniphon (John Wayne). The Stoddards are in Shinbone for his funeral; Doniphon was Hallie Stoddard's first love, and much is made of the commemorative cactus roses Hallie plucks from the ruins of Doniphon's home and places on his coffin. That those white, cactus roses are the focus of the film's meditative energies is the burden of many excellent analyses of the film. For our purposes it is enough merely to parallel the image's use by Ford with Thel's white paper roses in *Dead Man*. In addition to the lost love of Hallie and Tom, the plant suggests, as Tag Gallagher puts it, "the duality of order and liberty, the better dream, the loss of innocence, youth, perfection, beauty, the loss of a wilderness for a garden, of the physical for the verbal. . . ."[18] For Jarmusch, Thel's roses may suggest some of the same things but while Stoddard, in the final scene of Ford's film, has been sadly enlightened by what he's discovered of himself and of his wife's true feelings in Shinbone, Bill Blake remains oblivious. A moment in the brief courtship of Bill and Thel is telling—Blake is unable to detect any scent in the paper rose Thel offers him even after she has poetically described her plans to someday scent her flowers with perfume. To him, it merely "smells like paper"—an early sign of Blake's fatal lack of imagination.

Ford's cactus roses and Jarmusch's scattered paper flowers both suggest Edenic, garden worlds lost to time and civilization. Earlier westerns, however, associated the civilizing process with non-native flowers brought in from the East. Their jibes at Perley Sweet's flower garden serve to introduce the outlaws of *Three Godfathers* (Ford, 1948) to the lawman who will ultimately hunt them down. In *The Covered Wagon* (James Cruze, 1923), a feisty pioneer wife refuses to leave a walnut bureau behind when the film's wagon train must ford a dangerous river. "I've got rose cuttin's an' flower seeds in there!" she exclaims, "to say nuthin' of other things that I need to make a home." She gets her way. Ford's *My Darling Clementine* (1946) is subtler—the smell of Wyatt Earp's aftershave is confused by both his brother Virgil and the "girl from the East" (Clementine) with the native scents of "honeysuckle" and

The cactus roses of The Man Who Shot Liberty Valance.

"desert flowers," the barber's potent chemicals overwhelming true western scents. Indeed, they are mistaken for them. When Tom Doniphon gifts Hallie with a cactus rose in *The Man Who Shot Liberty Valance*, his rival from the East, Ransom Stoddard, shames her by asking her if she's ever seen "a real rose." "No," she says, "but maybe someday, if they ever dam the river we'll have lots of water, and all kinds of flowers!" By the end of the film, with Stoddard on his way back East to work on an "irrigation bill," both have learned just how real a cactus rose can be.

The wilderness/garden dichotomy as a structuring device of western myth was first discerned by Henry Nash Smith in his *Virgin Land* (1950), and then applied to the western film genre by Jim Kitses in *Horizons West* (1969). That dichotomy is illustrated so perfectly by *The Man Who Shot Liberty Valance* one would be very surprised if Ford could be proven not to have read Smith—as Hallie tells Stoddard at the end of that film, "it used to be a wilderness—now it's a garden." A contemporaneous survey of shifting ideas about that wilderness, Leo Marx's *The Machine in the Garden* (1964) is very useful in extending these ideas to Jarmusch's film. In the nineteenth century "Americans, so far as they shared an idea of what they were doing as a people, actually saw themselves creating a society in the image of a garden."[19] At the same time, however, American thought was all but unanimous in endorsing the regime of "progress" the coming of the Age of Machinery promised. That machinery was symbolized in the popular mind by the railroad, "a kind of national obsession" in the 1830s still being endorsed by westerns made over one hundred years later.[20] In the popular mind, the machine and the garden could co-exist. *Dead Man* reverses this, steeped as it is in the received, ecologically aware wisdom of our own era. The town of Machine is a "machine in the garden," but both Machine and garden are equally toxic.

Western Hits and Myths

At the time *Dead Man* was released, Jim Jarmusch commented that he liked the western as "kind of an allegorical open form . . . a fantasy world that America has used to process its own history through—often stamping its own ideology all over it." One thing that did annoy him, however, was "how mythological it becomes," referring specifically to the portrayal of indigenous peoples. His critique can be extended: when Jarmusch uses phrases like "a fantasy world that America has used to process its own history," it is clear what sort of Western myth he's alluding to. It is the same myth Howard Hawks defended in answer to a question about the 1970s trend "to debunk the mythology of the West." Hawks' answer—"You mean there are people around today who remember what it was like?"—says as much about the work of classical filmmakers like Hawks as it does the revisionist westerns of Altman and Penn, not to mention Jarmusch: all of them tell tales extrapolated from a legendary past.[21]

"Myth" is an elastic term that can be stretched to contain any component of the classical western from Manifest Destiny through to the laconic cowpokes and shootouts at high noon that form the stuff of Western lore. Jarmusch, parodic as he is of these devices, was careful while making *Dead Man* to be deeply respectful of another mythology, that of the indigenous peoples whose perspective Nobody represents. A more rigorous way of considering myth in the western might be to examine certain recurring elements of western narratives as examples of deeper cross-cultural patterns, myths or "master symbols" (to use Nash Smith's term) with powerfully affective resonance for large numbers of viewers. Works in the classical tradition are interested in affirming these verities, while revisionist works are, in their different ways, interested in interrogating, varying, and perhaps overturning them.

The classical western incorporates many such verities, symbols, and structuring narratives, many of which now seem outdated or simply wrong. The portrayal of indigenous cultures in many classical westerns is one obvious example. Less so, perhaps, is the continuing use of Frederick Jackson Turner's frontier thesis to structure western films, be they classical (*The Covered Wagon, Wagon Master, How the West Was Won*) or revisionist (the settling of the West by white men still organizes the narrative in films as disparate as *McCabe and Mrs. Miller* and *Dances With Wolves*). The New Western Historians whose work will be discussed later in this essay have rejected the very idea of a "frontier" as hopelessly ethnocentric, which presents classicists with another problem in defending that tradition, and revisionists a new frontier, as it were, for study and research.

Others of these myths operate on many levels across a culture, but for one reason or another take on particular resonance in the western genre. One of the most powerful myths in the classical western is of the moral regeneration of a flawed protagonist, a pattern that can be seen in westerns going at least as far back as the films of William S. Hart. In *The Return of Draw Egan* (Lambert Hillyer, 1916), for example, Hart plays an outlaw who reforms when given the opportunity to act as sheriff, his character gradually conforming to his position as lawman. Interestingly, the outlaw Draw Egan's adopted name as sheriff is none other than William Blake, although if this was a conscious reference to the British poet it's unsupported by the film. The reformed outlaw remained a common character in western films through the silent era, including more than one version of *Three Godfathers*, as well as Ford's *Three Bad Men* (1926).

This thematic pattern of character regeneration was extended in the postwar western to narratives involving the recovery and return to health of damaged psyches. *Pursued* (Raoul Walsh, 1947), the five westerns of the Mann-James Stewart cycle, and Richard Brooks' remarkable *The Last Hunt* (1956) are all prominent examples of this pattern. It is common to discuss these films as psychological westerns, but it might be just as valid to consider these works as myth-evoking spiritual journeys—the landscape of death which Howie Kemp (Stewart) and Lina Patch (Janet Leigh) leave at the end of *The Naked Spur* being suggestive of Kemp's former spiritual state, even as the frozen corpse of Charles Gilson (Robert Taylor) at the end of *The Last Hunt* suggests the living death his rival Sandy McKenzie (Stewart Granger) has avoided. Substantial evidence suggests that John Ford, at least, was widely read in classical mythology and that the references to classical myth in *The Searchers* and others of his works were deliberate. *Pursued's* screenwriter, Niven Busch, meanwhile, was well versed on the legend of Oedipus and its Freudian reading, as he indicated in his interviews.[22]

Whether thought of in psychological or mythic terms, *Pursued, The Last Hunt* and many other westerns all describe a movement by the film's hero toward mental health. And indeed, many commentators to the contrary, this may even be suggested of Ethan Edwards in *The Searchers*. This movement toward wholeness is signified by either the hero's foregoing of revenge or a violent exorcism of past trauma, and also by the hero's implied, or explicit, rejoining of the civilized community. In *The Naked Spur* Howie abandons his plans to return his dearly-purchased bounty, Ben Vandergroot's corpse, to his point of origin, preferring instead to go with Lina to California—a geographical analogue of his two choices at film's end: back to the site of his trauma, or forward into a better future. In *The Last Hunt* Brooks shows Sandy McKenzie turning his back on the white man's world, locating civilization in the starving Indian tribe McKenzie and his Native American lover heads for at film's end, his "half-breed" surrogate son going on ahead. In these films, the "hero's journey" Joseph Campbell spoke of becomes *literally* a journey across variegated western landscapes—a reading not irrelevant to *Dead Man* given that Campbell's popularized readings of world mythology are approvingly cited by *Dead Man's* producer, Demetra MacBride, in the film's pressbook.

This same pattern can be seen operating in later, revisionist westerns. In *Little Big Man* (Arthur Penn, 1970), the protagonist oscillates between corrupt white society and the idealized world of the Cheyenne "human beings." The film's tormented hero finally finds peace when reunited with his surrogate father, after much geographical and psychic travel across the at once mythic and historical West of Hickock, Custer, Washita and Little Big Horn. Only in the more politically conscious westerns of the later 1970s do we see a stasis that is the antithesis of the classic western journey: in Robert Altman's *Buffalo Bill and the Indians* (1976) Bill's arena never seems to travel from its point of origin. Instead, the film's movement is circular, around and around Bill's arena, even as Buffalo Bill never learns anything. His psyche remains stunted, his ego expanding as his soul withers. The endlessly circling choreography of dances and battles alike in Michael Cimino's *Heaven's Gate* (1980) describe a similar spiritual stasis that culminates in the living death we see a traumatized James Averill (Kris Kristofferson) inhabiting in that film's coda.

Unlike these revisionist works *Dead Man* is built around a classic journey across the entire American West, from Blake's train ride from the East into Machine in the film's prologue through to his flight from Machine to the Northwestern shore, aided and accompanied by his spiritual guide Nobody.[23] We last glimpse Blake traveling further west in his canoe, traveling across "the mirror of water," as Nobody calls the ocean.

Yet—and this is perhaps *Dead Man's* key difference from the classic (spiritual, psychological, moral) journey western—Bill Blake is a protagonist who never learns anything from his ordeal. He is a traveler across a mythic landscape who remains oblivious to it. At the very end of the movie, after Nobody tells him of his impending trip "back where you come from," Blake's response—"You mean Cleveland?"—demonstrates just how ignorant he is of where he's been, where he's going, or even his own fate: death in the sea canoe Nobody will shortly launch. This comic deflation of the very notion of a spiritual quest may be one of the most offputting elements of the film—at least to those who prefer goal-oriented as opposed to absurdist narratives. We are thus forced to consider *Dead Man* not as a classic western, a mythical western, or as a revisionist variant of same, but instead as a comic western—an approach which may prove instructive.

"A landscape of death": The Naked Spur.

The oblivious William Blake: "Cleveland?"

Dead Man Wearing Plaid

Comic westerns date back almost as far back as the first western films. The bulk of these comedies center around the real or perceived incompetence of the protagonist in attempting to fill the role of a classic western archetype. In *Wild and Wooly* (John Emerson, 1917), Douglas Fairbanks plays an eastern dude who learns the ways of the West and is a better man for it. In *The Paleface* (Norman Z. McLeod, 1948) "Painless" Peter Potter (Bob Hope), a dentist, is drafted into the role of gunslinging lawman and gets to display a battery of character traits usually not associated with the great western heroes: lechery, cowardness, false pride, incompetence at gunfighting.

Broadly speaking, these characters can be seen as failures in the roles that define manhood in the classical western. Janet Thumim's essay on *Unforgiven*, to be found in this volume, defines masculinity in terms of such competence (with guns, whoring, pig farming, carpentry), seeing the failures of most of the film's male characters in one of these areas or another as part of a pattern linking those failures to that film's final, apocalyptic violence. In *Dead Man*, Blake's passivity is explicitly read as feminine by the three strange men he meets in a forest clearing (one of whom grotesquely wears a dress himself): they finger him and wonder at his hair, "soft like a girl's." As if confirming Thumim, apocalyptic violence soon follows.

Comic westerns follow this pattern, with the final spasm of violence downplayed but still present. A very successful comic western of the immediate pre-war era, *Destry Rides Again* (George Marshall, 1939) is a paradigm of this: the James Stewart character, arousing universal amusement by his refusal to wear guns and by his willingness to take on women's chores like cleaning, ultimately proves to be a true western hero, traditionally masculine in his violent triumph over the outlaws. Stewart's character in *The Man Who Shot Liberty Valance*—at one point seen wearing an apron and serving food—is a variant of the pattern laid down for his star persona in the earlier film. In *The Paleface* Bob Hope is so unmanned that he introduces himself and his powerful wife (Jane Russell) as "Mr. and Mrs. Painless Peter Potter—I'm Mister." Yet he too is finally able to violently dispatch his and Russell's enemies.

Up to a point the same comic pattern can be seen at work in *Dead Man*. Arriving in Machine wearing ridiculously "dudish" clothing (a flat hat, a loud checkered suit), Bill Blake is given low-key bits of business that suggest comic routines in films past. His muttered excuses to Thel about why he did not remonstrate against the bully who had thrown her into the mud ("I had a sneaking suspicion that that large man back there was inebriated . . . I didn't want to cause trouble") is pure Bob Hope, or Woody Allen, as is his woozy inability to ride a horse later in the film. Blake's "goddamn clown suit," as Dickinson calls it, is together with his glasses and the boosterish greeting he offers his prospective employer ("I'm Bill Blake—your new accountant from Cleveland") suggestive of the clueless optimism of the classic Harold Lloyd character as reenvisioned by Preston Sturges in *The Sin of Harold Diddlebock* (1947). Even Blake's surprising skill with a gun later in *Dead Man*—he kills several of his pursuers—has antecedents, as we've seen, in *Destry Rides Again* and *The Paleface*.

Even more so than Stewart, Bob Hope or Harold Lloyd, however, Johnny Depp's performance in *Dead Man* is redolent of another actor who made his share of comic westerns, Buster Keaton. Complete to a chapeau suggesting the flat hat Keaton wore in most of his films, the long hair he wore in the Civil War western (of sorts) *The General* (1926), and the dudishly out-of-place suit Keaton sported in another quasi-western, *Our Hospitality* (1923), Depp in *Dead Man* seems at times to be continuing the Keaton pastiche he had already attempted in the contemporary comedy *Benny & Joon* (1993). Blake's scene in Machine's bar, seeking the solace of whiskey with his last few coins and having a larger bottle replaced with a smaller one when the bartender sees the size of his fee, strongly suggests Keaton's ill-luck while buying supplies in the opening scene of *Go West* (1925)—both films employing the same basic joke, shrinking resources purchasing less and less.

Keaton's films too can be thought of as critiques of traditional masculine roles, if only in the emphasis they place on the pain and difficulty Keaton's character has in meeting social demands for marital success (*Seven Chances*, 1925), military glory (*The General*), athletic prowess (*College*, 1927) or paternal approval (*Steamboat Bill Jr.*, 1928). Other films go further—the extraordinary *Battling Butler* (1926) mounts a sustained challenge to the notion of masculinity as brutality.

Keaton took full advantage of the western genre to expand on this critique. His short film *The Paleface* (1922) is a remarkable early example of a "pro-Indian western"—Buster playing a butterfly-collecting dude who becomes involved in a tribe's efforts to keep their oil rights. Another short from that same year, *The Frozen North*, is a ruthless parody of the ideas of masculinity the comedian found embodied in William S. Hart's westerns. Keaton's anti-hero knocks unconscious or kills various women, cries fake tears, and amorally proceeds on his way. Hart was reportedly deeply offended by the film, which evidently struck home.[24] Conversely, Keaton's one overtly western feature *Go West* presents as its hero one Friendless, probably the least traditionally masculine hero Keaton ever essayed, a lonely man in stark white clown makeup whose great love is a cow called Brown Eyes. The unsmiling Friendless parries a demand out of Wister's *The Virginian* ("when you call me that . . . smile") with a gesture drawn from silent cinema's great female victim, Lillian Gish in *Broken Blossoms*. Like Gish in that film, Keaton pushes up the corners of his lips in a ridiculous parody of a smile, responding to the macho demands of the genre with the ultra-"feminine" gesture of Gish. Keaton does ultimately take on the aspects of the classic male hero when he stages a cattle stampede in downtown Los Angeles as a means of rescuing Brown Eyes, and is rewarded by riding off into the sunset with his lady fair (the cow).

It is this ultimate turnabout, however parodic, by Keaton's hero that points up the one key difference between the comic hero of classical westerns and the Bill Blake of *Dead Man*—Blake's extraordinary passivity. Marking him off from comic western heroes as different as Stewart, Hope, and Keaton, Bill Blake drifts (at the end, literally) through the film, impelled this way and that by chance, Dickinson, Thel, and finally Nobody. Throughout the film Blake shows almost no agency whatsoever—he's passive, as even the most incompetent western hero never is.

Dead Man, then, can be seen not as a comedy but as an ironic work, as Northrup Frye defines the term. Frye distinguished irony from comedy—the latter

Buster Keaton as The Paleface.

was to Frye a mode of renewal, freedom, and joy. Despite its amusing moments, *Dead Man* lacks all of these qualities and instead can be seen to tally with Frye's definition: "Irony with little satire is the non-heroic residue of tragedy, centering on a theme of puzzled defeat."[25] "Puzzled defeat" is exactly the look on Blake's face in the film's penultimate moments—as he looks back on shore and tries to warn his friend Nobody of the killer sneaking up behind him. Like a silent movie comedian trapped in a talkie, he's fatally unable to speak.

The Dead Western Society

Our attempt to read *Dead Man* as a successor to the classic comic western only takes us so far, as did our earlier attempts to place the film in the lineage of classic, revisionist, psychological and mythic westerns. Jonathan Rosenbaum offers another subgenre to which *Dead Man* can be said to belong, "acid westerns" such as Monte Hellman's *The Shooting* (1966), Jim McBride's *Glen and Randa* (1971), Dennis Hopper's *The Last Movie* (1971), and Robert Downey's *Greaser's Palace* (1972), to which group could be added Alexander Jodorowsky's *El Topo* (1972) and Stan

Dragoti's *Dirty Little Billy* (1972), in which Michael J. Pollard, as Billy the Kid, spends most of the movie covered in mud from head to toe. Many of these films mixed visions of a grim West with counter-culture metaphysics; J. Hoberman was quite astute when he wrote that *Dead Man* suggests "an imaginary, post-apocalyptic 1970s, a wilderness populated by degenerate hippies and acid-ripped loners forever pulling guns on each other or else asking for tobacco."[26]

It is however another largely comic western that may help us better place *Dead Man* within the context of its genre. The title of this western is actually used as a line of dialogue in *Dead Man:* when Bill Blake first asks his new companion what his name is, the Indian replies "My name is Nobody." *My Name is Nobody* (Tonino Valerii, 1973) is an interesting Italian western which parodies the major works in the genre by Sergio Leone, who's credited as the film's supervisor. The parallels between the two films are quite marked—in the Valerii film Henry Fonda plays an aging gunfighter whose reputation (*a la* the Gregory Peck figure in *The Gunfighter)* has made him a target for every ambitious gunman in the West. Similarly, in *Dead Man* Blake's poster begins appearing all over the forest he's traveling through, his toll of victims and the amount of reward for his capture increasing as the film progresses. Like Blake in *Dead Man,* Fonda is aided by a fellow wanderer who latches onto him, also called Nobody (Terence Hill). In the Valerii film, Nobody forces Fonda to first augment his legend in a showdown with the Wild Bunch, and then aids him to escape America by boat. Paralleling this, in Jarmusch's film Nobody maneuvers Blake into a few gun battles he could have avoided, and then also helps Blake escape America by boat.

This reading, then, succeeds as it casts not the nominal protagonist, Bill Blake, as the film's hero, but instead foregrounds his "faithful Indian companion," as the Lone Ranger might put it. Like the poet William Blake and his filmic namesake, Nobody is exiled from his community, rejected by them in part due to his previous disappearance into the world of the white man (the film here subtly parodying *Little Big Man).* His tales of England have earned him the name "He Who Talks Loud, Says Nothing," "Nobody" being his preferred contraction of this.

Up to a point, Nobody can be seen as getting what he wants from his travels with Blake. Nobody uses Blake as a means of re-entering Native American culture, selling his vision of Blake as a spiritual heir of William Blake to the Makah community of the Pacific Northwest, and winning approval to use a sea canoe for the dying Blake.

In shifting from thinking of Blake as our hero to seeing the film's true protagonist as Nobody, we are making the same move many writers on the West have made over the last few decades, paying more attention to the fate of indigenous peoples and noting, with Elliott West, just how resilient those cultures have been: "If much has been lost, much has survived."[27] West notes that this new emphasis on the survival of both Indian and Hispanic cultures in the West contradicts "the usual 'triumphalist' view," which is certainly true, but it also contradicts the emphasis on Indian victimization common in much writing on the fate of America's indigenous peoples. *Dead Man* is part of this trend: Jonathan Rosenbaum is quite correct when he writes that the film's portrayal of Native American cultures is respectful without being "patronizing, idealizing, or otherwise simplifying."

A focal shift to seeing Nobody as the film's true hero might thus allow us after all to see *Dead Man* as a positive, mythical spiritual journey western. Bill Blake may be merely the protagonist of a postmodern Dunciad—it is Nobody who is this Odyssey's true hero. This is suggested once again by the line of dialogue which introduces the character: "My name is Nobody" is also the response given by Ulysses to the Cyclops as part of the former's scheme to blind and escape the monster in Homer's *Odyssey*. With his droll humor and seemingly magical skills, Nobody further suggests the Trickster legends of many indigenous cultures. Unfortunately, this reading also falters in the film's last moments: despite Blake's mute attempt to warn him, Nobody is slain by Cole Wilson, the Liberty Valance-like last survivor of Dickinson's hired guns. Granted, Nobody also slays his killer, but it's an empty victory, even as Blake's ascension to "the next level of the world" means nothing to him as he simply never understands what is happening to him.

    Dead Man, then, evades every attempt to affix a positive meaning to its narrative. Everything in it ultimately is canceled by something else: Thel's efforts to escape Machine, Charlie Dickinson's love for Thel, his father's quest for revenge. Dickinson's hired guns all die, as do the lawmen and other whites Blake encounters. Blake and Nobody also lose; they die, and there is no indication that their spiritual evolution has carried them anywhere. Like many another male couple on the trail, they have built up a strong friendship, but their touching good-bye is vitiated by the knowledge that if Nobody had not been convinced Blake was already a "dead man," he might have tried harder to save his friend's life. All the Indians lose—we see three separate scenes of abandoned, smoking, destroyed Indian villages. And white America (Machine) is presented as an industrialized hell. *Dead Man,* then, ultimately plays as a nihilist statement of protest, presenting no viable positive alternative to Machine civilization. As such, it suggests an alignment with an important contemporary school among historians of the West, the aforementioned New Western Historians who have rejected Frederick Jackson Turner's frontier thesis in favor of describing narratives of failure and loss. Elliott West puts it this way:

> Under the old frontier interpretation, the story shimmered with a romantic, heroic glow. Suffering and tragedy were redeemed by the glorious results presumed to have followed—the nurturing of American individualism and the coming of a civilized order into a wilderness. The new themes, by contrast, emphasize a continuing cultural dislocation, environmental calamity, economic exploitation, and individuals who either fail outright or run themselves crazy chasing unattainable goals.[28]

    Novelist Larry McMurtry has criticized this "new history of the West" as "Failure Studies."[29] A leading member of this group, Patricia Limerick, prefers to put it this way: "New Western Historians break free of the old model of 'progress' and 'improvement,' and face up to the possibility that some roads of western development led directly to failure and injury. . . . This is only disillusioning to those who have come to depend on illusions."[30]

    During his journey west Bill Blake looks out the window and sees signs of ruin and decay, images that tally with the harsh view of the West expressed by Limerick, West and others. In addition to iconographic shots of pine forests and a Monument

Valley-like rock formation, we see an abandoned covered wagon and abandoned teepees, balancing images of the doom of both white man and red. Later, Blake finds Machine decorated with skulls, coffins, piles of bones, while other images in the town's main street—unfriendly strangers, a pissing horse, a sickly looking woman and baby, a violent sex act—further unnerve him. Dickinson's office is decorated with mounted animal heads and a stuffed bear, while a skull is seen on his desk.[31] We continue to see bones and other markers of loss and decay throughout the film. A shot of a sewing machine in the mud of the Micah village near film's end recalls New Western Historian Richard White's description of the abandoned "cooking stoves, kegs and barrels . . . harnesses, clothing, bacon, and beans" scattered along the Oregon Trail, traces of many failures.[32]

Blake's fate resonates with the fate of the many western failures pointed out by the new historians, but the movie that tells his story shares the same problem the New Western History has had in gaining adherents. In White's words, "Old Western Historians usually write comedy, in the sense that they provide a happy resolution. . . . One reason the New Western History has failed to displace the Old Western History in the popular imagination is that it lacks an equally gripping and ultimately satisfying narrative." White's suggestion? "New Western Historians find people attempting one thing and very often achieving another. Consequently, their interpretations, and their narratives, become ironic, for irony is that figure of speech in which the meaning of a statement is the opposite of that seemingly intended."[33] Again, we return to the idea of *Dead Man* as an ironic text—in the view of these new historians, however, because it would represent a more truthful view of the West, as opposed to the satisfying lies of the classical western.

Is this a sufficient reading? More remains to be said.

ERASURE DEAD

To summarize: Jarmusch takes the contradictions of William Blake's *Songs of Innocence and Experience* and resolves them with irony. Where Blake the poet separated the innocent from the evil, and found the existence of both a "fearful symmetry" that cast doubt on the morality of God, Jarmusch seeks to find a synthesis in his William Blake. He is at once an innocent victim and a killer, oppressed by the Satanic Dickinson in the town of Machine, but also a representative of an Urizenic culture that oppresses the indigenous peoples it encounters. Blake's innocent presence in their midst harbingers their destruction. While Blake's actions parallel those of a Buster Keaton or a Bob Hope in their comic parodies of the West, they do not make the film a comedy. Keaton or Hope succeed as heroes in spite of their ineptness; their worlds are better for their presence. By contrast, William Blake's world seems either unaware of his presence, or is drawn with him into the void of his apparently empty and meaningless fate. The film's epigraph is a quote from novelist Henri Michaux: "It is preferable not to travel with a dead man." Nobody learns how true that is when his travels with Blake lead to his own death.

If Jarmusch synthesizes Blake's contradictions, like Blake, he also takes one of the myths of our contemporary culture and remakes it in order to critique it as at once both innocent and destructive. Jarmusch's West is not a place where people find themselves, but rather lose themselves. This tallies with the ideas of the New Western History movement, whose members emphasize that the real West was marked by cultural dislocation, environmental calamity, economic exploitation, and the traces of many individuals who failed to achieve their unreachable goals. "From the beginning," writes Donald Worster, "the agrarian myth was filled with all the unresolved contradictions of innocence." He cites Henry Nash Smith: while on the one hand the West was a place to escape the burdens of civilization, on the other the western myth "affirmed a doctrine of progress, of gigantic economic development."[34] To Worster the contradictions are insoluble:

> Logic says you cannot have it both ways. . . . Yet the agrarian myth was able to hold both possibilities together because it did not follow the rules of logical discourse; instead, it was a song, a dream, a fantasy that captured all of the ambivalence in a people about their past and future.[35]

There is however another approach that offers a way of reconciling these contradictions: postmodernist, deconstructionist, poststructuralist theories uninterested in achieving a final, definitive reading of any text—theories that deny such certainty is possible. The ambiguities of *Dead Man*, its evident hostility to fixed meanings, would seem to open it to such readings; at the very least as a late-twentieth century artist Jarmusch shares the same cultural moment with this thought.

In his influential essay "The Cultural Logic of Late Capitalism" (1984), Fredric Jameson advanced the argument that postmodernism is formally identifiable by its interest in pastiche ("mimicry . . . amputated of the satiric impulse"), and by its disinterest in the concept of a unified personality in favor of a "schizoid" experience of the loss of self.[36] If nothing else, *Dead Man* can be said to inscribe such a narrative, and as such it is at one with the disinterest in the humanist concepts—"Man," individualism, freedom, democracy—that underpin the classic western films of a John Ford. These concepts have fallen under withering critique in the works of many French thinkers of the 1960s and since, Michel Foucault and Jacques Derrida being only two of the most prominent. It is no accident that a critique of Ford was central to the first group of film theorists influenced by these doctrines, as in the celebrated *Cahiers du Cinema* rereading of *Young Mr. Lincoln*.

Jacques Derrida's poststructuralist, or "deconstructionist," criticism offers a particularly apt way of thinking about *Dead Man*. Derrida's work, to simplify greatly, has been concerned with the unresolvable contradictions and "undecidability" of language. Derrida has also argued the necessity of forcibly overturning accepted meanings as a key part of what he called, in a 1971 interview, the "general strategy of deconstruction."[37] Dan Miller, in an essay on Blake and deconstruction, stresses Derrida's interest in this, writing "That deconstruction involves the double gesture of reversal followed by displacement is well known."[38] *Dead Man*'s many gestures of reversal would seem to fit in with this strategy: every positive gesture, as we have seen, is canceled out by a negative one.

A term coined by Derrida may be perhaps the best way of grasping this dynamic. It is his concept of erasure (*sous rature*), introduced in *Of Grammatology* (1967). It is drawn from Martin Heidegger's habit of crossing out the word Being and letting both the word and its erasure stand: (~~Being~~). Heidegger felt that Being was prior to and beyond signification or meaning, and hence to signify it was inadequate, though there existed no alternative. Derrida extended this practice to all signs.

> This erasure is the final writing of an epoch. Under its strokes the presence of a transcendental signified is effaced while still remaining legible. Is effaced while still remaining legible, is destroyed while making visible the very idea of the sign.[39]

In Derrida's "Grammatology," any signifier has as its signified another signifier, any given word always defers meaning and, as such, always carries traces of other meanings. All words must therefore be studied as defective, incomplete, "under erasure." Derrida has no nostalgia for this "lost presence," as *Of Grammatology's* translator, Gayatri Chakravorty Spivak, puts it. The "strange 'being' of the sign" is that "half of it is always 'not there' and the other half always 'not that.'"[40] A concept is, but also simultaneously is not.

Dead Man, then, is the filmic equivalent of an erased, lined-out text: ~~Dead Man~~. As we've seen the film "erases," inverts, and upends all the various western conventions, from the idea of the western hero down through its final shootout. Its narrative forms a series of canceling operations: the fates of all the characters and the West itself are all equally null. Jarmusch's portrayal of the traditional western hero as an empty cipher is a further emptying gesture.

In this light Jarmusch's comments about his protagonist are of the greatest interest: "*Dead Man* is only kind of a western because Blake's such a passive character. He starts out as this blank piece of paper, and pretty soon everyone's trying to scrawl graffiti all over him. That's what's going on when Mitchum's saying, 'He's an outlaw, he's a killer, he's a scum.' And then Nobody does the same thing by telling him not only are you a killer of white men, you're the dead poet William Blake. Everyone's sort of writing and projecting things onto him."[41] One is reminded of all the famous heroes of westerns who are dismayed or delighted to find their exploits have been mythologized in dime novels (Buffalo Bill Cody in William Wellman's *Buffalo Bill*, or Billy the Kid in Penn's *The Left Handed Gun*) or who seek to shape that process (as in *Buffalo Bill and the Indians*, or *Unforgiven*). More broadly, the entire American West can be seen as a blank canvas onto which successive generations make their mark, leaving their traces behind.

Finally, *Dead Man* can be said to describe a narrative where the protagonist is indeed a Dead Man throughout the film. Nobody tells him as such early in their acquaintance: "Did you kill the white man who killed you?" Hoberman's review commented "There are ample clues to suggest that Blake has died and that Nobody is the spirit who guides his departing soul." Another layer of meaning comes from Nobody's

Nobody (Gary Farmer) and friend: "This Odyssey's true hero"?

name—a Dead Man's double would indeed be "nobody."

A new mythic reading of *Dead Man*, then, which I think the film supports, is that the film describes the posthumous journey of William Blake through the American West: presented here, as in "Failure Studies," as the land of the dead. The film, as noted, is saturated with images of death from beginning to end. What we see is ~~The West~~ not The West.

Just when does Blake die? In some sense Blake is a dead man not from the point of his shooting, but from a point *before the film's beginning*. In the film's prologue Blake tells the train's fireman that his parents are dead, his fiancée "changed her mind," and that he is heading west from Cleveland with the last of his cash in the expectation of a job in Machine. "You're just as likely to find your own grave," warns the fireman, as gunfire breaks out on the train—"The men are shooting buffalo!"— and the film's credit sequence begins with words formed from bones. Blake is presented as a man whose old life has ended before the film begins, and whose hold on his new life is tenuous indeed. As Crispin Glover's Fireman (whose face is as blackened as Blake's is pale) perceives, Blake may bear the mark of death already, the skull beneath his skin perhaps as open to his view as it is later to Nobody after his consumption of peyote. The Fireman is Blake's Charon, ferrying his body on an iron chariot across into Hades, the Land of the Dead, even as Nobody later attempts to guide him into the next world.

In one of her songs Laurie Anderson defines a detective story as one in which "the hero is dead from the beginning." It's easy to see this fatalism in such classic noirs as *The Killers* (1946), *Out of the Past* (1947), and *D.O.A.* (1950). *Dead Man* extends this spirit to the western genre in a way such noir-influenced westerns as *Pursued* never did. The classic western, as in *Pursued*, allows the doomed hero to be regenerated—or, if he's killed, as in *Colorado Territory* (1949), to have won a spiritual victory. In the revisionist westerns of Clint Eastwood, his character (as in *High Plains Drifter* and *Pale Rider*) is sometimes a ghost, but even as an avenging wraith he's unbeatable. As noted, Blake takes on some of this quality in the later stages of *Dead Man*.

Blake's death-bound journey may even be cyclical. The Fireman's opening words to Blake strongly suggest the film's final images: "Doesn't that remind you when you're in the boat . . . and the water in your head is not dissimilar to the landscape and you think to yourself, 'Why is it that the landscape is moving, but the boat is still?'" As his boat drifts away Blake looks back to the shore, shuts his eyes, and dies. If one wanted proof that Bill Blake is trapped in some sort of time loop, as Fred Madison is in David Lynch's *Lost Highway*—another postmodernist, circular narrative—the Fireman's monologue offers strong support.

Whether he's trapped in some sort of endlessly repeating cycle, dead from the beginning, or is merely a hapless easterner who meets his death in the Far West, Blake's ultimate fate is to be erased from memory, to disappear over the horizon, to vanish from sight. As such he suggests Foucault's last man, destined in the conclusion of *The Order of Things* to be "erased, like a face drawn in sand at the edge of the sea."[42] *Dead Man* presents us with a protagonist under erasure, and by extension, an entire genre.

A final paradox remains, however, in this paradoxical work: even as *Dead Man* erases its genre it confirms its ongoing vitality, dependent as this very interesting film is in so many ways on the genre's form and conventions for its very existence. What's always half "not there" and always half "not that" is by its very definition at least still half present, "there," and "that." What's alive is dead, but also what's dead is alive.

NOTES

1. Jonathan Rosenbaum, "Acid Western," *Chicago Reader* (June 28, 1996).

2. Jarmusch told interviewer Charlie Rose "This is the 1870s, although the film doesn't tell you so it's not important." (*Charlie Rose*, PBS, May 1996.)

3. Northrup Frye, *Fearful Symmetry* (Princeton, New Jersey: Princeton University Press, 1947), p. 227.

4. Harold Bloom, *The Visionary Company: A Reading of English Romantic Poetry* (Garden City, NY: Doubleday, 1961), pp. 45–6.

5. Hilda Hollis, "Seeing Thel as Serpent," *Blake: An Illustrated Quarterly* (Winter 1996-97), pp. 87–90.

6. Bloom, p. 47.

7. Ibid., pp. 47–8.

8. Ibid., p. 45; see also Hilda Hollis' essay and for example Brenda S. Webster, "Blake, Women, and Sexuality," in Dan Miller, Mark Bracher, and Donald Ault, *Critical Paths: Blake and the Argument of Method* (Durham, NC: Duke University Press, 1987), pp. 204–24.

9. Deborah McCollister, "The Seduction of Self-Abnegation in *The Book of Thel*," *Blake: An Illustrated Quarterly* (Winter 1996–97), pp. 90–95.

10. In the poem the Lilly urges Thel to sacrifice herself "passively and even thankfully." As McCollister suggests, the bloom that makes the Lilly "beautiful and sweet-smelling attracts the innocent lamb, who devours her while she 'sittest smiling in his face, / Wiping his . . . mouth.'" Compare Bill Blake's lamb-like appearance, his intervention in her life leading to Thel's death, and her sacrifice on his behalf.

11. See for all this Mark Schorer, *William Blake: The Politics of Vision* (New York: Vintage Books, 1959), pp. 229–44.

12. Edward Larrissy, *William Blake* (Oxford: Basil Blackwell, 1985), p. 83.

13. Ibid., pp. 125–6.

14. Schorer, p. 173.

15. Sam Whiting, "A Wilder Western," *San Francisco Chronicle Datebook* (May 5, 1996), pp. 35 ff.

16. Joseph McBride and Michael Wilmington, *John Ford (New York:* DaCapo Press, 1975), p. 175.

17. Jarmusch named the two lawmen who Blake kills "Lee" and "Marvin" in homage to the actor who played Liberty. Note the inversion—the villains are on the side of the law in *Dead Man*.

18. Tag Gallagher, *John Ford: The Man and His Films* (Berkeley: University of California Press, 1986), p. 413.

19. Leo Marx, *The Machine in the Garden* (New York: Oxford University Press, 1964), p. 143.

20. Ibid., p.191.

21. Jarmusch interview, *Charlie Rose* (PBS), May 1996. The Hawks quote is from Joseph McBride, *Hawks on Hawks* (Berkeley: University of California Press, 1982), p. 114.

22. While Busch claimed, during his appearance with the film at the 1980 San Francisco Film Festival, that the film's director hadn't understood *Pursued's* screenplay, this does

not mean that Raoul Walsh did not grasp what was truly important in his screenwriter's blueprint.

23. Jarmusch states in the film's pressbook that the town of Machine was actually based on the historical Virginia City, Nevada. Blake's last stop is the Olympic Peninsula in Washington state, home of the Makah tribe, whose traditional culture was recreated for the film.

24. See for this Gabriella Oldham, *Keaton's Silent Shorts: Beyond the Laughter* (Southern Illinois University Press, 1996), pp. 252–55.

25. Frye, *Anatomy of Criticism* (Princeton, NJ: Princeton University Press, 1957), p. 224.

26. J. Hoberman, "Promised Lands," *Village Voice* (May 14, 1996). In light of this linkage with these druggy westerns of the early 1970s, Jarmusch's comment at a public screening, quoted in the Sam Whiting interview, that the film might go better with the right drugs is more than a little interesting.

27. Elliott West, "A Longer, Grimmer, But More Interesting Story," in Patricia Nelson Limerick, Clyde A. Milner II, and Charles E. Rankin, eds., *Trails: Toward a New Western History* (Lawrence, KS: University Press of Kansas, 1991), p. 108.

28. West, p. 105.

29. Larry McMurtry, "How the West Was Won or Lost," *The New Republic* (Oct. 22, 1990), pp. 32–38.

30. Patricia Limerick, "What on Earth is the New Western History?," in Limerick, *Trails*, p. 86.

31. Chuck Stephens suggests that Mitchum's character is modeled after the patriarch played by Mitchum in Vincente Minnelli's *Home from the Hill* (1960), in which case the decor of Dickinson's office may be modeled after the similarly overdetermined furnishings of Wade Hunnicutt's den. Chuck Stephens, "Dead Man Talking," *San Francisco Bay Guardian*, May 8, 1996.

32. Richard White, "Trashing the Trails," in Limerick, *Trails*, p. 26. The silent epic *The Covered Wagon* perhaps achieved a more balanced view in 1923 than the New Western Historians do today when, after showing several images of the debris left behind on the Oregon Trail, it concludes with the title "Some found only bitter disappointment and defeat—and some found the end of the rainbow."

33. White, pp. 31–33.

34. Donald Worster, "Beyond the Agrarian Myth," in Limerick, *Trails*, p. 6, citing Henry Nash Smith, *Virgin Land* (Cambridge: Harvard University Press, 1950), p. 187.

35. Worster, pp. 6–7.

36. Fredric Jameson, "The Cultural Logic of Late Capitalism", in *Postmodernism, or the Cultural Logic of Late Capitalism* (Durham, NC: Duke University Press, 1991), p. 17.

37. Jacques Derrida, *Positions* (Chicago: University of Chicago Press, 1972), p. 41 .

38. Dan Miller, "Blake and the Deconstructive Interlude," in Miller, *Critical Paths*, p. 141.

39. Derrida, *Of Grammatology* (Baltimore: Johns Hopkins University Press, 1974), p. 23.

40. Gayatri Chakravorty Spivak, "Translator's Preface," *Of Grammatology*, xvi–xvii.

41. Stephens interview. In light of my earlier commentary on comic westerns it's interesting that Buster Keaton was dubbed "the Great Blank Page" by the British critic Penelope Houston.

42. Michel Foucault, *The Order of Things* (NY: Pantheon Books, 1970), p. 387.

NOTES ON CONTRIBUTORS

Sherman Alexie has written fiction, poetry, screenplays and criticism. His work includes *The Business of Fancydancing, First Indian on the Moon, The Summer of Black Widows*, and *Indian Killer*. The 1998 film *Smoke Signals* was scripted by Alexie from his book *The Lone Ranger and Tonto Fistfight in Heaven*. An enrolled Spokane/Couer d'Alene Indian, Alexie was born on the Spokane reservation in Wellpinit, Washington.

Robert Baird has worked as a post-production sound and picture editor on twelve films, including Alan Rudolph's *Trouble in Mind*. He is completing his dissertation at the University of Illinois, employing cognitive psychology to examine spectatorship and affect in the horror/thriller film text.

Michael Budd teaches film and media studies at Florida Atlantic University in Boca Raton. He is the editor of *The Cabinet of Dr. Caligari: Texts, Contexts, Histories* (Rutgers, 1990); and the author (with Steve Craig and Clay Steinman) of the forthcoming *Mapping the Wasteland: Television and the Environment of Commercial Culture* (Rutgers).

Edward Buscombe was until recently Head of Publishing at the British Film Institute. He is now a free-lance writer and teacher. He is the author of *Stagecoach* in the BFI Film Classic series, and the editor of *The BFI Companion to the Western*. With Roberta Pearson, he has co-edited *Back in the Saddle Again- New Essays on the Western*, due from the BFI in 1998.

Richard Combs was the editor of the *Monthly Film Bulletin* (British Film Institute) from 1974 to 1991, and a contributor to *Sight and Sound*, other periodicals and national newspapers. He now lectures at the National Film and Television School, is Managing Editor of the International Film Guide and writes for *Film Comment*, the *Times Literary Supplement*, and European periodicals.

405

Pam Cook is Professor of European Film and Media Studies at the University of Southampton. She is editor of *The Cinema Book* and the author of *Fashioning the Nation: Costume and Identity in British Cinema* (BFI, 1996). Her most recent book is *Gainsborough Pictures* (Cassell, 1997), and she is currently working on *I Know Where I'm Going* for BFI Film Classics.

Raymond Durgnat has taught film and aesthetics in England, America, Italy, India, Finland and New Zealand. His books include *Films and Feeling, Eros in the Cinema, Jean Renoir, Bunuel, The Crazy Mirror, A Mirror for England, Sexual Alienation and the Cinema,* and (with Scott Simmon) *King Vidor, American.*

Tag Gallagher is the author of *John Ford: The Man and His Films, The Adventures of Roberto Rossellini,* and many articles on *auteur* filmmakers. His ambition is to teach.

J. Hoberman is the senior film critic for *The Village Voice,* a contributing editor to *Sight and Sound,* and an adjunct professor of film at the Cooper Union in New York. He is the author of a history of Yiddish-language cinema and the co-author of *Midnight Movies,* a study of cult films. His writings have been collected as *Vulgar Modernism* (Temple University Press).

Jim Kitses was Deputy Education Officer for the British Film Institute in the 1960s, and a founding faculty member of the American Film Institute's Center for Advanced Film Studies. He is currently Professor of Cinema Studies at San Francisco State University. His books include *Horizons West,* now being expanded for reissue, and the recent *Gun Crazy* for the BFI's Film Classic series.

Marcia Landy is Professor of English and Film Studies at the University of Pittsburgh. She is the author of *Fascism in Film: The Italian Commercial Cinema, 1930-1943; British Genres-Cinema and Society, 1930-1960; Cinematic Uses of the Past*; and the forthcoming *The Folklore of Concensus: Theatricality in the Italian Cinema, 1930-1943.*

Peter Lehman is a professor in the Department of Media Arts at the University of Arizona. He is author of *Running Scared: Masculinity and the Representation of the Male Body* and editor of *Defining Cinema.* His essay "Texas 1868/America 1956: *The Searchers*" appears in *Close Viewings: An Anthology of New Criticism,* edited by Lehman. "'You just couldn't hit it on the nose': The Limits of Knowledge in and of *The Searchers*" appears in the forthcoming anthology *The Searchers: John Ford's Classic Western After Forty Years,* edited by Arthur M. Eckstein and James F. Brooks.

Blake Lucas has contributed over 100 essays to *Magill's Survey of Cinema* and *Magill's Cinema Annuals.* His writing has also appeared in the reference works *Film Noir, American Screenwriters,* and in *LA Woman* and, as a regular critic, the *Los Angeles Reader.* His monograph on John Ford was translated into French for the 1995 Cannes Film Festival retrospective. He has contributed to film programs at UCLA, the L.A. County Museum of Art, and Theater Vanguard.

Tania Modleski is Professor of Film and Literature at the University of Southern California. Her publications include *Loving With A Vengeance: Mass-Produced Fantasies for Women* and *The Women Who Knew Too Much: Hitchcock and Feminist Theory.*

Barrie Pattison's films include the documentaries *Mahattan Days—Disco Nights* and *I Am No*

God, and the feature *The Zombie Brigade from Lizard Gulley*. He has published across a range that includes *Positif, Age Monthly Review, Fatal Visions* and *Big Reel*, mounted programs for the London National Film Theater and the Paris Cinematheque, and was one of the founders of the Australian National Film Theater.

Jennifer Peterson is writing her Ph.D. thesis, "World Pictures: The Travelogue Genre in Film and Literature, 1895–1915," in the Department of English at the University of Chicago.

Gregg Rickman is the author of a number of books on Philip K. Dick, including *To the High Castle* and the forthcoming *Variable Man: The Lives of Philip K. Dick*. He reviews films regularly for the *SF Weekly*, and has an essay in the 1998 anthology *Twin Peaks Revisited*.

Lee Russell, the author of a series of auteur studies published in *New Left Review* in the 1960s, is Peter Wollen's doppelganger. Professor of Film at UCLA, Wollen is the author of *Signs and Meaning in the Cinema* and *Singing in the Rain*, co-editor of *Howard Hawks: American Artist* and *Visual Display: Culture Beyond Appearances*, and has made a number of films.

Scott Simmon is a film archivist, responsible for such Library of Congress restorations as Oscar Micheaux's *Within Our Gates*, and author of *The Films of D.W. Griffith* and (with Raymond Durgnat) *King Vidor, American*. Currently he is Visiting Associate Professor of English at the University of California, Davis, and producer of "The Library of Congress Video Collection." His *Dead West: The Dark Culture of the Western Film* will be published by Cambridge University Press.

Janet Thumim is senior lecturer in film and television at the University of Bristol. Her publications include *Celluloid Sisters: Women and Popular Cinema; You Tarzan: Masculinity, Movies and Men;* and *Me Jane: Masculinity, Movies and Women*. She is currently writing a book on early television in Britain for *Oxford Television Studies*.

Kenneth Turan is the film critic for the *Los Angeles Times* and the director of the *LA Times* Book Prizes. He has been book review editor for the *Times*, a staff writer for the *Washington Post* and *TV Guide*, and film critic for National Public Radio's *All Things Considered* and Monitor Radio. He is co-author of *Call Me Anna: The Autobiography of Patty Duke*.

Christopher Wicking has been writing for—and about—films and television since the 1960s, from cult Hammer and Vincent Price horror movies (*Scream and Scream Again, Blood From the Mummy's Tomb*) to *Lady Chatterly's Lover* and TV detectives—*The Professionals* and the upcoming *McGarr Mysteries*, based where he now lives, in Dublin, Ireland.

Paul Willemen migrated from Belgium to Britain where he was a member of *Screen's* editorial board in the 70s. He edited *Framework* in the 1980s, and is currently Professor of Critical Studies at Napier University, Edinburgh. His publications include *Looks and Frictions* and, with A. Rajadhyaksha, *The Encyclopedia of Indian Cinema*.

Doug Williams is a lecturer in Communications at the University of California, San Diego. His dissertation analyzes political uses of narrative to define American identity during the Cold War.

Robin Wood is the author of a number of books on film of which the most recent are *Hollywood From Vietnam to Reagan* and *Hitchcock's Films Revisited*. His final book of film criticism will be published in the spring of 1998. He is a founding editor and frequent contributor to *CineAction*.

Made in the USA
Lexington, KY
03 December 2013